SAN MIGUEL DE ALLENDE

JULIE MEADE

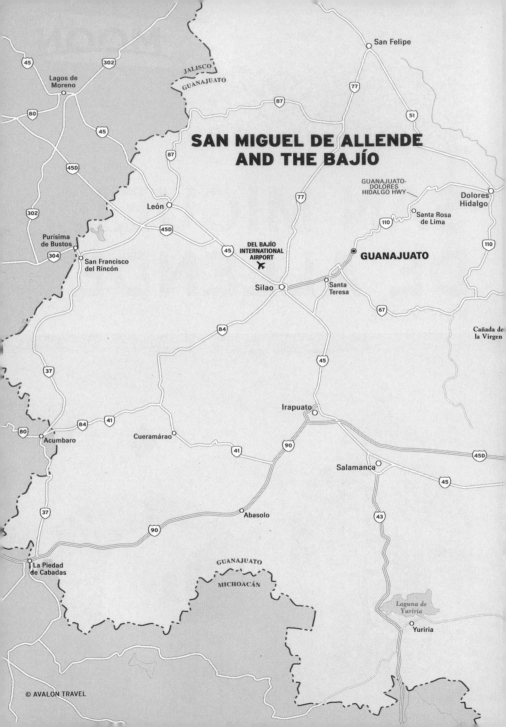

SAN MIGUEL DE ALLENDE
AND THE BAJÍO

San Felipe

Lagos de Moreno

JALISCO
GUANAJUATO

León

Purísima de Bustos

San Francisco del Rincón

DEL BAJÍO INTERNATIONAL AIRPORT

Silao

Santa Teresa

GUANAJUATO-DOLORES HIDALGO HWY

Dolores Hidalgo

Santa Rosa de Lima

GUANAJUATO

Cañada de la Virgen

Irapuato

Cueramárao

Acumbaro

Salamanca

Abasolo

La Piedad de Cabadas

GUANAJUATO

MICHOACÁN

Laguna de Yuriria

Yuriria

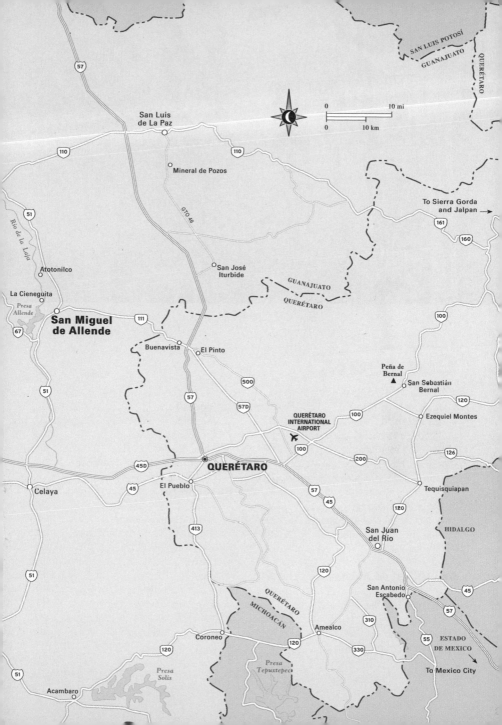

Contents

DISCOVER

San Miguel de Allende

As evening falls across the Sierra de Guanajuato, the brilliant blue skies above San Miguel de Allende warm to a rosy pink. Birds streak across the dimming sky, and clanging iron bells herald the end of the day. As the dry air drops to a pleasant chill, mariachis tune their instruments and the sidewalks hum with diners, gallerygoers, and revelers. This is Mexico *mágico,* a place both contemporary and old-fashioned, alive and thriving on the high plains.

San Miguel de Allende is located in Mexico's semiarid central highlands, a gateway between the vast northern deserts and bustling southern states. Built with the spoils of the colonial-era silver trade, San Miguel and its neighboring cities—Guanajuato and Querétaro—are some of the country's most splendid, renowned for their fine Mexican baroque architecture and historic city centers. The region is also known as the cradle of the Mexican independence movement: From the steps of the cathedral in nearby Dolores,

Clockwise from top left: cultural center at El Chorro; colonial-era architecture in Guanajuato; bell tower of the Templo de la Inmaculada Concepción; colorful tiles; celebrations during Día de San Miguel Arcángel; hillside in Guanajuato.

revolutionary hero Miguel Hidalgo raised his famous call to arms against the Spanish crown, igniting the country in war.

San Miguel is a quintessentially Mexican place, where tacos and tamales are standard fare, the midday siesta is still respected, and religious festivals are frequent, ritualistic, and raucous. Yet tradition and modernity are intertwined in San Miguel today, where a large expatriate population and a spate of new boutique hotels and concept shops have brought a sleek patina to a town once known for its quaintness. Here, the old cobblestone streets are now a mix of cultures and people: the modern art gallery and the antique apothecary, the French bistros and the buzzing taco stands, the young art students and the foreign retirees. And this mix of cultures and their joyous conviviality are precisely what makes San Miguel de Allende such a rewarding place to visit, to spend a season, and to become a part of *la vida mexicana*.

Clockwise from top left: traditional dancers in the central plaza in San Miguel; colorful pedestrian alley in Guanajuato; Parroquia de San Miguel Arcángel; artisan embroidering in Tequisquiapan.

10 TOP
EXPERIENCES

1 **People-Watching in San Miguel de Allende's** *Jardín:* This sun-drenched public plaza is the most popular gathering spot in town. It's also the best place to start a walking tour of the city's historic district (page 42).

∨ ∨ ∨
∨ ∨

2 **Historic Architecture:** With their unique Mexican baroque churches and well-preserved colonial-era mansions and haciendas, San Miguel de Allende, Guanajuato, and Querétaro are known for some of the most spectacular architecture in Mexico (page 24).

3 **Shop for Art and Craftwork:** With a range of shops specializing in everything from **traditional Mexican crafts** (page 64) to contemporary design, as well as a slew of artist-run galleries, San Miguel de Allende (page 62) is the ultimate shopping destination.

4 **Soak in the Hot Springs:** Spend a day soaking in the clear natural hot springs outside San Miguel de Allende; many believe the water has healing properties (page 113).

Folk-Art

5 **Celebrate the Visual Arts:** San Miguel de Allende's enthusiastic art scene is cozy, fun, and inclusive, celebrating local artists without the pretension of a big city (page 52).

6 **Festival Internacional Cervantino:** Every October, Guanajuato hosts Mexico's largest and most prestigious performing arts festival, with a bonanza of performances held in the Teatro Juarez (pictured) and other venues across the city (page 159).

> > >

7 **Countryside Excursions:** Experience the Bajío's countryside on horseback (page 76) or on a guided tour to the Cañada de la Virgen archaeological site and nature preserve (pictured, page 116).

∧∧∧

8 **Echoes of Independence:** Some of the most famous moments in the Mexican war for independence from Spain took place here. Visiting the region's historic sites provides an engaging look at this important era in Mexican history (page 31).

∧∧∧

9 **Renew Your Spirit:** Retreats like LifePath Center (pictured) are just one of the many ways to relax, learn, and spend some time off the grid in San Miguel (page 75).

10 **Savor Regional Cuisine:** Mexico is one of the world's top food destinations. Sample the Bajío's **local specialties** (page 32), eat at one of San Miguel's **top restaurants** (page 82), or take a **cooking class** (page 79) to immerse yourself in this burgeoning culinary scene.

<<<

Planning Your Trip

Where to Go

San Miguel de Allende

San Miguel de Allende is a small colonial town, known for its beautiful light, **charming atmosphere,** and artsy expatriate community. Irresistibly romantic yet surprisingly modern, San Miguel offers a little something for everyone, whether you are an artist, a history buff, or just looking for a great place to relax. Tour **colonial-era architecture,** visit contemporary **art galleries,** shop for **traditional crafts,** or linger over coffee in a sidewalk café. While there, visit the nearby **hot springs** for a relaxing afternoon in the desert, visit the fascinating former mining camps in **Mineral de Pozos,** or take a horseback ride through the desert chaparral.

Guanajuato

Guanajuato is one of Mexico's historic **silver cities,** built with the wealth of New Spain's lucrative mineral mines. It boasts a magnificent mix of baroque, neoclassical, and contemporary **art and architecture** as well as one of the world's most unusual urban maps. Here, the *centro histórico* was built within a steep ravine; automobile traffic passes through underground tunnels while pedestrians navigate a dizzying mess of hills and alleyways above. Home to a prestigious public university, Guanajuato is a spirited **college town** with a youthful atmosphere and an impressive tradition in the arts; it's particularly well-known for the spectacular **Festival Internacional Cervantino,** held every fall.

Día de Muertos altars in San Miguel de Allende's *jardín*

Querétaro

Querétaro is a handsome, bustling city, which is generally **overlooked by tourists** despite its important role in **Mexican history** and its remarkably well-preserved *centro histórico*, filled with sunny plazas and ornate baroque **mansions, convents,** and **churches.** A popular choice for Mexico City natives looking to relocate to a safer and more low-key metropolis, Querétaro has a cosmopolitan side, with some great **restaurants, galleries,** and **museums,** yet it remains old-fashioned and unpretentious all the same. From Querétaro, visit the charming country town of **San Sebastián Bernal** and its eponymous

monolith, stopping at one of the wineries or cheese producers along the way.

When to Go

San Miguel de Allende and the surrounding region are **year-round destinations,** though climate and costs vary depending on the season you choose to visit. North American winter is typically the tourist **high season** in San Miguel de Allende, when the region is cool, dry, and sunny. From **December through April,** large numbers of part-time residents from the United States and Canada arrive for their annual sojourn in San Miguel, and regular tourism surges. If you plan to visit San Miguel de Allende between **November and April,** make your hotel reservations in advance.

Throughout the region, the weather heats up significantly during the month of **May,** and tourism is more sluggish until the **rainy season** begins, around mid-June. With the rains, the climate cools off pleasantly, making it a nice time to visit. Although hotels and restaurants aren't as full during the summer as

they are during the winter, there is still a pleasant buzz of international tourism. **Summer** is also a popular time for college students to take language classes or volunteer in San Miguel or Guanajuato.

One thing to keep in mind when planning your trip to San Miguel de Allende, Guanajuato, or other nearby towns is that these destinations are popular with national tourists as well as international tourists. During long weekends, San Miguel is often thronged with families from Monterrey or Mexico City, while big holidays can transform the city with crowds of revelers. You will need to make advance hotel reservations if you plan to visit during **Holy Week** in the spring, **Independence Day** weekend in September, or during the **Christmas season** in December, or if you plan to visit Guanajuato in **October,** when the city hosts the annual Festival Internacional Cervantino.

- **A LONG WEEKEND:** Head straight to San Miguel de Allende and spend the weekend exploring the city's *centro histórico*.

- **ONE WEEK:** Follow the "Best of San Miguel" itinerary, allowing for a travel day at the beginning and end of the trip.

- **ONE MONTH:** Make San Miguel de Allende your home base and plan trips to the cities of Guanajuato, Querétaro, Mineral de Pozos, and Dolores Hidalgo.

- **A WINTER:** With a season in San Miguel, you can do it all: make friends, take a class, attend concerts, soak in the hot springs, and plan weekend trips throughout the region.

San Miguel de Allende's *jardín*

Before You Go

Passports and Visas

Since 2008, all foreign visitors must have a **valid passport** to enter Mexico. At the port of entry, immigration officials issue each visitor a six-month **temporary tourist permit,** or tourist card. You must keep your stamped tourist card and return it at the airport when you check in for your flight out of the country. If you enter by car, you must stop at an immigration office at the border to pick up your tourist card and, likewise, return it to immigration officials on your way home.

Transportation

San Miguel de Allende, Guanajuato, and other towns in northern Guanajuato state can be accessed by air via León's **Del Bajío International Airport** (BJX). Equidistant to San Miguel de Allende is the **Querétaro International Airport** (QRO), about half an hour outside Querétaro. Most travelers arrive in **León,** which offers more international flights than Querétaro, though both ports are about 90 minutes from San Miguel de Allende. The city of Guanajuato is about half an hour from the BJX terminal. Several tour operators offer shuttle service to and from the airport to San Miguel de Allende. For some travelers, it is easiest to book flights to **Mexico City** and then use ground transportation to reach their destination, which can also be arranged via tour operators in San Miguel de Allende.

There is plenty of **bus service** to and from the region, which is located in the very center of Mexico, including frequent departures to San Miguel de Allende, Guanajuato, and Querétaro from Mexico City. There is also frequent service between Bajío cities, including hourly departures to Querétaro and Guanajuato from San Miguel.

The Best of San Miguel de Allende

The perfect place for a getaway, San Miguel de Allende unites recreation, relaxation, and culture. In five days, you can see the city's historic sights, visit the countryside, eat memorable meals on rooftop restaurants and patio cafés, even take a day trip—and still have time to relax, soak in the hot springs, and thumb through a novel. The key is to plan, but not excessively: In this charming little town, you'll often encounter your most memorable moments by chance.

Day 1

Every tour of San Miguel de Allende should begin in the *jardín,* the city's heart both geographically and spiritually. The always-busy plaza is quietest in the mornings, though loyally attended by newspaper vendors and flocks of pudgy pigeons. Have a traditional Mexican breakfast beneath colonial-era arcades at **Rincón Don Tomás** while admiring the pink sandstone spires of the **Parroquia de San Miguel Arcángel,** San Miguel's singular neo-Gothic parish church.

Now it's time to perfect the art of the not-totally-aimless wander through the *centro histórico,* San Miguel's 500-year-old downtown district. You might choose to begin at the **Centro Cultural Ignacio Ramírez "El Nigromante"** (also known as Bellas Artes), an art school and exhibition space, then visit the adjoining **Templo de la Inmaculada Concepción,** San Miguel's largest domed church. Stroll east along Mesones toward the **Oratorio San Felipe Neri** and the **Templo de San Francisco,** two gorgeous baroque temples, then visit the **Mercado Ignacio Ramírez,** a colorful food and flower market in the center of town.

Spend a leisurely afternoon browsing the goods for sale at San Miguel's unique boutiques

the Parroquia de San Miguel Arcángel

the Centro Cultural Ignacio Ramírez "El Nigromante," popularly known as Bellas Artes

and galleries, like luxurious handwoven textiles at **Juana Cata,** contemporary Oaxacan art at **Noel Cayetano Arte Contemporáneo,** or interesting contemporary designs at eclectic boutique **Mixta.** Follow up the visual feast with a fine dinner at **The Restaurant,** one of nicest eateries in town and a truly beautiful one to boot, located in the patio of a colonial-era mansion.

Day 2

Now that you've got the lay of the land, give yourself the luxury of a lazy morning, lingering over a latte and a copy of *Atención San Miguel* at **Lavanda.** When you are ready to get moving, take a taxi to **El Charco del Ingenio,** the botanical gardens and ecological preserve located just above the city center. Spend some time amid the flowering cactus of El Charco's winding **nature trails,** framed by sweeping views of the city below.

Rest your legs over in the colorful dining room of Mexican restaurant **Marchanta,** then consider retiring for a well-earned siesta. After your nap (or in lieu of it), visit the galleries in the **Instituto Allende,** the country's oldest art school, and

climb the shady staircases of **El Chorro,** the site of San Miguel's founding. Enjoy a shady respite in **Parque Juárez** amid the cries of snowy egrets and the giggles of local children.

End the day in classic San Miguel style: on a rooftop with a view. Just beside the *jardín,* stylish **La Azotea** is a deservedly popular place for cocktails, snacks, and sunsets, with beautiful views of downtown. For a more low-key evening, wrap up the day with a fiery mezcal and some fried grasshoppers at relaxed Oaxacan bar and restaurant **Salón Oaxaca,** which also has a lovely open-air roof deck.

Day 3

Have a fresh, filling breakfast at stylish bistro and bakery **Cumpanio,** then join anthropologist Albert Coffee for a tour of the interesting **Cañada de la Virgen** archaeological site just outside San Miguel de Allende. Alternatively, visit the archaeological site on a daylong **horseback ride** with **Coyote Canyon Adventures,** exploring the gorgeous desert chaparral on your way to the pyramids.

Back in San Miguel, you might want to book

a treatment at **Float Sano** or **Jasmine Day Spa.** If you'd rather stretch your legs, head to the **Fábrica La Aurora,** a unique art and design center housed in a turn-of-the-20th-century former textile factory. You could spend the whole afternoon exploring its labyrinthine hallways, chockablock with art studios, design shops, and galleries.

In the evening, make it a point to attend an **art opening, concert,** or **film screening:** There's almost always something happening in San Miguel, and it's fun to rub elbows with locals at these well-attended events. Afterward, keep up the spirited mood at **El Manantial,** an atmospheric old cantina that serves local mezcal alongside some of the best fish tacos in town.

Day 4

By the time you've spent a few days in San Miguel, you've likely fallen in step with the city's easygoing rhythm. Now it's time to pick up the pace in **Guanajuato,** a lively college town just an hour-and-a-half drive northwest of San Miguel. Start your tour in the **Jardín de la Unión,** the city's music-filled central plaza, then cross the street

to visit the **Templo de San Diego,** which has numerous large-format oil paintings from the 17th century through the post-independence era, many by anonymous artists. Back outside, walk north toward the **Plaza de la Paz,** following Avenida Juárez until you arrive at the atmospheric **Mercado Hidalgo.** Grab a snack in the market, then head to the interesting regional museum inside the historic **Alhóndiga de Granaditas,** just a block away.

Have an artfully prepared lunch at modern-Mexican restaurant **Mestizo,** then spend the afternoon popping into museums, galleries, and shops along **Positos Street;** a highlight is the **Museo Casa Diego Rivera,** the childhood home of the famous muralist. Continue wandering toward the center of town, checking out the fine art galleries and climbing the iconic staircase on the main campus of the **Universidad de Guanajuato.**

Head back to the center of town to relax with a shot of top-shelf tequila at **Bar Tradicional Luna,** where you'll get a front-row view of the mariachi bands strolling the **Jardín de la Unión** plaza. Finish up the evening with tapas

downtown Guanajuato

Historic Architecture

During the 17th and 18th centuries, the silver trade brought prosperity to the towns and settlements along the Camino Real de Tierra Adentro, a route that ran from the northern reaches of New Spain's territory to Mexico City. Working with some of Mexico's most celebrated architects and artists, wealthy families built haciendas, churches, and other buildings in the cities of the Bajío, which continue to dazzle visitors today. Though taking cues from the Old World, the artisans who built these cities brought their own inventive flourishes to the work, adding unique elements to traditional European design.

MEXICAN BAROQUE

Downtown San Miguel de Allende, Guanajuato, and Querétaro are often compared to the Old World, and for good reason: During the colonial era, Mexican architecture followed trends from Spain, where baroque was the dominant aesthetic. An evolution of the classical style favored during the Renaissance, baroque architecture is characterized by its elaborate ornamentation, dramatic use of light, and monumental facades.

the Templo San Roque in Guanajuato

Where to Find It

In Guanajuato, the **Templo San Roque** (page 144) and the **Basílica de Nuestra Señora de Guanajuato** (page 143) are two beautiful representations of the baroque style. In San Miguel, the **Casa de Allende** (page 43) is an example of baroque civil architecture, built in the 18th century by one of the city's prominent families. The impressive baroque altarpieces in the **Templo y Ex-Convento Santa Rosa de Viterbo** (page 197) in Querétaro have been partially destroyed, but along with the building's interesting facade, they provide a wonderful example of inventive Mexican baroque.

CHURRIGUERESQUE

During the late 1600s, Spanish architect José Benito de Churriguera developed a style of ornamentation, called churrigueresque, that was a more elaborate offshoot of baroque design. Influenced by Churriguera's florid aesthetic, Mexican architects began to incorporate more extravagant embellishments onto the facades of 18th-century churches.

Where to Find It

In San Miguel, visit the **Templo de San Francisco** (page 46) for a fine example of early-18th-century churrigueresque ornamentation. You can see the direct influence of Churriguera's style in the elaborately carved sandstone columns. In Guanajuato's Valenciana neighborhood, the astonishingly detailed sandstone relief on the **Templo de San Cayetano** (page 154) is known throughout the country as one of the most beautiful representations of churrigueresque ornamentation.

GOTHIC REVIVAL

In Northern Europe, the mid-1700s saw a resurgent interest in medieval architecture, known as the Gothic Revival. Gaining popularity in the western hemisphere in the 1800s, this style was borrowed from traditional Gothic design and aesthetics.

Where to Find It

In San Miguel, there is one unmistakable neo-Gothic structure: the pink sandstone facade on the famous **Parroquia de San Miguel Arcángel** (page 42), inspired by Gothic cathedrals in Europe. Its towering spires and pointed arches are distinct trademarks of the style, though the design of the *parroquia* is largely original.

NEOCLASSICAL

During the late 1700s, classical architecture also experienced a revival worldwide. Typified by its clean lines and symmetry, neoclassical design often employs large arches, columns, and pilasters.

Where to Find It

In Guanajuato, there are many striking neoclassical buildings downtown, from the austere **Alhóndiga de Granaditas** (page 146) to the impressive columned facade of **Teatro Juárez** (page 140). In Querétaro, the elaborate **Fuente de Neptuno** (page 198), built in 1797, is neoclassical in style. Also note the massive neoclassical altarpieces in many of San Miguel's churches—including the **Templo de la Inmaculada Concepción** (page 46) and the **Parroquia de San Miguel Arcángel** (page 42).

THE HACIENDA

The hacienda—a large estate overseen by a Spanish family—was a major influence on Bajío architecture. Throughout the region, small towns, such as Dolores Hidalgo, were often founded as haciendas, eventually growing large enough to become cities in their own right. In downtown San Miguel, many present-day individual homes were once part of larger family estates.

the Templo de San Francisco

Where to Find It

For a glimpse into the lifestyle of 17th- and 18th-century haciendas, visit the **Ex-Hacienda San Gabriel de Barrera** (page 151) or the **Museo Gene Byron** (page 152) in Guanajuato.

gate at Museo Gene Byron

and cocktails at **El Midi Bistró,** a stylish French restaurant in the cultural and culinary center **Casa Cuatro.** At this second-floor spot, there's a full bar, a cool crowd, and often **live music** in the evenings.

Day 5

Back in San Miguel, it's worth getting an early start to visit the **natural hot springs** while the air is still cool and there aren't big crowds in the pools. Just 10 minutes from downtown San Miguel, flower-filled **La Gruta** is the best-known spot for soaking, but there are several other bathing pools along the highway to **Dolores Hidalgo.**

Enjoy the post-soak peace of mind as you visit the neighboring town of **Atotonilco.** The main attraction in this dusty outpost is the massive **Santuario de Jesús Nazareno de Atotonilco,** an unusual church with an important place in Mexican history. Inside, the walls are painted floor-to-ceiling with **inventive religious frescoes.**

Spend the remainder of the afternoon stopping into **galleries,** reading on the rooftop of your hotel, or digging into a slice of fig cake at French bakery **Petit Four.** As the sun sets, have a relaxing plate of tacos alfresco at **Jardín Rama,** or join the nightly crowds for jazz and *arrachera* at Mexican steak house **Tío Lucas** before crashing to sleep amid the clang of church bells.

Three Days of Design

San Miguel de Allende has a long tradition of excellence in architecture, the arts, and design. Today, this small city is home to an eclectic, entertaining mix of design shops, artist-run galleries, and contemporary boutique hotels, which contrast delightfully with the grand colonial-era architecture and old-fashioned ambience in the city center.

Friday

San Miguel is a wonderful place to learn about Mexico's unique traditions in handcraft, with

the elaborate carved-wood doors at the Casa del Mayorazgo de la Canal

Fábrica La Aurora

Hotel Matilda has an impressive art collection.

many well-curated shops that elevate craft to fine art status. Much of the gorgeous craftwork at gallery **Flor de Canela** has been signed by the artist, with many prize-winning artisans represented within the collection. Just across the street, **La Calaca** is a wonderful little shop that specializes in antique and one-of-a-kind artisan pieces, including ceremonial masks. It's also worth visiting the gift shop at the **Casa de Cultura Citibanamex** in the **Casa del Mayorazgo de la Canal,** just a few blocks away; though small, it represents top-quality artisan work, in addition to selling a nice collection of books about Mexican craft traditions, published by the Citibanamex Foundation.

See a joyous approach to popular craft at **La Esquina: Museo del Jugete Popular Mexicano,** a lovely two-floor museum that showcases the fine craftsmanship and creativity behind **traditional Mexican toys.** It's almost impossible to resist picking something up at their delightful on-site gift shop. Next, seek out the small shop **Juana Cata** on Recreo, which specializes in *huipiles*, embroidered blouses,

hand-loomed shawls, and other rare and beautiful textiles from the state of Oaxaca. From here, stop for lunch at stylish **La Mezcalería,** which has a chic Mexican ambience, or have tea and a vegan snack at **Néctar,** a little café inside the garden-and-bird-centric boutique **Camino Silvestre,** where you can sit at tables surrounded by flowers and pretty glass hummingbird feeders.

Now that you've had a thorough introduction to traditional craft, check out the city's contemporary art scene with a low-key gallery tour. In the heart of downtown, **Galeria Nudo** and **Noel Cayetano Arte Contemporáneo** are good spots to see contemporary work by Mexican artists. For some of San Miguel's most **avant-garde exhibitions,** as well as nice shows by local artists, walk out to **Yam Gallery** at the **Instituto Allende.** While there, be sure to stop into the gallery's sister shop, **Yam Gallery Silver,** which showcases work by legendary Taxco silver designer William Spratling. After browsing, wander around the Instituto Allende's historic stone courtyard, which is decorated with **colorful murals.** Wrap up the day with a

Cuna Quince

drink at the bar at **Nena Sky Bar** at boutique Hotel Nena, or snap pictures of the famous panoramic views at **Luna Rooftop Tapas Bar** in the Rosewood Hotel.

Saturday

Saturday's agenda is for the serious shopper. Start the day at the wonderfully curated boutique **Mixta**, where the **eclectic collection** of furniture, clothing, jewelry, original art, and accessories includes work by some interesting contemporary Mexican designers. Around the corner, there are several fun boutiques and a lovely showroom for furniture line **Namuh** in the **Cuna Quince,** a little shopping plaza in a historic building on Cuna de Allende. From there, visit upscale clothier **Recreo,** on the street of the same name, where a line of beautiful, high-quality wraps, shawls, and ponchos blend classic Mexican aesthetics with a contemporary, luxe look.

San Miguel's newly chic aesthetic is reflected in the many new "concept" boutiques and shopping centers in town, the best of which is the urban-esque dining and shopping complex **Doce**

18 Concept House. Here, you'll find dozens of small shops and galleries stuffed inside a restored colonial-era mansion (Mexico City–based designer Carla Fernández is a standout), plus a hip urban-style food court in the back of the building, if you'd like to grab a taco or a coffee on your way around town.

Next, hop a taxi north of the *centro* to the **Fábrica La Aurora,** a large art and shopping center in a converted turn-of-the-20th-century textile factory. With dozens of **galleries, studios, and shops** tucked into unexpected nooks and crannies, you'll find nearly endless visual inspiration in the goods on offer— from **Italian linens** at La Bottega di Casa to **handwoven textile art** at the studio of artist Nelly Lorenzo to **Mexican antiques** at atmospheric La Buhardilla. The space itself is enchanting, with an old-style industrial feeling, largely left intact despite the factory's reinvention as a shopping center. Finish the day with a glass of wine at **Food Factory La Aurora,** or relax in the expansive garden at **Geek & Coffee,** a mellow café in the old factory complex.

If you haven't yet been invited to an **opening**

Picture-Perfect San Miguel

San Miguel de Allende's colorful cityscapes and sweeping vistas are likely to inspire your inner photographer. Even camera-phone snapshots of the city can be surprisingly stunning, an auspicious situation for enthusiastic amateurs. If you want to bring home an impressive album of travel shots, here are some subjects to inspire point-and-shoot magic.

NIGHTTIME AT THE PARISH

Parroquia de San Miguel Arcángel is the most recognizable—and most frequently photographed—monument in town. Catching this unique church in the right light can be a bit of a challenge; for a shot worthy of any postcard, steady your hand and photograph the church at night, when its many arches are illuminated.

COBBLESTONE STREETS

Calle Aldama extends from the central square to Parque Juárez; its cobblestones give way to an iconic vista of the painted domes of the *parroquia*, rising above the multicolor jumble of colonial-era mansions.

MARKET ROSES

At the Mercado Ignacio Ramírez, San Miguel de Allende's covered market, the heaps of roses, lilies, carnations, gladiolas, and gerberas add a colorful flourish to the Mexican market scene.

MARIACHIS

A picture of the *jardín* becomes all the more alluring when you capture a group of mariachi musicians mid-tune, dressed in the traditional *charro* costume and singing in unison.

DYNAMIC PANORAMAS

If you are willing to huff and puff for a photo op, head up to El Mirador, a small rest stop on the Salida a Querétaro, which offers sweeping views of the city center, the reservoir, and the valley below town.

the cobblestone Calle Aldama

PARADES AND FESTIVALS

From the explosion of fireworks over the *parroquia* on Día de la Independencia to the giant papier-mâché figures that dance outside the church at traditional weddings, there is no shortage of festivals, color, and pageantry around San Miguel de Allende.

DONKEYS

The image of a packed donkey walking down a picturesque residential street is classic San Miguel de Allende. If you see the donkey's owner, it's customary to offer a small tip after you snap a shot of the beast.

colorful building in San Miguel de Allende

exhibition during your tour around town, pick up a copy of *Atención San Miguel* to see what's happening tonight. If a popular **local artist** is having a show, you can expect a flurry of attendees and little cups of cheap Chilean wine at the gallery.

Sunday

As beautiful as they are from the outside, San Miguel's grand old homes are often more stunning behind their colonial-era facades. If you'd like to peek behind closed doors, spend Sunday afternoon on the weekly **House and Garden Tour,** run by the **Biblioteca de San Miguel de Allende,** which will take you (and a busload of people) inside several of the city's most splendid houses. Though the itinerary changes frequently, the tour often includes properties that have been featured in magazines and coffee-table books.

Many of San Miguel's shops close early on Sundays (if they open at all), so continue your design tour with an afternoon drink at design-centric **Hotel Matilda,** a modern boutique hotel that has a happening bar and an excellent contemporary art collection. From Matilda, it's just a few steps to **Parque Juárez,** where sculptures made by local artists are on display throughout the shaded walkways. Wrap up the day with an early supper at **La Parada,** a Peruvian restaurant in a stylish open-air courtyard.

Echoes of Independence

Mexico's war for independence officially began in the small town of Dolores, where popular pastor and rebel leader Miguel Hidalgo raised the first battle cry against the Spanish crown on September 16, 1810. San Miguel de Allende, Querétaro, and Guanajuato also played major roles in the fight for independence. Today, the Bajío region, which celebrated 200 years of independence in 2010, boasts historic sites scattered throughout the major cities.

CASA DE ALLENDE

The seeds of independence were sown in early-19th-century San Miguel. At his home on the town square, Ignacio Allende held secret meetings to plan a revolt against the Spanish crown. Today, his home is the Casa de Allende (page 43), a museum chronicling the life and times of the city's most famous insurgent.

CASA DEL CORREGIDORA

Querétaro's *corregidor* (mayor), was a coconspirator against the Spanish crown, often meeting in secret with Allende and Hidalgo. The mayor's wife, Josefa Ortiz de Domínguez, was instrumental in saving the independence movement from being quashed: After the Spanish uncovered the independence plot, Ortiz de Domínguez sent warning to the conspirators, saving them from capture. The Domínguez home is today known as the Casa del Corregidora (page 194).

PARROQUIA DE NUESTRA SEÑORA DE LOS DOLORES

Once Allende and his coconspirators realized that their plot had been uncovered, they launched their revolt. Father Miguel rang the bell in the Parroquia de Nuestra Señora de los Dolores (page 123) to summon his forces. In front of a crowd, Father Hidalgo and the Mexican army declared independence from Spain, in the early morning hours of September 16, 1810. Today, the bell from the parish in Dolores hangs in Mexico City's Palacio Nacional, where the president reenacts Hidalgo's independence cry—known as the Grito de Dolores—on the night of September 15 each year.

SANTUARIO DE JESÚS NAZARENO DE ATOTONILCO

From Dolores, Father Miguel Hidalgo rode with his cavalry to the Santuario de Jesús Nazareno

statue of independence hero Ignacio Allende

de Atotonilco (page 112). There, he pulled down a banner bearing an image of the Virgen de Guadalupe, which became the new flag for the insurgent army. To this day, the virgin's image is a symbol of Mexican culture.

LA ALHÓNDIGA DE GRANADITAS

Though San Miguel and Celaya quickly fell to the insurgent army, Guanajuato's royalist leaders resisted. The first major battle in the war—and one of its bloodiest—took place at La Alhóndiga de Granaditas (page 146). Here, an indigenous miner nicknamed El Pípila became a hero of the independence movement, leading the rebels to victory. (Months later, Spanish forces would capture Allende and Hidalgo and hang their severed heads from the corners of the Alhóndiga.)

OTHER INDEPENDENCE SITES

In addition to historical sites, there are many Bajío streets and parks named after independence heroes, as well as monuments to the independence movement. Note the pretty Plaza de la Corregidora (page 194) in Querétaro and Guanajuato's titanic monument to El Pípila (page 150), as well as the statue to El Pípila at the southern entrance to San Miguel de Allende, among many other tributes to the region's war heroes.

The Bajío Palate

Mexico's color and creativity are reflected in its wonderful food. Every region in the country is distinguished by its own culinary traditions, as well as ingredients native to the land. In San Miguel de Allende and the surrounding region, there are several well-known local products and dishes worth seeking out on a trip to the Bajío. In addition, the growing organic and natural food movement, as well as a burgeoning wine industry, have made the Bajío a new culinary destination. If you want to get a taste of the highlands, here's what to try.

Nopal

Nopal, or prickly pear cactus, is a popular vegetable throughout Mexico and abundant in the highlands around San Miguel. It is often served as a stuffing in *gorditas* or grilled whole and served with cheese. One tasty stew served throughout the region features chopped *nopal* with garbanzo beans and cilantro. Find *nopal* in San Miguel at the **Mercado Ignacio Ramírez** (page 93), where you can buy it both fresh and prepared, and at **Hecho en México** (page 92), where you can order it as a grilled side dish.

Xoconostle

Throughout Mexico, the *tuna* (prickly pear fruit) is consumed whole or blended into ice cream and *aguas*. In the Bajío, a type of sour *tuna* called *xoconostle* is used in regional dishes as well as in sweets, where it takes on a pleasingly tart flavor. Buy some from Santa Rosa de Lima's **Conservas Santa Rosa** (page 185), or try a tangy *xoconostle*-mezcal cocktail at wonderful **Las Mercedes Banquetes y Restaurante** (page 173) in Guanajuato.

Queso Ranchero and Other Local Cheeses

Called *queso fresco* in other parts of Mexico, the Bajío's delicious *queso ranchero* is a fresh, white, salty cheese, often crumbled atop enchiladas or guacamole. Look for *queso ranchero* at supermarkets, at San Miguel's **Mercado de Martes** (page 95), or at the **Mercado de la Cruz** (page 200) in Querétaro.

In recent years, many small and artisanal cheese-makers have been cropping up around the Bajío. Many, like **Cava Bocanegra** (page 225) in Querétaro or **Remo's** (page 95) in San Miguel, have country stores where you can pick up their products (or take a tour of the ranch or cheese-making facilities). In San Miguel de Allende, drop by **Luna de Queso** (page 93) for a large and excellent selection of Mexican-made cheese and dairy, among other delicious local deli products.

Cajeta

Cajeta, caramelized milk candy, is a specialty of Celaya, a small industrial city just an hour east of San Miguel. Created with a mix of scalded goat and cow milk, *cajeta* sauce is served in crepes and on ice cream or slathered onto wafers. You can also find *cajeta* candy rolled in nuts. Try some at Guanajuato's **La Catrina** (page 166), or order a scoop of *cajeta*-flavored ice cream in the town square in **Dolores Hidalgo** (page 126). For excellent *cajeta* and other traditional sweets, stop into **Dulces Bernal** (page 227), in the state of Querétaro.

Wine

The Bajío's nascent wine industry has been growing rapidly over the past decade. If you'd like to taste some local wines, schedule a tasting at one of the new wineries near San Miguel de Allende, like **La Santísima Trinidad** (page 127), or in Querétaro state, like **Viñedos La Redonda** (page 224). Or look for local bottles at restaurants like **Nómada** (page 91) in San Miguel de Allende. **Folk** (page 228), a wine bar in the small town of Bernal, specializes in regional wines.

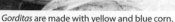
Gorditas are made with yellow and blue corn.

stew made with *nopal*

Mezcal

Though the most famous varieties of mezcal come from the state of Oaxaca, you can try locally produced mezcal, like the Guanajuato brand **Jaral de Berrio** (page 270), at bars and cantinas like **El Manantial** (page 53) in San Miguel de Allende or **Los Campos** (page 172) in Guanajuato.

Mixiote

Popular here and in the Valley of Mexico, *mixiotes* are slow-cooked meats (typically rabbit, chicken, lamb, and pork) wrapped in maguey leaves and steamed in an underground pit. While in San Miguel, you can order *mixiotes* at the rooftop restaurant **La Posadita** (page 87).

Gorditas

Gorditas are thick corn flatbreads, grilled and stuffed with fillings like cheese, chile peppers, chicken, or beans. *Gorditas* are sold by street vendors and in market stalls throughout the region. You'll find freshly made *gorditas* with a range of savory fillings on street corners throughout Guanajuato and San Miguel de Allende, or try the larger Querétaro-style *gordita* at the **Mercado de la Cruz** (page 200) in Querétaro.

Enchiladas Mineras

A hearty meal suited to a hungry laborer, these cheese-stuffed "miner's enchiladas" are bathed in *guajillo* chile sauce and topped with a generous serving of sautéed potatoes, carrots, and cheese. Fill your stomach with this regional specialty at **Truco 7** (page 169) or the **Mercado Hidalgo** (page 143) in Guanajuato. Very similar to *enchiladas mineras*, *enchiladas queretanas* are also bathed in a *guajillo* sauce; find them at **Cenaduria Blas** (page 210) in Querétaro.

San Miguel de Allende

San Miguel de Allende is a town of a thousand picture postcards, renowned for its Mexican baroque architecture and sparkling blue skies.

You can hardly turn a corner without finding a splendid scene before you. On one block, there is a crumbling stone chapel, its iron bells hanging crookedly in the belfry. On another, a flower seller stacks bushels of roses atop an 18th-century fountain. Along the winding streets of the *centro histórico* (historical district), vines of magenta bougainvillea spill over the walls of colonial residences. The setting sun throws a scarlet blanket across the sky throughout the winter and spring. It is precisely when everything seems too beautiful to believe that you stumble upon something new: an old wooden doorway, a wedding party led by a flower-wreathed donkey, an unexpected burst of fireworks over the starlit skyline.

San Miguel de Allende is much more than a beautiful facade. Warm, accepting, and amiable, it's a place of living culture and community. On the weekends, the sidewalks are pleasantly humming with diners, revelers, and families. Mariachi musicians fill the central *jardín*. Crowds spill from the doors of overstuffed galleries, where local artists host exhibitions fueled by glasses of cheap *vino tinto* (red wine). Join the crowd and you'll quickly learn that there are no tourists in San Miguel. Everyone's a local in this welcoming city, where cultures and people mix as easily as lime juice and tequila.

As San Miguel becomes bigger and more cosmopolitan, the cozy ambience that once defined the town has begun to transform into something more bustling. There are restaurants serving formal tasting menus, chic mezcal bars, and rooftop lounges with New York City price tags—as well as sprawling residential developments and big-box stores outside the city center. Luxury boutique hotels, once a rarity in a town known for its quaint bed-and-breakfasts and family-run inns, have cropped up throughout the *centro,* while high-end shops and food halls are now filling many colonial-era mansions.

Change, however, is part of San Miguel's identity. Since the 1940s, San Miguel has been home to a community of expatriates from

---

Previous: celebratory flags flying in San Miguel de Allende; courtyard of Bellas Artes. **Above:** marigold decorations for Día de Muertos.

Look for ★ to find recommended
sights, activities, dining, and lodging.

Highlights

★ **Parroquia de San Miguel Arcángel:**
San Miguel's iconic parish church is a symbol of
the town and one of the most original architectural sights in Mexico (page 42).

★ *El Jardín:* Since the early 18th century, the
central square, or *jardín*, has been the heart and
soul of San Miguel de Allende (page 42).

★ **Parque Juárez:** Spend a peaceful afternoon in the shade of fan palms and jacarandas
in this historic and family-friendly urban park
(page 47).

★ **El Chorro:** Located at the site of San
Miguel's founding, the cascading terraces of El
Chorro are among the most enchanting spots in
town (page 47).

★ **Fábrica La Aurora:** This interesting turn-of-the-20th-century textile factory has been
refashioned as an art and design center, with
more than 35 galleries, shops, and studios, plus
restaurants and cafés (page 49).

★ **El Charco del Ingenio:** An expansive
nature preserve and botanical garden, El Charco
offers sweeping views of the city, charming
nature trails, and excellent bird-watching along
a dramatic canyon ridge (page 50).

★ **Santuario de Jesús Nazareno de
Atotonilco:** One of the finest churches in all
of Mexico, the enigmatic sanctuary in Atotonilco
has been a site of religious retreat and refuge
since the 18th century (page 112).

★ **La Gruta:** Take a morning soak at La Gruta,
one of several bathing spots near San Miguel de
Allende, where thermal pools are surrounded by
lush gardens (page 113).

★ **Cañada de la Virgen:** See another side
of Mexican history at this small but fascinating
archaeological site, located within an expansive nature preserve just outside San Miguel de
Allende (page 116).

San Miguel de Allende

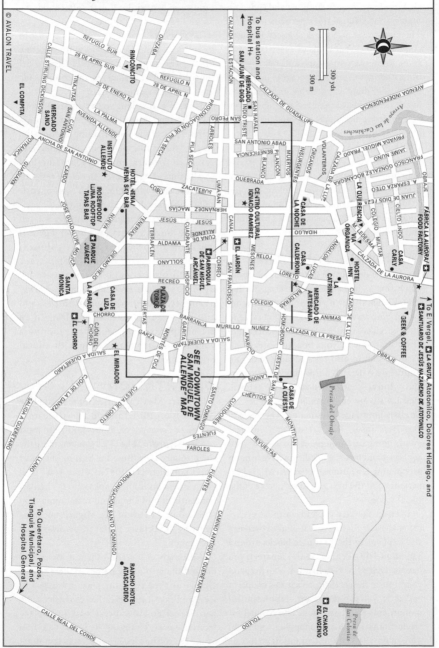

© AVALON TRAVEL

To bus station and
Hospital H+

To E Vergel, LA GRUTA, Atotonilco, Dolores Hidalgo, and
SANTUARIO DE JESÚS NAZARENO DE ATOTONILCO

0   300 yds
0   300 m

REFUGIO SUR

28 DE APRIL SUR

EL RINCONCITO

28 DE APRIL N

REFUGIO N

20 DE ENERO N

ORIZABA

CALZADA DE LA ESTACIÓN

MERCADO
SAN JUAN DE DIOS

CALZADA DE GUADALUPE

AVENIDA INDEPENDENCIA

Arroyo de las Cachinches

PRIVADA MIGUEL PRADO

JAIME NUNÓ

FRANCISCO GONZÁLEZ BOCANEGRA

FÁBRICA LA AURORA/
FOOD FACTORY

TINAJITAS

LA PALMA

CALLE STIRLING DICKINSON

EL COMPITA

AVENIDA ALLENDE

CJÓN SAN ANTONIO

SAN ANTONIO

INSTITUTO ALLENDE

ROSEWOOD/
LUNA ROOFTOP
TAPAS BAR

PARQUE JUÁREZ

MERCADO
SANO

ANCHA DE SAN ANTONIO

POTRANCA

GUADIANA

JOSÉ GUADALUPE TORRICA

CARDO

DIEZMO VIEJO DE LA

CUBO

NUEVA

ZACATEROS

SUBIDA

HERNÁNDEZ MACÍAS

JESÚS

ALDAMA

CUADRANTE

TERRAPLÉN

SOLLANO

RECREO

HOSPICIO

CORREO

SAN FRANCISCO

RELOJ

MESONES

HIDALGO

LUCAS

VIA
ORGÁNICA

LEDESMA

CIELO LINDO

MILITAR

JUAN DE DIOS PEZA

A. ESPARZA OTEO

CASA
CARLY

CASA
CARLY

HOSTEL
INN

CALZADA DE LA AURORA

CALZADA DE LA LUZ

CALZADA DE LA PRESA

GEEK & COFFEE

OBRAJE

Presa del Obraje

Presa de
las Colonias

EL CHARCO
DEL INGENIO

TOLEDO

NENA SKY BAR/
HOTEL NENA

HOTEL NENA

SANTA
MÓNICA

CASA DE
LIZA

CHORRO

EL CHORRO

CJÓN DEL
CHORRO

EL MIRADOR

SALIDA A QUERÉTARO

CUESTA DE SAN JOSÉ

LANDÍN

CASA DE
LA CUESTA

CUESTA DE LORETO

CJÓN DE LA DANZA

SALIDA A QUERÉTARO

PROLONGACIÓN SANTO DOMINGO

SANTO DOMINGO

CURTIDORES

CHEPITOS

FUENTES

FUENTES

FAROLES

REVUELTAS

MONTITLÁN

CAMINO ANTIGUO A QUERÉTARO

To Querétaro, Pozos,
Tianguis Municipal, and
Hospital General

RANCHO HOTEL
ATASCADERO

CALLE REAL DEL CONDE

LLANO

PARROQUIA
DE SAN MIGUEL
ARCÁNGEL

EL JARDÍN

PLAZA DE
TOROS

CUNA DE
ALLENDE

CENTRO CULTURAL
IGNACIO RAMÍREZ

CASA DE
LA NOCHE

CASA
CALDERÓN

LA
CATRINA

MERCADO DE
ARTESANÍA

LA QUIRENCIA

COLEGIO

ÁNIMAS

LORETO

BALDERAS

HOMOBONO

APARICIO

NÚÑEZ

MURILLO

COLEGIO

BARRANCA

GARITA

GARZA

MONTES DE OCA

SALIDA A QUERÉTARO

SEE "DOWNTOWN
SAN MIGUEL DE
ALLENDE" MAP

HUERTAS

LA PARADA

CALLE DE LA DANZA

ARBOLES

PILA SECA

PROLONGACIÓN DE PILA SECA

UMARÁN

CANAL

JESÚS

CÓDO

TENERÍAS

ORGANOS

VOLANTEROS

INSURGENTES

BENEFICENCIA

BLANCO

QUEBRADA

SAN ANTONIO ABAD

PLANCÓN

MUERTOS

SAN PEDRO

SAN RAFAEL

INDIO TRISTE

ESPARZA OTEO

several nations, predominantly the United States and Canada. Many of the city's first foreign residents came to study art and ended up making San Miguel their permanent home. The city draws foreigners of every ilk, who come here to live dreams of every type. For some, it's a place to escape and relax, while others come to start a new career or open a business. Today, expatriates are joined by Mexicans who have come to San Miguel from bigger cities, many opening businesses and buying homes.

What makes San Miguel so remarkable is its capacity to accept change yet never lose hold of its character. As the suburbs expand, prices rise, and gluten-free cookies become as ubiquitous as tamales, San Miguel is still a vivid and welcoming place, defined by culture and traditions, both old and new.

PLANNING YOUR TIME

San Miguel de Allende is just as much about downtime as it is about sightseeing. With a friendly, small-town atmosphere and year-round sunny weather, it's the perfect place to unwind, either on a bench in the town square or on the patio of your bed-and-breakfast. Visitors should also take advantage of San Miguel de Allende's surprisingly robust art and cultural scene. When you arrive in town, pick up a copy of *Atención San Miguel,* an English-language newspaper. The weekly *Que Pasa* insert lists artistic and cultural events going on throughout the week as well as classes and tours. Attending a lecture or an art opening is a quintessential San Miguel experience and the best way to get a taste of the social scene.

Even as the city expands, almost everything there is to do, see, eat, and experience still happens in the 10 square blocks around San Miguel de Allende's central square. If you have just **a day or two** in town, plan to spend your time in the *centro histórico.* In a couple of easy days, you can visit many of the beautiful monuments that have made San Miguel famous, fit in some quality shopping, and eat in a few of the city's best restaurants. If your time

is short, a **guided walking tour** can provide an interesting introduction to San Miguel's sights and history, leaving the afternoon free for an independent ramble.

If you plan to spend **more than a couple of days** in San Miguel, you will have time to visit the botanical garden El Charco del Ingenio, the hot springs, or the countryside for horseback riding or hiking.

No matter how long you are in San Miguel, take the opportunity to spend a few hours wandering the town. Strolling around the *centro,* you will stumble upon little alleyways barely fit for cars, gurgling fountains, and small stone chapels. Even the quiet residential streets are charming, with rows of rust-colored houses draped with flowers.

As many residents of San Miguel will tell you, the longer you stay, the better it gets. If you come to town for **a longer sojourn,** there are plenty of off-the-beaten-track places to visit, enough restaurants to fill up weeks, and a seemingly endless array of classes, educational opportunities, and cultural events. Consider enrolling in an art or Spanish-language class, joining a yoga group, or volunteering with a local organization.

ORIENTATION

Like most Mexican cities, San Miguel de Allende is organized around a town square—the *plaza principal* or, as it is known to most residents, **jardín.** The blocks surrounding the town square constitute the busiest and most important district in the city. Here, you'll find government buildings, banks, and the highest concentration of shops and restaurants. You will also find many of San Miguel's most interesting sights just a stone's throw away from each other.

Although city streets form a loose grid around the *jardín,* the names of these streets change as they cross the plaza from east to west and north to south. For example, Calle San Francisco runs directly into the plaza from the east, changing its name to Canal as it exits to the west. Even streets that don't run directly through the plaza will often take new names as they change latitude. One major street changes its name four times as it crosses downtown: from Pila Seca to Cuadrante to Hospicio to Garita.

To make everything more complicated, many of these streets have changed their names during the course of history. In many cases, the former street name is still posted on the corner! For the San Miguel novice, navigation can be a bit frustrating, if also a bit amusing and folkloric. When in doubt, look for the spires of the *parroquia* (church) in the town square, or just ask a local for directions. People in San Miguel are famously friendly, and most will gladly help you find what you are looking for.

There are some sights, restaurants, and accommodations in the residential neighborhoods that surround the city center. The **San Antonio** and **Guadiana** neighborhoods to the south, as well as the **Guadalupe** and **Aurora** neighborhoods to the north, are accessible on foot, or, more quickly, by taxi. Beyond these central neighborhoods, San Miguel de Allende is ringed by residential communities, predominantly inhabited by Mexican families and a smattering of expatriates.

HISTORY

When the Spanish arrived on the North American continent, the plains around modern San Miguel de Allende were populated by nomadic tribes, part of a culture known to the Spanish as La Gran Chichimeca. In 1542, Franciscan friar Juan de San Miguel arrived in the Laja River Valley. He founded the settlement of San Miguel de los Chichimecas along the river. Between 1548 and 1549, French friar Bernardo Cossin moved the settlement to the hill of Izcuinapan, site of a copious natural spring known today as El Chorro.

In the mid-16th century, the discovery of large silver veins near the cities of Zacatecas and Guanajuato changed the course of history for this small settlement. Located between the northern mines and Mexico City, San Miguel became a strategic town for traders traveling along the Camino Real de Tierra Adentro (Royal Inland Route). San Miguel's association with the silver trade led to tremendous prosperity. During the 17th century, San Miguel grew from a settlement of just a few hundred to a small city of about 15,000. The people of San Miguel commissioned architect Marcos Antonio Sobrarías to build a new parish church in 1683, and by the early 18th century, wealthy criollos (colonial-era

A wedding party departs the *parroquia* with a live band in tow.

term for Mexicans of Spanish descent) had begun to build luxurious homes around the town's main plaza, in addition to commissioning churches and monuments throughout the city. The opulence attracted some of the country's most celebrated architects and painters.

In the 18th century, San Miguel began to lose hold of its wealth as changes to Spanish governance of the colonies affected the silver trade, tobacco farming, and other industries. In the meantime, the seeds of independence were being sown across the region. In San Miguel, Ignacio Allende organized secret meetings with coconspirators in his home on the town square. When the fight for independence began in 1810, San Miguel fell peacefully to the newly formed Mexican army. There was no violent conflict in San Miguel, but the town was ruinously sacked after its surrender. A year later, Ignacio Allende was captured by the Spanish forces and executed for treason.

While Allende is the city's most celebrated name, San Miguel was the birthplace of many independence heroes, including Juan Aldama, the Malo and Lanzagorta brothers, and Juan José de los Reyes Martínez, or El Pípila, who became famous for his role at the Alhóndiga de Granaditas in the city of Guanajuato. After the protracted War of Independence ended, San Miguel was largely destroyed. Silver production dropped, and the city went into decline. By 1821, there were only 5,000 residents. The town was renamed San Miguel de Allende in 1826.

San Miguel remained sleepy, rural, and largely forgotten until the early 20th century. It was declared a national monument by the Mexican government in 1926. Shortly thereafter, Latin America's first art school, La Escuela Universitaria de Bellas Artes, opened in an 18th-century cloister downtown. After World War II, a handful of Americans came to study at the school under the GI Bill. Many never left. In 2008, the entire downtown district of San Miguel de Allende was named a World Heritage Site by the United Nations.

Sights

Located on the Camino Real de Tierra Adentro (Royal Inland Route), San Miguel de Allende grew rapidly during the 17th and 18th centuries, when it benefited greatly from the wealth of the colonial-era silver trade. Today, San Miguel's *centro histórico* is a unique example of city planning from that era, with an unusual mix of architectural styles. In particular, the town is recognized for its fine 18th-century Mexican baroque buildings. In 1926, San Miguel de Allende was declared a national monument by the Mexican government, a designation that, among other things, prohibits the construction of tall buildings or other structures that would compromise the city's historic downtown. As a result, the center of San Miguel de Allende has been remarkably well preserved, even as the city expands around it.

Most of San Miguel de Allende's historic architecture is religious, with many beautiful churches, chapels, and convents crammed into the narrow streets of the *centro histórico*. Many of these old churches are still used for religious services, though visitors and tourists are welcome to go inside. When entering a church, be respectful by speaking in a low voice and not using the flash on your camera. If a mass or ceremony is in progress, observe before entering. Tourists sometimes wander into churches during more personal events, like funerals, which are best left to the family. If you would like to avoid religious services altogether, most churches do not hold mass 1pm-5pm, though note that some also close their doors to the public at this time.

Downtown San Miguel de Allende

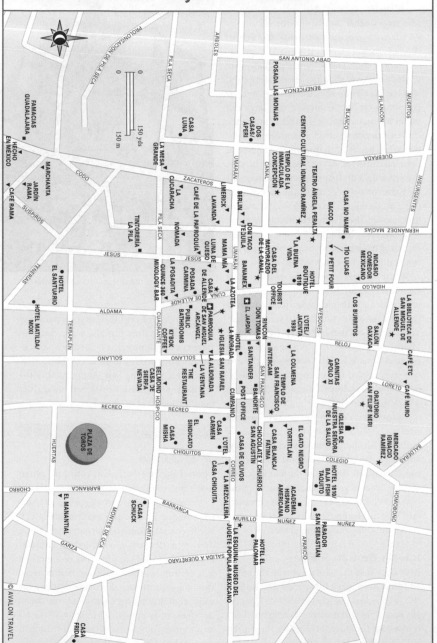

© AVALON TRAVEL

CENTRO HISTÓRICO

★ Parroquia de San Miguel Arcángel

The neo-Gothic sandstone towers of the **Parroquia de San Miguel Arcángel** (Plaza Principal s/n, tel. 415/152-4197, generally 7am-1:45pm and 3:30pm-9pm daily) are the rosy crown of the city. The building itself was constructed in the 16th century and, as old photographs corroborate, was large but rather unspectacular. In the 19th century, the church's facade received a complete renovation at the hands of an imaginative architect, Zeferino Gutiérrez. According to local history, this self-taught draftsman based his design for the parish on prints of the Gothic cathedral in Cologne, Germany. No matter what Gutiérrez had in mind, the results are entirely original, with cascading bricks of pink sandstone surrounding the peaked archways of the parish, concluding in three pointed bell towers.

While the exterior of the *parroquia* is elaborate, the interior's design is spare and neoclassical, with towering stone columns flanking the altar and chapels, some gilded. There is a carved statue of the eponymous San Miguel Arcángel on the altar; however, there is a more notable sculpture of Jesus in the east transept, carved from cane bark and highlighted by a backdrop of turquoise Byzantine mosaic and aging murals.

Today, the Parroquia de San Miguel Arcángel is still the parish seat (*parroquia* means parish church), mass is held here daily, and weddings take place almost every weekend. On days of celebration, the four iron bells of the *parroquia* are manually rung from the towers. When you hear their merry cacophony, look for the figures between the narrow arches, spinning the bells in circles.

Iglesia de San Rafael

Also known as the Santa Escuela, the small and often overlooked **Iglesia de San Rafael** (Plaza Principal s/n, tel. 415/152-4197, generally 8am-8pm daily) shares its courtyard entrance with the *parroquia*. Inside, the church is a wash of aqua, with turquoise tile floors

revelers in front of the *parroquia* during the Día de San Miguel Arcángel

and painted blue ceilings. Large oil paintings and wooden saints line the walls, some in rather dramatic dioramas. There is a particularly nice oil painting to the left of the neoclassical altar depicting San Miguel. Above the Iglesia de San Rafael, a brick bell tower rings out the time every 15 minutes.

TOP EXPERIENCE

★ El Jardín

The town square—officially called the *plaza principal,* but known to all as the *jardín*—is the heart and soul of San Miguel de Allende, surrounded by colonial-era mansions and bordered to the south by the *parroquia*. From dawn to dusk, the *jardín* is filled with a pleasant crowd of locals and tourists resting their legs on iron benches, walking their dogs, or stopping for a chat in the shade of the many well-manicured laurel trees. Above them, hundreds of happy birds tweet away the afternoon, while balloon sellers and fruit vendors make a slow turn through the crowds, tempting the children who've come to play on the flat stone expanse. Sit on a bench to soak up the sun with an ice cream or watch people go by.

Those who've traveled in other parts of Mexico often wonder why San Miguel's square is referred to as the *jardín,* not the *zócalo.* Generally, the term *zócalo* refers to a central plaza adjoining a cathedral. Despite its multitiered opulence, San Miguel's *parroquia* is not a cathedral but a parish church. The cathedral and the seat of the bishop overseeing San Miguel de Allende's parish are in the city of Celaya, about an hour south of San Miguel.

WALKING TOURS OF *EL JARDÍN*
Patronato Pro Niños (tel. 415/152-7796, www.patronatoproninos.org, US$20), a local nonprofit organization, offers cultural walking tours of San Miguel de Allende's *centro histórico* with knowledgeable English-speaking guides. Tours depart from the *jardín* every Monday, Wednesday, and Friday at 9:45am, cover about 10 blocks, and last about 2.5 hours. There is also a special Thursday morning tour, which focuses on architecture. All of the proceeds from the tour benefit Patronato Pro Niños' medical and dental services program, which provides free or very low-cost medical care to 2,500 children in the San Miguel area, as well as dental services to over 9,000 children.

Casa de Allende
A famous hero in Mexico's War of Independence from Spain, Ignacio Allende was born to a prominent family of San Miguel el Grande in 1769. His family's home, an opulent colonial-era mansion on the southeast corner of the central square, is now the **Museo Histórico de San Miguel** (Cuna de Allende 1, tel. 415/152-2499, www.inah.gob.mx, 9am-4.30pm Tues.-Sun., US$3) The museum is commonly known as Casa de Allende. Today, the space is dedicated to the history of the town and to the life of its most famous former resident.

During the 17th century, the first floor of a colonial mansion was generally reserved for servants' activities and quarters. The museum dedicates these rooms to the history of San Miguel de Allende, from its founding through the independence. The rooms contain a few nice artifacts from the colonial era and a surprising number of informational videos, all in Spanish. Upstairs, the Allende family's living quarters have been restored and re-created. The replica of the kitchen is particularly interesting, since it deviates so greatly from the modern version. It is also worth noting that there were no bathrooms in the opulent Allende home, though a toilet did exist near the horse stables in the pretty back patio.

Casa del Mayorazgo de la Canal
A wealthy businessman from Mexico City, Don Manuel Tomás de Canal moved to San Miguel in 1732. He bought numerous haciendas in the region, took control of San Miguel's textile industry, and made major investments in buildings and infrastructure

Iglesia de San Rafael

throughout the city. He is remembered as one of San Miguel's most generous benefactors. In addition to the money that Canal spent on religious and municipal projects, he spent thousands of pesos lavishly refurbishing his magnificent mansion, which still stands on the corner of Canal and Hidalgo on San Miguel's central square. His home, the **Casa del Mayorazgo de la Canal,** is one of the most spectacular examples of 17th-century civil architecture in the region. Its massive red facade runs along the side of the *jardín,* where a row of balcony windows from the family's living quarters overlook the *parroquia.* Take note of the elaborately carved wooden doorways on the north side of the building, flanked by towering stone columns. The niche above them holds a stone figure of Our Lady of Loreto and the family coat of arms.

Today, the Casa del Mayorazgo de la Canal is officially the **Casa de Cultura Citibanamex** (Canal 4, tel. 415/152-7584, www.casasdeculturabanamex.com, 9am-6pm Mon.-Fri., 10am-6pm Sat.-Sun., free), owned and operated by Citibanamex's excellent cultural foundation. Visitors can peek inside the home's impressive inner courtyard and back patio, where soaring archways separate the first floor from the second. Several small exhibition spaces are dedicated to rotating exhibits of work by important Mexican and international artists. In addition, the foundation runs a small but beautifully curated gift shop, featuring high-quality Mexican crafts, as well as a selection of books from the foundation's publishing imprint.

Oratorio San Felipe Neri

During the 18th century, the congregation of San Felipe Neri was rapidly gaining popularity throughout New Spain. In San Miguel de Allende, the congregation constructed the beautiful **Oratorio San Felipe Neri** (Insurgentes s/n, tel. 415/152-0521, generally 9am-6pm daily) in 1714, along with a school, the Colegio San Francisco de Sales. The pink sandstone facade of the *oratorio* is delicately carved and represents the beginning of a shift in architectural aesthetic, from baroque to churrigueresque. Above the facade, the church has five beautiful bell towers, which were recently restored. The unpainted pink sandstone tower to the northwest of the church is particularly lovely.

Inside the oratory, delicate pink frescoes on the ceiling, old tiled walls, and worn floors reflect the church's long history. As in the majority of baroque churches in San Miguel,

Casa del Mayorazgo de la Canal

most of the original paintings and altarpieces in the *oratorio* were lost or looted; however, there are still several of the original 18th-century wooden saints and *retablos* on the walls of the nave. In the 19th century, the famous architect of the *parroquia,* Zeferino Gutiérrez, designed the building's neoclassical altar. As you walk out, look up at the beautiful gilded organ above the entryway. On occasion, the oratory will host organ concerts with this unique instrument.

You will have to make an extra effort if you want to visit the chapel **Santa Casa de Loreto** and the adjoining **Camarín de la Virgen,** a jewel of colonial architecture located in the precept to the left of the oratory's altar. Commissioned and paid for by Don Manuel Tomás de Canal in the 18th century, this elaborate gilded chapel is possibly San Miguel's finest historic structure. The chapel is not normally open to the public. However, the priests do occasionally unlock the chapel's old iron doors during morning and evening masses.

Iglesia de Nuestra Señora de la Salud

Just to the east of the *oratorio* and overlooking the Plaza Cívica, the **Iglesia de Nuestra Señora de la Salud** (Church of Our Lady of Health, Plaza Cívica s/n, no phone, generally 9am-6pm daily) is distinguished by the scalloped stone dome that presides over the church's curved entryway. An influential figure in San Miguel de Allende, Father Luis Felipe Neri de Alfaro erected this church in the 17th century as an accompaniment to the adjoining school, San Francisco de Sales. The school was an important institution in San Miguel de Allende, teaching philosophical thought to many of the young criollo heirs who would oversee the town and, eventually, instigate the independence movement.

Inside the Iglesia de Nuestra Señora de la Salud, the altar surrounds an azure-dressed Virgin Mary in a gilded glass box. Like the oratory, this small church was looted, and most of its original pieces were destroyed. However, to the right of the altar, there is still a beautiful collection of 17th-century oil paintings depicting the Stations of the Cross, some punctured or damaged.

Outside, the **Plaza Cívica** is a popular place to sit in the shade, and it is occasionally the site of crafts or book fairs (during late October, there is a large market selling crafts, candies, and candles for Día de Muertos altarpieces). For many years, the Plaza Cívica

the spires of the Oratorio San Felipe Neri rising over San Miguel's skyline

was also the site of San Miguel de Allende's municipal market.

Templo de San Francisco

The many pigeons perched on the stone facade of the **Templo de San Francisco** (San Francisco s/n, esq. con Juárez, tel. 415/152-0947, 10am-2pm and 4pm-7:30pm Mon.-Sat., hours vary Sun.)—despite the city's attempts to ward them off with chicken wire—have found plenty of places to nest amid the ornate carvings of this church's churrigueresque entryway. A fine example of Mexican baroque architecture, this church was constructed at the end of the 18th century. The principal facade is the site's most striking feature, with cascading sandstone columns carefully carved with saints and figures. Walk east around the church to get a sense of its size and grandeur. There is another less ornate but also beautiful facade on its eastern wall. Above it, the church's large dome towers over Calle Mesones. In contrast to its ornate exterior, the Templo de San Francisco's interior is austere, with very high ceilings and glass chandeliers, a neoclassical altar, and walls lined with rows of wooden saints and dark *retablos.*

Directly to the east and adjoining the same small plaza as the Templo de San Francisco, the **Capilla de la Tercera Orden** is a far simpler Franciscan church. Like its neighbor, it was constructed in the 18th century, though it appears much older. The lovely, crumbling belfry that tops this old stone building has recently been restored and repainted, and it wears its age handsomely.

Teatro Ángela Peralta

The neoclassical **Teatro Ángela Peralta** (Hernández Macías 82, tel. 415/152-2200, open only during events) was built at the end of the 19th century. The sandstone facade was restored during the 1980s, but the building is basically unchanged since its construction. Its namesake, Ángela Peralta, was a famous opera singer of her day, and she personally inaugurated the theater with a concert on May 20, 1873. Since its inauguration, the theater has been and continues to be one of San Miguel's most important venues for music and performance. Though not open to the public on a regular basis, the theater opens its doors frequently for concerts and events.

Templo de la Inmaculada Concepción

The massive dome that dominates San Miguel's skyline belongs to the **Templo de la Inmaculada Concepción,** most widely known as **Las Monjas** (esq. Canal y Hernández Macías s/n, generally 9am-6pm daily). According to local history, it was originally commissioned and funded by a young nun and heiress, Josefina Lina de la Canal y Hervas, as a church and nunnery (hence its popular name, Las Monjas, which means "the nuns"). The first child of Manuel Tomás de Canal, Josefa was a devout Catholic and a close confidante of Father Luis Felipe Neri de Alfaro. After spending a week at his religious retreat in Atotonilco, Josefa decided to spend her entire inherited fortune building a lavish new temple and religious convent for an order of nuns in San Miguel. Construction on the massive building began in 1755, though funds ran out before its conclusion in 1842. Josefa died in 1770, at age 33.

Today, this massive church is one of San Miguel's most iconic structures. Although the temple's architect is unknown, the dome was said to be a copy of Les Invalides in Paris. At night, this massive structure often out-glitters the Parroquia de San Miguel Arcángel, with a ring of bright lights illuminating the dome and the parade of stone saints that surrounds it. Pass through the worn wooden doors of the church to admire the massive dome from the inside, where it illuminates a towering neoclassical altar, with numerous niches containing life-size statues of saints. On your way out, note the large conch shell that is embedded into the stone column as a receptacle for holy water.

Centro Cultural Ignacio Ramírez "El Nigromante"

The large stone building adjoining the Templo de la Inmaculada Concepción was once the cloister for the temple's order of nuns. Today, it is the **Centro Cultural Ignacio Ramírez "El Nigromante"** (Hernández Macías 75, tel. 415/152-0289, http://elnigromante.inba.gob. mx, office 10am-2pm and 4pm-6pm Mon.-Fri., galleries and installations 10am-6pm Mon.-Sat., 10am-2pm Sun., free), popularly known as **Bellas Artes.** Owned and managed by Mexico's Instituto Nacional de Bellas Artes (National Fine Arts Institute), Bellas Artes is both a small art school and a cultural center. Although this building was constructed for religious purposes, the center's namesake, Ignacio Ramírez, was an outspoken writer, thinker, lawyer, and atheist born in San Miguel de Allende during the early 19th century. Ramírez defended the rights of indigenous peoples in independent Mexico and served on the country's supreme court.

Bellas Artes is one of the most peaceful places in downtown San Miguel. The school's lovely courtyard is filled with swaying reeds of bamboo, blooming orange trees, and a lovely old stone fountain. Beneath the arcades that surround the courtyard, there are several exhibition spaces open to the public, showing work by local artists as well as itinerant exhibitions from across the country. Notably, one of the back salons contains an incomplete mural by famous postrevolutionary artist David Alfaro Siqueiros, painted in 1948. On both the first and second floors, the school's enchanting classrooms are housed in the tiny rooms of the former cloister; each is dedicated to a discipline, such as ceramics, oil painting, guitar, and piano.

Biblioteca de San Miguel de Allende

A nonprofit, nongovernmental organization, the **Biblioteca de San Miguel de Allende** (Insurgentes 25, tel. 415/152-0293, http://biblio tecasma.com, 10am-7pm Mon.-Fri., 10am-2pm Sat.), formerly known as the Biblioteca Pública, is home to a large bilingual lending library, a nice open-air café, and a small theater. As a part of its mission to serve the community, the library manages a scholarship program for local children as well as free art and music classes, a language exchange program, and other educational opportunities. For many expatriates, the library is something of a social hub, where people come together to lend a hand, have a cappuccino, take a class, or see a speaker in the Teatro Santa Ana. The newspaper *Atención San Miguel* is published by the library and its sales support the organization's social programs, as do frequent book sales, fundraising events, and the weekly House and Garden Tour. Check the library's corkboard for information about upcoming programs, or pick up a copy of *Atención San Miguel* for the full list of events, movies, and volunteer opportunities.

★ Parque Juárez

A few blocks south of the central square, beloved **Parque Juárez** (between Aldama and Diezmo Viejo) is one of the freshest and greenest spots in San Miguel de Allende. Take a stroll along the park's old curving walkways, admiring the old stone fountains and the wild, tropical vegetation that flourishes throughout the park. Throughout the day, you'll find teenage couples holding hands, ambitious joggers, seniors reading the paper, exuberant Zumba classes, or dogs and their owners wandering along the shaded footpaths. Bring a book and stake out a spot on one of the weathered stone benches, or simply enjoy the people-watching. The park is also a favorite nesting spot for white egrets, and the birds in the trees above can become surprisingly noisy.

★ El Chorro

After its founding on the banks of the Río Laja, the settlement of San Miguel de los Chichimecas moved to the hill of Izcuinapan, site of a copious natural spring. According to local legend, the Purépecha people from Michoacán had originally discovered the spring after their *xoloitzcuintle* dogs dug up water along the hillside. Today, the site of San Miguel's founding is a verdant corner of the city, known as **El Chorro** (the spring). On the hillside, San Miguel's **Casa de la Cultura El Chorro** (Bajada del Chorro 4) is a cultural center that offers art, dance, and music classes to local children.

In the shade of breezy trees, El Chorro is among the most beautiful spots in town. The steep hill leading up to the Casa de la Cultura is lined with cascading patios and winding staircases, a lovely place to rest amid the lush foliage and the sound of squabbling egrets. Just to the north, a stone staircase leads you to a pretty plaza and **La Capilla de Santa Cruz del Chorro,** a 16th-century church and one of the oldest structures in San Miguel de Allende. From there, you can huff and puff up the tiny pedestrian alleyway La Bajada del Chorro, an enchanting, if challenging, ascent to the Salida a Querétaro.

Just below El Chorro, take notice of the row of red *lavaderos públicos* (public washtubs), which surround a small plaza below the hillside. For years, the natural spring has fed water into these washtubs, where local families came to do their laundry. According to some historians, these washtubs were among the municipal projects financed by Manuel

Canal in the 18th century. Even today, some San Miguel residents will wash their clothes and linens in the *lavaderos,* and on the weekends there is a casual art market in the plaza they adjoin.

Instituto Allende

A legacy of the oldest art academy in the Americas, the **Instituto Allende** (Ancha de San Antonio 22, tel. 415/152-0929, http://instituto-allende.edu.mx) has a huge stone facade that dominates the busy avenue below. Originally built by the wealthy Canal family as a country residence, this massive building became an art school in the 1950s, when Cossío del Pomar moved his academy from its original location in the ex-convent at the Templo de la Inmaculada Concepción to this colonial-era mansion. (The Centro Cultural Ignacio Ramírez is now housed in the ex-convent of the Inmaculada Concepción, but that school is under the direction of the Mexican government, whereas the Instituto Allende is a private college.)

Today, the institute is divided into two parts. In the back, the buildings and gardens continue to function as an art college, offering an undergraduate program for Mexican students alongside noncredit public classes for

The colorful cultural center at El Chorro is one of the most enchanting spots in San Miguel de Allende.

tourists and residents. The front of the building is a nice **commercial plaza** (Ancha de San Antonio 20, tel. 415/152-0226, www.institutoallende.com, generally 11am-6pm daily, though individual business hours vary) with a comfortable café and several good galleries.

NORTH OF THE *CENTRO*
★ Fábrica La Aurora

Many longtime residents of San Miguel remember the cry of the steam-generated whistle that sounded every morning from the **Fábrica La Aurora** (Calzada de la Aurora s/n, Col. Aurora, tel. 415/152-1312, www.fabricalaaurora.com, generally 9am-11pm Mon.-Sat., 10am-5pm Sun., hours vary by shop). Until the early 1990s, La Aurora was one of Mexico's largest textile factories and the single biggest employer in the town of San Miguel. After cotton imports began flooding the Mexican market, domestic production was greatly affected. The factory closed in 1991, and the space was converted to a warehouse. A few years later, some local artists and designers began to express interest in renting the old factory rooms as studios and workspaces. The first shops and studios opened in 2001. The project quickly grew, and today the former factory houses more than 35 studios,

galleries, design shops, antiques dealers, boutiques, restaurants, and a café. Many of San Miguel's most beloved artists and exhibition spaces are located in the Aurora. Its unique ambience is perfect for strolling and passing a morning.

Typical of turn-of-the-20th-century constructions, the factory's long sandstone facade, concrete floors, and industrial architecture provide a contrasting (yet complementary) backdrop to modern art and design. Wandering around the corridors, you can see some of the old equipment from the factory's former days in textile production, and old photographs of the space line the walls of the principal hallway. Hours vary by shop, so visit during the morning or early afternoon, Monday through Saturday, to see the most spaces open.

EAST OF THE *CENTRO*
El Mirador

If you have a set of wheels or strong legs for walking, you can follow the Salida a Querétaro up the hill to **El Mirador,** a small outlook with panoramic views of the city below. From here, you can see the river valley stretching beyond the town, including the large reservoir beyond the city and the distant Sierra de Guanajuato.

Fábrica La Aurora

The bust of Pedro Vargas, a famous singer and actor from Mexico's golden age of cinema, presides over the *mirador*. Vargas was born in San Miguel; his former home adjoins this small plaza.

★ El Charco del Ingenio

San Miguel de Allende's unique botanical garden, **El Charco del Ingenio** (Paloma s/n, tel. 415/154-4715 or 415/154-8838, www.elcharco.org.mx, 9am-7pm daily, US$3) is located along the ridge of a canyon overlooking the city center. Bring a hat and good walking shoes to explore the rustic and meandering footpaths within this ecological preserve, which covers more than 100 acres of natural habitat along the canyon's edge and the shores of a small reservoir. With admission, staffers will give you a map to the grounds; a highlight is the covered conservatory, which houses a rare and weird collection of cacti and succulents. El Charco del Ingenio frequently hosts special events, such as full moon ceremonies, nature talks, yoga classes, or traditional *temazcal* steam baths. There is also a small coffee shop and gift store at the entrance, where visitors can support the project by purchasing a live cacti, books, or handicrafts made in local villages.

SIGHTSEEING AND CULTURAL TOURS

A local nonprofit organization, **Patronato Pro Niños** (tel. 415/152-7796, www.patronatoproninos.org, US$20), offers cultural walking tours of San Miguel de Allende's historic center with knowledgeable English-speaking guides. Tours depart from the *jardín* every Monday, Wednesday, and Friday at 9:45am, cover about 10 blocks, and last about 2.5 hours. There is also a special Thursday morning tour, which focuses on architecture. All of the proceeds from the tour benefit Patronato Pro Niños' medical and dental services program, which provides free or very low-cost medical care to 2,500 children in the San Miguel area, as well as dental services to over 9,000 children.

Helene Kahn's tour group **And You Thought You'd Seen Everything...** (tel. 415/152-0849, cell tel. 415/153-5944, www.helenekahn.com, US$80-400) offers informative walking tours of downtown San Miguel de Allende for individuals and private groups. A guided introduction to the city's major sights usually takes about an hour or two, and the route can be tailored depending on your interests (and how many hills you are willing to climb). A delightful host with a passion for local history, Helene has spent many years in Mexico. She can offer tips on where to eat, where to shop, and what to do around San Miguel, so one of her walking tours can be a nice way to start your trip. In addition, the group offers day trips to various destinations like Dolores Hidalgo, Guanajuato, Pozos, and Querétaro, with optional excursions to artist workshops for those interested in crafts or ceramics.

Ever wondered what's behind those old wooden doors and big stucco facades? You're not alone. One of the most popular activities in town, the weekly **House and Garden Tour** (meeting point Biblioteca de San Miguel de Allende, Insurgentes 25, tel. 415/152-0293, sandra@bibliotecasma.com, noon Sun., US$20, cash only) gives participants a chance to peek inside several historic and lavishly decorated homes in San Miguel de Allende. Drawing from a roster of over 300 historic homes in San Miguel, the lineup changes weekly, but usually includes at least four properties. The tour departs from the Biblioteca de San Miguel de Allende every Sunday at noon in large buses. You can buy tickets ahead of time at the gift shop (10am-2pm and 3pm-6pm Mon.-Fri.), or just show up on Sunday morning.

Arts and Entertainment

Since the early 20th century, San Miguel has been home to a community of artists and writers, both national and international. Today, there are many small galleries, some artist-run, where new exhibitions open seemingly every weekend, often drawing overflowing crowds.

Live music, dance, and even theater are performed at a few city venues. Jazz music is universally popular, and a few cool nightclubs make San Miguel a semi-chic destination for Monterrey and Mexico City weekenders.

NIGHTLIFE

For most visitors and residents, evenings are best enjoyed in the company of friends, kicking back with a book, or lingering over a good meal. During the week, nightlife is usually limited to hotel bars and a few old standbys, where locals convene for drinks and conversation. Weekends are much livelier, when large crowds of tourists or day-trippers arrive from Mexico City, Querétaro, Monterrey, and beyond. On Friday and Saturday nights, San Miguel's bars extend their hours, and a good party can be found throughout the *centro histórico*. Though not a major city, San Miguel offers just enough style to feel cosmopolitan and just enough folklore to feel like Mexico.

Right beneath the spires of the *parroquia* and overlooking the dome of Las Monjas, **La Azotea** (Umarán 6, tel. 415/152-8265, 1pm-midnight daily) has one of the most attractive views in San Miguel. This chic rooftop restaurant and bar is a good choice for a pleasant drink in the early evening as the sun sinks behind the distant mountains, bathing the town in a rosy glow. Here, you can lounge on a couch, order some tapas, and watch as flocks of birds glide across the sky. For more excitement, hang around a little longer. As the evening wears on, the crowd swells and the music gets louder. On Friday and Saturday nights, La Azotea draws a trendy crowd of locals and

weekenders, and there is often a live DJ. You may not see La Azotea from the street; to get there, enter through the Pueblo Viejo restaurant (once you're inside, the host will direct you to the bar) and take the stairs or elevator to the top floor.

Just a block from the main plaza, **Berlin** (Umarán 19, tel. 415/154-9432, www.berlin-mexico.com, 5pm-1am Mon.-Sat.) is a small bar and restaurant that serves well-prepared German and continental food, like grilled chicken and savory crepes, as well as oft-praised hamburgers (dinner is served till 11:30pm). While the restaurant has many loyal patrons, the bar is the true locus of this convivial joint. Any evening at Berlin, you're likely to find a crowd of graying expatriates nursing inexpensive cocktails and chatting with the waitstaff. You can do like the locals and order dinner or appetizers at the bar while eavesdropping on the night's voluble conversations.

With its spectacular views of the *parroquia* and the surrounding city, **360 Mixology Bar** (Cuna de Allende 15, tel. 415/154-9776, http://quincerooftop.com, noon-midnight Sun.-Thurs., noon-2am Fri.-Sat.) at the upscale restaurant **Quince** has become a popular hangout for locals and visitors; the party can go late on nights when they host a DJ or other live music in-house. As the bar's name indicates, cocktails are a specialty here, with creative drinks like cucumber margaritas on offer, and there is also a late-night food menu available on the weekends. For an afternoon respite, stop in during the bar's excellent weekday happy hour: From 4pm to 6pm every Monday through Thursday, domestic beer, house wine, and margaritas are half price, and there are discounts on bar snacks, like rosemary potatoes and the cheese board.

The younger and rowdier crowd gathers at **Limerick Irish Pub** (Umarán 24, tel. 415/154-8642, 6:30pm-3am Tues.-Thurs. and

Celebrate the Visual Arts

During the early 20th century, Mexican and Latin American bohemians began to gather in then-sleepy San Miguel de Allende. Mexican scholar Alfonso Reyes came to visit San Miguel, as did the celebrated Chilean poets Gabriela Mistral and Pablo Neruda. Oaxacan painter Rufino Tamayo and his wife, Olga, were among the city's most famous fans. After World War II, with the help of American artist Stirling Dickinson, American artists began to arrive, often studying at the school that is today known as the Instituto Allende. Over the next 100 years, San Miguel de Allende became a well-known expatriate community as well as a haven for artists.

Though now removed from its bohemian roots, San Miguel continues to be a mecca for visual artists, and there are dozens of artist studios and artist-run galleries scattered around town, in addition to a never-ending slate of arts-related events taking place at public institutions, galleries, and other more unusual venues. Here are some of the best places to go.

OUTSTANDING INSTITUTIONS

Despite its ties to the visual arts, San Miguel does not have many fine art museums or public galleries. Two institutions worth noting, however, are the **Casa del Mayorazgo de la Canal** (page 43), a cultural center and exhibition space in the city's grandest colonial-era mansion, and the **Centro Cultural Ignacio Ramírez "El Nigromante"** (page 47) also called Bellas Artes, an art school and cultural center with several public galleries. It's worth seeking out the unfinished mural by Mexican master **David Alfaro Siqueiros,** located in one of Bellas Artes' back salons.

GALLERIES

There are dozens of **art galleries** throughout San Miguel, some amateur but enthusiastically run, others professional and representing well-known names in art. One of the best, **Yam Gallery** (page 71) often shows work by local artists, as well as talent from around Mexico and Latin America. Another spot worth seeking out is **Noel Cayetano Arte Contemporáneo** (page 71), which is run by a well-known Oaxacan gallerist and represents a number of well-known Mexican artists, chiefly painters, sculptors, and printmakers.

PUBLIC ART

There are numerous sculptures by local artists beneath the trees of the beautiful **Parque Juárez** (page 47). The **Guadalupe neighborhood,** just north of the *centro histórico,* is known for its many colorful murals. Stroll along the street Margarito Ledesma to see a few.

EVENTS

There is a well-attended **Art Walk** at the **Fábrica La Aurora** (page 49) on the first Saturday of every month, during which most galleries and artist studios stay open late and serve refreshments. It's a good opportunity to talk with working artists in town while enjoying a glass of wine and a night under the stars. As part of the annual **La Calaca festival** (page 61), which runs in early November, public works of art are installed throughout town.

HOTELS

The much-beloved boutique property **Hotel Matilda** (page 104) is known for its excellent collection of contemporary art, which fills the lobby and shared spaces of the building. The hotel also occasionally hosts special events and exhibitions. Though smaller, the **Rosewood San Miguel de Allende** (page 103) also has a nice collection of art by contemporary visual artists, some collected in San Miguel.

Sun., 6:30pm-5am Fri.-Sat.), an expansive Irish-inspired bar with a billiard table, cheap beer, and loud music. This casual pub is a longtime favorite with locals, and it is filled to the brim on the weekends, when there is often a live band or DJ in addition to the big crowds. On Saturday nights, the staff sometimes turns off the lights to force revelers out the door.

The wonderful cantina **El Manantial** (Barranca 78, tel. 415/110-0007, 1pm-midnight Tues.-Sat., noon-midnight Sun.) is one of San Miguel de Allende's oldest watering holes and one of the nicest places to have a casual drink in town. The lovely old building has thick adobe walls and old wood beams crossing its incredibly high ceiling. Locals flock here for inexpensive drinks, jovial company, and the delicious menu of fish tacos and tostadas. Here, many classic Mexican dishes are prepared with fish rather than meat, so *tacos al pastor, chilorio,* and carnitas take on a new, delicious twist. It remains one of the most popular and pleasant places to have a snack while tipping back a drink in a low-key, historic setting.

For a different cantina experience, **El Gato Negro** (Mesones 12, no phone, 11:30am-11pm daily) is an old multistory watering hole with some of the cheapest drinks downtown. Push through the swinging wooden doors and into the small bar, where they have been serving drinks for decades. Those in the know take their beers up to the teensy rooftop terrace, where a few plastic chairs overlook the historic sandstone towers of San Miguel de Allende. It's a top-dollar view at a discount price.

Of all the cantinas in San Miguel de Allende, **La Cucaracha** (Zacateros 22, tel. 415/152-0196, 7pm-5am daily) is clearly the granddaddy of them all, the oldest and most fabled spot for a drink in town. This incredibly cheap and often rowdy dive bar is a favorite of students, youthful expatriates, oldtimers, riffraff, and young ranchers from the towns surrounding San Miguel. Opened in the 1940s, this historic bar used to be located in the Casa del Mayorazgo de la Canal on San Miguel's central square—today, a Banamex branch. At the current site on Zacateros, the walls are decorated with original artwork from local artists (in the true spirit of San Miguel, La Cucaracha will occasionally host an art exhibition). Bathrooms leave something to be desired (and may house a few of the bar's namesake critters), but beers are among the cheapest in town, and the laid-back vibe will appeal to dive-bar aficionados. The booming jukebox often determines the humor of the evening, depending on who's controlling the shuffle. Late at night, the atmosphere can be jovial or aggressive. Use your judgment if you stay into the wee hours.

For dining, drinking, and taking dozens and dozens of photos, **Luna Rooftop Tapas Bar** (Nemesio Diez 11, tel. 415/152-9700, www.rosewoodhotels.com, Mon.-Thurs. 2pm-11pm, Fri. Sun. 1pm-11pm), an upscale lounge on the top floor of the massive Rosewood Hotel, attracts both tourists and locals with an international style that wasn't common in San Miguel until recently. The decor is minimal, but given the spectacular views of San Miguel—beautiful anytime, but especially dramatic at sunset, when the town is often bathed in a rosy light—the food and drinks off the chef-driven menu are far better than they need to be. Try the refreshing cucumber-and-mezcal cocktail rimmed with chile salt and a flavorful plate of tuna-ceviche tostadas.

Across the street from the Rosewood Hotel, the more intimate atmosphere at **Nena Sky Bar** (Nemesio Diez 10, tel. 415/154-7128, www.hotelnena.mx, noon-10:30pm daily) impresses with its prime view of the *parroquia* and the surrounding *centro histórico*. It's often blissfully quiet here in the afternoons, making it a great time to take advantage of the on-site pool (open to drop-ins with a minimum purchase of about US$30 per person). Children are not allowed.

LIVE MUSIC

Live music plays an important role in Mexican culture. In San Miguel de Allende, marimba musicians play jubilantly on busy avenues for tips from passersby, while merry

Top Spots for Sunset

During the winter and early spring, the sky turns vibrant pink as the sun sets over the Sierra de Guanajuato. A rosy glow blankets the city as the church bells clang and birds streak home against a darkening sky. It's a romantic, moving spectacle from any spot in the city, but if you want to truly experience a San Miguel de Allende sunset, here are the best views in town.

THE CLASSIC VIEW

Everyone's favorite spot for sundown, the Rosewood hotel's open-air rooftop lounge, **Luna Rooftop Tapas Bar** (page 53), has a spectacular panoramic view of the city. This spot gets extra points for being one of the only rooftops in San Miguel de Allende that has an elevator and is fully wheelchair-accessible.

UP CLOSE WITH THE *PARROQUIA*

It's hard to decide which way to look from the **360 Mixology Bar** at **Quince restaurant** (page 51): On one side, the spires of the *parroquia* seem impossibly close, lighted against a darkening sky. On the other, there are views of San Miguel's rooftops, the plains below, and the Sierra de Guanajuato in the distance.

VISTA OF LAS MONJAS

The bar tables along the balcony at **La Azotea** (page 51) have a prime view of the dome of Las Monjas, which is illuminated with amber floodlights at sundown. Once the stars come out, though, the party gets started at this popular nightspot.

IN PAJAMAS AND SLIPPERS

The views from the west-facing guest rooms at **Hotel El Palomar** (page 101) are among the best in town. Book a room and you can watch the sunset from your windows. Or, if you're not quite ready to retire, head to the hotel's top-floor restaurant, Antonia Bistro, for an early-evening cocktail and stunning views.

JUST THE VIEW, PLEASE

Take a taxi or huff up the steep but ultra-charming alleyway Bajada del Chorro to get to **El Mirador** (page 49), an outlook on the Salida a Querétaro with a perfect view of downtown San Miguel.

THE LOCAL FAVORITE

Low-key, inexpensive, and with lovely views of the *parroquia* and the many rooftops of San Miguel, **La Posadita** (page 87) is a relaxed spot for an early dinner and drinks as the sun goes down.

SIMPLE PLEASURES

No tamarind margaritas or tapas plates here, but locals know there are lovely views from the rooftop of old-time, no-nonsense cantina **El Gato Negro** (page 53).

marching bands accompany wedding parties as they make their way out of a chapel. Roving guitarists play songs by request in San Miguel's fancy restaurants, and *norteño* trios entertain the taco rush at the weekly Mercado de Martes. In the *jardín*, mariachis make the rounds on Friday and Saturday nights, their joyous sound floating over the *centro*.

Many of San Miguel de Allende's popular restaurants have live musicians accompanying the nightly dinner crowd. There is nightly live jazz at Mexican steak house **Tío Lucas Restaurant and Bar,** and a changing lineup of classic guitar, Andean music, and rock at the main stage at **Mama Mía** during the weekend brunch hour as well as at dinner. Many other restaurants schedule special musical events with local talent. The guitarist Gil Gutierrez is one of San Miguel's most talented and popular performers, who often plays ticketed events in fine restaurants. Jazz trumpeter Doc Severinsen of *Tonight Show* fame is a San Miguel resident, and he plays at local venues as well (often accompanied by Gil). As always, you can see what's going on in *Atención San Miguel,* or just follow your ears to the party.

Throughout the year, there are frequent live music and dance performances in the *jardín,* sponsored by the municipal and state government. These free concerts really run the gamut, from lively traditional dance performances to wailing rock shows by San Miguel teenagers. Sometimes wonderful, sometimes painful, most performances in the town square draw a multigenerational crowd. To see what's coming up, you can check the monthly schedule in the *jardín,* which is usually posted beneath the arcades on all four corners of the square.

For a formal concert, the historic **Teatro Ángela Peralta** (Hernández Macías 82, tel. 415/152-2200) presents an ongoing program of live music, film, dance, theater, and other performances. It is one of the major venues for the annual Festival Internacional de Música San Miguel de Allende in July, which features a wonderful two-week program of classical music ensembles. To see what's playing while you are in San Miguel, check the newspaper *Atención San Miguel,* or drop by the Ángela Peralta box office, a cubbyhole on the west side of the theater.

The second Saturday of every month, the organization behind San Miguel's excellent summer music event Festival Internacional de Música San Miguel de Allende, in conjunction with the national fine arts institute, sponsors **Music Under the Trees** (www.festivalsanmiguel.com), a free concert series at the Centro Cultural Ignacio Ramírez.

ART MUSEUMS

For a town of its size, San Miguel has built a strong reputation for its commitment to the visual arts, boasting numerous art schools, a surprising number of galleries, and a slew of working artists, both newbies and professionals. Notably, there is great interest in the visual arts throughout every sector of the community. Here, even coffee shops, dive bars, and real estate offices are known to host an art exhibition or two.

The majority of local artists show their work in private galleries; however, there are several public exhibition spaces on the first floor of the government-run **Centro Cultural Ignacio Ramírez "El Nigromante"** (Hernández Macías 75, tel. 415/152-0289, http://elnigromante.inba.gob.mx, 10am-6pm Mon.-Sat., 10am-2pm Sun., free). These spaces are often dedicated to work by local artists, and opening events are well attended. The center also hosts several new and itinerant exhibitions by Mexican artists outside of San Miguel every year. The galleries are free and open to the public. Wander in to see what's on show, or check *Atención San Miguel* to see if a new show is being inaugurated while you are in town.

An enchanting little museum located in a beautifully renovated colonial home, **La Esquina: Museo del Jugete Popular Mexicano** (Nuñez 40, tel. 415/152-2602, www.museolaesquina.org.mx, 10am-6pm Tues.-Sat., 11am-4pm Sun., US$3 adults, US$2 kids, seniors, students, and teachers) is dedicated entirely to traditional Mexican toys. Behind the museum's glass display cases, the permanent collection includes a wide range of antique and contemporary toys, including painted papier-mâché dolls, corn-husk figurines, clay whistles, little wooden chairs, toy planes and automobiles, wool stuffed animals, toy instruments, and many other lovely and imaginative designs. There are also changing exhibitions on the top floor dedicated to regional toy designs from different Mexican states. The light and colorful space is appropriate for kids (plus they get a discount on the admission cost), but visitors of any age will enjoy the diversity and imagination of traditional toy design from across Mexico. If the project inspires you, the museum operates two small gift shops where you can pick up your own *jugetes* (toys), on-site and in the *jardín.*

FESTIVALS AND EVENTS

Many people in San Miguel de Allende claim that this small town has more municipal festivals than any other city in Mexico. While that may or may not be true, it is easy enough to believe. In San Miguel, barely a day goes by that does not celebrate a patron saint, a beloved chapel, or a revolutionary hero. Every neighborhood has its own annual party, and on any given night loud fireworks crackle through the sky in celebration.

In addition to the near-constant festivities rumbling through San Miguel's neighborhoods, there are several important events and dozens of popular celebrations that take place every year, with much anticipation and fanfare. San Miguel enthusiastically participates in every national holiday, from Cinco de Mayo to Constitution Day. You'll also see plenty of festivities during the numerous unofficial but incredibly important holidays like May 10—Mother's Day.

Visiting during one of San Miguel's festivals can be a memorable experience; however, you should plan ahead if you want to visit during the most popular dates, especially the weeks around Semana Santa and Día de la Independencia.

January

While not a national holiday, **Ignacio Allende's birthday** is celebrated in San Miguel on January 21. The life and achievements of San Miguel's native son are recognized with a parade downtown put on by local schoolchildren.

LA CANDELARIA
On **El Día de los Reyes Magos** (Three Kings' Day, celebrated annually on January

6), children receive gifts from the *reyes magos* (the three wise men) and families get together to share a *rosca de reyes,* a wreath-shaped sweet bread topped with crystallized fruit and sugar; during the first week of the year, you'll see them in every bakery in town. The person who finds a figurine of a baby baked inside their slice is appointed godmother or godfather to the baby Jesus in the family's nativity scene. The godparent is responsible for dressing baby Jesus and taking him to the church for blessing on February 2, the day of **La Candelaria.** On the same day, the godparent must also invite friends and family to their home for a traditional dinner of tamales, *atole,* and hot chocolate. While La Candelaria is a Catholic tradition, the tamales and *atole* may have derived from a pre-Hispanic tradition in honor of the rain god Tlaloc.

In addition to the family gatherings throughout town, San Miguel de Allende celebrates La Candelaria with the opening of the annual plant and flower sale at Parque Juárez. This lovely and aromatic market fills the winding walkways of the already verdant park with an impressive array of plants, flowers, hanging vines, trees, fresh herbs, cacti, and succulents. Vendors come from as far away as Veracruz and Puebla, and many set up tents to camp in the park during the 10 market days. If you are on an extended sojourn in San Miguel de Allende, La Candelaria is an excellent occasion to buy well-priced plants and flowers. If you are just visiting, be sure to stop by the park to see the many exotic plants and cacti on sale.

February

SAN MIGUEL WRITERS CONFERENCE
Just as it has attracted many visual artists, San Miguel de Allende is home to writers of every stripe, from memoirists to poets. Organized by the English-language writers' group, the San Miguel Literary Sala, the annual **San Miguel Writers Conference** (www.sanmiguelwritersconference.org) is a very high-quality, well-organized five-day

event that invites dozens of editors, publishers, literary agents, and published authors to give talks and workshops to conference participants. Throughout the long weekend, there is a full schedule of panel discussions, readings, classes, and parties, including keynote presentations by internationally famous writers. Programs range from practical advice on getting published to fiction- and memoir-writing workshops. Past speakers include such famous names as Wally Lamb, Rita Dove, Emma Donoghue, Barbara Kingsolver, Laura Esquivel, Alice Walker, and Tom Robbins. Admission costs include meals.

March-April

For the ultimate cute fix, don't miss the parade on March 20 heralding the **first day of spring.** Just as San Miguel's many jacaranda trees begin to bloom, all the town's children dress up as flowers, bumblebees, butterflies, and bunnies, then process through the streets of downtown as their proud parents snap photos.

SEMANA SANTA

San Miguel de Allende is well known for its beautiful and solemn **Semana Santa** (Easter week) celebrations. There is amazing color and pageantry throughout the week, with major events drawing thousands of spectators. Semana Santa technically begins on Palm Sunday, but in San Miguel, the festivities begin earlier. One of the first major events related to Holy Week takes place two weeks before Easter. On the fifth Sunday of Lent, a massive pilgrimage departs from the Santuario de Jesús Nazareno, and the sacred figure of **El Señor de la Columna** is carried, along with La Virgen de Dolores and the Señor de San Juan, from Atotonilco to San Miguel de Allende. The journey is made slowly and in silence, with a mass held at the midpoint. Just before daybreak, the procession passes through San Miguel de Allende via the Avenida Independencia, where families have lined the streets with palm leaves, balloons, and flowers. With much fanfare, the figure of El Señor de la Columna is carried to the church of San Juan de Dios, where it will stay until Easter Sunday.

A lovely local tradition, **Viernes de Dolores** is celebrated on the final Friday of Lent, two days before Palm Sunday. This holiday is dedicated to La Virgen de Dolores (Our Lady of Sorrows), who is remembered with special masses in the town's churches, fresh flowers in the city fountains, and the

In early February, plant and flower vendors set up in Parque Juárez for La Candelaria.

distribution of *aguas de fruta* in the local community. At the workplace, employers will often provide *aguas* or ice cream to their employees, and some will also give out miniature popsicles to clients and passersby. The *aguas* are said to be symbolic of the virgin's tears.

The same evening, Our Lady of Sorrows is honored with hundreds of small home-built altars, erected in the windows and doorways of family homes throughout San Miguel de Allende. These altars are traditionally adorned with a statue or image of the virgin, chamomile, purple flowers, and little parcels of green wheat sprouts. All the town's lovely altars are open to the public, so there is quite a buzz on the street. As children go from house to house visiting with their neighbors, they are served hibiscus juice, ice cream, and popsicles.

Two days later, **Domingo de Ramos** (Palm Sunday) officially begins the Holy Week festivities. All day long, beautifully woven palm crosses and other palm adornments are sold outside every church in San Miguel. Local families buy their palms and take them to the church for blessings. There are also several religious processions on Palm Sunday, commemorating Jesus's arrival in Jerusalem.

Viernes Santo (Good Friday) is the single most important day during Semana Santa. In fact, it is more likely that a shop or restaurant will close to business on Good Friday than on Easter Sunday. Good Friday is not a day of celebration so much as a day of mourning, with solemn processions throughout the town. The *jardín* is the locus of activity, with huge crowds gathered there from morning until evening.

The events of Viernes Santo begin when the cross from Atotonilco is carried to the *parroquia,* followed shortly thereafter by the statue of El Señor de la Columna. The revered statue will spend the weekend in the *parroquia* before being returned to Atotonilco on the following Wednesday. Around midday, there is a live and unflinching reenactment of the Stations of the Cross, which concludes with Jesus's trial by Pontius Pilate in the esplanade of the *parroquia.* In preparation, a slow and serious procession weaves through town, carrying statues of Jesus and the saints aloft. The men are dressed in dark suits, and the women, or *mujeres dolientes,* are clothed in mourning attire. Among them, young girls in white dresses with bright purple sashes drop chamomile along the path to the *parroquia.* As evening falls, another mournful parade, the **Procesión del Silencio,** weaves through town toward the *parroquia.* For this beautiful and solemn event, capped men and women dressed in black proceed slowly and silently to the *jardín,* holding flickering candles.

In the days before Easter Sunday, or **Domingo de Pascua,** colorful papier-mâché Judas figures are hung over the *plaza principal,* between the Presidencia Municipal and the *jardín.* Just after Easter mass, a crowd gathers to burn the Judases, which have been rigged with explosives. One at a time, these paper giants spin in circles until they burst into flame, to the delight and applause of onlookers. Today, many of the Judas figures are fashioned to look like politicians or other famous (but controversial) figures. Other than this colorful event, Easter Sunday is generally a quieter day, spent with family and attending mass.

Most Mexican schools have a break in the weeks preceding and following Easter Sunday, bringing a flood of domestic tourists to town. If you are planning a visit during this time, make hotel reservations in advance and be prepared for a more bustling version of the city. Once you touch down, be sure to pick up a copy of *Atención San Miguel,* which publishes a detailed list of Semana Santa events. Alternatively, you can look over the week's schedule on the municipal message boards in the town square.

May-June

During May, four historic neighborhoods in San Miguel de Allende hold their annual celebrations. On the fourth Sunday in May, the most raucous of these celebrations, the

Fiesta de la Santa Cruz, is held in the Valle del Maíz. This major block party has roots dating back to the 16th century and includes live music, pageantry, and plenty of libations.

SAN ANTONIO DE PADUA: FIESTA DE LOS LOCOS

Saint Anthony is one of San Miguel's most popular saints as well as the namesake for one of the city's biggest neighborhoods. On the Sunday after Saint Anthony's feast day (June 13), San Miguel has a very particular way of feting this favored figure. On this auspicious day—also dubbed **Los Locos**—thousands of San Miguel residents march through the streets in silly and sometimes provocative costumes, from political masks to gorilla suits. The prevalence of cross-dressing is a particularly noticeable aspect of this parade, as many of San Miguel's mustachioed *señores* don dresses, lipstick, and wigs for the tour around town. Ogle all you want, but remember that onlookers are routinely pegged (and with gusto!) by handfuls of hard candy from the marchers. After the parade ends, the party continues well into the evening. From morning through afternoon to the wee hours of the night, wigged and costumed revelers dance ceaselessly, until they finally run out of steam the following morning.

July-August
EL FESTIVAL INTERNACIONAL DE CINE DE GUANAJUATO

What began as a small, shorts-only festival is now one Mexico's largest film events, co-hosted by the cities of San Miguel de Allende and Guanajuato. Held annually at the end of July, **El Festival Internacional de Cine de Guanajuato** (www.giff.mx), or the Guanajuato International Film Festival, shows hundreds of films selected from thousands of international entries. Screenings are free and open to the public, and they take place in more than 20 different venues—from the breathtaking (the *jardín principal* in San Miguel de Allende, Teatro Juárez in Guanajuato) to the unusual (a tunnel beneath Guanajuato's city center, the municipal graveyard). While the festival is still largely dedicated to shorts, there are numerous feature-length films included in the program, some of which make their debut at the festival. Many films are in Spanish; in most cases, international selections are subtitled in both Spanish or English (language is indicated in the program).

FESTIVAL INTERNACIONAL DE MÚSICA SAN MIGUEL DE ALLENDE

Every summer, the **Festival Internacional de Música San Miguel de Allende** (International Music Festival of San Miguel de Allende, Hernández Macías 75, tel. 415/154-5141, www.festivalsanmiguel.com), formerly the **San Miguel Chamber Music Festival,** invites renowned quartets, soloists, and other classical ensembles from around the world to play in a series of concerts in San Miguel de Allende. Often excellent and sometimes avant-garde, concerts take place in a variety of venues and vary in price, though there are always several free events included in the program. Proceeds from this not-for-profit festival benefit the music education programs, also run by the organization, through which promising young musicians from across Mexico are invited to San Miguel to work directly with acclaimed international musicians.

September
INDEPENDENCE CELEBRATIONS AND EL GRITO

The birthplace of many of Mexico's independence heroes and an important meeting ground for Mexican pro-independence conspirators in the 19th century, San Miguel de Allende is often described as "the cradle of independence." Today, this party-loving town is a major destination for the national Día de la Independencia de México (Independence Day) celebrations. In the weeks leading up to the festivities, public spaces are festooned with tricolor decorations, local families hang Mexican flags outside their windows, and vendors appear in the streets with every manner of patriotic kitsch. Festivities technically begin on the night of September 15 with the traditional cry *"¡Viva Mexico!"* delivered in the *jardín* by the town's mayor. After the crowd is riled up, fireworks explode over the *parroquia* while special, semi-precarious pyrotechnic towers constructed for the event burst into multicolored flames. Seriously, you must watch out that your hair does not catch on fire.

During the independence celebrations, the town is flooded with national tourism, including the inevitable and noisy crowd of youngsters who've come to party in San Miguel's nightclubs. After the pyrotechnics, Independence Day is a big night out. Bars and clubs are packed and riotous until daybreak. While September 15 is the biggest party, the anniversary of the independence movement is actually September 16, a national holiday, with banks and most business closed. Needless to say, the parties continue.

DÍA DE SAN MIGUEL ARCÁNGEL

The gorgeous festivals in honor of San Miguel's patron saint begin almost immediately after the Independence Day parties end. **Saint Michael's feast day** is technically September 29. However, if the 29th falls on a weekday, the festivities are pushed to the following weekend, culminating with the largest and most well attended fiestas on Sunday.

The festivities in honor of San Miguel actually begin with a novena, nine days of prayer and celebration leading up to the saint's feast day. During each of these nine days, one of the city's neighborhoods, along with various civil and religious groups, organizes processions around the city. The sounds of drums or marching bands echo through the narrow streets as those in the procession dance through town, eventually arriving at the Parroquia de San Miguel Arcángel, where the festivities often continue.

On Friday afternoon (two days before the official feast day celebrations), a procession departs from the Aurora neighborhood, accompanied by the Aguascalientes Brothers band. They arrive at the *parroquia* at dusk, just as vendors are setting up hot punch and taco stands in preparation for the night ahead. At this point, marching bands, dancers, and devotees of Saint Michael have begun to arrive from across Mexico—some coming from as far as the United States. At 4am on Saturday, the festivities officially begin with **La Alborada,** an astonishing hour-long fireworks display over the *jardín*. During this endless spray of pyrotechnics, the town square

dancers performing during Día de San Miguel Arcángel

is filled with smoke, and the sound of explosions is almost deafening. The party continues until 6am, when the revelers sing "Las Mañanitas" (Mexico's birthday song) to San Miguel and then attend mass.

The weekend continues with dances, masses, and celebration. On Saturday afternoon, a long and beautiful procession of dancers and indigenous groups heads up Canal Street to the *parroquia*. When they arrive, they decorate the *parroquia* with flowers and banners. The beautiful **Voladores de Papantla** from Veracruz perform their unique treetop ceremony as the dancing continues, and inevitably, there are more fireworks. The party continues through Sunday, with another procession of dancers up Zacateros street to the *jardín*. The fireworks and dancing don't stop until late Sunday night.

October-November
DÍA DE MUERTOS

Día de Muertos (Day of the Dead) is one of Mexico's most well-known holidays. The name is a bit of a misnomer, as the holiday is actually celebrated during two days, November 1 and November 2, with November 2 recognized as a national holiday. In San Miguel de Allende, like everywhere in Mexico, regional traditions distinguish local Day of the Dead festivities. During the final week of October, San Miguel families and prominent organizations build traditional altars in the town square using sugar skulls, *pan de muerto,* gourds and jicama, colored sand, and *cempasúchil* (marigolds), the flower of the dead. You may notice that traditional altar design in this region tends to be neater and more geometrical than in other parts of Mexico.

Throughout the two-day holiday, the municipal cemetery (behind the Real de Minas hotel on the Salida a Celaya) is packed with families who have come to leave flowers and treats on the graves of loved ones. Many families spend the entire day there, cleaning the gravesite, laying flowers, offering food and drink to their ancestors, or eating a picnic lunch together. By the evening, the crowds are so dense that it can take several hours to get into the cemetery.

LA CALACA

Occurring at the same time as traditional Día de Muertos festivities, **La Calaca** is a public art and cultural festival that made its first run in 2012. Taking place over four days, La Calaca celebrates Day of the Dead traditions

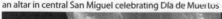
an altar in central San Miguel celebrating Día de Muertos

through themed art installations and special performances in the town's parks and public squares, all of which are free and open to the public. Adding Halloween-style revelry to an otherwise solemn holiday, La Calaca also puts on a bevy of raucous costume parties, processions, and music concerts in the evenings.

December

Mexico's long holiday stretches from the day of the Virgin of Guadalupe, on December 12, to Three Kings' Day, on January 6. This span is informally referred to as "Guadalupe Reyes." In most of the country, it's a relaxed, celebratory time, often spent with family. Cities are quieter and businesses run with reduced hours. In San Miguel, however, it is a bustling, busy season, when many domestic and international visitors flood the city.

Preparations for Christmas begin in November, but the season really kicks off on December 12, the day of **La Virgen de Guadalupe.** Although December 12 is not a national holiday, it is widely celebrated throughout Mexico. In San Miguel de Allende, you can expect to hear loud fireworks exploding throughout the night in the Virgin's honor. From December 12 onward, families gather for *posadas,* parties that occur during the nine days leading up to Christmas.

On the night of a *posada,* guests gather at a neighbor's house with candles and costumes, asking the host family for shelter (and thereby reenacting Mary and Joseph's search for shelter on the night that Jesus was born). Once inside, the families say a rosary and sing Christmas songs. Then children may break a piñata while adults sip on punch. *Posadas* conclude on December 24, the most important night of the season. Traditionally, Mexican families gather for a late dinner, attending midnight mass afterward. December 25 is a quiet day, usually spent relaxing with family.

In San Miguel de Allende, **New Year's Eve** is similar to most cities: lots of parties, people, and bubbly. There are often live music performances in the town square and, at midnight, a large fireworks display over the Parroquia de San Miguel Arcángel (a perfect chance for that postcard-perfect photo). If you want to follow Mexican tradition, eat 12 grapes for good luck when the clock strikes midnight— one grape for each month of the year. But be aware that the price of grapes in the market is always much higher on December 31! The season officially ends with **El Día de los Reyes Magos** (Three Kings' Day), on January 6.

Shopping

With a slew of unique stores and many creative minds at work, San Miguel de Allende is a wonderful place to shop. Although there are a few chain supermarkets and large department stores in San Miguel's outskirts, the *centro histórico* is still largely populated by mom-and-pop bakeries, corner stores, specialty boutiques, and artist-owned galleries. Here, local proprietors usually tend their own shops, and many are on a first-name basis with their clients.

San Miguel excels in everything related to art, design, craft, and interiors, and among shops there is quite a bit of diversity for a town of its size, as a few hours of window-shopping will quickly reveal. From small gifts and contemporary art to a unique piece of jewelry or even a new couch for your living room, San Miguel's creative climate is reflected in the many unique and local products it sells.

SHOPPING CENTERS

Located in a beautifully restored colonial-era mansion, just half a block from the *jardín,* the **Doce 18 Concept House** (Relox 18, tel. 415/154-9201 or 415/152-1398, http://doce-18.com, 10am-10pm daily, individual vendor hours vary) is a chic, city-style culinary and shopping center where you can wander through dozens of small shops featuring contemporary art, clothing, jewelry, and accessories, some representing well-known designers, including clothier Carla Fernández and jeweler Sangre de Mi Sangre, both from Mexico City. The centerpiece of the plaza is Mexican restaurant Jacinta, helmed by chef Matteo Salas. For a more casual meal, head to Doce 18's food hall, known as **The Kitchen,** where you can pick up a burger or a taco from one of multiple food stands, or just sip a cup of coffee or a cocktail from the in-house bar.

TRADITIONAL CRAFTS

From elaborately woven textiles to simple palm baskets, Mexico's rich traditions in art and handcraft are amply represented in San Miguel de Allende. You'll find a lot of work made by local artisans, including regional specialties like stamped tin, copper, and aluminum, forged iron, glass boxes, decorative and carved wooden figurines, leather goods, and hand-painted majolica-style ceramics. In addition to local products, San Miguel's best craft shops show the work of master artisans from across Mexico. In many cases, shop owners are knowledgeable about the traditional art they sell and can give you insight into a piece's origins or the artist's technique.

A delightful shop across the street from the Capilla de la Tercera Orden, **El Nuevo Mundo** (San Francisco 17, tel. 415/113-0324, 9am-8pm Mon.-Thurs., 10am-9pm Fri.-Sun.) sells a colorful range of crafts from central and southern Mexico. Handmade clothing and textiles are a specialty here, including beautiful hand-embroidered shirts, *huipiles,* rebozos, shawls, woven bags, tablecloths, bedspreads, and scarves. An excellent place to pick up a small gift to take home, El Nuevo Mundo also has an assortment of tin ornaments and boxes, miniatures, painted wooden animals, and other well-selected curiosities and trinkets. The friendly staff is knowledgeable about their products and patient if you'd like to try on a piece of clothing or two.

The two floors at **Flor de Canela** (Mesones 76, tel. 415/152-2749, 10am-3pm and 4pm-7pm Mon.-Sat., 11am-3pm Sun.) are amply stocked with beautiful folk art and crafts. Most of the work comes from the state of Michoacán, which borders Guanajuato to the west. Come here to see some of Mexico's most interesting craft traditions, like *árboles de la vida,* lacquered wooden trays and dishes, intricately hand-painted clay pots and platters, and large

Evoke sells a beautiful selection of wool rugs from Oaxaca.

Shopping for *Artesanía*

Shopping for traditional craftwork, or *artesanía,* is one of the great pleasures of a trip to Mexico. It's also an important way to support the country's historic artistic traditions. San Miguel de Allende is a wonderful place to shop for traditional craftwork, with a range of styles and techniques represented in its many well-stocked shops, most run by knowledgeable buyers.

MAJOLICA-STYLE CERAMICS

Since the 16th century, the states of Puebla and Guanajuato have been major producers of tin-glazed **majolica-style ceramics,** with the finest and most expensive ceramics produced in Puebla. Puebla's pottery is generally referred to as **Talavera.**

Dolores Hidalgo is also a major producer. Dolores pottery is more loosely painted and brightly colored than traditional *poblano* ceramics, and generally far less expensive.

Shopping tip: When shopping for ceramics from Dolores, seek out individual quality in each piece. Although there may be 25 ceramic plates of the same design, some are more beautifully painted than others.

Where to buy it: JMB (page 125) and **Azulejos y Loza Talavera Vázquez** (page 125) in Dolores Hidalgo; **Casa Benito** (page 66) in San Miguel de Allende.

CERAMICS

Santa María Atzompa, Oaxaca, produces distinctive **forest-green glazed pottery and cookware.** Another distinctive tradition is the elaborate **ceramic pineapples** from the towns of Patamban and San José de Gracia in Michoacán, where potters produce their wares without the use of a potter's wheel.

Unglazed burnished clay pottery, known as *barro bruñido,* is polished with pyrite and prolifically produced in several colorful and distinctive styles in Tonalá and Tlaquepaque, Jalisco. Another type of **burnished clay pottery** is native to Michoacán, specifically the town of Capula. The most recognizable Capula pottery is painted with hundreds of white dots. Also look for the shiny **glazed platters, plates, and pots** from Huancito and the typical **green and black pottery** from Tzintzuntzan, among other Michoacán pueblos. **Burnished black-clay pottery** from San Bartolo Coyotepec, Oaxaca, is also distinctive and well known, available in some shops in San Miguel.

Where to buy it: Flor de Canela (page 63) has decorative ceramics from Michoacán, often signed by the artisan. **Casa Benito** (page 66) and **Artes de Mexico** (page 66) carry a range of ceramic work. **Hilo Negro** (page 66) in the Fábrica La Aurora sells contemporary polished-clay pieces.

TEXTILES AND CLOTHING

Manta, a light cotton muslin, was mass-produced throughout Mexico and has long been the base for traditional Mexican clothing. Throughout town, you can find beautiful embroidered *manta* tunics and *huipiles* from the state of Oaxaca as well as the geometrically stitched Magdalena *huipiles* from Chiapas. In addition to *manta,* Oaxaca is a major producer of beautiful textiles and clothing, the best of which are hand-loomed and embroidered.

Chales, rebozos, and *mantillas* are different types of wraps and shawls produced throughout Mexico. The famous silk rebozos of Santa María del Río are so finely woven that, despite their large size, they can pass through a woman's ring.

Shopping tips: The best (and priciest) shawls are made with natural fibers, usually silk or cotton. Mexican-made textiles and clothing using natural dyes are the most sought-after and priciest.

Where to buy it: Juana Cata (page 67) has a stunning selection of textiles from the state of Oaxaca, handmade and colored with natural dye. **El Nuevo Mundo** (page 63) has colorful embroidered blouses, *manta* clothing, and other textiles from across Mexico. Boutique **Mixta** (page 67) has an eclectic selection of contemporary and traditional Mexican clothing.

HAND-LOOMED RUGS

There are few local producers of **wool rugs** in the state of Guanajuato. The most famous rugs in Mexico come from Teotitlán del Valle in Oaxaca; many feature pre-Columbian designs.

Shopping tip: The best and most expensive rugs are made with natural fibers. However, acrylic thread is commonly used in modern rugs. To test for acrylic, take a rug out into the sun. Unlike wool, acrylic will shine.

Where to buy it: You can sometimes find locally made rugs, as well as Oaxacan wool rugs, in craft shops in and around the **Mercado de Artesanía** (page 66). The boutique **Evoke** (page 66) sells beautiful wool rugs from Teotitlán del Valle.

HOJALATERÍA AND GLASS BOXES

Hojalatería (tin products) are a specialty in the San Miguel region, most often used in stamped-tin lamps and candelabras, wastepaper baskets, mirrors, and picture frames. San Miguel has also long been known for its delicate **blown-glass lanterns and boxes,** fused with iron.

Where to buy it: Los Botes Chilo (page 70) specializes in stamped tin and is one of the oldest craft shops in San Miguel de Allende. **Artes de Mexico** (page 66) sells blown glass.

WOOD FIGURINES

Whittled wooden toys and figurines, as well as wooden spoons and cutting boards, are produced locally and sold in many of the older craft shops in San Miguel de Allende. *Alebrijes,* delicately carved and brightly painted animals and figurines, are principally produced in San Antonio Arrazola, Oaxaca.

Where to buy it: Tiny **La Casa** (page 66) sells old-fashioned unpainted wood figurines and kitchen utensils. **Casa Benito** (page 66), along with many other craft shops, carries *alebrijes*.

LACQUERWARE

Gorgeously detailed **lacquered wood trays, boxes, chests, and platters,** as well as decorative gourds, are produced in the states of Michoacán and Guerrero.

Shopping tip: The most famous lacquerware artisans often sign their work, and many have won prizes for their talent; award-winning pieces are the most expensive.

Where to buy it: The shop inside the **Casa de Cultura Citibanamex** (page 44) often stocks lacquered trays and gourds from Michoacán. **La Calaca** (page 72) maintains a lovely selection of vintage hand-painted platters and wood figurines.

CEREMONIAL MASKS

Wooden masks are often used in traditional ceremonies, principally in the states of Oaxaca, Michoacán, and Guerrero. The original designs can range from the head of a jaguar to a garish devil.

Shopping tip: Masks are very individualized artisanal products, and they carry more significance (and a higher price) if they have already been used in a ceremony.

Where to buy it: La Calaca (page 72) almost always carries a selection of ceremonial masks, some antique and very rare.

glazed pineapples typical to the region. You'll find pieces at a range of price points, but the store specializes in high-quality decorative work often signed by the artisan, including a number of special pieces that have won national awards for excellence.

Located in a lovely old stone building on historic Hidalgo, unique interior decor shop **Evoke** (Hidalgo 19, no phone, http://evoketh-espirit.com, 10am-6pm daily) has a small but well-chosen selection of contemporary *arte-sanía* and handmade decor, like handwoven curtains and wall hangings, delicately hand-painted Mexican ceramics, decorative beaded cow skulls made by Huichol artisans, and beautiful, high-quality handmade wool rugs from Oaxaca state. Evoke started out as a workshop and showroom in the Pacific resort town of Sayulita, and its second shop in San Miguel de Allende retains a beachy bohemian-chic aesthetic.

For a taste of many Mexican craft traditions, **Casa Benito** (Mesones 55, tel. 415/150-0224, http://casabenitofolkart.com, 11am-7pm Mon.-Sat., 11am-3pm Sun.) features a range of colorful painted figurines, ornaments, decorated gourds, and ceramics from Michoacán, Puebla, Guanajuato, and other regions in Mexico known for their artisan productions. It's hard to get a sense of what's on offer from the shop's windows on Mesones Street, so take a moment to pop inside this surprisingly welcoming shop. You'll find pieces here at a range of price points, from high-end one-of-a-kind items to fun and inexpensive souvenirs for the folks back home.

There is a large selection of inexpensive and predominantly regional handicrafts at the **Mercado de Artesanía** (Andador Lucas Balderas, tel. 415/152-6590, hours vary by shop daily), an outdoor artisan market located in a descending alleyway between the Mercado Ignacio Ramírez and Calle Loreto. Here you'll find *milagritos* (painted tin ornaments) and other metalwork, as well as beautiful handmade mesquite bowls and utensils, ceramics, beaded jewelry, papier-mâché, and textiles. A few shops specialize in art and

crafts from Oaxaca and Michoacán as well as clay miniatures. There is some good work here, but it takes a sharp eye to find the best pieces amid the jumble of storefronts. Along the exit of the *mercado* on Calle Loreto, there are many more small shops selling craft work from across Mexico.

A dusty little storefront with over 75 years in operation, the small but adorable **La Casa** (Pepe Llanos 11, no phone, 10am-3pm and 5pm-8pm Mon.-Sat.) sells a variety of natural wicker baskets, plaited fans, and tortilla holders as well as a zoo full of unpainted, hand-carved wooden animals and statues. It is a shoebox of a space, with everything stacked in pleasing disorder and smelling of fresh wood, it is a charming throwback in increasingly chic San Miguel de Allende.

Just a few steps from the Fábrica La Aurora art and design center, the well-stocked shop **Artes de Mexico** (Calzada de la Aurora 47, tel. 415/152-0764, www.artesdemexi-cosanmiguel.com, 9am-7:30pm Mon.-Fri., 9am-6pm Sat.) has a large, diverse, and yet well-selected stock of furniture, lamps, blown glass, stamped-tin-frame mirrors, ceramics, papier-mâché, and other crafts. With such a huge variety, this store can feel like a small *artesanía* warehouse, yet quality is very good. Of particular note, Artes de Mexico stocks a range of *equipales:* large chairs, couches, and round tables made of lightweight natural wood and pigskin. Based on pre-Hispanic designs, *equipales* are pieces of comfortable and inexpensive traditional furniture from Jalisco.

A small and stylish shop in the Fábrica La Aurora, **Hilo Negro** (Local 3D, Fábrica La Aurora, Calzada de la Aurora, tel. 415/152-4835, www.hilo-negro.com, 10am-6pm Mon.-Sat., 11am-3am Sun.) features beautiful traditional crafts as well as imaginative decorative pieces by the shop's owner, Ricardo Garcia. Garcia's interest in traditional Mexican games, like *lotería* and *pissota,* often inspires his work, which is playful yet handsome, and elaborated with a mix of materials like wood, burnished clay, and antique coins. Though inspired by *artesanía,* Garcia's pieces are more akin to fine art, with the prices to match. In addition, the store has a fine collection of hand-painted majolica platters.

CLOTHING AND ACCESSORIES

Owned by a family of well-known Oaxacan craft experts, **Juana Cata** (Recreo 5A, tel. 415/152-6417, 10:15am-8pm Mon.-Sat. and 10:15-6pm Sun.) sells gorgeous handmade clothing and textiles from the state of Oaxaca. Take your time perusing the stacks of expertly woven shawls, thick hand-dyed cotton fabrics, and lovely velvet *huipiles,* lavishly embroidered with colorful flowers in the Isthmus of Tehuantepec. Here, every piece is painstakingly created and expertly selected. For those interested in Mexican textiles and weaving traditions, this shop is essential. In addition to textiles, Juana Cata has a nice collection of Oaxacan silver jewelry, known for its delicate filigree details.

A sister shop to the long-running home-design emporium Namuh, **Munah** (Cuna de Allende 15, tel. 415/152-8848, www.munahbysami.com, 11am-2pm and 3pm-6pm Mon., 11am-8pm Tues.-Sat., 11am-6pm Sun.) is a clothing and accessories boutique at the entrance of the pretty shopping plaza Cuna Quince. Much of the merchandise at Munah has a noticeably Mexican aesthetic, with a selection of embroidered blouses and tasseled jewelry in vibrant colors, cashmere sweaters, leather accessories, contemporary silver jewelry, and a small but delightful selection of children's clothing.

Spend some time browsing the beautifully selected mix of crafts, collectibles, art, and clothes at **Mixta** (Pila Seca 3, tel. 415/152-7343, www.mixtasanmiguel.com, 11am-7pm Mon.-Sat., noon-5pm Sun.), an excellent and eclectic design-centric boutique on Calle Pila Seca. Set in the romantic old salons of an 18th-century mansion, the always-changing collection here includes bangles, shawls, beaded necklaces, greeting cards, unique home furnishings, original art, scarves, totes, tunics, oilcloth wallets, votive candles, throw pillows,

furniture, and photographs, culled from a range of Mexican and international designers. The shop's warm Australian owner is often behind the register; she selects all the work for the shop, looking far and wide for unusual items you won't find elsewhere in San Miguel.

The blast of color at **Abrazos** (Zacateros 24, tel. 415/154-8580, www.sanmigueldesigns.com, 10am-7pm Mon.-Sat., 10am-4pm Sun.) comes from the lighthearted, Mexican-themed cotton fabrics that form the base of the store's product line. A great place to pick up a gift for yourself or someone at home, Abrazos has a range of cute and colorful aprons, dish towels, handbags, kimonos, eye masks, pajamas, and men's ties as well as funky jewelry, buttons, and notebooks. All the shop's products are handmade in San Miguel de Allende by a cooperative of local seamstresses.

Inspired by traditional Mexican design, the luxe line of ponchos, wraps, shawls, and dresses created at **Recreo** (Recreo 26, tel. 415/154-4820, http://recreosanmiguel.com, 10am-7pm Mon.-Sat., 10am-4pm Sun.) has garnered a loyal clientele over the boutique's many years in San Miguel. If you are looking for a high-quality and elegant piece to take home from Mexico, this is the place to go. Though focused on women's accessories, there is also a small line of men's clothing. Prices are high, but the designs are original and the quality is excellent. The spacious stone-floored boutique has a swanky ambience, with gleaming chandeliers, polished clay floors, and clothing hung neatly on the racks, and the staff is friendly and generous with their time.

JEWELRY

Yam Gallery, a contemporary art space in the Instituto Allende, represents William Spratling's estate, selling sterling-silver pieces made by the legendary designer, as well as jewelry and silver accessories produced by artisans in his Taxco workshop. Recently, Yam's owners debuted a small boutique dedicated entirely to silver design, **Yam Gallery Silver** (Instituto Allende, Ancha de San Antonio,

11am-6pm Mon.-Sat., 11am-3pm Sun.), also in the Instituto Allende, which showcases Spratling's iconic work, jewelry from the Spratling workshop, and other unique pieces by several high-quality contemporary designers.

Located in the Fábrica La Aurora, **Alquimia4** (Local 16A, Fábrica La Aurora, Calzada de la Aurora s/n, tel. 415/152-6012, www.alquimiacuatro.com, 10am-6pm Mon.-Sat., 11am-3pm Sun.) is a gallery and jewelry shop. Large stone, metal, and clay sculptures by Victor Hugo Nuñez dominate the space, but there are also plentiful display cases dedicated to Lila Parilla's original and highly varied jewelry designs. Parilla works in silver, but pieces often incorporate precious and semi-precious stones, leather, and pearls. Some of her collections are inspired by pre-Columbian art and architecture, while others take their designs from natural forms.

HOME AND FURNITURE

Decorating a colonial mansion calls for some serious furnishings, but **Maria Luisa** (Canal 40, tel. 415/152-0130, 10am-7pm Mon.-Sat., 10am-4pm Sun.) has all the iron fixtures and monumental accessories that an 18th-century home deserves. The ceilings of this shop's large showrooms are filled with tin lamps and chandeliers of every conceivable design, while metal candlesticks, vintage-style furniture, tableware, elaborate mirrors, stately clay urns, picture frames, and other housewares cram the floor space. Impressive home accessories blend old San Miguel style with the polish of contemporary design. On the outdoor patio, there is also a selection of iron tables and chairs along with concrete fountains.

Namuh (Camino a Alcocer, Km 2.2, tel. 415/154-8080, www.namuhmex.com, 9am-6pm Mon.-Fri., 10am-6pm Sat., 11am-4pm Sun.) is a furniture design shop and importer that provides a range of beautiful furnishings and home accessories, with a particular emphasis on Asian-inspired designs and products from countries such as Thailand, China, and Indonesia. The work is of high quality, yet the aesthetic is earthy and comfortable, with merchandise ranging from leather armchairs and hanging lamps to weathered chests and clay urns. Though the main warehouse is

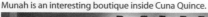

Munah is an interesting boutique inside Cuna Quince.

Shipping Items Home

With the many galleries, boutiques, and home decor shops in San Miguel, it's easy to buy more artwork and *artesanía* than can fit into your suitcase. Some visitors even find themselves contemplating the purchase of a new dresser for the bedroom or an oil painting for the library, among other oversize, unpackable pieces. Fortunately, San Miguel de Allende's shops and shipping services have ample experience sending items overseas, and, in many cases, the cost of shipping an item home isn't prohibitive.

COSTS

Shipping prices vary widely, and always depend on a combination of factors: weight, size, value of the item, and the item's destination. Of these, weight and size are the most important factors. If you are buying in bulk, you can often reduce the per-item price of shipping.

Because the cost of shipping items home can vary widely, make sure you or the shop owner gets an accurate quote from a trusted shipping company before you make a purchase.

SHIPPING SERVICES

In most cases, shopkeepers will assist you in getting a shipping estimate on a larger item or a bulk purchase. If you are buying from a less established shop or an artist's home studio, or if you'd like to talk directly to the shippers, the following are long-running and reliable companies operating in San Miguel.

Solutions (Recreo 11, tel. 415/152-6152, 9am-6pm Mon.-Fri., 9am-noon Sat.) provides insured overseas shipping services in conjunction with several ground transportation companies in the United States. Solutions estimates that the cost of sending an item from Mexico to the United States through their service is between 30 and 50 percent of the item's value, though especially large or heavy pieces can cost much more. With Solutions, shipping a standard 60- by 40-centimeter (24- by 16-inch) cardboard box that weighs under 20 kilograms (44 pounds) to the United States runs about $80-90. If you are in a shop and debating whether to purchase a piece, you can send a photo of the piece to Solutions via WhatsApp, and they will send you an estimate on the spot.

Another shipping company in San Miguel de Allende, **La Union** (Zacateros 26A, tel. 415/185-8870, www.launionsanmiguel.com, 10am-6pm Mon.-Fri., 10am-3pm Sat.) provides packing and insured shipping services domestically and internationally through DHL and UPS, among other services. Though they do not have a fixed rate for any items, size and weight are the factors that most affect the cost of shipping. They can also provide assistance for importing items or households from the United States or Canada to Mexico.

La Conexión (Aldama 3, tel. 415/152-1599, 9am-5pm Mon.-Sat., 10am-2pm Sun.; Plaza Real del Conde Local BA14, tel. 415/152-2312, 9am-5pm Mon.-Fri.; Libramiento a Dolores Hidalgo 11, tel. 415/152-4223, 9am-5pm Mon.-Fri.; Zacateros 83, tel. 415/152-2190, 9am-5pm Mon.-Sat., www.laconexionsma.com) is a certified U.S. Postal Service agent for expatriates living in San Miguel de Allende. La Conex can ship smaller packages via U.S. mail for a cost of US$1 per pound, plus 17 percent on the declared value of the merchandise; anything larger than 24 square inches must be quoted separately.

There is also a **FedEx** (Canal 148, 415/688-1271, www.fedex.com, 9:30am-3pm and 4pm-7pm Mon.-Fri., 10am-1pm Sat.) in downtown San Miguel, through which you can ship boxes overseas or send expedited mail. For fast service, it's a good option, though FedEx's services are generally far more expensive than those of the companies listed above.

located on a country road west of town, you can get a sampling of Namuh's furnishings, antiques, and textiles at their charming little downtown shop (Cuna de Allende 15, no phone, 11am-7pm Mon.-Fri., 11am-8pm Sat., 11am-6pm Sun.) in the Cuna Quince plaza.

With two locations downtown, **Camino Silvestre** (Zacateros 46, tel. 415/121-3359, and Correo 43, tel. 415/152-3918, www.caminosilvestre.com, 10am-7pm Mon.-Sat., noon-5pm Sun.) stocks all the essentials for a romantic garden party, from wind chimes and candlesticks to blown glass and hand-painted ceramics. Inspired by a love of forest birds, this store is romantic and crafty; it's a great place to pick up a unique gift for the garden or thumb through one of the store's glossy, well-selected coffee-table books. At the Correo location, you can see the store's creative line of glass hummingbird feeders swaying from trees over the popular courtyard cafe, **Néctar** (8:30am-5:30pm Mon.-Sat., 10am-4:30pm Sun.), where tea, coffee, and herbal infusions, vegan sandwiches, and desserts are served.

La Bottega di Casa

Located within the same beautifully renovated mansion that houses dining hot spot The Restaurant, **Sollano 16**'s (Diez de Sollano 16, tel. 415/154-8872, www.sollano16.com, 10am-6pm Tues.-Thurs., 10am-8pm Fri., 11am-9pm Sat., noon-4pm Sun.) high-end line of furniture and home accessories matches the upscale ambience. In this expansive, high-ceilinged shop, you'll find a range of chic and unusual decor from across the world, from French pottery to New York-designed jewelers. There's also a small, curated selection of menswear, accessories, and art.

In the Fábrica La Aurora, the lovely home-goods store **La Bottega di Casa** (Local 17A, Fábrica La Aurora, Calzada de la Aurora s/n, Local, tel. 415/152-8636, www.labottegadicasa.com, 10am-6pm Mon.-Sat., 11am-3pm Sun.) is best known for its proprietary collections of fine bed linens, table dressings, and other textiles made with Italian fabrics, most specially designed by the store's sophisticated Italian owner. La Bottega di Casa also sells unique home goods, like Merino vases and 19th-century lithographs, culled from the owner's travels around the world, particularly Europe, as well as Mexican-made blown-glass pitchers and drinking glasses, hammered copper lamps, and white-glazed ceramic table settings, elegantly produced and presented.

Sisal (Local 2A, Fábrica La Aurora, Calzada de la Aurora s/n, tel. 415/152-0338 or 415/152-8944, 10am-7pm Mon.-Fri., 10am-5pm Sat.) sells an eclectic yet tasteful mix of modern furniture, imported Asian antiques, Mexican rugs, and contemporary art. The store's owner, a Querétaro businesswoman with a flair for design, is constantly seeking out new merchandise; every time you go back, there's something different on the floor. Sisal also carries accessories, like colorful throw pillows, baskets, onyx lamps and accessories, luxe bath products, and mirrors.

On a busy street just outside the *centro histórico*, **Los Botes Chilo** (Prol. Calzada de la Luz 51-B, tel. 415/152-2789, 11am-6pm Mon.-Sat., noon-3pm Sun.) produces decorative tin accessories, an artisanal specialty of the San Miguel de Allende region. Here, you'll find both ready-made and custom tin lamps, mirrors, and frames. The tiny showroom is packed with examples of their work, some quite original. Although you can buy directly, Chilo specializes in custom-designed products for San Miguel de Allende homeowners.

GALLERIES AND ARTIST STUDIOS

Blessed with ornate baroque architecture and lovely natural light, San Miguel de Allende is a feast for the eyes. As such, it is hardly surprising that this small town has been home to a cozy community of artists since the early 20th century. Free of the pretension you'd find in major cities, San Miguel is a welcoming place to see, make, or buy art. Here, amateurs and art students can quickly find a place to show their work, and opening events feel like lighthearted social gatherings among a group of friends. Every weekend, new exhibitions are inaugurated in San Miguel's galleries or an art walk is hosted by a group of exhibitors and studios. Visiting these spaces is a quintessential part of visiting San Miguel.

Right next to the Teatro Ángela Peralta, **Galería Izamal** (Mesones 80, tel. 415/154-5409, www.galeriaizamal.com, 11am-3pm and 4pm-8pm daily) is one of the longest-running artist-owned collective galleries in town. This tiny, overstuffed storefront features diverse drawings, paintings, and jewelry by the exhibiting artists and co-owners, who each work a weekly shift in the gallery. Their techniques vary, but all are good-quality artists with many years of recognition in San Miguel. Two of the gallery's artists also give informal drawing and creativity workshops behind the gallery; inquire in the shop for more information. Depending on when you stop in, you may have the opportunity to chat with one of the creative folks behind the space.

The well-known Oaxacan gallery operator Noel Cayetano has opened a branch of his eponymous gallery **Noel Cayetano Arte Contemporáneo** (Hernández Macías 68, tel. 415/121-1227, 10am-8pm daily) in San

Miguel de Allende, just across the street from Bellas Artes. Featuring work by well-known Oaxacan names like Ruben Leyba, Ixrael Montes, Guillermo Olguin, and Sergio Hernandez, this well-curated, white-walled space mostly features large-format oil painting, though it also boasts a small outdoor sculpture garden. It's a good place to get a primer on the Oaxacan tradition in fine art or shop for a unique piece.

The interesting **Galeria Nudo** (Recreo 10B and Recreo 36, tel. 415/154-7179, www.galerianudo.com, 10am-6pm Mon.-Sat., 10am-3pm Sun.) shows a range of painting and work on paper by artists from across Mexico, with an emphasis on Oaxacan names, including the master Francisco Toledo, Damián Flores, and Guillermo Olguin. If you'd like to know more about a piece's provenance, the knowledgeable staff can answer your questions.

Occupying the southeast corner of the Instituto Allende, **Yam Gallery** (Instituto Allende, Ancha de San Antonio 20, Int. 1, tel. 415/150-6052, www.yamgallery.com, 11am-5pm Mon.-Sat.) is a unique space that has distinguished itself through a number of original and even controversial exhibits in its two-story space. In 2006, Yam made international news for exhibiting 20 works on paper by artist Donald Johnson, a prisoner in solitary confinement at Pelican Bay State Prison in California. More recently, the gallery has shown work by contemporary Mexican, South American, and European artists, including several talented San Miguel locals, and it is always represented at a booth at the annual Zona Maco in Mexico City, the country's most prestigious art fair.

Born in Florence, Italy, but raised in Mexico, artist and architect Pedro Friedeberg was one of the country's most prominent artists of the 20th century. When Friedeberg moved to San Miguel de Allende, he redecorated the colonial interior of **Casa Diana** (Recreo 48, tel. 415/152-0885, www.galeriacasadiana.com, 10am-7pm Mon.-Tues. and Thurs.-Sat., 11am-4pm Sun.), which now houses an art gallery in the downstairs living spaces. The gallery is open to the public and hosts rotating exhibitions of local artwork, with an emphasis on sculpture. Friedeberg is one of the gallery's permanent artists. Needless to say, Friedeberg's unique decorating style is one of the main reasons to visit Casa Diana, where you can see his imagination at work as well as some of his iconic chairs in the shape of giant hands.

Many visitors find themselves taking something home from **Vintage Posters International Gallery** (Zacateros 57, tel. 415/149-7327, www.mrposter.com), which maintains a wonderful collection of Soviet-era posters, as well as contemporary posters, most produced in Poland. Thumb through hundreds of original and diverse posters dedicated to films, sports, politics, and theater, among other topics, many sold at reasonable prices. The owner and staff are knowledgeable about the work they sell.

San Miguel's most avant-garde gallery, **Kunsthaus Santa Fé** (Santa Fé 22A, Col. Allende, tel. 415/152-5608, www.kunsthaussantafe.com, by appointment) was founded as a nonprofit organization designed to showcase emerging talent from Latin America and beyond. Today, the gallery is a commercial space but continues to promote its original concept of supporting new proposals in contemporary art, with many interesting shows by both national and international artists. Kunsthaus's galleries are located on the bottom floor of owner Lothar Müller's home in the residential Allende neighborhood, a decidedly funky atmosphere for the gallery's frequent opening exhibitions. Guests often wander through the living spaces on the second floor, where more artwork is on view. Expect a wide range of offerings here, from sculpture and installations to photography and large-scale painting.

Numerous working artists have studio space in the **Fábrica La Aurora** (Calzada de la Aurora s/n, Col. Aurora, tel. 415/152-1012, www.fabricalaaurora.com), many of which are open to the public. While their hours vary, most of the Aurora's artists hold open studios 11am-5pm on Thursday and welcome visitors throughout the week. If you'd prefer to view artwork accompanied by a glass of wine, the Fábrica La Aurora also hosts an art walk on the first Friday of each month.

One of San Miguel's most beloved and recognizable painters, **Juan Ezcurdia** (Calzada de la Aurora s/n, Col. Aurora, tel. 415/101-2622, hours vary, but usually 11am-3pm and 4pm-5pm Mon.-Sat.) has a workshop in the Fábrica La Aurora where he creates his distinctive whimsical, color-saturated paintings and prints of anthropomorphic animals riding in cars, flying in planes, and other merriment. His spacious stone-walled studio, tucked into the back of the Fábrica La Aurora, doubles as a showroom, and his doors are usually open to curious visitors and buyers.

ANTIQUES

The opulence of 17th- and 18th-century San Miguel left behind its share of spoils. Today, the former finery from old haciendas and colonial mansions often turns up in dusty antiques shops around town. While the number of antiques is beginning to dwindle, those interested in vintage wares will still find good places to buy them in town, in addition to antique popular art and pottery.

It is easy to walk right past the little storefront, so keep an eye out for **La Calaca** (Mesones 93, tel. 415/152-3954, US tel. 512/695-0489, www.lacalaca.com, 11am-2pm and 4pm-6pm Mon.-Sat.), which specializes in antique popular and ceremonial art from around Mexico. The store's owner, Evita, has been trading *artesanías* for more than 25 years, and her experience has helped compile a lovely collection of masks, platters, ceramics, textiles, and other special objects that wear their age with dignity. A cozy little spot on a bustling street, this tiny store is a good place to find a special piece for your home and to hear a little bit about its history from Evita.

Stepping through the door of **La Buhardilla** (Local 4A, Fábrica La Aurora, Calzada de la Aurora s/n, tel. 415/154-9911, www.arteyantiguedades.mx, 10:30am-6pm Mon.-Sat.,

Respect the Siesta

In every tourist resort or border town, you can buy a ceramic figurine or a hand-painted shot glass depicting a Mexican *muchacho* asleep against a cactus, sombrero pulled over his eyes. The famous siesta, or midafternoon nap, has become a symbol of living the good life in Mexico.

In reality, the siesta is an important part of family life in many parts of the country, including San Miguel de Allende. Here, the midday meal, known as the *comida*, is the biggest and most important meal of the day. Traditionally eaten at 2pm, the *comida* is a time that families spend together, just after children come home from school. Often, people take a short nap after lunch; hence, the entire midday break is often referred to as the siesta.

Although the traditional siesta is losing is prevalence in big cities, it continues to be very much a part of daily life in smaller towns like San Miguel. Notice the operating hours at many small businesses, like pottery shops, galleries, or real estate offices. They usually close 2-4pm, a time during which the shop's proprietors will go home for lunch and relaxation. For tourists, the siesta can be a bit of a nuisance, since few expect to find a gift shop or clothing boutique closed during the bright light of day. Most, however, learn to do like the locals and enjoy a long and leisurely lunch.

Like the siesta, Sundays are an important family day in Mexico, often undisturbed by the necessity of running a business. Frequently, when a shop's proprietors say it is open "every day," they are excluding Sunday. It can be very surprising to learn that the majority of shops—and even restaurants—are closed or have very reduced hours on Sunday, when tourists flock to San Miguel from nearby towns like Celaya and Querétaro. Yet personal time, family, and tradition are still a priority here.

---

noon-3pm Sun.) is almost like stepping into another world. Inside this vast and artful shop in the Fábrica La Aurora, the walls are covered with antique masks and old oil paintings, vintage lamps swing from the ceiling, and worn but beautiful carpets cover the floors. Owned by experienced antiques dealers and restoration experts from Monterrey, Mexico, La Buhardilla is one of the best places to browse fine Mexican antiques in town. In recent years, the shop has also been at the center of an international controversy after it announced the possession of a chest full of artifacts from artist Frida Kahlo's home, a collection that is as yet unrecognized by Kahlo experts.

ART SUPPLIES

For paints, brushes, canvases, colored pencils, drawing paper, notebooks, and other artistic necessities, head to **Lagundi's: La Esquina de Arte** (Umarán 17, tel. 415/152-0830, 10:30am-2pm and 4pm-6:30pm Mon.-Fri., 11am-3pm Sun.). In addition to art supplies, Lagundi's also mats and frames artwork at a reasonable cost.

A favorite with locals for its good selection and low prices, **El Pato** (Margarito Ledesma 19, Col. Guadalupe, tel. 415/152-1543, 10am-3pm and 4pm-8pm Mon.-Fri., 10am-3pm Sat.) is a well-stocked art supply store in the Guadalupe neighborhood, about a 10-minute walk from the central square. Here, you can stock up on inexpensive national and imported oil, acrylic, and watercolor paint, a variety of natural bristle and synthetic brushes, canvases and frames, notebooks, drawing pads, pencils, pastels, linseed oil, and other essential art supplies. El Pato also has a small but good selection of heavy stock paper, sold by the sheet.

BOOKSTORES

In the Centro Cultural El Nigromante (Bellas Artes), the bookstore **Educal** (Hernández Macías 75, tel. 415/154-9179, www.educal.com.mx, 10am-6pm Mon.-Sat., 10am-2pm Sun.) is operated by CONACULTA, the Mexican government's department of art and culture. This small store sells numerous titles from CONACULTA's own press, principally covering art and international literature written in or translated into Spanish (almost all titles at this small but well-stocked bookstore are in Spanish). There is also a small collection of world music for sale.

A little cubbyhole of a shop stocked floor-to-ceiling with used books, **Garrison & Garrison** (Hidalgo 26, tel. 415/109-7387, 11am-6pm Mon., Wed., and Fri.-Sun.) offers a small, changing selection of fiction, nonfiction, and children's books in both English and Spanish (and even some in French). You never know what you'll find on the shelves, but it's worth looking through the stacks if you're in need of some reading material. Despite its diminutive size, the store has a sweet literary atmosphere.

Sports and Recreation

With its leisurely pace, near-perfect climate, and breathtaking architecture, it is easy to give in to San Miguel's relaxing atmosphere—except that it's so hard to sit still! There is always something to do in San Miguel, whether it's horseback riding through desert canyons or relaxing away the morning in natural hot springs. Taking the time to explore the peaceful, cactus-filled, starkly beautiful semiarid landscape around San Miguel de Allende may be one of the most memorable parts of a trip to the area and a pleasing contrast to the vibrant colors and bustling activity in downtown.

YOGA, MEDITATION, AND THERAPY

LifePath Center (Riconada de la Aldea 29, tel. 415/154-8465, U.S. tel. 214/432-5711, www.lifepathretreats.com, hours vary) is a multifaceted center for wellness, healing, and personal growth, owned and operated by a collective of alternative practitioners. The center has many comfortable consultation and massage rooms, where a range of therapists offer counseling, body work, and alternative therapies, like acupuncture, craniosacral therapy, therapeutic massage, naturopathy, counseling, and reflexology. LifePath also operates as a small bed-and-breakfast, with four lovely, well-priced rooms ideal for those who would like to join classes or workshops.

A thoughtful, skilled teacher in the Iyengar tradition, **Jennifer Kagan** (tel. 415/149-9668, www.jenkagan.net) offers group classes and private yoga instruction at her lovely studio in the Atascadero neighborhood. Her studio is fully equipped with props, mats, and blankets, and she can design an individual program of study for those who want an intensive yoga retreat. In addition to her home studio, Jennifer teaches regularly in Querétaro and Mexico City. One month (four classes) costs about US$40.

Jennifer Kagan also teaches at **Float Sano** (Hernández Macías 12, tel. 415/121-1314, www.floatsano.com, 8am-6pm Mon.-Fri., 9am-8pm Sat., 10am-4pm Sun.), along with recommended teacher Usha Leason. This unique spa and fitness center is named for its therapeutic float tank, but it offers a range of wellness treatments, including infrared sauna and deep-tissue massage. The spa offers packages of unlimited yoga plus spa treatments for a very reasonable price, as well as reduced-price packages for yoga classes.

The friendly **Meditation Center of San Miguel** (Callejón Blanco 4, tel. 415/156-1950, www.meditationsma.org) provides three sitting meditation sessions Monday-Friday, at 8am, 8:50am, and 5:30pm, plus a single session on Saturday at 10am. There are also occasional talks and classes offered in the center's peaceful main room. The center is Buddhist-oriented, though nondenominational, and participants are welcome to practice any form of still, silent mediation.

Renew Your Spirit

LifePath Center

For many, San Miguel isn't a traditional tourist destination, where sightseeing and recreation are the priority. Instead, it's a place to relax, learn, and spend some time off the grid. For dharma bums, burgeoning artists, or stressed-out city types looking for a respite, San Miguel is a wonderful place for a low-key retreat.

MIND

· Reflect in a still and silent **meditation** session at the welcoming **Meditation Center of San Miguel** (page 74).

· Sweat it out during a meditative session of **Iyengar yoga** with **Jennifer Kagan** (page 74).

BODY

· **LifePath Center** (page 74) offers a range of therapies with local practitioners, including **acupuncture, Ayurvedic massage, Reiki,** and **craniosacral therapy.** There are also workshops in **yoga, qigong,** and silent **meditation,** all held in a lovely old mansion.

· Book an aromatherapy massage at **Jasmine Day Spa** (page 76), a float therapy session at **Float Sano** (page 74), or a thermal stone fusion at **Sense** (page 76), a spa at the Rosewood hotel.

· Soak in the covered pools at **La Gruta** (page 113), where the natural warm water that fills the pools is believed to have **healing properties.** Just down the road, **Escondido Place** (page 114) has a series of progressively warmer pools, filled daily by **natural springs,** as well as **cold-water pools.**

SPIRIT

· **El Charco del Ingenio** (page 50), San Miguel's unique botanical gardens and nature preserve, is a peaceful place to spend a few hours wandering and reflecting under the Mexican sun. They also host frequent special events, like *temazcal* steam baths, morning **yoga** sessions, and **wildlife workshops.**

· Visit the **Cañada de la Virgen** (page 116), a small but beautiful archaeological site located within an expansive **ecological reserve.**

SPAS AND MASSAGE

San Miguel de Allende begs you to relax. But if stress persists, despite the soothing sunlight and strong margaritas, it may be time to visit one of the many day spas in town.

The low-key atmosphere at **Jasmine Day Spa** (Jesús 25A, tel. 415/152-7973, www.jasminedayspasma.com, 10am-6pm Mon.-Sat.) feels pleasantly in tune with the casual vibe of San Miguel de Allende. The simple spa rooms are cozy with brightly painted colors—comfortable but not fancy. Treatments include Swedish, shiatsu, and deep-tissue massage, manicures and pedicures, facials, and body scrubs. Deep-tissue massage is a particular specialty of the spa. For a single treatment, prices are very reasonable.

Upon arrival for your treatment at **Sense** (Nemesio Diez 11, tel. 415/152-9730, www.rosewoodhotels.com, 8am-8pm daily), the upscale spa on the top floor of the Rosewood hotel, you'll receive a bathrobe and slippers and a chance to enjoy the facilities, which include gender-separate saunas and relaxation areas stocked with high-end toiletries. The spa offers a robust line of treatment options, from facials and massages to manicures and pedicures—even package deals that combine spa and tour-guide services in San Miguel.

Warm and talented Italian massage therapist **Fabrizio Crisafulli** (Guadiana 5, Col. Guadiana, tel. 415/118-1771) is certified in a range of healing traditions, including iridology and aromatherapy, and he offers relaxing, well-priced therapeutic massages (starting at US$35) at his pretty Guadiana neighborhood studio—or, if you prefer, Crisafulli will bring a table to your home. Make an appointment by telephone or WhatsApp.

Trained in California, **David Galitzky** (cell tel. 415/114-8469, www.essentialmassageandwatsu.com) is a highly recommended and licensed massage therapist specializing in watsu, a form of aquatic body work. He has a

pool equipped for watsu at his home, but he will also make house calls.

HIKING, BIKING, AND HORSEBACK RIDING

A friendly, family-run tour group, **Coyote Canyon Adventures** (tel. 415/154-4193 or 415/121-0340, www.coyotecanyonadventures.com) leads half-day and full-day horseback riding tours in the beautiful ranchland near the Cañada de la Virgen ecological preserve. The day of your scheduled outing, someone from the team will pick you and your group up in San Miguel and take you out to the country. Beautiful scenery and fun but manageable rides suitable for any skill level characterize this tour group. While horseback riding is Coyote Canyon's specialty, they also offer adventure sports like rappelling, hiking and camping tours, biking, and nature walks. Prices range from US$90 per person for a half-day tour to around US$195 for an overnight trip.

Ride a horse across stark, scenic ranchlands at family-owned-and-operated **Rancho Xotolar** (tel. 415/154-6275, cell tel. 415/105-2622, www.xotolarranch.com). Guided half-day rides (US$95 pp) include transport to and from San Miguel as well as a homemade lunch of products grown on the ranch. The ranch also offers donkey rides for children, hiking tours, and on-site camping as well as guided tours of the Cañada de la Virgen archaeological site.

Bici-Burro (Hospicio 1, tel. 415/152-1526, www.bici-burro.com, 9am-2pm and 4pm-7pm Mon.-Fri., 9am-2pm Sat.) is a family-run bike shop and tour operator leading both hiking and off-road biking trips in the countryside around San Miguel de Allende. Some of the bicycle tours will take you along the former silver route (which was used to bring goods to and from San Miguel during the colonial era) and out to the beautiful Santuario de Atotonilco. It is a great way to see the countryside while also checking out some of San Miguel's cultural sights. A half-day tour runs about US$95 per person, including a tour guide and the rental of an aluminum mountain bike, helmet, and gloves.

GYMS AND FITNESS

The gym and pool at Rosewood's **Sense** (Nemesio Diez 11, tel. 415/152-9730, 7am-8pm daily) is open to hotel guests or those receiving a treatment. They also offer annual (US$2,500) and monthly (starting at US$135) memberships for long-term users. Memberships include discounts on classes, like yoga and Pilates, as well as use of the spa facilities and locker rooms.

Upbeat, positive, and a bit of a taskmaster, **Sue Lawrence** (Col. Guadiana, tel. 415/109-0240) is a Classical Pilates instructor offering classes by appointment (7:30am-6:30pm Mon.-Sat.) in her private studio. With toned abs across the town, Sue's students are dedicated champions of her excellence.

TENNIS

Weber Tennis Courts (Callejón de San Antonio 12, Col. San Antonio, tel. 415/152-0659, U.S. tel. 561/429-7017, www.sanmigueltennis.com, sunrise-sunset daily) has three clay tennis courts popular with locals, both Mexican and expatriate, which you can use for about US$10 per hour. Courts are open to the public by reservation (though walk-ins are also welcome). If you want to improve your backhand, Weber will also help set up private lessons (US$35/hour).

Tennis courts are available at the **Club de Golf Malanquín** (Carretera San Miguel-Celaya, Km 3, tel. 415/152-0516 or 415/154-8210, www.malanquin.com.mx, US$20 per hour weekdays, US$25 weekends), right outside the city center. Reservations aren't necessary. They also allow hourly access to the on-site pool.

GOLF

San Miguel's oldest course, **Club de Golf Malanquín** (Carretera San Miguel-Celaya, Km 3, tel. 415/152-0516, www.malanquin.com.mx, 6:30am-9pm Tues.-Sat., 7am-7pm Sun.) maintains a well-groomed nine-hole golf course right on the edge of town. During the weekdays, greens fees are accessible; they also offer temporary memberships, for those who'd like to play multiple times or take advantage of the club's other facilities. If you want to practice your stroke, two excellent golf pros offer beginning, intermediate, and advanced golf clinics throughout the week. Membership allows access to the club's tennis courts, swimming pool, steam bath, clubhouse, restaurant, and coffee shop.

The **Ventanas de San Miguel Golf & Resort** (Carretera San Miguel Allende-Dolores Hidalgo, Km 1.5, tel. 415/688-0061, toll-free Mex. tel. 800/465-3762, www.club-ventanasdesanmiguel.com, 7am-5:30pm Mon.-Fri., 7am-4:30pm Sat.-Sun.) has an 18-hole Nick Faldo-designed Championship Course at par 70, plus a number of lots and residences for sale. The course hosts several annual golf tournaments, with daily greens fees for the public as well as membership options. Private classes are also available with a golf pro throughout the week.

BIRD-WATCHING

Mexico's only Audubon chapter, **Sociedad Audubon de México** (tel. 415/119-4671, www.audubonmex.org) runs monthly birding walks around San Miguel de Allende, by the Río Laja, and in the area around the Allende dam, where you can spot ducks, shovelers, hawks, kites, egrets, and many other beautiful bird species. Tours depart from the Instituto Allende on the third Sunday of every month and generally cost about US$10 for nonmembers.

Classes and Volunteering

San Miguel de Allende is a friendly and livable town, making it an excellent place to spend a few weeks, a few months, or even a few years studying language and arts or pursuing new hobbies.

SPANISH LANGUAGE STUDY

Serious students should take a look at the excellent and centrally located **Academia Hispano Americana** (Mesones 4, tel. 415/152-0349, www.ahaspeakspanish.com, 8:30am-4:30pm Mon.-Fri.). Established in 1959, this is the oldest Spanish school in San Miguel de Allende and one of the best. Throughout the year, AHA offers intensive and semi-intensive Spanish curricula, which include grammar, pronunciation, and Spanish-language lectures on Mexican culture. New sessions begin each month, and class size is capped at 12. The school will also arrange for students to stay in the homes of local families, where they can eat, sleep, and keep practicing their Spanish. College students can earn credit at AHA, which is associated with the University of Guanajuato.

A popular and effective language school with a proprietary system of Spanish instruction aimed at adult learners, **Warren Hardy Spanish School** (San Rafael 6, tel. 415/154-4017 9am-noon, tel. 415/152-4728 afternoons, www.warrenhardy.com) offers a series of intensive, half-day courses that span two and a half weeks per session. Students must purchase the series of Warren Hardy books and CDs, which complement in-class work. Classes run continuously throughout the year and are very popular with American and Canadian expatriates. This school is not only a great place to brush up your *español*, it is also a great place to make new friends in San Miguel.

A family-run language school, **Instituto Habla Hispana** (Calzada de la Luz 25, tel. 415/152-0713, www.mexicospanish.com) offers monthlong intensive language programs throughout the year. Typically, monthlong Spanish programs include 20 hours of classroom instruction per week with additional cultural activities, like walking tours and cooking classes, during the afternoon. Upon arrival, students are tested and placed at a class appropriate to their level; class size is capped at 10 students. While studying at Habla Hispana, students may choose to stay in the simple, inexpensive accommodations on the school's campus, or the school can arrange for students to stay with a local family. Most of the year, Habla Hispana's students are principally adults and seniors; however, in the summer months, the school enrolls a range of ages.

Based in Mexico City, the **Universidad Nacional Autónoma de México** (UNAM, Mesones 71, tel. 415/120-3461, http://enes.unam.mx) is the country's largest and most prestigious university. The school operates a number of extension programs in smaller cities across Mexico, including San Miguel de Allende. For foreign residents, UNAM offers classes in Spanish language as well as TOEFL certification courses, in addition to occasional continuing education classes in Mexican history and culture. Classrooms are located on the second floor of San Miguel's **Casa de la Cultura on Mesones,** though the school's offices—where you can get information about schedules and tuition fees—are on the first floor.

ART, PHOTOGRAPHY, AND CRAFTS

The historic art school at the **Centro Cultural Ignacio Ramírez "El Nigromante"** (Hernández Macías 75, tel. 415/152-0289, http://elnigromante.inba.gob.mx) offers instruction in painting, collage, ceramics, and guitar, among other disciplines. The tiny classrooms were once nuns' cloisters, and the quirky atmosphere adds to the charm. Run by the Mexican government's Instituto Nacional de Bellas Artes (National Fine Arts Institute), tuition is reasonable, though there is often a waiting list for popular courses.

The **Instituto Allende** (Ancha de San Antonio 22, tel. 415/152-4538, http://instituto-allende.edu.mx, office 9am-2pm Mon.-Fri.) is one of the country's oldest art academies, and many of San Miguel's artists have taken (or taught) a class or two there. Though it discontinued its master's program for foreign students, the school still offers an undergraduate fine arts program for Mexican nationals as well as continuing education courses in disciplines such as jewelry-making, sculpture, weaving, drawing, and painting. The institute also offers a series of adult continuing education classes in history, science, art, classical music, and other disciplines.

For serious instruction in jewelry creation and design, **Sterling Quest** (Guty Cardenas 3, Col. Guadalupe, tel. 415/119-4381, www.sterlingquestschool.com) offers ongoing group workshops with class size capped at six people. Spirited instructor Billy King has been teaching silverwork for more than 20 years, and he is a talented jeweler himself. His exacting style receives high praise from former students, many of whom later became professional jewelers themselves. Classes cost US$380 for 36 hours of individualized instruction and do not include the cost of silver or stones (though vendors come to offer these products during class time each week).

In a spacious house adjoining the Fábrica La Aurora, **Gerardo Ruiz** (Casa 4, Fábrica La Aurora, tel. 415/152-6110, www.gerardoruiz.com) gives printmaking, etching, painting, and drawing courses in his large working studio. Students get plenty of individual attention, yet the environment is laid-back and casual. A master printer and a bit of a character, Ruiz has many students who return to work with him year after year. Those with no printmaking experience can get started here, though Ruiz can mentor more experienced printers as well.

If you're inspired by all the colorful rugs and textiles produced in Mexico, you may want to channel that feeling into an off-loom weaving or macramé workshop with **Nelly Lorenzo** (Local 2A-1, Fábrica La Aurora, tel. 415/152-1833, www.nellylorenzo.com) at her studio and gallery at the Fábrica La Aurora. Lorenzo is a warm teacher and talented weaver; she offers classes appropriate for both beginners and more experienced weavers. Appointments are scheduled 11am-4pm weekdays year-round, and class size is capped at four students.

German-born artist **Edina Sagert** (Local 8A, Fábrica La Aurora, tel. 415/120-8088, www.edinasagert.com) offers year-round watercolor workshops in her light and airy studio. Sagert has years of experience teaching watercolor, and her popular small-group classes are appropriate for students of any level. Many return to San Miguel to work with Sagert again, year after year.

CHILDREN'S COURSES

A multipurpose community and cultural center, **El Sindicato: Espacio Cultural Alternativo** (Recreo 4, tel. 415/152-0131, www.elsindicatoespaciocultural.com) offers a variety of dance and workout classes at very reasonable prices as well as cultural workshops, performances, talks, and theater, much of it designed for children and teens. Swing by to check the upcoming schedule, which may include ballet, belly dancing, *danza conchera,* traditional Mexican dance, and popular Zumba, an energetic aerobic dance class. There is special summer programming for children. For most classes, instruction is in Spanish.

TOP EXPERIENCE

COOKING

Paco Cardenas (tel. 415/154-4010, www.elpetitfour.com), owner of the wonderful French bakery Petit Four, is not just a pastry chef, but a true aficionado (and master cook) of Mexican cuisine. Every Monday by appointment, he offers lively market tours followed by Mexican cooking classes held in his spacious home kitchen, which was specially designed to comfortably accommodate a group of students. After learning to make mole or *chiles en nogada,* the class sits down to feast on the results. Half-day small-group classes with market tours are about US$150 per person and are capped at six students, though you may also choose to just take a market tour with Paco.

Gaby Green (tel. 415/119-2195, www.chefgabygreen.com, from US$100 per person) is a talented chef with a deep knowledge of Mexican culinary traditions. She offers cooking classes and market tours, which can be tailored to a student's interest—whether that's making tortillas by hand or creating elaborate Mexican sauces and salsas. Formerly the chef at the much-beloved but now-shuttered restaurant Aguamiel, she now gives classes in the restaurant's professional kitchen, to topnotch reviews from participants.

Wellness and nutrition are at the heart of the cooking classes offered by New York native Alicia Wilson Rivero at **Pura Vida Kitchen** (Mercado SANO, Ancha de San Antonio 123, www.puravidakitchen.com, US$80-125 per person), set in a pretty, light-filled kitchen on the second floor of the Mercado SANO. Workshops generally run several hours and cover topics like cooking with grass-fed beef or fermentation basics. Rivero also offers wonderful monthly classes at the Posada Corazón, a beautiful old property with extensive gardens (from which she may gather some of the day's ingredients) in the heart of the *centro histórico.*

Marilau Traditional Mexican Cooking School (Calle de la Luz 12, Col. San Antonio, tel. 415/152-4376, http://mexican-cooking-school.com, from US$115 per person) offers Mexican cooking classes to groups of up to 10 people, all taught by the knowledgeable Marilau herself. Depending on your interests and how much time you wish to dedicate, Marilau can organize a single-day class based on a culinary theme like working with corn masa or making tamales. She also offers detailed multiday workshops on salsas and moles. With a long culinary tradition in her own family, Marilau shares family recipes from central Mexico.

WRITING

Many published and aspiring English-language writers live in San Miguel de Allende. The well-organized **San Miguel**

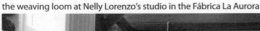
the weaving loom at Nelly Lorenzo's studio in the Fábrica La Aurora

Literary Sala (tel. 415/185-2225, http://san-miguelliterarysala.org) offers monthly literary readings and events at the Posada de la Aldea hotel (Ancha de San Antonio 15), book discussion groups, and summer literary workshops. The organization is involved in numerous community projects and recently opened a new library and event space in the Centro Cultural Ignacio Ramírez "El Nigromante," in conjunction with the Mexican government's department of fine art. Most notable, the Literary Sala also organizes the annual San Miguel Writers Conference each winter, an excellent event that brings world-famous names in fiction to speak to the San Miguel community.

VOLUNTEERING

Numerous nonprofit organizations and an active expatriate community make San Miguel de Allende an excellent place to get involved. Foreigners routinely volunteer for these organizations (or host benefits to support them); here's a short list of the many opportunities for big-hearted visitors and residents.

The **Sociedad Protectora de Animales** (SPA, Los Pinos 7, Col. Lindavista, tel. 415/152-6124, www.spasanmiguel.org, office 9am-3pm Mon. and Wed.-Fri., 9am-4pm Tues. and Sat., volunteer hours 11am-2pm Mon.-Sat.) operates a no-kill shelter for strays as well as an animal clinic with low-cost veterinary care, sterilizations, and vaccinations. Most visibly, SPA has a very active animal adoption program, placing hundreds of stray dogs and cats in family homes each year. Walking through the town square, you often see SPA members showing off the newest dogs available for adoption.

SPA is always looking for animal-loving volunteers to help with fundraising, animal training, dog walking, or simply socializing with resident dogs and cats. You can also help SPA by adopting a pet; the animals seeking homes are listed on their website.

CASA (Santa Julia 15, Col. Santa Julia, tel. 415/154-6060 or 415/154-6090, U.S. tel. 212/234-7940, www.casa.org.mx) is a multi-faceted nonprofit organization that provides health services, social services, and health education to rural families. In 1994, CASA also opened a maternity hospital, where thousands of babies have been delivered. Two years later, this unique organization officially opened the first accredited school of midwifery in Mexico, which has since trained midwives from dozens of Mexican states and foreign countries.

El Sindicato: Espacio Cultural Alternativo

Patronato Pro Niños (Av. Reforma 75C, Fracc. Ignacio Ramírez, tel. 415/152-7796, www.patronatoproninos.org, 9am-4pm Mon.-Fri.) is a nonprofit organization that provides free or very low-cost medical care to needy children in San Miguel de Allende and environs, in addition to free or very low-cost dental care in their three mobile dental vans, which visit small towns throughout the area. Patronato Pro Niños is always looking for volunteers who can work in the office, support caregivers in the field, and lead walking tours of the *centro histórico* (a part of their fundraising programs), as well as experienced doctors and dentists to work in the field.

The **Biblioteca de San Miguel de Allende** (Insurgentes 25, tel. 415/152-0293, http://bibliotecasma.com, 10am-7pm Mon.-Fri., 10am-2pm Sat.) uses volunteers to help with their numerous education and literacy programs. Positions could range from a newsletter author to a children's art teacher to fundraising support.

Jóvenes Adelantes (c/o La Conexión, Box 49A, Aldama 3, www.jovenesadelante. org) is a tutoring and college scholarship program for promising students at an economic disadvantage. The program seeks out exceptional rural high school students, who can receive up to five years of college scholarship money through the program. In addition, participating students are linked with mentors and tutors and can participate in free English-language classes. Volunteers can get involved with the nonprofit's activities through academic mentoring, academic tutoring, and as personal counselors.

Food

Eating out is a big part of life in San Miguel de Allende. There is a constant buzz about new restaurants opening (or old ones closing) and a spirited debate about the best bites in town. Satisfying all manner of tastes and appetites, San Miguel's streets are peppered with fruit stands, ice cream carts, traditional bakeries, casual eateries, charming bistros, and upscale establishments.

San Miguel has many beautiful sit-down restaurants serving food from all over the world. However, some of the best and most authentic Mexican fare can be found in the little market stalls and taco stands across town. If you are new to Mexico, open-air taco joints can be tougher on the stomach than sit-down restaurants. That said, most of San Miguel de Allende's eateries—even the most casual—are hygienic and clean, and adventurous eaters will be well rewarded with memorable meals.

CENTRO HISTÓRICO
Tacos and Quick Bites

Early in the morning, **fresh juice stands** appear throughout the city, casually operating from the windows of local houses or in the doorway of a corner store. For a wide range of juices (from fresh carrot to custom *jugo verde*), fruit smoothies made with milk, *aguas frescas,* and fresh fruit cocktails throughout the day, try San Miguel mainstay **El Compita** (Salida a Celaya 55, tel. 415/185-9000, 6am-6pm Mon.-Sat., US$2), a two-floor eatery that specializes in *jugos*. The blenders are always whirring behind the counter, and the seating is as casual as they come. But the fruit is fresh and the service lickety-split. If you want something more substantial, El Compita also sells inexpensive *tortas*—sandwiches served on a soft, white roll called a *telera*—and fruit with granola.

Like juice, **tamales** are a ubiquitous breakfast meal. There are plenty of places to buy tamales throughout San Miguel; however, some of the very best are sold from a stand on the

Best Restaurants

the elegant courtyard dining room at The Restaurant

★ **La Colmena:** Pick up a sweet roll, pastry, or cookie at this traditional Mexican bakery, which has been in operation in San Miguel de Allende for more than 100 years (page 84).

★ **Don Taco Tequila:** This casual restaurant's appealing menu is entirely vegan, with creative and delicious tacos and a list of inventive cocktails, Mexican spirits, and craft beer (page 86).

★ **Salón Oaxaca:** Half bar, half restaurant, this excellent evening spot serves top-notch Oaxacan-inspired bar snacks and a changing selection of fiery Oaxacan mezcal (page 87).

★ **Marchanta:** Two young chefs experiment with traditional Mexican flavors at this colorful, low-key, yet sophisticated little eatery (page 88).

★ **Lavanda:** At this bistro, start the day with a fresh, creative, and beautifully prepared breakfast and an outstanding cup of coffee (page 88).

★ **The Restaurant:** With more than a decade in operation, San Miguel's most popular chef-driven restaurant is still one of the best eateries in town (page 90).

★ **Áperi:** Book ahead for the chef's table at this destination restaurant, which builds its nightly menu around fresh and locally sourced ingredients (page 90).

★ **Petit Four:** Buttery croissants, miniature raspberry-topped tarts, delicate fig cake, and handmade dark-chocolate candied oranges are among the many perfectly made sweets at this beloved French bakery (page 92).

corner of Insurgentes and Pepe Llanos, right in front of the Oratorio San Felipe Neri (no phone, 7am-11am, US$1). There are always crowds of locals lining up to order savory tamales with *salsa verde, salsa roja,* cheese, or chile pepper. To accompany your *tamal,* try a steaming mug of *atole,* a sweet corn-based drink with pre-Columbian origins. Get there early; the stash can be depleted as early as 10:30am.

In operation since the early 1900s, ★ **La Colmena** (Relox 21, tel. 415/152-1422, 8:30am-2pm and 4pm-9pm Mon., 6am-2pm and 4:30pm-9pm Tues.-Sat., 6am-10am Sun., US$1) is a traditional Mexican bakery just off the main square, known to many as the "blue door bakery." Every day, La Colmena's ovens turn out an astounding variety of traditional *pan dulce* (sweet bread) as well as empanadas, cookies, cinnamon rolls, and whole-wheat breads. If you haven't tried Mexican sweet breads, *conchas* (a sweet roll topped with a sugary crust) are a classic introduction; at La Colmena, *conchas* come fresh out of the oven every morning and are some of the best in Mexico. When buying bread, pick up a metal tray and a pair of tongs, then pick out breads you want; the bevy of shop assistants will bag and total your purchase at the end. It is always filled with a crowd of locals and residents, plus (with a name that means The Beehive) some sugar-loving bees.

For a more familiar assortment of bakery items, **La Buena Vida** (Plaza Golondrinas, Hernández Macías 72, Int. 14, tel. 415/152-2211, 8am-3pm daily) has been baking fresh artisan breads for decades. In a small plaza across the street from Bellas Artes (walk past the small café to find La Buena Vida's window on the right side), La Buena Vida's glass display case is always filled with a tempting variety of chocolate chip and peanut butter cookies, fluffy muffins, cinnamon rolls, pastries, and donuts. Behind the case is an assortment of whole-wheat loaves, multigrain rolls, and sourdough bread. The bakery also has a kiosk in the **Mercado SANO** (Ancha de San Antonio 73, no phone, 9am-7pm daily), which sells breads, empanadas, and a selection of other treats from the store.

For a quick, cheap, and tasty meal, seek out **Los Burritos** (Hidalgo 23, tel. 415/152-3222, http://losburritos1986.com, 10:30am-5:45pm Mon.-Sat., 11:30am-5:15pm Sun., US$5), a popular lunchtime spot that serves tiny burritos made with fresh flour tortillas and filled with *pipián* (green mole), *picadillo* (spiced ground beef), or potatoes. First, pay

fruits and vegetables for sale at Bodega Orgánica at the Mercado SANO

for the number of burritos you want at the register (four or five will make a filling meal). Next, proceed to the steamy kitchen in back, where you select your fillings. You can see the fresh tortillas being rolled and warmed as you order your food! Fresh fruit drinks round out the meal, which can be had for just a couple bucks. You can also do like many locals and get a package of their fresh tortillas to go.

Braised pork tacos, or carnitas, are one of Mexico's most popular dishes, usually eaten for breakfast or lunch. You can try some very tasty carnitas in downtown San Miguel at **Carnitas Apolo XI** (Mesones 42A, tel. 415/154-6252, 9am-5pm daily, US$4). If you order your tacos *surtido,* they will be prepared with mixed meat, including everything from snout to ear. If you order *maciza* instead, your tacos will be made principally with shoulder. For two people, a quarter or half kilo of carnitas is a good amount to share, served with warm tortillas, salsa, and garnishes. There are casual tables on the roof of Apolo XI (which overlooks the *parroquia*), but the place is pretty self-service. Order downstairs before you sit down, then grab a beer from the fridge.

Tortas are hot sandwiches served on a soft roll, and **Tortitlán** (Juárez 17, tel. 415/152-3376, 9am-7pm daily, and Ancha de San Antonio 43, tel. 415/152-8931, 9am-6pm Mon. and Wed.-Fri., 10am-6pm Sun., US$5) makes some of the best (and biggest) in town. The surprisingly extensive menu includes a chicken *torta* with cheese and poblano peppers as well as a vegetarian sandwich with avocado and fresh cheese. Juice and a variety of *aguas frescas* are made at the moment you order. Many people order their food for delivery (you'll see Tortitlán's motorcycles whizzing across town midday), though you can also eat in. Both branches of this popular *tortería* are casual, though the Tortitlán on San Antonio is a bit nicer for a sit-down meal, with a small dining area where you can watch dozens of *tortas* being assembled at breakneck speed.

For a low-key lunch, head to the rooftop terrace at friendly **Baja Fish Taquito** (Mesones 11-B, tel. 415/121-0950, 11:30am-8pm daily, US$5), where you can fill up on marlin tacos, shrimp cocktail, and ceviche-topped tostadas, accompanied by a cold and spicy *michelada.* The combination plates, which include several selections from the menu plus the *agua del día* (drink of the day) are a particularly good bargain, and the relaxed ambience is perfect for a warm afternoon. They also sell craft beer and cocktails.

After night falls, **taco trucks** appear throughout San Miguel de Allende, spreading their savory aroma for blocks and drawing a flock of diners like flies to honey. One of the most aromatic pit stops is on the corner of Mesones and Pepe Llanos (7pm-midnight, US$3), just behind the Templo de San Francisco. Push through the crowds for *longaniza* (sausage), rib, or *pastor* tacos, which are served with double tortillas. If you get your tacos *con todo* (with everything), they will come with cilantro, grilled onion, and salsa. There are no stools (though some folks perch on the bumpers of automobiles parked nearby), so diners should be prepared to eat standing up, balancing a plate in one hand and eating with the other.

Although Dolores Hidalgo is famous for its *nieves* (ice cream), San Miguel's offerings are just as tasty. There are **ice cream carts** all over town, but one of the best and most popular is on the corner of Hernández Macías and Canal, just down the street from the entrance to Bellas Artes; another is on the corner of Reloj and Insurgentes, just across from the Biblioteca de San Miguel de Allende. At both spots, a family of ice cream vendors scoops heaping cones in exotic flavors like rice, rose petal, cheese, guava, mango, walnut, and peppermint. A single serving includes two flavors, favorable to the indecisive. You can order them in a cup, but the handmade sugar cones are almost as sweet and delicious as the ice cream that fills them.

Mexican

On the northwest corner of the town square, **Rincón Don Tomás** (Jardín Principal 2, tel. 415/152-3780, 8:30am-10pm Mon.-Sat., 8:30am-9pm Sun., US$8) is a good place to kick off your visit to San Miguel de Allende, with a prime location right on the *jardín* and a tasty menu of traditional Mexican food. Here, you can linger over a filling lunch while enjoying some excellent people-watching beneath the shaded arcades of the *plaza principal*. Don Tomás's tasty *sopa azteca* and squash blossom soup are popular ways to start a meal; follow them up with a Mexican specialty like *enmoladas,* chicken in yellow mole, or enchiladas in *chile pasilla,* a mild but flavorful dried chile. This restaurant is also a nice place to have breakfast accompanied by an early-morning view of the *parroquia*.

A casual dinner spot favored by locals, **La Alborada** (Sollano 10, tel. 415/154-9982, 1pm-10pm Mon.-Sat., US$5) specializes in traditional pozole, a hearty hominy soup that has been consumed in Mexico since the pre-Columbian era. Pozoles are popular fare throughout Mexico, and the preparation varies by region. At La Alborada, they serve red pozole with chicken, pork, or beef (or all three!), accompanied by small plates of garnishes—typically, dried oregano, radishes, chopped onion, and dried chile pepper. When everything arrives at your table, you sprinkle the condiments over your soup to taste. In addition, La Alborada serves a variety of Mexican *antojitos,* like quesadillas, guacamole, tostadas, and enchiladas, as well as inexpensive beer and *aguas frescas.*

The perennially popular **Chocolate y Churros San Agustín** (San Francisco 21, tel. 415/154-9102, 8am-11pm daily, US$10) is well known for its eponymous hot chocolate and fresh, crunchy churros. From morning until night, this bustling little eatery is filled with folks getting a serious sugar fix, and on busy weekends there is often a wait for a table. In the spirit of pure excess, every hot chocolate includes an order of three sugarcoated churros, made fresh on the premises and still warm when they arrive at your table. On the savory side, the restaurant is also a nice place for breakfast or lunch, with a tasty menu of

egg dishes, spicy *chilaquiles,* sandwiches, and salads, plus espresso drinks, beer, wine, and spirits. During San Miguel's chilly winters, this café is a good destination for its warm and cozy (if quirky) atmosphere. It's owned by Argentine actress Margarita Gralia, and the walls of the lovely, high-ceilinged dining room are festooned with memorabilia from her screen career.

You don't have to be a vegetarian to enjoy the flavorful vegan tacos and bar snacks at cozy cantina-esque ★ **Don Taco Tequila** (Hernández Macías 83, tel. 415/154-9608, 2pm-10pm Mon. and Wed.-Thurs., 2pm-11pm Fri.-Sat., 2pm-8pm Sun., US$6). Choose from jackfruit seasoned with achiote, tequila-spiked wild mushrooms, or soy chorizo tacos, among other interesting options, and accompany your meal with one of their excellent creative cocktails, like the margarita made with spicy chile and hibiscus. They also have a nice selection of craft beer and Mexican spirits, including unusual liquors like *sotol,* from the state of Chihuahua. The cozy dining room is unpretentious and comfortable, with affable service and low prices making it a perfect spot for an evening out.

In a simple second-floor dining room off busy Hidalgo, the ultracasual ambience and surprisingly low prices at **Nicasio Comedor Mexicano** (Hidalgo 28, no phone, 9am-7:30pm Mon. and Wed.-Sat., 9am-5pm Sun., US$6) do not prepare you for the kitchen's sophistication. At this spot, you'll find a short but interesting menu of creative takes on traditional Mexican recipes, using native ingredients, all beautifully plated. At breakfast, try the handmade *tlacoyo* (a torpedo-shaped corn flatbread), which is stuffed with black beans and topped with cactus, goat cheese, and herbs. Afternoon lunch service (which starts after 1:30pm) includes creative takes on a fried-tongue *torta* (sandwich) or a unique version of the Yucatec specialty *papadzules,* which here are prepared stuffed with potatoes, smothered in a spicy habanero sauce, and topped with a poached egg.

★ **Salón Oaxaca** (Insurgentes 44, tel. 415/121-1840, www.salonoaxaca.mx, 5pm-11pm Mon. and Wed.-Fri., 9am-11pm Sat.-Sun., US$7) describes itself as a *gastro-mezcalería,* a well-chosen descriptor for this excellent bar-restaurant. Here, a menu of traditional Oaxacan and Oaxacan-inspired snacks are accompanied by a changing list of Oaxacan mezcal, craft beer, and hot chocolate. Try the crisp, umami-rich *tlayuda* or the tacos stuffed with fried *chapulines* (grasshoppers), which go well with a double serving of mezcal. Stake out a table on the simple yet lovely roof deck, which has pretty views of the surrounding churches and cupolas, or in the funky-cool bar downstairs. Service is a bit relaxed, but there's no reason to come here in a hurry.

A modern Mexican restaurant, **Jacinto 1930** (Doce 18, Relox 18, tel. 415/150-0075, http://jacinto1930.mx, 1pm-9pm Sun.-Thurs., noon-10pm Fri.-Sat., US$20) is run by the same chef behind beloved fine-dining restaurant Áperi. Here he focuses his attention on Mexican food, taking traditional dishes and reimagining them with a blend of old and modern techniques. The menu takes risks, infusing corn with smoke, for instance, to create a new take on the common street food *esquites* (boiled and seasoned corn). Some dishes, like the wild-mushroom-stuffed tacos, are less experimental and just straight-up delicious. The dining room, at the center of the Doce 18 Concept House, is light, airy, and contemporary, with some Mexican-style touches; the setting feels like something you might see in Mexico City.

San Miguel de Allende can spoil you with beautiful views, and **La Posadita** (Cuna de Allende 13, tel. 415/154-8862, noon-10pm Thurs.-Tues., US$8) has one of the nicest views in town. From La Posadita's open-air rooftop dining room, you can have lunch beneath the spires of the *parroquia,* overlooking the sweeping river valley beyond San Miguel. The menu is diverse, with Mexican classics like guacamole and enchiladas as well as more unusual plates like *mixiotes* (steamed meat in banana leaves) and *cochinita pibil* (spiced pulled pork). Food is generally decent, if not excessively seasoned (add their delicious salsas if you want some kick), and the kitchen can occasionally get backed up—though you're unlikely to be in a hurry here. The margaritas, including the tasty version made with tamarind, are the best choice on the cocktail menu, although they also have a nice wine selection, including many Mexican bottles.

Try a creative chef-inspired approach to

Marchanta is a stylish, creative Mexican restaurant run by two young chefs.

traditional Mexican food at standout new-comer ★ **Marchanta** (Nemesio Diez 2, tel. 415/121-9163, noon-9pm Mon.-Sat., US$8), founded by the duo of young chefs behind beloved local restaurant Nómada. Located in the original Nómada space, the dining room is casual, eclectically decorated, and stylish, with colorful murals on the walls and an open kitchen where you can see the chefs at work. The well-executed, appealing menu, which changes frequently, might feature a cured cactus salad with goat cheese and grilled avocado, fish tacos topped with shredded red cabbage, or pork belly with candied figs. Complement the meal with one of the restaurant's creative cocktails, a craft beer, or their delicious coconut-infused *limonada* (limeade).

For visitors and locals, **Jardín Rama** (Nemesio Diez 8, tel. 415/185-8919, www.caferamasanmiguel.com, noon-7:30pm Tues.-Sat., 11am-6:30 Sun., US$5-7) is a blessing, providing a much-needed spot for an inexpensive and relaxed afternoon enjoying a craft beer and a plate of tasty fish tacos. Owned by the same folks who run Café Rama across the street, here the menu of classic Mexican dishes—like tortilla soup, refried beans, guacamole, and battered-shrimp tacos—is nicely executed and economical. Whether you sit at the plant-fringed outdoor tables or inside the cheerful green-painted dining room, the atmosphere is casual and breezy, perfect for lingering on a summery day.

Tío Lucas Restaurant and Bar (Mesones 103, tel. 415/152-4996, noon-midnight daily, US$12) is a lively Mexican steak house right across the street from the historic Ángela Peralta theater. Starters and salads are good here, but Tío Lucas is best for enthusiastic carnivores. Try one of the Mexican cuts of beef, like *arrachera, puntas de filete,* or *norteña,* which are served with beans, rice, and guacamole. Cocktails are also a specialty, and the bar serves powerful margaritas with your choice of tequila. The atmosphere is among the best in town, with a nightly jazz band, constant crowds, and Mexican pottery and

stamped metal decorations adorning the walls of the open-air dining room.

Chef Enrique Olvera became an international food celebrity for his fine-dining restaurants in Mexico City (Pujol) and New York (Cosme). In San Miguel de Allende, the celebrity chef oversees **Moxi** (Hotel Matilda, Aldama 53, tel. 415/152-1015, www.moxi.com.mx, 8am-11pm daily), an elegant restaurant on the ground floor of the Hotel Matilda. The space is beautiful, particularly the outdoor patio, with its stone floors, white tablecloths, and soft natural light. The restaurant offers both a daily tasting menu and à la carte selections, often fusing surprising ingredients and techniques in dishes like guava tacos or eggplant mole, though there are also more traditional pastas, risotto, and meat dishes on the menu. Although Moxi serves the hotel, it focuses on high-concept food; culinary compositions are elegantly presented but not nearly as generously portioned as what you'd find in other Mexican spots around town.

Breakfast and Brunch

For fresh, lovingly prepared breakfasts and brunches, ★ **Lavanda** (Hernández Macías 87, tel. 415/152-1610, http://lavandacafe.com, 8:30am-5pm Mon. and Wed.-Sat., 8:30am-2pm Sun., kitchen closes at 3pm, US$5-7) is the perfect place to start the day. Try the clay pot with shaved potatoes, cheese, razor-thin slices of bacon, and a baked egg. Or see how the restaurant's unique egg-poaching technique—which somehow renders the eggs perfectly cooked into little basket-shaped pockets—puts a new twist on classic Mexican dishes like spicy huevos rancheros. The coffee bar is quite possibly the best in town, with expertly prepared espresso drinks and pour-overs; they also serve lavender lemonade, high-quality loose-leaf teas, a delicious "green juice," and unusual fruit-sweetened cold drinks made with the shell of the cacao seed, making it difficult to choose. (Though the kitchen closes at 3pm, breads and beverages are available until 5pm.) There can be an occasional wait for a table during peak brunch hours at this local favorite, but once you're seated in the serene plant-filled courtyard, the experience is unhurried.

Though open till evening, the inexpensive and centrally located **Café de la Parroquia** (Jesús 11, tel. 415/152-3161, http://cafedelaparroquiasma.com, 8am-10pm Mon.-Sat., 8am-2pm Sun., US$6) is a beloved breakfast spot, frequented by locals and tourists alike. Set in a colonial courtyard surrounding a gurgling fountain, it is one of the most relaxing places to brunch alfresco while flipping through the latest edition of *Atención San Miguel*. While there is always a pleasant hum of diners during the morning hours, this popular café is packed on the weekends. The delicious morning menu includes a range of traditional Mexican dishes, like fried eggs in *mole negro,* huevos rancheros, and chicken and cheese tamales in black bean sauce.

A local favorite, the eclectically decorated **Juan's Café Etc.** (Relox 37, tel. 415/154-8636, 9am-4pm Mon.-Sat., 9am-2pm Sun., US$5) is a popular place for a meal or a coffee, often drawing a crowd of expatriates who've come to relax away the morning. Until midday, the kitchen prepares filling Mexican-style breakfasts, like *chilaquiles* and huevos rancheros, while Juan himself mans the coffee bar. In the afternoon, this super-casual café also sells a surprisingly luxe *comida corrida.* For those who need a caffeine fix, Juan's coffee is strong and inexpensive, and there is a large selection of loose-leaf black and herbal teas. Several plastic tables sit within the tiny plant-filled courtyard, so you'll definitely overhear your neighbor's conversation in this cozy coffee shop—but that's part of the fun.

Hanging ferns swing above the rows of cloth-dressed tables at low-key **Café Muro** (Loreto 10B, tel. 415/152-6341, 8:30am-4:30pm Thurs.-Tues., US$6), where a homey, well-priced menu has made this breakfast-and-lunch spot a local staple. Service is warm, and the food is traditional, well prepared, and generously served. You'll find Mexican classics like huevos rancheros and eggs with chorizo on the breakfast menu (juice and coffee included in the price), plus international faves like omelets and eggs Benedict. For lunch, there are à la carte options (the giant burrito is a popular choice) as well as a daily *comida corrida,* an inexpensive three-course, set-price meal that changes daily and includes coffee and dessert.

On a bustling corner of Zacateros and Pila Seca, **La Mesa Grande** (Zacateros 49, tel. 415/154-0838, www.lamesagrande.com, 8am-5pm Mon.-Fri., 9am-5pm Sat., 9am-2pm Sun., US$4-7) makes wonderful European-style breads and pastries fresh every day, including the tangiest, chewiest sourdough outside of San Francisco. You can pick up sliced multi-grain loaves, crusty baguettes, soft cinnamon rolls, and buttery croissants to go, or order a baked treat and an espresso drink to enjoy at the large communal table. For a heartier meal, the attractive breakfast and lunch menu includes egg dishes, French toast, enchiladas, made-to-order sandwiches, and salads—all savory, generously served, and well-priced.

Italian and Pizza

Right off the main plaza, the perennially popular **Mama Mía** (Umarán 8, tel. 415/152-2063, www.mamamia.com.mx, 8am-midnight Sun.-Thurs., 8am-3am Fri.-Sat., US$10) is a San Miguel de Allende institution. There are two bars, a gift shop, and a rooftop terrace inside Mama Mía's expansive Umarán location, anchored by a large, bustling, family-friendly restaurant in a tree-filled open-air courtyard. The bars draw big crowds at night, but the restaurant is Mama Mía's flagship, consistently filled with local families and national tourists enjoying a lazy afternoon in the shade of magnolia trees. Food is decent Italian fare—pastas, lasagna, and doughy homemade-style pizzas. Come early on the weekends for the restaurant's best culinary offering: a breakfast buffet with eggs in salsa, beans, chiles rellenos, *chilaquiles,* fresh quesadillas, menudo, pozole, and other traditional Mexican dishes served in big clay pots. To make the mood especially pleasant, there is always live music in the restaurant during peak hours.

Within the handsome plant-filled courtyard of the Hotel Sautto, **Bacco** (Hotel Sautto, Hernández Macías 59, tel. 415/154-5513, 1pm-10:30pm Tues.-Sat., 1pm-6pm Sun., US$12) is a lovely Italian restaurant that has maintained quality and charm over many years in San Miguel. Start with a plate of smoked provolone or a salad, then move onto flavorful pastas, served properly al dente, or thin-crust pizza baked in a huge stone oven and topped with fresh ingredients, like eggplant, fresh basil, or prosciutto. During the warm spring and summer seasons, it is particularly pleasant to sit in Bacco's lush courtyard, and there is often live music during peak hours. Throughout the year, the restaurant also hosts a popular *cineclub*, **Cine Bacco** (http://cine-bacco.com), screening both recent releases and classics.

International

★ **The Restaurant** (Sollano 16, tel. 415/154-7862, www.therestaurantsanmiguel.com, noon-11pm Tues.-Sun., US$18) caused a huge splash when it opened in 2008, heralding a new era of gourmet dining in San Miguel de Allende. Even today, it remains one of the nicest places to eat in town, housed in a gorgeously restored colonial-era mansion with neoclassical and Moorish details. The courtyard seating plays perfect accompaniment to the seasonal, chef-driven menu, which incorporates both Asian and Mexican influences. For a town with generally uninspired wine lists, The Restaurant does well for itself, offering an excellent assortment of Mexican and Latin American glasses and bottles as well as a full bar and specialty cocktails (many made with local mezcal or tequila, like the popular watermelon margarita). On Thursday evenings, The Restaurant hosts the popular Mo-Betta Burger Night, a popular destination for locals looking for a juicy cheeseburger (or salmon burger or veggie burger) and some good company.

Occupying the busy corner of Correo and Recreo, **Cumpanio** (Correo 29, tel. 415/152-2327, www.cumpanio.com, 8am-10pm daily, US$8-10) is a stylish, well-done bakery, bistro, and bar, appealingly decorated with hanging lamps, wooden floors, and modern furnishings. Stop in for a homemade pastry and top-notch cappuccino, or sit down for a plate of scrambled eggs and salad for breakfast. At lunch, try soup in a bread bowl, a fancy sandwich, or the *burrata* appetizer. If you don't stay for dessert, Cumpanio's daily selection of lovely breads and pastries are available to go, many quite tasty. Peek into the kitchen from large windows on Recreo to see the bakers at work. There is a second location of the bakery and café on the Salida a Celaya (Salida a Celaya 69, 8am-10pm daily).

The **Casa Blanca Cafe** (Hotel Casa Blanca, Juárez 7, tel. 415/688-1438, http://casablanca7.com, 8am-11pm daily, US$15), located in the ground floor of boutique hotel Casa Blanca, is run by Donnie Masterson, the chef behind San Miguel's beloved eatery The Restaurant. At this casually elegant spot, the menu reflects the hotel's decor, mixing Moroccan-inspired dishes with traditional Mexican ingredients. It's a nice place to stop in for cocktails in the evening, which are served in a tranquil open-air courtyard or in one of the cafe's high-ceilinged dining rooms. The hotel's more formal restaurant, **Fátima,** is also a Masterson project, with a second-floor dining room framed by gorgeous views of the churrigueresque sandstone facade and towering cupolas of the Iglesia de San Francisco.

For a memorable meal or special occasion, ★ **Áperi** (Dos Casas, Quebrada 101, tel. 415/152-0941, www.aperi.mx, 2pm-4pm lunch and 6:30pm-10pm dinner Wed.-Mon., US$30) is a widely heralded fine-dining restaurant in the ground floor the Dos Casas hotel. Make reservations for the evening's tasting menu, designed by chef Matteo Salas, and reserve well in advance for the chef's table, which is located just beside the kitchen. Alternatively, you can dine on à la carte options, such as ceviche served with turnip, cucumber, and citrus or grilled duck with fruits and beet. No matter which way you go, Áperi receives consistently rave reviews for its contemporary, flavorful food, which uses unique local ingredients, including heirloom tomatoes and gigantic mushrooms from local farms and fish caught off Mexico's Pacific coast.

Located in a modern dining room in the lobby of the Casa 88 hotel, **Nómada** (Hernández Macías 88, tel. 415/121-9163, http://nomada-cocina.mx, 9am-4pm and 5pm-10pm Wed.-Mon., US$10-12) quickly earned its place among San Miguel de Allende's most beloved eateries. Overseen by two young Mexican chefs, the international menu is constantly changing, but might include a selection of dishes like grilled chicken, wild-mushroom risotto, and ceviche, accompanied a nice selection of mezcal, Mexican wine, and craft beer. Service can be a bit slow, so don't come in a rush—this is slow food at its best. If you'd like to try the popular Wednesday night tasting menu, which the chefs design specially each week, book ahead.

With its pretty multicolor tile floors, low lighting, and long bar adjoining the doorway, **La Mezcalería** (Correo 47, tel. 415/121-5354, 5pm-11pm Mon.-Fri., 1pm-11pm Sat., 1pm-9pm Sun., US$15) is, true to its name, a cool place for mezcal—served straight or in one of the bar's wonderful signature cocktails, like the flavorful chile-guero-and-espadin concoction. Though it's an appropriately attractive, dimly lit spot for a drink, most visitors come to eat as well, picking shareable plates from the menu of Mexican and Spanish-style dishes, like grilled shrimp over roasted cherry tomatoes, mezcal-cured salmon, and asparagus wrapped in *jamón serrano*. The place is stylish enough that you might expect pretension, but fortunately, it isn't. Servers are friendly, and the atmosphere is welcoming.

Whatever your mood, you're likely to find something satisfying at **Café Rama** (Calle Nueva 7, tel. 415/185-8919, www.caferama-sanmiguel.com, 8am-midnight Tues.-Sat., US$10), a funky, low-key café just down the street from the Rosewood hotel. Covering breakfast, lunch, and dinner, the menu here is super-diverse—even mismatched—with dishes like fish-and-chips, borscht, a polenta bowl, bagels with smoked salmon, potpie, and potato flautas all on offer. Fortunately, everything is nicely prepared and generously served, making Rama a great value; there are plenty of options for vegetarians. Just as nice, there's plenty of space within the two big dining rooms, which are colorful and decorated with funky furniture. If you find a table you like, linger with your laptop (there's free Wi-Fi) or a book through dessert.

Cumpanio is a stylish bistro and bakery, right off San Miguel's main square.

For warm and filling comfort food, head to **Hecho en Mexico** (Ancha de San Antonio 8, tel. 415/154-6383, www.hechoenmexicosma. com, noon-10pm Sun.-Thurs., noon-11pm Fri.-Sat., US$8). This inexpensive and casual restaurant serves big, tasty soups, salads, burgers, and sandwiches as well as meat and seafood plates accompanied by indulgent side dishes like creamed spinach, coleslaw, and onion rings. Despite the name, cuisine is not strictly Mexican, though you will find guacamole and well prepared *arrachera,* fajitas, and chiles rellenos on the menu, plus tasty side dishes like grilled *nopales* (prickly pear) and black beans. Cocktails, big desserts, and consistently satisfying food make this comfortable courtyard restaurant perennially popular with the local crowd.

South American

The perfect spot for lunch on a warm afternoon, the modern open-air dining room at **La Parada** (Recreo 94, tel. 415/152-0473, www. laparadasma.com, noon-10pm Wed.-Sat., noon-9pm Sat.-Sun., US$10) is something of a surprise, tucked behind the doorway of an old colonial home on the quiet end of Recreo. Settle in the shade beneath a big turquoise umbrella to sample the restaurant's interesting Peruvian menu, which features tasty, fresh ceviche served in a wide variety of creative styles (fish with corn and sweet potato, for example). If you want something more stick-to-your-ribs, there are also South American-style sandwiches, rice plates, and appetizers, many featuring *ají,* a popular Peruvian chile pepper with a tingly spice. Pair anything with one of La Parada's delicious pisco sours in flavors like cucumber-mint, pineapple-ginger, and orange, made in-house with fresh fruit.

Coffee Shops and Dessert

The second location of Tulum coffee shop **Ki'bok** (Diez de Sollano 25, no phone, www. kibokcoffee.com, 8am-6pm daily) is in the center of San Miguel de Allende. Like the original, it is a stylish, laid-back spot for top-notch drinks and a bohemian-chic ambience.

Perch on a wood bench in the eclectically decorated downstairs café, or head up to the rooftop terrace on a sunny day to sip a pour-over coffee or a perfectly pulled espresso, made with beans from Coatepec, Veracruz. Drinks are beautifully served on natural wood boards and with fabric napkins beside them.

For a cup of hot organic coffee and a sweet snack, stop by **La Ventana** (Diez de Sollano 11, tel. 415/154-7728, 8am-9pm Mon.-Sat., 9am-3pm Sun., US$1). This popular coffee shop does most of its business from a small window that opens onto Calle Sollano. Sidle up to the open window, order an espresso to go, and then take it around the corner to sip in the *jardín.* You can also go inside the café (enter through La Alborada restaurant) to have a seat or order roasted beans to take home.

★ **Petit Four** (Mesones 99-1, tel. 415/154-4010, www.elpetitfour.com, 10am-6pm Tues.-Sun., US$5) is the best place to satisfy your sweet tooth in San Miguel de Allende. This lovely French-style bakery has a glass display case that features a mouthwatering daily selection of perfectly prepared confections, like delicate vanilla-fig cake, tangy lemon-meringue pie, chocolate-covered fruit, assorted truffles, decadent brownies, crisp biscotti, and individual fruit tarts. They also serve espresso drinks as well as savory baguette sandwiches, croissants, and danishes. From the tiny dining room, a large glass window lets you peek into the goings-on in Petit Four's kitchen, where white-clad pastry chefs prepare cakes and truffles right before your eyes.

Markets and Specialty Foods

The Bajío is a major agricultural region, producing a bounty of fruits and vegetables, local meats, and dairy. Here, farmers markets brim with an abundance of beautiful produce year-round. In addition, the organic and local food movement has taken hold in San Miguel, and there are now numerous specialty shops selling handmade and local products, from organic milk to sourdough bread. San Miguel's discerning consumers have also created a large market for specialty products, like sushi rice and Greek olives. You can find everything you need for a fancy dinner party or healthy lunch in San Miguel's lovely food shops.

Behind the Iglesia de Nuestra Señora de la Salud and the Plaza Cívica, the **Mercado Ignacio Ramírez** (Colegio s/n, 8am-7pm daily, vendor hours vary) is a small covered market selling an abundance of fresh fruits, vegetables, meat, chicken, and fresh flowers as well as dry goods like chile peppers, rice, and beans. There is plenty of nice produce at this pretty urban market, and some of the vendors will offer samples to convince you of their fruit's quality. Behind the fruit and flower sellers, there are several food counters, where you can get a *torta,* a fresh juice, or a full meal for just a few dollars. Just behind the market (at the entrance to the Mercado de Artesanía), there are more casual stands selling handmade tortillas, farm-style cheese, roasted corn, steamed fresh garbanzos, and prickly pear.

A market collective dedicated to organic and healthy locally produced food, **Mercado SANO** (Ancha de San Antonio 123, no phone, 8am-7pm daily, hours vary by vendor) brings together some of the best farms, food producers, bakeries, and other food purveyors in the area. The name is an acronym—*saludable, artesanal, natural, orgánico* (healthy, artisanal, natural, organic)—and every one of the businesses involved has to comply with at least two of the four descriptors. Come here to pick up something for the kitchen or to take home to a foodie friend. Among the dozens of products on offer, you'll find artisanal salsas, rare wild mushrooms, local cheeses, freshly made juices, organic coffee, and roasted nuts. On the first floor, **Bodega Orgánica** sells organic fruits and vegetables from a local farm, and it also maintains a large takeout salad bar with ultra-fresh produce—a popular lunch stop for locals.

If you are planning to do a little cooking during your stay, centrally located **Bonanza** (Mesones 43, tel. 415/152-1260, 8am-8pm daily) is a small but well-stocked grocery store, where you can stock up on kitchen basics. This little grocery sells a range of dry goods, like rice, beans, pasta, nuts, raisins, bread, and crackers, as well as milk, yogurt, and cheeses. They also carry a selection of pricey luxury items, like jars of pesto, oyster sauce, dry sea vegetables, canned salmon, coconut milk, and tahini.

When you are in the mood for a treat, head to **Luna de Queso** (Jesús 2, tel. 415/154-8122, 10am-6pm Mon.-Sat.). This lovely deli has the largest selection of high-quality cheeses in town, many of which are local—some made by the owner's mother—including tangy French-style camembert and brie, fresh mozzarella, and aged Chihuahua (a Mexican cheese). In addition to the deli counter, Luna de Queso stocks all sorts of hard-to-find specialty items, like miso, yellow lentils, hummus, Italian pastas, Mexican olive oil, halvah, couscous, teriyaki sauce, a wide variety of rice, and marinated olives, among other treats. It's also an excellent place for lunch: Take a seat in the courtyard café for a homemade sandwich and a craft beer or coffee, listening to the gurgling fountain as you eat. Service is amiable, the food is tasty, and the prices are very economical. Luna de Queso has a bigger second location, with garden seating and parking, on the Salida a Celaya (Salida a Celaya 79, 9am-7pm Mon.-Fri., 10am-5pm Sat.).

A few blocks southeast of the central plaza, **Mercado San Juan de Dios** (between Calle San Rafael, Indio Triste, and San Pedro, 8am-7pm daily, hours vary by vendor) is a large food market just a few blocks east of the town square, which is more diverse and bustling than the smaller market downtown. At Juan de Dios, there are numerous large fruit and vegetable stands in the covered area, plus smaller vendors selling handmade tortillas, fresh cheese, and cactus paddles on folding tables. Its low prices and variety make this market very popular with locals. Crossing Calle San Rafael, the market continues down a covered pedestrian walkway, where you'll find assorted shoe stores and toy shops as well as several fragrant and inexpensive flower stands. On Sunday mornings, there are always bustling families gathered around the food stalls in the market, which sell *tortas,* fruit juices, tamales, deep-fried quesadillas, *huaraches,* and many other popular snacks. If you want tamales, go early; they usually run out by midday.

SOUTH OF THE CENTRO
Mexican

An inexpensive and super-casual lunch spot, **El Rinconcito** (Refugio Norte 7, Col. San Antonio, tel. 415/154-4809, 12:30pm-9pm Mon. and Wed.-Sat., 1pm-7pm Sun., US$6) has garnered a loyal following with folks who live the San Antonio neighborhood. This family-run eatery has three nice outdoor tables on a tiny patio, where you can watch the cooks whip up your food the moment you order it. When the weather's chilly, they also have a few tables inside. Everything on the menu has a pleasing, homemade quality, from the grilled chicken salad to the guacamole. The giant vegetarian or shrimp quesadillas are particularly tasty, and you can accompany it all with a beer or fruit drink.

NORTH OF THE CENTRO
International

Shoebox-size **La Querencia** (Julián Carrillo 4B, Guadalupe, no phone, 9am-3pm Mon.-Fri.) is an ultracasual, bohemian coffee shop with a short menu of breakfast and lunch items, as well as coffee, homemade kombucha, and a selection of imported Chinese and Japanese teas. The café's chef-owner is always in the kitchen, calmly preparing your order while also keeping an eye on the fresh bread and pastries she's baking in the kitchen's industrial oven (the homemade German-style bread is excellent and comes served with homemade jam and butter). A standout is the eggs prepared in a leaf of fragrant *hoja santa,* which comes served in a small iron pan. With its eclectic, messy atmosphere and delicious home-style cooking, breakfasting here feels a bit like eating at a gourmet friend's home.

Cap off a trip to the Fábrica La Aurora with a leisurely meal at the lovely **Food Factory La Aurora** (Local 1A, Fábrica La Aurora, Col. Aurora, tel. 415/152-3982, noon-10pm Mon.-Sat., noon-5pm Sun., US$12), where a menu of European dishes like Caprese salad, French onion soup, and stuffed artichokes are complemented by a few Asian-inspired options, such as pad Thai with shrimp. There is a full bar, wines by the glass, and a wide selection of imported beers as well as a large temperature-controlled wine cellar on-site. Food Factory's indoor dining room is comfortable and elegant, though you can best enjoy the historic ambience of La Aurora on the restaurant's patio, right below the sandstone arches of the factory's facade. Food Factory La Aurora is at the very end of the left hallway, just as you enter the factory.

Coffee Shops and Dessert

After walking around Fábrica La Aurora art and design center, stop for an hour (or two) at relaxing **Geek & Coffee** (Fábrica La Aurora, Calzada de la Aurora s/n, Col. Aurora, tel. 415/152-3554, 10am-7pm daily). Tucked just behind the factory's old duck pond (east of the main entrance), the shop has a small, fairly ordinary menu of sandwiches, sweets, and coffee, which you can order inside the funky-cute café. Next, take your drinks outside to enjoy on the café's super-spacious lawn or in one of the chairs beneath shady palms. Given all the expansive outdoor space, it's no surprise that this spot is popular with dog owners and families—there's even a small playground for kids.

Specialty Food and Markets

Vía Organica (Margarito Ledesma 2, tel. 415/152-8042, http://viaorganica.org, 8am-9pm daily, US$9) is an organic supermarket, café, and nonprofit organization, located in a residential neighborhood just north of the *centro.* Come to shop for organic peanut butter, local greens, ranch eggs, or almond milk, or sit down at one of the café tables for fresh, vegetable-heavy, and often very tasty meals from breakfast through dinner. Though not entirely vegetarian, the menu has a large selection of meat-free options among its salads, burgers, sandwiches, pizzas, and Mexican plates, like enchiladas, tostadas, and tamales. High-quality, organic ingredients are sourced right from the farms that the store operates. How well the food is prepared varies, depending on the day and the hour, but it can often be very good. There are four tables in the first-floor grocery store and more on the upper patios, where you can eat amid the organization's pretty and functional rooftop gardens, where workshops are held on planting and sustainability.

EAST OF THE CENTRO
Specialty Food and Markets

The weekly municipal market, casually referred to as the **Mercado de Martes** (Plaza Municipal, no phone, 8am-5pm Tues.), descends upon San Miguel's upper municipal plaza once a week. You can find almost anything you're looking for at this busy open-air marketplace, whether it's blender parts, new Converse sneakers, drill bits, or a birdcage. For food shopping, this is the best deal in town. Fruits and vegetables in season often come at rock-bottom prices—think kilos of mangoes for a dollar. There are also plenty of little places where you can grab a bite to eat,

though strong stomachs are best for those who want to dig into the delicious green chorizo tacos or deep-fried fish plates. Come prepared for dust and bustle, and bring a shopping bag if you plan to buy. Located on the plains above town, the market is too far to comfortably reach by foot from downtown, but a taxi will get you there in five minutes.

Just outside of town on the highway to Querétaro, **Remo's** (Carretera San Miguel-Querétaro, Km 3, tel. 415/152-0453, www.prodremo.com, 10am-5pm daily) sells a homemade selection of Italian-style cheeses, like mozzarella and provolone, as well as numerous locally produced soft cheeses, including camembert and brie. The shop's Italian owner stocks well-priced imported parmigiano-reggiano and grana padano, Italian sausages and salamis, and a nice selection of imported pastas, sun-dried tomatoes, olives, and Italian wine and bubbly. For cheese lovers, this country shop is worth a stop.

WEST OF THE CENTRO
International

Just outside town, down a bumpy road off the highway to Dolores, **El Vergel** (Camino a La Alborada No. 17, Predio la Alborada, tel. 415/110-2254, http://elvergelsanmiguel.

You could spent hours relaxing in the gardens at Geek & Coffee.

com, 9am-6pm Tues.-Thurs., 9am-9pm Fri.-Sat., 9am-6pm Sun.) is a country bistro with a largely French-inspired menu of attractive and well-prepared dishes like salad Nicoise, roast chicken, eggplant galette, and roasted-beet salad. Though there is a cozy indoor dining room, it's nicest to dine in the bright tree-shaded patio (though note that it adjoins the parking lot, which is occasionally a nuisance). In addition to the bistro, El Vergel operates a small gourmet market, which sells many local treats like honey, cheese, wine, and chocolate. If you have a set of wheels (or don't mind taking a taxi to and fro), it's a nice place to spend an afternoon, away from the bustle of downtown.

Accommodations

There is a wide range of accommodations in San Miguel de Allende, with something to fit every style and budget. Hotels in every price range cater to the laid-back atmosphere with lovely gardens and comfortable common spaces. Though it is more expensive than other small Mexican towns, in San Miguel de Allende you won't have to pay a bundle to get warm service or a good location near the town square. Some of San Miguel's beautiful boutique hotels are a destination in and of themselves.

Every bed-and-breakfast, posada, or hotel has its own individual character. For romantic travelers, San Miguel has its share of dark and creaky ex-haciendas, while modernists can sleep in sleek accommodations with smartphone docks and flat-screen TVs. Some hotels are decorated with original art and traditional *artesanía,* while others are decked out with vintage furnishings and hand-painted tile.

San Miguel attracts tourists throughout the year, with the largest number of foreign visitors coming to town between December and April, its high season. National visitors flock to San Miguel year-round but especially on weekends and during Holy Week, Independence Day, and the Christmas holidays, as well as Mexican holidays and three-day weekends. In some cases, hotels may raise their rates 10-15 percent on the weekends (especially Saturdays) and during peak holidays, though many maintain the same rates all year. The prices listed are for a double room during San Miguel's high season, though rates can fluctuate.

CENTRO HISTÓRICO
Under US$50
In the blocks surrounding the town square, there are numerous casual hotels that cater to budget travelers. For a very low price, you can find a clean and centrally located crash pad, sometimes just a block or two from the *jardín.* While budget accommodations may not be the most luxurious, some are surprisingly pleasant, boasting roof decks or common courtyards. In almost every budget hotel, some bedrooms are nicer, lighter, or quieter than others. When you check in, ask to see a few different options.

Popular with young backpackers and solo travelers, the centrally located **Hostal Alcatraz** (Relox 54, tel. 415/152-8543, US$12 dorm) is one of the few youth hostels in San Miguel de Allende. Single-sex dorm rooms are clean, though a bit cramped, and bathrooms are shared. Guests can also make use of the communal kitchen downstairs, lockers, and the computers with Internet access. The friendly owners are happy to give tips about the town, and the location is excellent.

Just five minutes away, the same family that owns the Hostal Alcatraz manages the **Hostel Inn** (Calzada de la Luz 31A, tel. 415/154-6727, www.hostelinnmx.com, US$12 dorm, US$20 private double), which has both shared and private rooms for two, three, or four people. The accommodations here are simple and

Best Accommodations

Hotel Posada de las Monjas

★ **Hotel Posada de las Monjas:** The best option for budget travelers, this rambling building was once a convent. Today, the nuns' quarters are simple but lovely bedrooms (page 98).

★ **Casa Schuck:** This beloved bed-and-breakfast is quintessential San Miguel, with spacious, colorful rooms decorated with traditional crafts, a top-notch breakfast, and friendly hosts (page 101).

★ **Casa No Name:** A gorgeously restored colonial-era mansion is the backdrop for this central six-room boutique hotel, which distinguishes itself with its lovely design and warm service (page 101).

★ **Hotel El Palomar:** You will find some of the most beautiful views in San Miguel de Allende from the spacious suites at this upscale boutique hotel, a good pick for small groups or families (page 101).

★ **L'Otel:** This excellent boutique hotel has two locations. Romantics will love the lavishly decorated original location on Chiquitos (page 102).

★ **Casa Carly:** This comfortable and reasonably priced inn, just a few steps away from the Fábrica La Aurora art and design center, has spacious and colorful rooms (page 104).

utilitarian but very clean. The staff is warm and friendly, and there are lots of shared facilities to make your trip to San Miguel easy and inexpensive, including free wireless Internet, a shared kitchen, a washing machine, and a living area to lounge in.

Just around the corner, **La Catrina** (Loreto 80, tel. 415/121-4545, www.lacatrinahostel.com, US$10 dorm, US$25-45 private room) is a clean and genial hostel located on quiet Loreto Street. A newer addition to the backpacker scene and one of the better deals in town, La Catrina has shared dormitories (both single-sex and mixed) and private rooms, some with their own bathrooms and some without. Downstairs is a kitchen for guests and a lounge with a Sky-equipped television, plus several upstairs terraces for relaxing. There's also Wi-Fi and a simple breakfast—coffee, tea, and toast—included in the price.

US$50-100

Housed in a former cloister, the historic and charming ★ **Hotel Posada de las Monjas** (Canal 37, tel. 415/152-0171, www.delasmonjas.com, US$55) is a central and simple place, which is among the town's best values. This sprawling ex-convent sits on lower Canal, ideally located just a block and a half from the main plaza. Guest rooms are minimally decorated—they were once the residence of nuns, after all—but they are comfortable and clean, and the building itself has a wonderful historic ambience. When you arrive, ask to see a few available rooms: Some have beautiful views and semiprivate balconies. The nightly price includes a basic breakfast and, for those with wheels, parking.

A good centrally located option with an accessible price tag, **Parador San Sebastián de Aparicio** (Mesones 7, tel. 415/152-7084, US$55) is on the most easterly block of Mesones, right past the Plaza Cívica and around the corner from the municipal market. The hotel's 30 guest rooms are nothing fancy, but they are nonetheless spacious and clean, with old wooden furnishings and small private bathrooms with showers. Bottom-floor rooms are a bit dark but have windows overlooking the hotel's sunny courtyard, surrounded by archways and hanging vines. Ask to see more than one room at check-in, and then pick the best available. The reception desk can be a bit lackadaisical, but for the price, it's easy to overlook the drawbacks of this budget hotel.

Unless you are rather spry, getting to and from **Casa Frida** (Cuesta de Loreto 24, tel. 415/152-7518, www.casafrida2.net, US$70-95) can be a bit of a challenge. However, if you don't mind making use of San Miguel's many taxis, the rooms at this hilltop bed-and-breakfast are very spacious, clean, comfortable, and reasonably priced. Accompanying bathrooms are decorated with pretty colored tiles, and some have tubs. The Matisse room is particularly nice, with a private balcony and a pretty view of the city below. The largest suite has a private sitting area with a table and chairs. Breakfast (included in the price) is served downstairs in the shared dining room, and there are several common areas for relaxing. However, given its location, Casa Frida is best for visitors who plan to spend most of their days in town, heading back to the hotel for a good night's rest.

Occupying a narrow multistory home on the corner of Correo and Chiquitos, **Casa Chiquita** (Correo 45, tel. 415/152-3327, toll-free Mex. tel. 800/890-2173, www.casachiquita.mx, US$70-150) has four individually decorated guest rooms, each equipped with soft lighting, a pillow-strewn bed, book-filled shelves, and wood floors. There's no lobby, but the prime location, just a few blocks from the *jardín*, gives you plenty of places to hang out outside the hotel. Just a few blocks away, the same small hotel operates **Casa Real** (Salida a Querétaro 15, tel. 415/152-1938, US$70-150), which is also located in a historic building, and has a similar aesthetic and prices to the original spot on Chiquitos.

The quirky-creative style at **Casa Luna** (Quebrada 117, tel. 415/152-1117, U.S. tel. 210/200-8758, www.casaluna.com, US$80-175) is quintessential San Miguel. Behind the unassuming door of this brick-red colonial house, there is a charming maze of 14 individually decorated guest rooms, each equipped with a private bath and a chimney for cool winter nights. Many rooms also open onto small private balconies. The decor is warm and eclectic, with lots of traditional Mexican touches, like embroidered textiles and hand-painted wooden chests. Downstairs, an old pepper tree keeps the house shady and cool. Full breakfasts are included in the price and served in the downstairs dining rooms.

Casa Carmen

US$100-200

The paradigm of a successful bed-and-breakfast, **Casa Calderoni** (Callejón del Pueblito 4A, tel. 415/154-6005, toll-free U.S. tel. 713/955-6091, www.casacalderoni.com, US$110-140) is a cute, centrally located, and reasonably priced place to stay, with comfortable rooms, friendly proprietors, and delicious made-to-order breakfasts. At Casa Calderoni, each bedroom is named after a famous artist, and the decor subtly reflects its namesake. The Diego Rivera room, for example, is gussied up with colorful textiles and serapes and decorated with several Rivera posters on the wall. No matter which artist you call home, the cozy rooms are all brightly painted and have large beds with fluffy comforters, cute tiled bathrooms with brass sinks, cable TV, and special touches like painted desk lamps and skylights. The hotel's gregarious owners are meticulous about keeping the lodging clean and up-to-date, and the service is friendly and attentive.

The large 18th-century mansion that houses the **Hotel Posada Carmina** (Cuna de Allende 7, tel. 415/152-8888, www.posadacarmina.com, US$140) seems to have been trapped in time. Spacious and sparely decorated rooms retain a lot of the mansion's original charms, with little luxury but plenty of character. The impossibly high, wood-beamed ceilings and thick white walls attest to the building's age. With the exception of three smaller rooms with double beds (which run about US$90/night), all the other rooms in the old mansion are the same price. However, their size, furnishings, and view can be quite different, so ask to see a few at check-in. The best bedrooms overlook the *parroquia* from a small private balcony, though be aware that these rooms can also be noisy at night.

Staying in a bed-and-breakfast becomes an experience in itself at **Casa de la Cuesta** (Cuesta de San José 32, tel. 415/154-4324, www.casadelacuesta.com, US$180), located on a bustling residential street above the Mercado Ignacio Ramírez. Throughout this colonial home, the owners' passion for traditional Mexican crafts is amply reflected in the decor—clay figurines, ceremonial masks, and ceramic urns artfully complement the cozy atmosphere. Rooms are decorated with traditional crafts and textiles, painted in bright colors, and equipped with king-size beds. There are views of downtown from many of the shared spaces as well as some of the guest rooms. A lovely **Mexican mask museum** (by appointment only, US$3) on-site, which showcases the owners' collection of ceremonial masks, draws visitors who aren't staying at the hotel.

Just one block from the town square, **Casa Carmen** (Correo 31, tel. 415/152-0844, U.S. tel. 707/771-3054, www.casacarmenhotel.com, US$160-180, with discounts for weekly and monthly stays) is San Miguel de Allende's oldest bed-and-breakfast. With more than 50 years in operation, this friendly, family-run establishment makes it easy to imagine the quiet days before San Miguel was a tourist town. The hotel's 10 guest rooms are simple yet charming, with creaky high ceilings, clean bathrooms, and vintage accessories like old wooden armoires and little glass chandeliers. Suites are more spacious; some are two-story, with a spiral staircase leading up to a creaky loft bed. The pretty Caballeriza Suite is housed in the home's former stables. The cost of a room at Casa Carmen includes both breakfast and a three-course lunch in the hotel's airy dining room—unique in San Miguel. Guests can also relax in the small sitting room or the sunny courtyard.

Adjoining the town square, the incredibly central **Hotel La Morada** (Correo 10, tel. 415/152-1647, toll-free Mex. tel. 800/221-7432, http://lamoradahotel.com.mx, US$160-200) has 15 large bedrooms and suites upstairs, in the colonial style, with vaulted ceilings, chimneys, and Saltillo tile floors. The two-story Terraza Suite has a large private balcony overlooking Sollano and the *parroquia*—a piece of paradise, all to yourself. Downstairs, the hotel's patio suites are clean and minimalist, with big white beds, abstract art on the walls, and modern bathrooms. If you prefer a room downstairs, note that the high-ceilinged, one-story rooms are airier than the two-story rooms (which have a loft bed above the sitting area). No matter where you choose to stay, the hotel's location is smack-dab in the middle of everything. You'll enjoy an easy stroll to any destination in town and get used to the sound of church bells ringing through the night.

Situated in a beautifully restored colonial home, **Casa de los Olivos** (Correo 30, tel. 415/152-0309, www.casadelosolivos.com, US$135-150) is a sweet five-room bed-and-breakfast that unites cushy comforts with the atmosphere of old San Miguel. Spacious and clean bedrooms open onto the shared courtyard, and each is equipped with a white canopy bed with Italian linens, terra-cotta tile floors, rustic wooden furnishings, and a big bathroom with a Jacuzzi tub. Despite modern comforts, the high-beamed ceilings, thick walls, and architectural details retain a distinctly Mexican aesthetic. Upstairs, the hotel's tiny bar serves hotel guests in the afternoon and evening; they can take their drinks out to the terrace and relax amid the historic domes and bell towers of San Miguel. Service is friendly, and the location is ideal, just a block and a half from the town square.

Charming **Casa de la Noche** (Organos 19, tel. 415/152-0732, U.S. tel. 831/373-8888, www.casadelanoche.com, US$115-190) was once a bordello; today, it is a charming guesthouse with sunny rooms of varying size and amenities. Working with the unusual structure of the original house and its many nooks and crannies, the proprietor redesigned all the guest rooms with a delightfully colorful touch. For those on a budget, smaller rooms can accommodate two people in a double bed for a reasonable price. Suites are spacious and have lovely tiled kitchens, comfortable sitting areas, and often small patios and pretty views. All rooms are impeccably clean and sunny with cute private bathrooms. For large groups, the owner also rents a seven-bedroom home near the *centro* as well as a five-bedroom colonial property.

There may be no more peaceful place in San Miguel than the cascading gardens of the **Casa de Liza** (Bajada del Chorro 7, tel. 415/152-0352, www.casaliza.mx, US$75-150). Located along the lush Bajada del Chorro, Casa Liza's sloping grounds are filled with giant maguey, flowering fruit trees, winding stone walkways, and the happy motion of attending butterflies. Scattered across the property, each room at this unusual bed-and-breakfast feels like its own private cabin, with sloping wood-beamed ceilings and big comfortable beds. Some are more spacious than others, though each is individually decorated with Mexican crafts, original art, and unique furniture, some of which has been designed by surrealist artist and architect Pedro Friedeberg. Your best bet is to choose a room with a private patio, though all guests share the beautiful gardens as well as the small outdoor Jacuzzi.

Over US$200

San Miguel de Allende's luxury hotels are much more than a place to lay your head.

Decorated with love and attention, thoughtfully attended, and incredibly comfortable, these places can become destinations themselves.

Every bedroom at the ★ **Casa Schuck** (Garita 3, tel. 415/152-0657, U.S. tel. 937/684-4092, www.casaschuck.com, US$250-350) is decorated with tremendous flair. Housed in a massive colonial-era mansion, the spacious guest rooms are decked out with jewel-colored walls, delightful crafts, stone chimneys, and colorful bedspreads. Second-floor bedrooms have large French windows that open onto the leafy trees of the central courtyard. Guests can relax in the home's various shared spaces, including a comfortable living area, a roof deck with views of the *parroquia,* and a garden patio. Morning breakfasts are included in the price and served in the beautiful blue dining room downstairs.

When the owners of ★ **Casa No Name** (Hernández Macías 52, tel. 415/152-1768, http://casanoname.com.mx, $340-600) were restoring the colonial-era mansion in which the hotel is housed, they uncovered a stunning 18th-century religious mural that had been painted in the home's main courtyard. The mural, as well as the historic Moorish arches that surround the patio, has been restored and is among the first of many beautiful details you'll notice at this top-notch boutique hotel. Here, each of the six guest rooms is romantic yet comfortable, with high ceilings, wood furnishings, and warm decor, including original artwork and antiques specially selected for the room. Upstairs, there is an open-air bar on the roof, with lounge chairs and a cactus garden. Downstairs, the garden in back is an enchanting place to read with a cup of coffee.

Among of the first boutique hotels to open in San Miguel de Allende, **Dos Casas** (Quebrada 101, tel. 415/154-4073, www.doscasas.com.mx, US$210-420) is a contemporary six-room property that doesn't sacrifice comfort for style. This upscale establishment occupies a colonial home on a busy street corner in the *centro histórico.* Behind its dark wood doors, the building's original architecture is complemented by carefully designed interiors: Clean lines and neutral colors define the bedrooms, where choice Mexican crafts and textiles make an elegant accompaniment to the modern atmosphere. To unwind, guests can order drinks in the first-floor bar or relax on the lovely roof deck with its pretty views of downtown San Miguel; the in-house restaurant, Áperi, is widely considered one of San Miguel's best.

Judging by its grand colonial entryway, spacious lobby, and large sun-drenched patios, you'd expect **Hotel Nena** (Nemesio Diez 10, tel. 415/154-7129 or 415/154-7128, www.hotelnena.mx, US$250) to house more than just six guest rooms. But the charm of this boutique property is its intimate feel, despite its grand surroundings. Located in a colonial mansion just across the street from the mammoth Rosewood hotel, Nena mixes traditional colonial decor—Saltillo-tile floors, high wood-beamed ceilings, and colorful tiled bathrooms—with decidedly modern touches, like contemporary artwork on the walls, shaggy throw carpets below the beds, and LCD televisions. The common areas, including a spacious lobby, rooftop bar, and a courtyard restaurant, are beautiful, and the service is notably friendly and helpful.

Perched just above the *centro histórico,* ★ **Hotel El Palomar** (San Francisco 57, tel. 415/152-0656 or 415/152-0339, http://hotelelpalomar.com.mx, US$150-250) has 10 remarkably spacious, individually decorated guest rooms, each done up in soft grays and neutral tones, decorated with artwork, and comfortably stocked with bathrobes, air-conditioning, and Wi-Fi. Depending on which suite you book, you might have a fireplace in the sitting room, a private balcony, or, best yet, gorgeous views of San Miguel's rooftops and church spires. For bigger families, there are two enormous and well-appointed double suites, which have two bedrooms and two full baths in each. Anyone staying at the hotel can enjoy spectacular views from the rooftop restaurant, Antonia Bistro.

Few hotels can boast the sheer history of

Santa Mónica (Fray José Guadalupe Mojica 22, tel. 415/152-0451 or 415/152-0427, http://santamonica.mx, US$200-270). Housed in an enchanting 17th-century mansion bordering the Parque Juárez, guest rooms at this beautiful hotel are entirely comfortable yet retain the original charms of the historic setting. Furnishings lean toward the romantic, with white canopy beds, tile floors, and antique accessories. In the courtyard, the hotel's restaurant serves breakfast and lunch. Lush gardens are filled with lime, jacaranda, and palm trees with well-tended lawns and a very small but pretty swimming pool. Suites are more expensive than standard doubles but are incredibly spacious, with sitting areas and in some cases private terraces.

On a small cobbled street just a few blocks from the town square, ★ **L'Otel** (Chiquitos 1A, tel. 415/154-9850, U.S. tel. 210/745-1457, http://l-otelgroup.com, US$350-400) is an intimate spot with a luxe, get-away-from-it-all ambience. Occupying a beautifully restored colonial home, guest rooms are lavish but tasteful, decorated with old-fashioned furniture, well-chosen antiques, Mexican crafts, contemporary art, and gorgeous rugs. Yet rooms are fully equipped with modern conveniences, like flat-screen TVs and air-conditioning, ensuring a comfortable stay as much as a romantic one. Though the house itself is rather small, the four guest rooms are spacious and luxurious, decked out with high-thread-count sheets and all-natural toiletries. Service is as friendly and elegant as the hotel.

In 2017, **L'Otel** (Doce 18, Relox 18, tel. 415/154-7114, http://l-otelgroup.com, $300-420) opened a very different location on the top floor of the Doce 18 Concept House, half a block from the central *jardín*. Like the rest of the "concept house" downstairs, the hotel feels far more contemporary than what you'd usually find in San Miguel de Allende, with an ultramodern look. The interior design is unique but comfortable; guest rooms mix ultramodern furnishings with romantic touches, each outfitted with king-size beds, 500-thread-count sheets, satellite TV, and Nespresso coffeemakers. In a particularly nice touch, several of the larger suites have outdoor tubs in the bathrooms. You can order room service from any of the downstairs eateries, like Taco Lab or Birdie's Burgers, or snack beside the black-and-white-tiled outdoor pool, which is surrounded by lounge chairs.

With a distinct old-world style, **Casa Misha** (Chiquitos 15, tel. 415/152-2021, U.S. tel. 646/688-4862, www.casamisha.com, US$320-375) is a small seven-room hotel that drips with opulence. Here, every single room has been lavished with attention, from the guest suites to the library downstairs, filled with gilded furniture, fine china, crystal chandeliers, and oil paintings. Rooms are all different, yet every one is lavishly appointed with armoires and antiques, silky bedspreads, and four-poster beds as well as a gorgeous private bathroom with ample space, a big tub, and French toiletries. There are several rooftop terraces with panoramic views of San Miguel de Allende and beautiful gardens throughout the central courtyard. The hotel is small yet fully staffed, and service is incredibly hospitable, attentive, and friendly.

One of the best features of **Hotel Boutique 1810** (Hidalgo 8, tel. 415/121-3501 or 415/121-3506, www.casa1810.com, US$200-300) is its location, just a half block from the *jardín*. Set back from the bustle of the street, the guest rooms, which surround a central atrium, have clay floors, iron lamps, and Mexican-inspired wood furnishings, giving them a homey, wholly Mexican, and luxe feeling. Unlike many hotels in San Miguel, 1810 is equipped with an elevator for guests on higher floors, and there is a small, upscale restaurant on the top floor, with pretty views of the surrounding city. For the price, however, service could be a bit more attentive.

Housed in a grand centuries-old mansion, the 10-suite boutique hotel **Casa Blanca** (Juárez No. 7, tel. 415/688-1438 or 415/688-1439, http://casablanca7.com, $250-500) brings together the best elements of a stay in San Miguel de Allende: history, romance, and luxury. In the guest rooms, a simple, elegant design combines modern furnishings with Morrocan-style details, like Berber carpets and embroidered pillowcases, an aesthetic that blends remarkably well with the old Mexican mansion's original details. Each comfortable, spacious room is done up in luxuries like high-thread-count sheets and rainfall showers. On the second floor, Mediterranean restaurant Fátima provides room service to the guests, though you're likely to prefer eating in the stunning dining room, with its breathtaking views of the Templo de San Francisco.

A classic San Miguel establishment, **Belmond Casa de Sierra Nevada** (Hospicio 35, tel. 415/152-7040, Belmond central reservation office U.S. tel. 843/937-9066, toll-free U.S. tel. 800/237-1236, www.belmond.com, US$300-400) is the oldest full-service luxury hotel in San Miguel de Allende; it was purchased in 2006 by Belmond Ltd. (formerly Orient-Express Hotels), and the name changed in 2014. There are 37 guest rooms located in five different colonial mansions in San Miguel de Allende's *centro histórico*. With so many properties, rooms vary widely, though each is decorated with colonial-style headboards, overstuffed furniture, and terracotta floors. Comfort is key, with twice-daily housekeeping, fluffy bathrobes, and in-room

spa services. Grounds are lovely and quiet in the hotel's Casa del Parque directly across from the *lavaderos públicos* on the Bajada del Chorro. The Recreo location has a small swimming pool, a sculpture garden, and deck chairs. If you have a preference, you can request the house you'd like to stay in when you make your reservation.

Opened in 2011, **Rosewood San Miguel de Allende** (Nemesio Diez 11, tel. 415/152-9700, toll-free Mex. tel. 800/363-7373, toll-free U.S. tel. 888/767-3966, www.rosewoodsanmiguel.com, US$595-750) is a large 67-room retreat operated by the international hotelier Rosewood Hotels and Resorts. Occupying a large swath of land between the Ancha de San Antonio and Parque Juárez, the grounds mirror the city's colonial aesthetic but in mammoth proportions, with oversize stone arches, gurgling fountains, and saturated colors throughout. In keeping with the brand's focus on luxury, an on-site spa gets top reviews, while the terraced pool is a particularly dreamy place to sip a drink under an umbrella or in a private cabana. Spacious guest rooms are designed for comfort, dolled up with Italian bedsheets, gilt-framed mirrors, and Mexican rugs. The Rosewood is a popular weekend destination for tourists from

Belmond Casa de Sierra Nevada is housed in a colonial-era mansion.

Mexico City, Monterrey, and other cosmopolitan cities in Mexico, and their influence is noticeable throughout the hotel.

In a town where crimson facades and crumbling fountains are the norm, **Hotel Matilda** (Aldama 53, tel. 415/152-1015 or 415/152-0883, www.hotelmatilda.com, US$285-500) is an anomaly. From the moment you enter, the multicolored art installation glowing behind the reception desks affirms this boutique hotel's commitment to the contemporary. Bedrooms are modern, comfortable, and chic; overstuffed furniture and king-size beds play nice accompaniment to modern art and cozy tan-and-chocolate colors. Private baths are comfortably minimalist, with marble tubs, big mirrors, square porcelain sinks, luxury toiletries, and stacks of fresh towels. The hotel's popular DJ bar draws a local and tourist crowd, while famed chef Enrique Olvera operates ground-floor restaurant Moxi. In 2018, it was voted Best City Hotel in the world by *Travel + Leisure* readers.

NORTH OF THE CENTRO
US$50-100

At ★ **Casa Carly** (Calzada de la Aurora 48, tel. 415/152-8900, U.S. tel. 202/391-0004, www.casacarlysanmiguel.com, US$90-100),

proprietor Carly Cross designed her bed-and-breakfast to feel like the places she likes to stay in when she travels, at the prices she wants to pay. The result is spacious and comfortable guest rooms at surprisingly good rates. Seven large suites surround a pretty courtyard with a stone fountain, leafy trees, and a fishpond. Large, comfortable, and cheerfully decorated, each suite is painted with bright colors and adorned with Mexican crafts. Rooms are all illuminated by ample windows and fully equipped with comfy beds and a small kitchen. The location on the Calzada de la Aurora is a few steps farther from the town square but right across the street from the Fábrica La Aurora art and design center.

EAST OF THE CENTRO
US$100-200

On the eastern edge of San Miguel de Allende, the historic **Rancho Hotel Atascadero** (Prol. Santo Domingo s/n, tel. 415/152-0206 or toll-free Mex. tel. 800/466-0000, www.hotelelatascadero.com, US$85-200) was built on the grounds of a sprawling ex-hacienda originally constructed in the 1880s. The property has changed hands many times, belonging once to a famous bullfighter, Pepe Ortiz, and

the Rosewood San Miguel de Allende

later to a Peruvian scholar (and founder of the Instituto Allende) Felipe Cossío del Pomar. As a hotel, the Rancho Atascadero has been in business for more than 60 years, and it retains the distinct feeling of a mid-20th-century family-style resort. Rooms are simple affairs, with old, oversize colonial furniture, red tile floors, and woven Mexican bedspreads—and a log fire is included in the price during chilly winters. Amid the stone fountains and pomegranate trees of the hotel's extensive gardens, there is a swimming pool, tennis courts, and racquetball for guests.

SOUTH OF THE CENTRO
Under US$50

On a small street in the residential Allende neighborhood, **Casita de las Flores** (Calle de las Flores, Col. Allende, tel. 415/117-7223, www.casitadelasflores.com, US$35-45, with discounts for weekly and monthly stays) has five small guest rooms with shared bath surrounding a tranquil central courtyard. It can be a challenge to find this place the first time around, but once you make your reservations, the managers will send you a map with detailed directions. Rooms are small but clean, comfortable, and attractive, with painted walls, tin-framed mirrors, and Mexican bedspreads. In the small communal kitchen, each guest has their own basket to store food as well as their own shelf in the refrigerator. Though the managers are friendly, the guesthouse is rather self-service and located 20 minutes from the *centro histórico*; it is best for fairly independent travelers.

VACATION RENTALS

For those planning to spend a week or two in San Miguel de Allende, renting a private home can be a nice way to visit the town and have a bit more space and independence than a hotel offers. From simple apartments to lavish mansions, there are literally hundreds of private homes available for short-term rental in San Miguel. Although a private home does not offer all the services of a hotel, many have cleaning and kitchen staff, gardens or outdoor spaces, and parking.

Unless you will have a set of wheels, look for rentals in central neighborhoods, like the *centro histórico,* Guadalupe, Aurora, San Antonio, La Aldea, and Guadiana, all of which are walking distance from the city center.

Airbnb (www.airbnb.mx) arrived in San Miguel de Allende a little later than other online vacation-rental agents, but once it did, it swept the market. Today, it seems like most San Miguel homeowners rent out their home when they are out of town, while many others offer shared apartments, private rooms, and dorm-style beds for rent. The cost of renting via Airbnb is higher in San Miguel than in other parts of Mexico— it can be cheaper to stay in a hotel, in some cases, unlike in other tourist destinations. **VRBO** (www.vrbo.com) also lists many San Miguel properties and has been operating here longer than Airbnb. Though you're less likely to find bargain prices on VRBO, there are some really lovely listings.

Though Airbnb and other online home rental services are now major players in San Miguel, many wonderful vacation rentals are still principally available through agents. For every type of rental property, from simple apartments to lavish multi-bedroom haciendas, **Premier San Miguel** (tel. 415/154-9460, www.premiersanmiguel.com) can help you book a place to stay for short- or long-term excursions to San Miguel. The very friendly staff will answer your questions about rental properties, which are listed (along with pictures) on their website, and they can help arrange airport pickup and other tourist services for your stay in San Miguel de Allende.

Information and Services

TOURIST INFORMATION

San Miguel's **tourist office** (Plaza Principal 10, tel. 415/152-0900, U.S. tel. 646/536-7634, www.visitsanmiguel.travel, 9am-8pm Mon.-Sat., 10am-5pm Sun.), on the main square, can offer you an annotated map of the town and arrange for accommodations or a tour of the city. For those new to the city, there are various flyers in the office advertising tour guides, hotels, restaurants, and other tourist attractions.

Media

The weekly bilingual periodical *Atención San Miguel* (www.atencionsanmiguel.org) is required reading for anyone visiting San Miguel. Each week, *Atención* publishes a few news articles in Spanish and English about municipal events as well as a slew of advertisements and promotional pieces about cultural happenings, art events, and upcoming speakers, which can be very helpful in planning your trip. The journalistic quality can be hit or miss, but there is no question that *Atención* is the number-one source of information about events in San Miguel de Allende. Published principally for San Miguel's expatriate community, the classifieds are a good place to turn if you are looking to rent an apartment or take an art class.

The Spanish-language newspaper *El Sol del Bajío* (www.elsoldelbajio.com.mx) is published in Celaya and occasionally covers news and events in San Miguel de Allende. If you can read text in Spanish, it is a good place to get regional news. The newspaper *am* (www.am.com.mx) is based in the state capital, León, and also covers regional news in Spanish.

Travel Agents

The only travel agent left standing, **Viajes Vertiz** (Hidalgo 1A, tel. 415/152-1856, toll-free U.S. tel. 800/861-6423, www.viajesvertiz.com) can book plane tickets, cruises, and travel packages, with an emphasis on all-inclusive national tours. Viajes Vertiz is also an American Express representative.

Visas and Officialdom

Thanks to the large American expatriate population, there is a **U.S. Consular Agency** (Plaza La Luciérnaga, Libramiento Jose Manuel Zavala No. 165, Locales 4 y 5, Colonia La Luciernaga, toll-free Mex. tel. 800/681-9374, toll-free U.S. tel. 844/528-6611, conagencysanmiguel@state.gov, http://mexico.usembassy.gov, 9am-1pm Mon.-Thurs.) in San Miguel de Allende, which can process passport renewals (including reports of lost or stolen passports) and provide notary services, among other consular functions.

To report a missing tourist card, complete paperwork for a resident visa, or perform any other immigration-related paperwork, go to the **Instituto Nacional de Migración Delegación Guanajuato** (Mexican Immigration Services Guanajuato Branch, Calzada de la Estación de FFCC s/n, tel. 415/152-8991, 9am-1pm Mon.-Fri.), just outside the center of town and almost to the railroad station. With so many foreigners in such a small town, Migración can get a bit backed up. Lines often form before the offices even open, so set aside several hours to account for long wait times and arrive with a lot of patience.

SERVICES
Internet Access

In San Miguel de Allende, even 17th-century mansions are wired. In most hotels, there is free wireless or a personal computer that guests can share. There are also plenty of places to hop online throughout town, from coffee shops to restaurants.

If you didn't bring a web-enabled device, **La Conexion** (Aldama 3, tel. 415/152-1599, www.laconexionsma.com, 9am-5pm

Mon.-Sat., 10am-2pm Sun.) has computers in their main office as well as a fax machine, a scanner, and a wireless printer.

Laundry

Right in the center of town, **Tintorería Lavandería La Pila** (Jesús 25, tel. 415/152-5810, 8am-7pm Mon.-Fri., 8am-6pm Sat.) washes and dries your clothes for about US$5 for five kilos of laundry. They also have dry-cleaning services.

Franco Tintorería (Cinco de Mayo 29A, tel. 415/154-4495 or 415/154-4495, 9am-7pm Mon.-Fri, 9am-4pm Sat.) offers inexpensive laundry and dry cleaning, with pickup and delivery service available to your home or hotel on weekdays. They will launder four kilos of clothes for about US$5.

Medical and Emergency Services

For all types of ailments from stomach flu to altitude sickness, many expatriates turn to **Dra. Silvia Azcarate** (Codo 9A, tel. 415/152-1944), a general medicine doctor who speaks Spanish, English, and French. Another good English-speaking general practice doctor, **Dr. Ricardo Gordillo** (Hidalgo 28, tel. 415/154-9976 or cell tel. 415/109-5961 emergencies) runs a clinic with labs and a pharmacy just a block from the main square.

Dial **911** from any telephone to reach the government-operated emergency response system. You can reach the police force, or **Protección Civil** (Civil Protection Department, Bulevar de la Conspiración 130, Salida a Querétaro) directly at tel. 415/152-0911. Unlike other Red Cross operations worldwide, the amazing, volunteer-run Cruz Roja Mexicana not only participates in disaster relief work and humanitarian aid but also plays an essential role in emergency response throughout the republic. The San Miguel chapter of the **Cruz Roja Mexicana** (Libramiento Manuel Zavala 17, office tel. 415/152-4225, www.cruzrojasanmiguel.org) responds to medical emergencies, traffic accidents, and other life-threatening situations.

They can be reached at tel. 415/152-4121 or 415/152-1616 and will often be summoned via 911.

The general hospital, **Hospital General Dr. Felipe Dobarganes** (Primero de Mayo s/n, Fracc. Ignacio Ramírez, tel. 415/120-4746 or 415/120-4799), has a 24-hour emergency room. **Hospital H+** (Libramiento a Dolores, tel. 415/152-5900, http://hmas.mx/sanmiguel, 7am-7pm Mon.-Sat., 7am-5pm Sun.) is a small private hospital, affiliated with a larger hospital group (an additional larger branch is located in the city of Querétaro, and takes emergencies within business hours. Many foreigners, however, prefer to use the larger private hospitals in Querétaro, a 45-minute drive from San Miguel de Allende.

Money

In most cases, the easiest and most efficient way to **change money** is to use ATMs at Mexican banks, which are located throughout the *centro histórico*. If you do bring cash, you can change dollars to pesos at any bank in town (most will post their exchange rates in the window) or at one of several exchange houses around the central plaza. There are teller services with currency exchange and 24-hour ATMs at **Banorte** (San Francisco 17, tel. 415/152-0019, 8:30am-4pm Mon.-Fri., 9am-2pm Sat.). There are **Citibanamex** ATMs on the corner of the *Jardín* (Canal 4, toll-free Mex. tel. 800/021-2345, 24 hours daily) and a **Santander** branch (Calle Portal de Guadalupe 4, tel. 415/152-2334, branch 9am-4pm Mon.-Fri., ATMs 24 hours) with two ATMs on the other side of the plaza.

When changing dollars to pesos, remember that Mexico has recently imposed much stricter controls on cash exchange. In any bank or exchange house in San Miguel de Allende, you will need to present a valid passport in order to change money. Some exchange houses will also cap the amount of money you can change per day or per month.

In addition to changing American dollars, Canadian dollars, and euros, **Intercam**

(Correo 15, San Francisco 4, and Plaza La Luciérnaga, Local 53, tel. 415/154-6707, www. intercam.com.mx, 9am-5:45pm Mon.-Fri., 9am-1:45pm Sat.) will also change travelers checks. For clients in San Miguel de Allende, Intercam can also change American checks to pesos, though you must be registered as an Intercam client to use this service.

Postal Services
The Mexican **post office** is at Correo 16, on the corner of Correo and Corregidora. Inside, MexPost provides certified and expedited mail services through the regular postal system.

Veterinary Services
Dr. Michael Kronish at **Animal Medical Center SMA** (Salida a Celaya 67, tel. 415/185-8185, cell tel. 415/109-9957, 9am-7pm Mon.-Fri., 9am-2pm Sat.) cares for pets at his office to the south of the city center or at your home.

Transportation

GETTING THERE
Air
Getting to San Miguel from overseas can be a bit of a challenge. While well connected to other Mexican cities by highway, it is nonetheless a small town and relatively remote. If you are coming from outside of Mexico, the two airports closest to San Miguel de Allende are the Del Bajío International Airport (BJX) just outside the city of León, Guanajuato, and Querétaro International Airport (QRO), outside the capital city of Querétaro. Many travelers find it is just as easy to fly to Mexico City (MEX), then take ground transportation to San Miguel. Many hotels can help arrange transport to San Miguel from any airport.

DEL BAJÍO INTERNATIONAL AIRPORT (BJX)
The most popular choice for visitors to San Miguel de Allende, the **Del Bajío International Airport** (BJX, Carretera Silao-León, Km 5.5, Col. Nuevo México, Silao, Guanajuato) has daily direct flights to and from U.S. cities, including Dallas-Fort Worth, Houston, and Los Angeles, as well as several flights to and from Mexico City, Los Cabos, Cancún, and Monterrey, among other national destinations. The airport is in Silao, Guanajuato, just outside the city of León, about a 90-minute drive from San Miguel de

Allende. From the airport, most people hire a shuttle or car service to drive them to San Miguel de Allende.

QUERÉTARO INTERNATIONAL AIRPORT (QRO)
Querétaro International Airport (QRO, Carretera Estatal 200, Querétaro-Tequisquiapan 22500, tel. 442/192-5500, www.aiq.com.mx), northeast of the city of Querétaro, is about a 90-minute drive from San Miguel de Allende. This airport is much newer, smaller, and less trafficked than its counterpart in León. Routes and rates change frequently, though there are direct flights from Houston, plus connecting service to other international destinations throughout Mexico City. You can schedule a shuttle pickup from Querétaro or hire a taxi to take you to San Miguel.

MEXICO CITY INTERNATIONAL AIRPORT (MEX)
The country's busiest airport is **Mexico City International Airport** (MEX, Capitan Carlos León s/n, Peñón de Los Baños Venustiano Carranza, Distrito Federal, www.aicm.com.mx), officially named the Aeropuerto Internacional Benito Juárez, in the capital. There are direct flights from Mexico City to more than 100 cities around the world. Flights to Mexico City can often be

considerably less expensive than those to León or Querétaro, both much smaller airports.

From the airport in Mexico City, travelers must arrange for ground transportation to San Miguel de Allende, usually by bus or through one of San Miguel de Allende's transport companies, which can meet you at the airport. **Primera Plus** (toll-free Mex. tel. 800/375-7587, www.primeraplus.com.mx) offers hourly direct bus service from both Terminal 1 and Terminal 2 in the Mexico City airport to Querétaro's main bus station, for about $20; from there, you can take a second-class bus to San Miguel de Allende, or hire a taxi in the bus station to drive you the last 45-minute leg for a flat rate of about US$45.

The trip from the Mexico City airport to San Miguel by bus takes about five hours, depending on road conditions and the infamous Mexico City traffic.

SHUTTLE SERVICE

Many hotels and home rental agents will help you arrange shuttle service from the airport in León or Querétaro to San Miguel de Allende. If you are making your own arrangements, highly professional **BajioGo** (Jesús 11, tel. 415/152-1999, toll-free Mex. tel. 800/225-4040, U.S. tel. 202/609-9905, www.bajiogoshuttle.com, 8am-8pm Mon.-Sat., 9am-3pm Sun.) is the go-to private transport service to and from León and Querétaro. They offer comfortable shared shuttles (which seat around nine) at about US$30 per person as well as private cars, with discounts for seniors. BajioGo can also arrange private transportation to and from the airport in Mexico City. BajioGo offers a round-the-clock answering service should anything come up during your travels.

Bus

A network of comfortable and reasonably priced bus lines connects all of Mexico. There is ample first- and second-class bus service between San Miguel de Allende and Mexico City as well as direct service to all major cities in the Bajío and Guadalajara. Both first-class and second-class buses are comfortable, though all

first-class buses also have a bathroom, which is convenient on longer trips. The major difference is that second-class buses tend to stop along the roadways to pick up and drop off passengers; therefore, travel on a second-class bus can be slower and more tiring, though also a bit cheaper. Note that bus fares change frequently.

A first-class bus company covering central to northern Mexico, comfortable and efficient **Primera Plus** (tel. 415/152-0084, toll-free Mex. tel. 800/375-7587, www.primeraplus.com.mx) offers direct service between the Terminal Central del Norte in Mexico City and the Central de Autobuses in San Miguel de Allende (US$24). Primera Plus also operates direct routes from San Miguel de Allende to Morelia, Guadalajara, Guanajuato, León, and Lagos de Moreno, with connecting service to more distant cities, like Puerto Vallarta and Manzanillo. Comfortable buses include bathrooms, snack packets, and reclining seats, plus televisions projecting noisy Hollywood movies—usually dubbed into Spanish.

If you are arriving on a flight to Mexico City International Airport, Primera Plus also offers direct service from both airport terminals to Querétaro's main bus station (about US$31). From the bus station, you can hop a second class bus for the remaining 80 kilometers (50 miles) to San Miguel de Allende. Alternatively, Querétaro's city taxis will drive you all the way to San Miguel de Allende from the bus terminal for about US$45. Before you go outside to grab a taxi, you must buy a ticket from the registered taxi stand inside the bus terminal and let them know you are going to San Miguel.

The poshest bus line in central Mexico, **ETN** (tel. 415/152-6407, toll-free Mex. tel. 800/800-0386, www.etn.com.mx) also provides comfy first-class bus service between the capital and San Miguel de Allende (about US$31), with five departures daily. These stylish coaches have reclining seats, bathrooms, snacks, and coffee service. ETN's routes are a bit more limited than Primera Plus, but the company also offers direct service to Guadalajara, León, Guanajuato, and Querétaro, with connecting service elsewhere.

For shorter trips or a more spontaneous agenda, it can be easiest to use second-class bus service, especially when traveling between San Miguel de Allende and Querétaro (about US$4) or San Miguel de Allende and Dolores Hidalgo (about US$3). Second-class buses depart from San Miguel de Allende to Querétaro, and vice versa, every 20-30 minutes until about 10pm. **Herradura de Plata** (tel. 415/152-0725) and **Servicios Coordinados Flecha Amarilla** (tel. 415/152-0084, toll-free Mex. tel. 800/375-7587), the latter of which is run by the same company that operates Primera Plus, both offer second-class service to Querétaro and Dolores Hidalgo. No need to book ahead; it's easiest to simply arrive at the bus terminal and get on the next departing bus. The ticket sellers loudly announce each departure.

Car
FROM THE UNITED STATES
From the southernmost tip of Texas, San Miguel de Allende is just one (very long) day's drive from the U.S.-Mexico border. For decades, many Texan families drove down to Mexico's high plains to escape the summer heat in the Lone Star State. Unfortunately, driving to San Miguel de Allende from the United States has become less safe due to the widespread drug-related violence along Mexico's border. If you plan to drive to San Miguel de Allende from the United States, use precaution by traveling **during daylight hours** and **using toll roads,** which tend to be in better condition and less dangerous than free highways.

Most drivers coming to San Miguel de Allende cross the border at the well-trafficked **Laredo/Nuevo Laredo crossing;** this remains the best choice, as opposed to the more southerly crossing at Brownsville/Matamoros. From there, head south toward Monterrey then on toward Matehuala. From Matehuala, take the toll highway south toward San Luis Potosí, passing outside the city, and continue

on Highway 57 toward Querétaro. Turn off at the Dr. Mora/San Miguel de Allende exit (just past San Luis de la Paz), heading west until you arrive in San Miguel de Allende. The drive from the border should take about **10-12 hours,** but getting lost in the outskirts of a major city can make the trip much longer. If you are going to do the drive, make sure your phone's GPS will be activated and order a *Guia Roji* (www.guiaroji.com.mx), Mexico's most complete road map.

FROM MEXICO CITY
San Miguel de Allende is about 255 kilometers (160 miles) northwest of Mexico City. The drive takes **3-4 hours** on fairly well-maintained toll highways. From Mexico City, exit the city via the Periférico Norte and head north toward Tepotzotlán. After passing through the *caseta* (tollbooth), continue on Highway 57 north toward Querétaro. Just past San Juan del Río (but before arriving in Querétaro), turn off at San Luis Potosí/San Miguel de Allende Via Corta. You will pass another tollbooth and then cross Highway 57 again; continue straight on the overpass and follow the winding two-lane road for another 30 minutes until you arrive in San Miguel de Allende.

If you miss the turnoff for the Via Corta, you can continue straight on Highway 57 all the way to Querétaro. Once you pass the city, keep an eye out for the turnoff to San Miguel de Allende on the right-hand side. Cross the overpass and follow the two-lane highway all the way to San Miguel de Allende. This is also the route you take to and from the downtown districts in Querétaro.

GETTING AROUND
If you come to San Miguel, you should be prepared to use your legs. This hilly little town is best for walking, and it will give you quite a workout! When you're worn out, there are several other ways to get around.

Car
With everything just a stone's throw away, it

isn't necessary to have a car in San Miguel de Allende. However, a car can make it easier to visit the hot springs or the botanical gardens or to eat at some of the nice restaurants outside the downtown area. Generally, drivers are courteous in San Miguel, even if streets feel a bit narrow for those used to suburbs and highways.

If you are itching for your own set of wheels, **San Miguel Rent-a-Car** (Codo 9, tel. 415/152-0198, www.sanmiguelrentalcar. com) rents compact cars, sedans, Jeeps, and vans for a day or more. They also rent ATVs. All you need is a valid driver's license and a credit card. Prices are very reasonable.

The most difficult part about driving in San Miguel is finding a place to park downtown. Fortunately, there are several low-cost parking garages, if you get fed up with circling. There are covered spots at **Estacionamiento Hidalgo** (Hidalgo 57) between Callejón del Pueblito and Insurgentes, for about a dollar an hour. There is also a large lot on Tenerías, right where the small street Jesús dead-ends.

Taxi

Taxicabs constantly circle San Miguel, providing the most convenient and inexpensive way to move around town. Anywhere within the town limits, a taxi ride costs about US$2. Longer trips to outlying neighborhoods, like the residential Los Fraile, will cost a buck or two more. Taxis will also take you out to the hot springs for around US$10, and if you ask, most will be happy to return to pick you up at an appointed time. You can also call **Taxis San Miguelito** (tel. 415/152-0124 or 415/152-0395) to pick you up.

Ride-Hailing Services

Uber operates in San Miguel de Allende, though there are still very few cars available through their service. In most cases, the low cost and general abundance of taxis have kept demand for ride-hailing companies very low.

ATV

Traffic in San Miguel is slow-moving and courteous, making it generally safe for smaller vehicles like ATVs to circulate along with automobiles. If you want to cruise around town on four wheels, **Bicentenario Todo Terreno** (Jesús 4, tel. 415/152-7342) will rent you an ATV by the hour, by the day, or by the

Motorcycles can be a nice way to get around town and avoid San Miguel's traffic

week. They also run ATV sightseeing tours of the surrounding countryside with trained guides. Although their loud motors can make an unpleasant echo down San Miguel's narrow streets, ATVs are a popular way to move around the city center. They can also be a great way to get up to the botanical gardens or explore more outlying neighborhoods.

Bus

Inexpensive **city buses** crisscross the city of San Miguel, improbably turning around tight corners, barreling down narrow colonial streets, and filling the air with the sweet aroma of exhaust fumes. For around 50 cents, the city buses will get you anywhere you need to go, though finding a direct route can be a bit of a challenge.

Generally speaking, it is much easier to find your way into the downtown district than to get out to a distant neighborhood. Buses head to the *centro histórico* from every corner of the city, and they will almost always have a sign in the front window that reads Centro.

Downtown, a major **bus stop** is located on Insurgentes and Pepe Llanos, across the street from the Oratorio San Felipe Neri. Here, you can catch a bus to the Independencia, San Rafael, and San Antonio neighborhoods, among others. If you are going to the Tianguis Municipal, you can get a bus on Calle Colegio, to the east of the Plaza Cívica. Buses depart from the Mercado San Juan de Dios for the La Cieneguita neighborhood. Most buses have their destination posted in the front window, and in many cases, the driver's assistant will shout out the bus's destination to the crowd at the bus stop. When in doubt, ask the driver where the bus is going.

Vicinity of San Miguel de Allende

ATOTONILCO

The small town of Atotonilco is 13 kilometers (eight miles) from downtown San Miguel de Allende, just off the highway to Dolores Hidalgo. Atotonilco is a small, sleepy, and dusty place, where little seems to have changed in the 400 years since its founding. Despite its wee size (there are fewer than 1,000 residents), Atotonilco has an important place in history and culture. Originally conceived as a religious retreat from San Miguel, it has attracted Catholic pilgrims for centuries. During the War of Independence, Atotonilco was the first place that Father Miguel Hidalgo rode with his cavalry after giving the historic call to war from the steps of the Dolores church. Hidalgo and his men borrowed a banner of La Virgen de Guadalupe from inside Atotonilco's Santuario de Jesús Nazareno, carrying it as a flag into San Miguel de Allende. Thereafter, a banner bearing the image of La Virgen de Guadalupe became a symbol of the independence movement.

Today, Atotonilco is a sleepy town that experiences just a small cultural overflow from San Miguel de Allende. There are always a few tourists wandering around the town's famous church, some resort hotels have opened in the nearby countryside, and a number of American and Canadian expatriates have bought homes here, preferring the rural setting to the bustle of San Miguel.

Sights
★ SANTUARIO DE JESÚS
   NAZARENO DE ATOTONILCO

The main attraction in Atotonilco is the magnificent **Santuario de Jesús Nazareno de Atotonilco** (Plaza Principal s/n, 8am-6pm daily), one of the finest examples of baroque art and architecture in New Spain. Luis Felipe Neri de Alfaro, the same wealthy Catholic priest who oversaw the construction of the Iglesia de Nuestra Señora de la Salud in downtown San Miguel de Allende, originally conceived of the shrine in Atotonilco as a religious sanctuary for the people of San Miguel. The majority of the church was constructed between 1740 and 1776, beginning with the facade, the main nave, and several adjoining chapels. After its construction, the artist Miguel Antonio Martínez de Pocasangre spent more than 30 years painting the walls and ceiling of the nave with detailed religious histories and personages. As you walk through the creaky entryway into the church, the visual stimulation from floor-to-ceiling murals is momentarily overwhelming. One could easily spend hours examining the many unusual figures and strange histories related on the sanctuary's walls.

In 2008, the United Nations named the Santuario de Atotonilco a World Heritage Site, together with San Miguel de Allende's downtown. Thereafter, the church underwent a massive restoration project. Today, it is easier to appreciate the incredible masterwork inside the church, as Martínez's frescoes have been nicely restored. There are occasionally Spanish-speaking tour guides at the church's entryway who can help illuminate the fantastic meaning behind the elaborate painting (you can also hire a tour guide in San Miguel de Allende to accompany you to the site).

In addition to its historical and architectural significance, the Santuario de Atotonilco is an important pilgrimage destination for Mexican Catholics throughout the region. In particular, many come to see and give thanks to the wooden figure of **El Señor de la Columna,** widely revered for its ability to perform miracles. Not far astray from its founder's intentions, the *santuario* also continues to serve as a religious retreat of the most austere variety, with dorm dwellers sleeping on cold stone floors and often subjecting themselves to corporal punishment. On some days, the plaza in front of the church is packed with pilgrims and vendors, some of which sell rough twine ropes for self-flagellation and real crowns of thorns. Other days, the town is as quiet as history, with nothing but the sound of wind whipping dust into the air.

Right next door to the Santuario de Atotonilco, there is a small **gift shop** (Plaza Principal s/n, no phone, 8:30am-6pm Tues.-Sun.) operated by the nuns of Atotonilco, which sells religious souvenirs, rosaries, stuffed animals, and beaded jewelry as well as a few small booklets (in English and Spanish) with information about the church. Within the shop, the nuns also run a small **café,** with an appealing row of cloth-covered wood tables and a simple menu of quesadillas, sandwiches, and instant coffee. The food here is nothing spectacular; for a better (and even less expensive) lunch, try one of the small stands right across the street, where they serve handmade *gorditas* and other quick bites for just a few dollars.

Hot Springs and Swimming

In the region surrounding the town of Atotonilco (about 13 kilometers/eight miles from downtown San Miguel), volcanic activity under the earth has produced copious natural, nonsulfurous hot springs. Many locals believe the water has healing properties, and after a dip you may agree. If you want to try the hot springs, there are a number of low-key places to enjoy this amazing natural resource. No matter where you choose to soak, don't forget to bring a towel! Besides cafés and small snack shops, there are very few services at most of these family-style swimming spots.

★ LA GRUTA

La Gruta (Carretera San Miguel Allende-Dolores Hidalgo, Km 10, tel. 415/185-2162, www.lagruta-spa.com, 7am-5pm Wed.-Sun., US$11, children under 3 free) is the most popular bathing spot near San Miguel. On La Gruta's ample grounds, lush gardens surround several large outdoor pools. From the warmest outdoor pool, you can swim down a covered hallway to a domed cave that is filled with even warmer water, fed directly from the spring. (This is the *gruta,* or grotto, for which the spot is named.) After a dip, you can relax in the pretty gardens, which are shaded by fig trees and dotted with picnic tables and recliners. La Gruta's small café serves breakfast and lunch—fruit, scrambled eggs, *chilaquiles,* quesadillas, guacamole, and the like—plus juice, soft drinks, beer, and margaritas. During the summer months, the pools are filled with splashing children and families; it's much quieter in the winter, when chilly air makes getting in and out of the warm water slightly torturous. For the most Zen experience, get there early in the morning, when the pools are just filling up with water and few people have arrived.

ESCONDIDO PLACE

There are several thermal pools amid the gardens at **Escondido Place** (Carretera San Miguel Allende-Dolores Hidalgo, Km 10, tel. 415/185-2202, http://escondidoplace.com, 8am-5:30pm daily, US$10, children under 3 free), both indoor and enclosed. Every morning, water is pumped into the barrel-shaped caves that cover several adjoining pools, filling them with steam. There are also several outdoor pools, a small snack bar, and a picnic area with outdoor grills. The gardens are extensive, filled with towering trees and a lily-covered pond. Though the gardens are beautiful and the pools are warm, Escondido is less popular with locals than La Gruta, so early birds often have the place to themselves.

TABOADA

A members-only private swim club, **Taboada** (Carretera San Miguel Allende-Dolores Hidalgo, Km 8, tel. 415/152-9250, www.taboada.com.mx) has an almost-Olympic-size swimming pool fed by a natural spring. The slightly warm water makes Taboada's pool a nice place for laps during the cool winter months. There is also a smaller hot bath, fed by the springs, for soaking, and two shallow children's pools, as well as an expansive lawn and playground. Facilities are a bit run-down, but the vintage look is part of the charm. You must be (or go with) a member in order to use Taboada's facilities; friends and family of members can visit for a day rate of about US$15. Just beyond the pool, Taboada also runs a large hotel with a hot-spring-fed pool.

XOTE

Family-friendly **Xote** (Carretera San Miguel Allende-Dolores Hidalgo, Km 5.5, tel. 415/155-8330, www.xoteparqueacuatico. com.mx, 9am-6pm daily, US$8 adults, US$3 children, $4 seniors) is more water park than

Even on a cloudy day, the pools are warm at La Gruta.

relaxation center. This large, hilltop spot caters to children; not only is there a large swimming pool at the park's summit, there are several high-speed waterslides, plus a playground for children. If you arrive during the week, there are often just a few bathers (in the event that you are alone, the park staff will turn on the waterslides so you can use them); summer afternoons can become quite crowded, when Xote also allows families to camp on the grounds. Once children are taller than 1.35 meters (four feet, four inches), they must pay adult prices.

Shopping

Anyone with an interest in Mexico's rich folk art traditions should plan a visit to **Galeria Atotonilco** (tel. 415/185-2225, www.folkart-sanmiguel.com, by appt. only), which sells and exhibits high-quality handcrafts, art, and *artesanía* from across the republic, including ceremonial masks, antiques, handmade textiles and serapes, silver jewelry, Huichol yarn paintings, hand-carved wooden sculptures, detailed ceramic work, and other decorative pieces by a range of traditional Mexican artists, many of whom owner Mayer Schacter has built a relationship with over the years. Housed in an airy, magenta-hued gallery (and adjoined by Schacter's own home, also on the property), the gallery's clean lines and bright colors make a lovely contrast to the works on display. All visits are by appointment, though the gallery occasionally hosts open houses when inaugurating a new exhibition of artwork.

Food and Accommodations

A giant mesquite-fired grill is the centerpiece of the casual country dining room at **La Burger** (Carretera San Miguel Allende-Dolores Hidalgo, Km 7.3, tel. 415/185-2247, www.laburger.mx, 1pm-7pm Sun.-Thurs., 1pm-8pm Fri.-Sat., US$14), located on the highway to Dolores Hidalgo. Simple tables surround this aromatic pyre, which feels worlds away from the bustle of downtown San Miguel. If you can take your eyes off the kitchen's near-constant activity, there are spacious views of the mesquite-studded grasslands behind the restaurant. The namesake hamburgers are made of very finely ground beef and served very rare, with a side of shoestring potatoes. The restaurant also grills generous and juicy steaks, served on simple wooden cutting boards. You need a car to get here, so the crowd is mostly local, though visitors can take a taxi to the restaurant and arrange for a pickup a few hours later.

Just a few minutes' drive from the center of Atotonilco, **Nirvana Restaurant and Retreat** (Camino Antigua Estación FFCC 11, tel. 415/185-2194, www.hotelnirvana.mx, noon-10pm Wed.-Mon.) is a small hotel on a beautiful ranch in the Atotonilco countryside. For those who'd like to spend a day or two in the tranquility of the country, Nirvana has seven guest rooms (US$135-215), some of which are in freestanding cottages surrounded by trees and gardens. If you aren't staying overnight, you can still enjoy the atmosphere over a cocktail and a snack at their on-site restaurant (noon-10pm Mon.-Sat., noon-8pm Sun., US$10), which has particularly nice outdoor seating with lovely views of the gardens. The menu here is eclectic, ranging from sushi plates to steaks, but the real attraction is the scenery. To get there, turn down the dusty Camino Antigua Estación (the first major road after Atotonilco's east entrance) and continue for a few kilometers until you see signs for the ranch.

Many San Miguel families like to have a leisurely Sunday lunch at **Casa de Aves** (Los Fresnos 1, Col. Montecillo de Nieto, tel. 415/155-9610, www.casadeaves.mx, 1pm-7:30pm Fri.-Sun., US$6-9), a hotel and restaurant with an outdoor dining room overlooking a small pond home to a resident flock of ducks. The menu includes good Mexican and international dishes, and while nothing is mind-blowing, eating here is more about the low-key, country atmosphere than the food. Like Nirvana, Casa de Aves is also a hotel, with eight individually decorated guest rooms (US$115-200).

Getting There and Around

Atotonilco is located about 18 kilometers from San Miguel de Allende on the highway to Dolores Hidalgo (Mexico 51); the main turn-off for Atotonilco is near kilometer 62. Look for the large billboard announcing La Gruta hot springs.

City buses run from the Calzada de la Aurora in San Miguel de Allende to Atotonilco every 30 minutes or so during the day. The ride can be bumpy and full, as they stop to pick up riders along the route. An easier alternative for those without a car is to hire a driver or simply flag down a taxi to take you to Atotonilco. If you are visiting the hot springs, any city taxi can drive you out there (about US$10), and they will often be willing to pick you up again at a set time. Most tour guides in San Miguel can also arrange an informative walking tour of Atotonilco and its sanctuary, including transportation to and from the site.

TOP EXPERIENCE

★ CAÑADA DE LA VIRGEN

The area around San Miguel de Allende, Querétaro, and other cities of the Bajío was sparsely populated when the Spanish arrived in the Americas, and for centuries, anthropologists believed that the great sedentary civilizations of Mesoamerica only extended as far north as Tula, in the state of Hidalgo. Abandoned cities have been rediscovered throughout the Bajío region in recent decades, showing evidence of complex civilizations here, most of which developed during the Post-Classic Period of Mesoamerican history.

To get a taste of Mexico's grand pre-Hispanic history, visit the interesting local archaeological site known as the **Cañada de la Virgen** (Carretera Guanajuato-San Miguel s/n, Carretera Federal 51, Km 10+800, 10am-6pm Tues.-Sat., US$2 adults, US$1 seniors and children), about 30-40 minutes southeast of San Miguel de Allende. Opened to the public in 2011 after a preliminary excavation and study, the ruins of this pre-Columbian city are believed to be tied to the Panteca people of the greater Toltec empire, who once lived along the floodplain of the Laja River. Occupied around AD 540-1000, the site contains five groups of monuments, including a 15-meter temple-pyramid and a large sunken plaza. Here, as in many Mesoamerican cities, the main architectural structures were constructed to align with

The Cañada de la Virgen archaeological site was opened to the public in 2011.

the sun's path. However, unlike in cities like Teotihuacán, Xochicalco, and Palenque, the sun rises in front of the main temple at the Cañada de la Virgen, rather than behind it. Archaeological study of the site is ongoing, and plans for more extensive excavation of the area are under way.

The Cañada de la Virgen is operated by the Instituto Nacional de Antropología e Historia (INAH), Mexico's bureau of history and anthropology, and the site itself is located on federally protected land. However, that land is encircled by a large private ranch owned by a German-American family that has long been reluctant to allow access to the ruins. As a result of the landowners' restrictions, there aren't any food stalls, shops, or other businesses operating around the ruins, as you'll see at many other of archaeological sites in Mexico. In addition, visitors must comply with some unusual rules. Notably, visitors to the site are shuttled by van from the main parking lot to the entrance to the ruins. From there, visitors must walk about a kilometer uphill to the ruin site. Note that backpacks are not permitted at the site, and neither is food. Water, good walking shoes, and sunscreen are necessities.

If arriving at the site by car, park at the main entrance and buy a ticket in the office (US$2, including shuttle and guide). All visitors to the Cañada de la Virgen must be accompanied by a guide licensed by the state of Guanajuato. The service is included in the cost of a ticket, though note that tours are only given in Spanish. Tours to the site depart hourly, from 10am to 4pm. On weekends or holidays, tour groups may fill up (the number of people allowed at the ruins is limited), in which case, you could be required to wait up to an hour for the next tour.

For excellent, authoritative English-language tours of the site, contact **Albert Coffee** (tel. 415/102-5583, U.S. tel. 225/963-0870, www.albertcoffeetours.com, US$50), a professional anthropologist and Guanajuato-state-certified tour guide who worked on the ruins' excavation. Coffee is passionate and knowledgeable about Mesoamerican cultures and provides a rich and detailed explanation of the different structures at the site, as well as an introduction to local ecology, Mesoamerican history, and local customs. Generally departing in the morning (though he may offer additional afternoon tours during the high season), tours include transportation to and from downtown San Miguel.

Getting There and Around

The Cañada de la Virgen is just over 24 kilometers (15 miles) from San Miguel de Allende, just past the Presa Ignacio Allende reservoir on Federal Highway 51. For visitors, there is a parking lot just off the highway to Guanajuato; from there, a van run by the site will take you from the visitors center to the archaeological site.

MINERAL DE POZOS

It seems that time swept right past Mineral de Pozos, a chilly, half-abandoned city perched on a sloping hillside in the high desert chaparral. A place of whispers and legends, this crumbling little pueblo was a prosperous city during the 19th century, home to an estimated 70,000 people and several prolific mineral mines. Slowly, the town's resources were depleted, the mines flooded, and the population dwindled. Without industry or stewards, Pozos was left to the elements.

Today, Pozos exudes the eerie, half-ruined romance of a ghost town, filled with crumbling adobe walls and muddy roads where tiny cacti grow freely in the rocky nooks and crannies. It is surprisingly beautiful, with some fascinating ruins from the former mining camps just outside the city's small but charming *centro*. A wonderful place to visit, the town has made a modest resurgence over the past few decades. Not far from the tourist capital of San Miguel de Allende, travelers have begun to take notice of this unusual destination, and the romance of a desert ghost town has inevitably convinced some artists and expatriates to settle down there permanently. Around downtown Pozos, there is now a small selection of restaurants, hotels, and shops, some with a rather sophisticated feeling. In fact, many speculate that Pozos will become the next San Miguel de Allende (Pozos residents think otherwise, though). Whatever the future holds for Pozos, it is a wonderful place to spend a day, offering the perfect blend of off-the-beaten-track charm and contemporary panache.

While Pozos is definitely one of the most interesting places to visit near San Miguel de Allende, visitors should keep in mind that it is a very small town and a relatively quiet place. On weekdays, most shops and galleries are shuttered, and the town's few sights, though fascinating, are also limited. If you plan to spend more than a day in Pozos, bring a book, a camera, or some other peaceful form of self-entertainment. While the tranquility in Pozos is undeniably inspiring, the town isn't as tourist-ready as San Miguel. Romantic self-starters will be happiest here.

Iglesia San Pedro

History

The Spanish arrived in Pozos in the mid-16th century, as they expanded their settlements northward to accommodate the new silver industry in Zacatecas. Located near the Camino Real de Tierra Adentro silver route, the first settlement in Pozos was established as a protective fort for merchants traveling by donkey train to the capital. Not long after the settlement was founded, Jesuit missionaries arrived and discovered that the indigenous people of the region had been mining minerals from a large open pit. With this discovery, the Jesuits immediately began metal extraction in the same pit mine, which is known today as Santa Brígida. When the Jesuits were expelled from Mexico in 1767, the mining industry in Pozos ceased.

Toward the end of the 19th century, the mines in Pozos were reopened under new direction. Metal deposits were discovered near the city's western edge, and the industry began to boom. By the end of the century, there were more than 300 active mines in Pozos. The president of Mexico renamed the city after himself, christening it Ciudad Porfirio Díaz. The ruins of this era can be witnessed just outside Pozos, in the mining camps and ex-hacienda Cinco Señores.

When the Mexican Revolution broke out in 1910, mining operations in Pozos abruptly ceased. Though their closure was meant to be temporary, the mines flooded and the global price of silver dropped significantly, making it impossible for them to reopen when the revolution ended. The final mine closed in 1927. Without income from the silver industry to support its population, Pozos was quickly abandoned. By the mid-20th century, only a couple hundred residents remained in town.

For many years, Pozos was a ghost town, supporting a teeny population in crumbling old buildings. Still, its beauty and historical significance remained intact. In 1982, the president of Mexico named Pozos a National Historic Monument Zone. Today, it has a modest population of several thousand residents and a burgeoning tourist industry.

Sights

For a taste of Old Mexico, the entire city of Pozos is a sight in itself. Here, the windswept dirt roads are lined with crumbling adobe houses, stray dogs mill through the sleepy central plaza, and the desert landscape is stark and beautiful. The mines, both sorrowful and majestic, are one of the most interesting places to visit in the Bajío region.

PLAZA PRINCIPAL

It is easy to imagine tumbleweeds rolling through the dusty *plaza principal* in Pozos, a shady gathering place in the center of town. Catering to very opposite needs, this lovely little square is equipped with a cantina on one corner and a church on the other. The **Iglesia San Pedro** and its massive dome preside over the square, while a little string of galleries and hotels occupies the east side. On the weekends, there are many more tourists in town, and vendors arrive in the square to sell *pan dulce* (sweet bread), roasted corn, *aguas frescas,* and other small snacks. Look for the unusual bright pink beverage *pulque de tuna* (a fermented prickly pear beverage) during the late summer or early fall.

TEMPLO DEL NUESTRO SEÑOR DE LOS TRABAJOS

Just east of the main plaza, the large **Templo del Nuestro Señor de los Trabajos** stands on the hillside. Most notable for its giant half dome, this church appears to be a ruin. In fact, it is simply unfinished. The wealthy patron of this church was struck by the ruin of the silver trade and never completed construction.

SANTA BRÍGIDA MINE

The former mining camps in Pozos, now magnificent and mysterious ruins, are one of the most interesting sights in the Bajío. They are also a good exercise for the imagination as you wonder about the maze of unmarked structures, half-reclaimed by the desert wilderness. Out in Pozos, there are no informational placards posted at historic sites, no tourist office to feed your need for information, and no books or brochures published about the city's great silver boom and bust.

Just outside the city center, **Santa Brígida** was the very first mine in Pozos. Uniquely in the region, Santa Brígida was actually mined by indigenous people before it came under Spanish control. As you approach the mine, you can see three large smokestacks that were the mine's smelting ovens. If you've come without a guide, park near the large red-and-white building, which was the mine's former management offices (it isn't open to the public). From there, you can easily wander into the mining camp.

Santa Brígida was a pit mine, so it doesn't have a traditional mine shaft. Instead, a large crevice runs through the earth, bordered on the north side by the beautiful arched ovens used for mercury amalgamation, which extracts metals from the rock. The rubble surrounding the mines still gleams with mineral-rich rocks. Without a guide, you should watch your step everywhere around Pozos, and especially here. The mouth of the mine is unmarked and gravelly, plunging deep into the earth. In addition to the mine, there are several deep wells around the mining camp, with no signs to indicate their existence. Keep a close eye on dogs and children!

To reach the Santa Brígida Mine, follow the highway through town north toward San Luis de la Paz. Just as the pavement begins, take a right on a large, unmarked dirt road. At the first major fork, go left (or north) toward the mine. After a kilometer or so, you will see the smokestacks in the distance. Unfortunately, there is no signage for Santa Brígida; however, you can get detailed instructions from the locals in town.

CINCO SEÑORES MINE

Though the city was long home to a mining industry, Pozos reached its height during the Porfiriato era of the late 19th century. The incredible ex-hacienda **Cinco Señores** offers a fascinating glimpse into the splendor of Pozos's former wealth and prestige. This expansive mining camp and its associated buildings covered a complete hillside on the southwest of the city; today, you can wander among roofless buildings, crumbling porticoes from 19th-century offices, huge stone tubs filled with moss-rich water, and the dark mouths of numerous abandoned mine shafts. Within the site, there are several of the wells, or *pozos,* for which the city is famous. They are marked with barbed wire and, if you dare to lean over the edge, dizzyingly deep and cavernous. Likewise, there are several mine shafts littered throughout the property. Use care when walking near the edge of these, as the ground can be uneven, and some shafts are only minimally marked.

Just as spectacular as the ruins, the hills around the ex-hacienda afford a lovely view of the surrounding valley and a rather stunning collection of wild plants, cactus, and succulents, which are often occupied by birds, butterflies, and other insects.

To reach Cinco Señores, head west up Manuel Doblado from the main square. Continue one block past the Plaza Zaragosa (only about three large blocks from the square) and then veer left on a dirt road. You will pass a shop, Venado Azul. Continue along the dirt road for a few kilometers, passing tiny homes and agave farms, until you see the mining camps on the hillside. There is no admission, though often there are local people in front of the site selling rocks and minerals from Pozos.

ESCUELA MODELO
A former textile factory was gorgeously restored and reopened in 2017 as the **Escuela Modelo** (Calle Centenario 10, tel. 442/348-1333 http://escuelamodelo.mx, 11am-6pm Sat.-Sun.), a multidisciplinary arts academy that aims to become the largest art school in the Americas. In addition to offering creative workshops for children in the Pozos community, the school offers a wide range of workshops and classes on topics as diverse as museography, design, jewelry-making, and photography, which are open to the public.

The space itself is gorgeous and includes an on-site museum. Note that it is generally only open for visitors on weekends, though classes may take place during the week.

Food and Accommodations
Right on the main square, **Hotel Casa Mexicana** (Jardín Principal 2, tel. 442/293-0014, http://casamexicanahotel.com, US$60-80) is precisely the type of place you'd like to rest your head during a romantic weekend in Pozos. The very first guesthouse in town, this establishment has a distinctly Mexican ambience; rooms with clay floors, vaulted ceilings, and whitewashed walls surround a sunny courtyard. Each has been lovingly decorated with special details, like antique furniture, old chandeliers, original artwork, and traditional crafts. Loft beds and sitting areas in the larger suites can be nice for reading and relaxing when you've finished visiting the limited attractions in surrounding Pozos.

Although the **Posada de las Minas** (Manuel Doblado 1, tel. 442/293-0213, www.posadadelasminas.com, US$60-120) is the largest establishment in Pozos, there are only eight rooms in this attractive boutique hotel. Housed in a restored 19th-century mansion, the guest rooms are comfortable and nicely decorated with a Mexican flair, with cute tiled bathrooms with tubs, oversize wooden furniture, and handwoven comforters on the beds. Since the hotel is situated on a small hill a block above the city center, some rooms have nice views of Pozos; the largest has a small balcony and chairs. Downstairs, the in-house restaurant (8:30am-10pm daily, US$10) is set in a wildly pleasant courtyard. Mexican specialties like guacamole, enchiladas, and stuffed peppers are the best dishes here (and are appropriately accompanied by a nice list of tequilas by the glass), though they also serve a range of sandwiches, burgers, fish, and pastas. The service is attentive, if a bit slow, and the atmosphere is casually luxurious. Thanks to the restaurant's great prices and friendly, family-style atmosphere, it is always busy on the weekends with local tourists and families.

Services

Mineral de Pozos has a nice buzz on the weekends, when a handful of tour groups and families arrive from Querétaro or San Miguel de Allende. Although the atmosphere can feel rather posh for a ghost town, Pozos offers very little to the visitor in terms of services. There are **no banks or ATMs** in town, so you must bring cash with you. It has no tourist office, no local publications, and no taxis. Sometimes, even phone service and electricity can be unexpectedly cut off, so be prepared for anything when visiting Pozos.

Getting There and Around

The best way to get to Mineral de Pozos is in a car. Although there is occasional bus service to and from the town, you will not be able to visit the town's fascinating mines without a set of wheels. Driving to Pozos from San Miguel de Allende or Querétaro is rather easy; it takes about 45 minutes to an hour from either city. Pozos is about four hours north of Mexico City.

To get to Pozos from San Miguel de Allende, follow the Salida a Querétaro out of the city. Arriving at the traffic circle, head east, following the signs toward Doctor Mora and Los Rodríguez. Follow this two-lane highway through Los Rodríguez (watch out for speed bumps!), crossing over Highway 57 on an overpass. About eight kilometers (five miles) from the highway, you will reach an intersection indicating the turnoff for Pozos and San Luis de la Paz; turn north toward these cities. About 16 kilometers (10 miles) down the road, the highway turns to dirt, and you have arrived in Pozos.

From Querétaro or Mexico City, take Highway 57 north toward San Luis Potosí. About 80 kilometers (50 miles) north of Querétaro, exit toward Doctor Mora and head east. About eight kilometers (five miles) later, you will reach an intersection; turn north toward San Luis de la Paz and travel about 16 kilometers (10 miles) to reach Pozos.

DOLORES HIDALGO

The small city of Dolores Hidalgo is about 32 kilometers (20 miles) northeast of San Miguel de Allende and about 48 kilometers (30 miles) southeast of Guanajuato. The city is well known for its lovely ceramic artisan work as well as for its important role during the Mexican War of Independence. There are a number of small but interesting sights in the city's downtown district as well as good shopping for pottery and hand-painted ceramic tiles. If rather less spectacular than its neighbors, San Miguel de Allende and Guanajuato, Dolores has nonetheless won some loyal fans with its low-key and traditionally Mexican atmosphere.

Most of the activity in Dolores Hidalgo is concentrated in the few blocks around the city center. The exceptions are the ceramics workshops along the highways near town, which also draw their share of visitors. If you come to Dolores by bus, the terminal is conveniently located just a few blocks from the city's central square. From there, almost everything is accessible on foot.

History

An early settlement in the Bajío region, the town of Cocomacán (today, Dolores Hidalgo) was founded in the 1540s. Cocomacán, meaning "place where they hunt herons" in Otomí, was part of a large ranch, Hacienda de la Erre, which originally fell under the jurisdiction of San Miguel el Grande. In 1710, La Erre was incorporated into the new parish of Nuestra Señora de los Dolores (Our Lady of Sorrows). The first stone was laid for Dolores's parish church on February 2, 1712.

A small agricultural outpost in the state of Guanajuato, Dolores would not be well known if it weren't for its native son, Miguel Hidalgo, and his role in the Mexican War of Independence. The parish priest of Dolores, Miguel Hidalgo was an early conspirator

Dolores Hidalgo

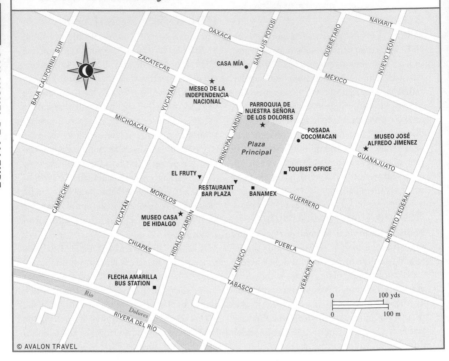

© AVALON TRAVEL

against Spanish rule. He attended the famous meetings in Querétaro and San Miguel de Allende, hosted by wealthy criollo families who wished to free Mexico from the tightening grip of the Spanish crown. Hidalgo was an important element to the conspiracy, as he was extremely popular with the large mestizo and indigenous population that lived in and around Dolores.

In 1810, Spanish royalists uncovered the criollo plot against the crown. To avoid arrest, the Mexican conspirators quickly jumped to action, and Miguel Hidalgo was named general of the Mexican army. Though he was only a parish priest with no formal experience in war, Hidalgo oversaw a force that included numerous high-ranking Queen's Dragoon Army officers, like Ignacio Allende. To rally soldiers to the cause, Hidalgo arrived on the steps of the Dolores parish church on September 16, 1810, where he issued his famous cry, *"¡Viva México!"* From there, he rode with his cavalry to San Miguel de Allende, which became the first town to fall (though peacefully) in the independence movement. Thereafter, the War of Independence was arduous and protracted. Hidalgo himself was captured and executed in July 1811. The Mexican army finally took the city of Dolores on September 10, 1811, almost a full year after Hidalgo issued the call to arms.

After the war ended, the city was renamed Dolores Hidalgo on May 21, 1824. Regarded as the birthplace of an independent Mexico, Dolores Hidalgo continues to be an important site in the country's history. Many of Mexico's important leaders have passed through here during their tenure, and each Mexican president comes to celebrate at least one independence day in town. The *grito* (the nickname for the annual reenactment of Hidalgo's cry on Día de la Independencia of each year, delivered by the town's mayor) in Dolores always draws big crowds.

Sights

PLAZA PRINCIPAL

Like many cities, the downtown district in Dolores Hidalgo is organized around a *plaza principal* (central square). The plaza is at the heart of the city's busiest commercial zone, and it is a popular spot with local families. In the very center of the plaza, there is a bronze statue of the famous pastor Miguel Hidalgo, originally commissioned by President Benito Juárez. On the west side, the plaza is bordered by the **Casa de Visitas** (Plaza Principal 25), an 18th-century mansion. During the War of Independence, Dolores's Spanish governor and his wife were held in the Casa de Visitas as prisoners of the rebel army.

PARROQUIA DE NUESTRA SEÑORA DE LOS DOLORES

One of the most famous churches in all of Mexico, the **Parroquia de Nuestra Señora de los Dolores** (Parish Church of Our Lady of Sorrows, Plaza Principal s/n, generally 8am-8pm daily) is the jewel of Dolores Hidalgo's central square. This impressive sandstone church has an elaborate churrigueresque facade, topped by two soaring bell towers. Inside, wood floors and rows of creaky wood pews stand before a neoclassical altar. In the left transept, there is an ornate, hand-carved baroque altar washed in gold leaf. Even more impressive is the walnut altar to the right, which has been carefully carved in wood but left without gold leaf or paint. Not only is the untreated wood especially beautiful, it really illustrates the incredible craftsmanship behind many of Mexico's baroque altarpieces. On your way out, note the large organ in the balcony over the entryway.

MUSEO CASA DE HIDALGO

Just a block from the central square, the **Museo Histórico Casa de Hidalgo** (Morelos 1, tel. 418/182-0171, www.inah.gob.mx, 9am-5:45pm Tues.-Sun., US$2.50), also known as the Casa de Diezmo, is the former home of Mexico's most famous pastor, Miguel Hidalgo. This large colonial building has been outfitted with period furnishings

the Parroquia de Nuestra Señora de los Dolores

and didactic texts about the life of the parish priest. The kitchen is particularly interesting. There is also a small collection of artifacts from the War of Independence, including an antique banner with the image of the Virgen de Guadalupe—Father Hidalgo's improvised flag for the Mexican army. Don't bother paying the extra camera fee; most of the scenery is behind glass.

MUSEO DE LA INDEPENDENCIA NACIONAL

The sprawling **Museo de la Independencia Nacional** (National Independence Museum, Zacatecas 6, tel. 418/182-8277, 9am-4:45pm Mon.-Fri., 9am-3pm Sun., US$1) is in the city's former jailhouse. From this very building, Miguel Hidalgo freed the city's prisoners before issuing his famous *grito,* or call for independence, from the steps of the parish church. Today, the former jail is filled with dioramas and colorful oil paintings depicting scenes from the War of Independence, accompanied by long didactic texts, principally in Spanish. There are also a few artifacts from the era, including old coins and weapons used in the rebellion, as well as facsimiles of famous documents signed by Miguel Hidalgo. This spacious and rather unusual museum drags on a bit too long, though it's not an unworthy pit stop if you are in town.

MUSEO JOSÉ ALFREDO JIMÉNEZ

The great *ranchera* singer and songwriter José Alfredo Jiménez was born to a middle-class family in Dolores Hidalgo. Located in the composer's childhood home, the charming **Museo José Alfredo Jiménez** (Guanajuato 13, tel. 418/154-4070, http://museojosealfredojimenez.com.mx, 10am-5pm Sun.-Thurs. 10am-6pm Fri.-Sat.., US$3) offers a nostalgic look into the life of the legend. Through photographs, quotes, and artifacts, the museum chronicles the life of this gentleman singer, showing his humble beginnings as a musician in Mexico City and highlighting his notable influence on traditional *ranchera* music. Alfredo's old family house provides a nice backdrop to the singer's life story. In the back, the family's original blue-and-white tiled kitchen is still intact. Just beside the kitchen, the museum operates a small café where you can soak up the ambience with a coffee and snack. For fans of this celebrated composer, the Museo José Alfredo Jiménez is a must-see; however, even those who aren't familiar with Jiménez's music may still get a charge out of the exhibits about his life, which include artifacts like his beautiful old *charro* suits with silver buttons, old letters and telegrams, and photographs from the 1950s golden era of Mexican cinema.

TOMB OF JOSÉ ALFREDO JIMÉNEZ

José Alfredo Jiménez's original **tombstone** was just a simple granite block decorated with a quotation from one of his most famous songs, "Caminos de Guanajuato." It read, *La vida no vale nada* ("Life is worth nothing"). Today, the simple headstone that once marked his resting place has been replaced by a giant concrete sombrero and serape, decorated with multicolored ceramic tiles from Dolores. Visitors can walk inside the serape to leave flowers at the grave of the singer. Beloved throughout the country, José Alfredo's unique tomb receives its fair share of visitors each year.

Shopping

After the conquest, the Spanish introduced tin glazing to indigenous artisans, who were already skilled potters. The result was a new and wholly Mexican craft tradition, based on both European and American craft. While the state of Puebla is home to the oldest Talavera workshops in Mexico, the town of Dolores began its line of ceramics a bit later, under the direction of famous pastor Miguel Hidalgo. Generally speaking, the painting on Dolores's ceramics is freer and less detailed than the work produced in Puebla. As a result, it usually is far less expensive as well. While not as painstakingly created, the saturated colors and whimsical designs from Dolores can be incredibly sophisticated and also very charming. Today,

José Alfredo Jiménez

José Alfredo Jiménez was born in 1926 to a middle-class family in the small town of Dolores Hidalgo. With no formal training as a musician—or even the ability to play an instrument—Jiménez became one the most prolific and beloved songwriters in Mexican history.

Jiménez began composing songs during his childhood in Dolores. After the death of his father, his family relocated to Mexico City. As a young man, he wrote and performed throughout the capital, singing on the radio with the group Los Rebeldes in 1948. He rose to prominence with the breakthrough hit "Yo" two years later. Thereafter, he continued to pen one hit song after another. As his fame grew, he appeared in cinema, radio, and television, frequently traveling overseas to perform.

Jiménez wrote music principally within the traditional Mexican genre *ranchera*, and his melodic songs recall a romantic Mexico of cantinas, tequila, serenades, small towns, and country life. Jiménez wrote hundreds of songs during his lifetime, which were recorded by some of the biggest names in Mexican music, such as Pedro Infante, Lola Beltran, Javier Solís, and Lucha Villa. Jiménez also performed his own songs, often dressed in a *charro* suit and serape. Visitors to the Bajío may be particularly interested in Jiménez's wonderful tribute to his home state, the song "Caminos de Guanajuato." In this lovely and well-known ballad, Jiménez immortalizes the Bajío cities of León, Salamanca, and Santa Rosa as well as his beloved home town of Dolores Hidalgo.

Like many of Mexico's golden age stars, Jiménez died at an early age, at just 47. Today, José Alfredo Jiménez's body is buried in the cemetery of Dolores Hidalgo, his grave lovingly adorned with a giant concrete sombrero and tiled serape.

Dolores is a major exporter of ceramic tile and craft throughout the world.

For many tourists, the main reason to visit Dolores is to shop for low-cost and high-quality Talavera ceramics. It is especially useful to visit if you plan to buy in bulk; for instance, if you are looking for a complete dinner set or tiles for the bathroom, you'll find unbeatable deals here. There are inexpensive factory stores throughout Dolores Hidalgo; although many produce the same products (principally flatware, flowerpots, and tiles), each has its own creative flair. Check out a few different shops to find your favorite. Most will gladly help with shipping overseas.

Stocking a selection of anything and everything that can be created in ceramic, **JMB** (Puebla 60, tel. 418/182-0749, www.dtalavera.com, 10am-6pm daily) is a huge ceramics shop near the city center. Don't be fooled by the small storefront; this cavernous factory store contains room after room of hand-painted ceramic goods. The staff will turn on the lights to each showroom as you make your way down the narrow hallways. Anything you've ever dreamed of owning in brightly colored Talavera can be found here, including hand-painted flowerpots, liquid soap dispensers, light-switch adornments, platters, side plates, demitasses, toothbrush holders, segmented salsa dishes, and more. There is also a pretty line of lead-free products.

Just across the street from JMB, **Azulejos y Loza Talavera Vázquez** (Puebla 56 and 58, tel. 418/182-2914, 9:30am-7pm daily) is easily recognizable, thanks to its blue-and-white tile facade. Inside, this spacious factory store stocks an extensive selection of beautifully painted ceramic work. You'll find lots of oversize products, like large ceramic urns and flowerpots, as well as decorative wall pieces and tile sets. Vázquez also stocks a really lovely selection of delicately painted platters, dishes, and other housewares. The quality of the work is high, and prices are excellent.

On the highway between San Miguel de Allende and Dolores Hidalgo, several large factory stores offer a wonderful range of Talavera at surprisingly low prices. Among the most popular, **Arte San Gabriel** (Carretera

Avocado Ice Cream

Dolores Hidalgo is famous for its unusual ice cream flavors.

A country famous for its warm and sunny weather, Mexico has also perfected the art of creating delicious cold sweets. *Raspados* (shaved ice), ice cream, and popsicles are all popular throughout the country. First-time visitors to Mexico should try a cup or cone of *nieve*, a refreshing and icier version of ice cream sold in plazas, markets, and street corners.

In literal translation, the word *nieve* means snow. Most resembling ice milk or sorbet, *nieve* is not as creamy as ice cream, though some flavors are made with milk while others are water-based. Throughout Mexico, *nieves* are still a cottage industry, made by hand with family recipes and scooped on street corners from metal containers lodged in ice. These highly flavorful ices are almost always made with fresh ingredients (you may even find pieces of fruit) in a range of flavors, from vanilla and walnut to mango and peppermint.

Though *nieve* is popular (and delicious) throughout the Bajío, **Dolores Hidalgo** has developed a particular culture with regard to creating and scooping flavors. In Dolores, massive *nieve* vendors occupy the four corners of the main plaza, each offering an extensive menu of flavors. Of course, you can find classics, like chocolate or vanilla; however, Dolores vendors head toward the wacky, with ice cream flavors like shrimp, tequila, cheese, beer, pork rind, and avocado. You can ask to sample a flavor before taking the plunge or take your chances; most flavors, even the most bizarre, are surprisingly sweet and appealing.

Just as fun for the foreign palate, Dolores *nieves* always include more unusual tropical fruits like *tuna* (prickly pear), *guayaba* (guava), *zapote* (sapodilla), *guanabana* (soursop), and other delicious exotics. If you really want to taste a range of sweets, keep an eye out: Dolores has hosted several ice cream festivals and flavor competitions in the past.

San Miguel Allende-Dolores Hidalgo, Km 14, tel. 418/185-5037, www.artesangabriel.com.mx, 10am-6pm Mon.-Sat., 10am-5pm Sun.) has been in business since 1973. This vast store sells a large selection of flatware and dinner sets as well as larger pieces, like urns, flowerpots, and statues. They are also a major ceramics exporter.

Food

Quick and tasty snack food abounds in Dolores Hidalgo's central plaza. Around the square, there are numerous informal carts selling sliced fruit, roasted corn, and, most famously, delicious *nieves* (ice cream). In fact, Dolores has made a bit of a reputation for itself with its diverse selection of *nieves* in flavors that range from exotic (*guanabana*) to downright bizarre (shrimp). Gregarious ice cream vendors will allow you to sample a few flavors, if you are curious about the taste of seafood ice cream. Great for the indecisive, cones or cups can come with two (or three) flavors.

For a more formal meal, there are several places to eat around Dolores's central plaza. Popular with locals, **Restaurant Bar Plaza** (Plaza Principal 17B, tel. 418/182-0259, 8am-10pm Mon.-Sat., 9am-10pm Sun., US$10) is a nice place to relax over a leisurely if somewhat unspectacular lunch. On the south side of the central plaza, this restaurant's big open windows give you a nice view of the action in the center of town. Grilled meats and creamy pastas dominate the menu, and there is a full bar. The food and service can feel a bit old-fashioned in this longtime Dolores establishment.

The tree-shaded patio at lovely little Mexican spot **El Fruty** (Hidalgo 2, tel. 418/182-3679, 8:30am-10:30pm Mon.-Fri., 9am-10:30pm Sat.-Sun.), which is half a block from Dolores's main square, is a perfect place for breakfast, with a menu that covers traditional dishes like huevos rancheros, as well as fruit-topped house-made organic yogurt and espresso drinks. Come in the afternoon for *sopes* (round corn cakes topped with beans and shredded meat) and an artisanal beer, all served by efficient and friendly waiters. The prices are low, and there is always a crowd of locals dining here, giving the spot a lively ambience.

A couple blocks from the main square, the small and unassuming **Cafeteria Damonica** (Nayarit 67, tel. 418/182-4587, 10:30am-10:30pm Wed.-Sun., US$8-10) has become something of a sleeper hit for its generously served and wonderfully prepared

Italian cuisine. Dishes like pasta with clams and shrimp, meat ravioli, carbonara, homemade focaccia, and lasagna are made with skill, in house, by the chef and her family and can be followed up with a homemade dessert and espresso. This little place has gained enough of a loyal following that San Miguel locals make the trip to Dolores for lunch, and it is worth seeking out on a day trip to the city.

Just outside the city center, famously tasty **Carnitas Vicente** (Mariano Balleza 61, no phone, 8am-4pm daily, US$3-5) is an inexpensive and casual place for a filling *almuerzo* or lunch. Specializing in carnitas, this excellent little eatery serves delicious braised pork, either by the kilo or wrapped in individual tacos. Their *maciza* is richly flavored yet not greasy, well complemented by the *pico de gallo* and other salsas laid out on the tables, and you can order it in tacos, *tortas,* or *gorditas.* Get food to go or eat in the ultracasual, colorful dining room.

Wineries

There are a number of burgeoning wineries operating in the Bajío region, many on former ranches near Dolores Hidalgo. If you'd like to taste some local wine, one beautiful spot creating very nice wines is **La Santísima Trinidad** (Carretera San Miguel Allende-Dolores Hidalgo, Km 25, cell tel. 473/134-1086, www.lasantisimatrinidad.com.mx, by appointment only, tasting and tours by reservation at 11am, 1pm, and 3pm Wed.-Mon., US$40) in the countryside right outside Dolores Hidalgo. It's worth visiting for the beautiful Napa-meets-Mexico-style grounds, which include a pond, lavender fields, and many palms and poplars. Reserve ahead for a wine tasting and tour; they are often booked solid on the weekends.

One of the best-known wineries operating near Dolores Hidalgo, **Cuna de Tierra** (Dolores Hidalgo-San Luis de la Paz, Km 11, Rancho el Rosillo, tel. 415/152-6060, http://cunadetierra.com.mx, 10am-8pm

Tues.-Sat., tasting with tour by appointment only, US$60) produces both red and white wines, some of which have won awards for their quality. Though open to the public for less than a decade, it is one of the oldest wineries in the region. They offer guided tours and wine tastings, accompanied by a sampler platter of products grown on the ranch, by appointment, Tuesday through Sunday, at 11am, 1pm, and 3pm. Their bottles are sold in quite a few San Miguel de Allende establishments.

Accommodations

Most people don't choose to spend a night in Dolores Hidalgo, and because the town is so close to the numerous hotels in San Miguel de Allende and Guanajuato, they really don't need to. However, those who'd like to spend the evening in Dolores can choose between plenty of inexpensive options in the downtown district. Luxury hasn't quite hit Dolores Hidalgo yet, but many Dolores hotels are a good bargain for the price, clean, and well attended.

Dolores Hidalgo's reputation as an inexpensive city to visit is amply confirmed at **Casa Mia** (San Luis Potosí 9B, tel. 418/182-2560, www.hotelcasamia.com.mx, US$26-30). Just around the corner from the central square, rooms at this super-friendly inn are cozily decorated with printed bedspreads, curtained windows, and terra-cotta tile floors and equipped with a small private bath decorated with ceramic tile. Decor is cute and comfortable enough to make this hotel feel like a serious bargain. Rooms upstairs surrounding the hotel's back patio are the nicest, getting more natural light than those downstairs. All rooms include television and parking.

Right on the main plaza, **Posada Cocomacan** (Plaza Principal 4, tel. 418/182-6086, www.posadacocomacan.com.mx, US$35) is one of Dolores's larger hotels. Bedrooms are decidedly small and simple—even a bit stuffy. However, staying right on a town's main square is a pleasure that doesn't usually come at such a reasonable price. Most rooms surround a central courtyard and restaurant; the nicest are on the second floor and have windows that overlook the Dolores parish. There is a restaurant in the lobby, which caters to the hotel's largely national clientele as well as to tourists passing through Dolores.

Services

Dolores Hidalgo's friendly **Oficina de Turismo** (Tourist Office, Callejón Casiano Éxiga s/n, tel. 418/182-1164, www.doloreshidalgo.gob.mx, 10am-5pm Mon.-Fri.) is just beside the *parroquia* on the *plaza principal*. They can provide a sightseeing map of the downtown district as well as tips on what to see and do in Dolores. When the tourist office is closed on the weekends, you can pick up a map and other tourist information from a kiosk in the Jardín Principal.

There are several banks and ATMs in Dolores Hidalgo's main plaza. There is a **Citibanamex** (Plaza Principal 15, toll-free Mex. tel. 800/021-2345, 9am-4pm Mon.-Fri.) branch on the plaza's south side as well as a 24-hour ATM on the west side of the square. There is also an **HSBC** (Plaza Principal 23, tel. 418/182-1530, 9am-5pm Mon.-Fri.) on the plaza.

In a medical emergency, you can call the **Cruz Roja** (Red Cross, Calzada de los Héroes 179, tel. 418/182-0000) day or night. **Seguridad Pública** (México 2, tel. 418/182-0021 or 911) is also available to respond to emergencies.

Getting There and Around

The drive to Dolores Hidalgo from San Miguel de Allende is fairly quick and easy. A benefit to driving is that you can stop in some of the ceramics factory stores on the way. To get to Dolores, take Highway 110 from San Miguel for about 48 kilometers (30 miles), then follow the Centro signs for Dolores Hidalgo's downtown. After passing through Dolores, you can continue on Highway 110 to Guanajuato. From here, the highway becomes incredibly scenic, climbing into the Sierra de Guanajuato and passing through the small town of Santa Rosa.

Though most of Dolores's attractions are easy to access on foot, there are inexpensive taxis throughout Dolores Hidalgo's city center. You can also call **Radio Taxi** (tel. 418/120-0069).

Operated by **Flecha Amarilla** (tel. 415/152-0084, toll-free Mex. tel. 800/375-7587), second-class buses depart for Dolores Hidalgo from the main bus terminal in San Miguel de Allende every 30 minutes; the ride takes 30-45 minutes. Flecha Amarilla also operates second-class buses every 20 minutes between Guanajuato and Dolores Hidalgo. If you are traveling to Dolores from Guanajuato, you can pick up the bus at the terminal or on the highway passing through La Valenciana. There is no first-class bus service between Dolores Hidalgo and San Miguel de Allende or Guanajuato.

Guanajuato

As if plucked from the pages of a fairy tale, Guanajuato is almost mythical in its beauty.

From above the classical theaters and baroque churches crammed within the labyrinthine alleyways of the city center, haphazard stacks of sherbet-colored houses rise along the hillsides in perfect disorganization. Even higher above, rocky peaks rise over the valley floor, while the clear mountain sky complements the scene like a crystal-blue canopy.

Guanajuato is a city to stroll in, to observe from courtyard cafés or from a shady bench in the Jardín de la Unión. The city is best explored on foot; it is a pleasure to get lost in the twisted maze of picturesque streets, where people walk uninhibited by traffic—in a pedestrian-friendly innovation, many roads in the *centro histórico* occupy a circuit of tunnels below the ground. Even with fewer automobiles, the streets of Guanajuato are surprisingly busy, crowded with tourists and families, street musicians, candy sellers, and fruit stands. The atmosphere is decidedly bustling, bordering on frenetic, during any of the city's large arts festivals or religious holidays.

Home to the prestigious Universidad de Guanajuato, the city is a place of students, intellectuals, and the arts. The university influences the local culture in many ways, most noticeably in its lively and youthful spirit. Visitors will enjoy all the perks of student life, like dusty bookstores, cheap eats, and cool outdoor cafés, which are well suited to a leisurely afternoon reading and drinking coffee. For foreign exchange students and happy backpackers, Guanajuato is an appealing and inexpensive place to spend a few days (or a few months) relaxing in coffee shops and meeting up with other travelers. Despite the youthful atmosphere, the city also offers a good measure of cultural sophistication. Visitors of every ilk will enjoy Guanajuato's unique architectural sights and the smattering of international and gourmet restaurants, while the fantastic Festival Internacional Cervantino brings an array of world-class art and performance events to town every year.

Like much of the surrounding region, Guanajuato is a town with a tremendous role in Mexican history. Once home of the world's largest and most prolific silver mines, the city rose to prominence during the 17th century. It was among the first cities invaded by Miguel Hidalgo's army in the War of Independence,

Look for ★ to find recommended sights, activities, dining, and lodging.

Highlights

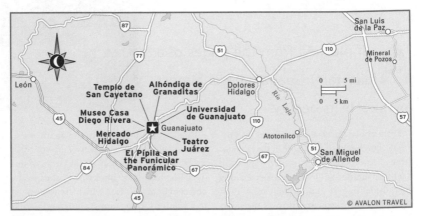

© AVALON TRAVEL

★ **Teatro Juárez:** A majestic turn-of-the-20th-century theater and one of Guanajuato's principal performance venues, which is worth touring even if you aren't seeing a show (page 140).

★ **Universidad de Guanajuato:** Guanajuato's university campus makes an enormous cultural contribution to the city, architecturally and culturally (page 141).

★ **Mercado Hidalgo:** Inside this unique municipal market are plenty of places to shop or grab a snack, and the atmosphere is one-of-a-kind (page 143).

★ **Alhóndiga de Granaditas:** The fortress-like public granary holds a grisly place in history; it is now a regional museum illustrating the city's past with artifacts and old photographs (page 146).

★ **Museo Casa Diego Rivera:** The childhood home of the great Mexican muralist and painter Diego Rivera is now a museum showcasing some of the artist's early work (page 149).

★ **El Pípila and the Funicular Panorámico:** Take a ride on the funicular to visit the monument to El Pípila and snap some photos from one of Guanajuato's most sweeping vistas (page 150).

★ **Templo de San Cayetano:** This ornate sandstone chapel is one of the most spectacular examples of baroque architecture in Mexico (page 154).

★ **Festival Internacional Cervantino:** During Mexico's largest and most prestigious performing-arts festival, a massive program of music, theater, and dance performances are presented in Guanajuato's theaters, public plazas, and churches (page 159).

Guanajuato State

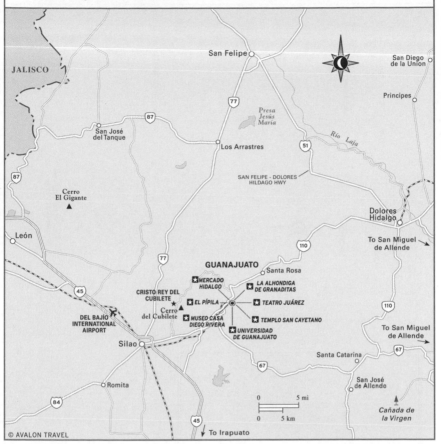

© AVALON TRAVEL

where the Alhóndiga de Granaditas granary became the site of one of the war's most important and bloody battles. Today, Guanajuato's many historic buildings and interesting museums bring the visitor close to the city's history, yet the vibe is never stuffy or old-fashioned. Here, contemporary art exhibitions take place in 17th-century cloisters while medieval troubadours play songs for groups of Mexico City weekenders. The mix is appealing, unusual, refreshing, and unique. As visitors to this special city quickly learn, there is no place on earth quite like Guanajuato.

PLANNING YOUR TIME

Guanajuato is a popular destination, welcoming national and international tourists, visiting artists, and exchange students throughout the year. Though well accustomed to crowds, Guanajuato does not feel touristy, nor does the city particularly cater to its many visitors. There are a few information booths in the town center, trolley tours of the major sights, and plenty of friendly locals to give advice. However, visitors to Guanajuato should not expect to find a well-oiled tourist machine at work. In this

Guanajuato City

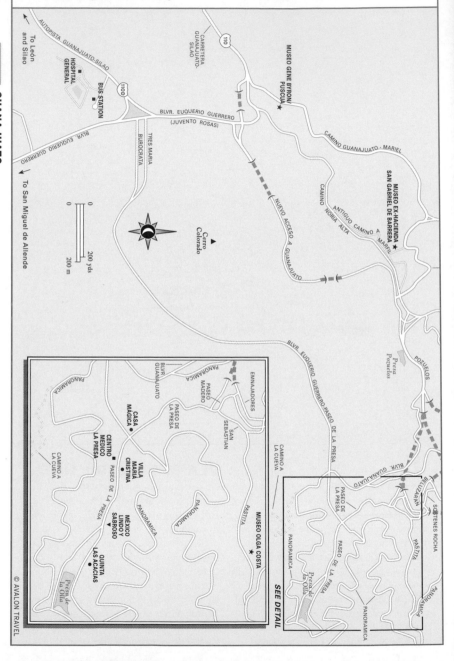

To León
and Silao

AUTOPISTA GUANAJUATO-SILAO

CARRETERA
GUANAJUATO-
SILAO

110

MUSEO GENE BYRON/
PUSCUA

HOSPITAL
GENERAL

BUS STATION

110D

BLVR. EUQUERIO GUERRERO
(JUVENTO ROSAS)

BLVR. EUQUERIO GUERRERO

CAMINO GUANAJUATO - MARIEL

To San Miguel de Allende

TRES MARIA

BUROCRATA

NUEVO ACCESO A GUANAJUATO

CAMINO NORIA ALTA

ANTIGUO CAMINO A

MARIEL

MUSEO EX-HACIENDA
SAN GABRIEL DE BARRERA

0   200 yds
0   200 m

Cerro
Colorado

BLVR. EUQUERIO GUERRERO/PASEO DE LA PRESA

Presa
Pozuelos

POZUELOS

PANORAMICA

BLVR
GUANAJUATO

PANORAMICA

PASEO
MADERO

EMNAJADORES

CASA
MAGICA

PASEO DE
LA PRESA

SAN
SEBASTIAN

CENTRO
MEDICO
LA PRESA

CAMINO A
LA CUEVA

VILLA
MARIA
CRISTINA

PASEO DE LA PRESA

PANORAMICA

PANORAMICA

CAMINO A
LA CUEVA

MEXICO
LINDO Y
SABROSO

QUINTA
LAS ACACIAS

Presa de
la Olla

PASTITA

MUSEO OLGA COSTA

SEE DETAIL

BLVR. GUANAJUATO

PASEO DE
LA PRESA

PASEO DE LA PRESA

PANORAMICA

PANORAMICA

Presa
de la Olla

BELAUNZARAN

SOSTENES ROCHA

PASTITA

PANORAMICA

© AVALON TRAVEL

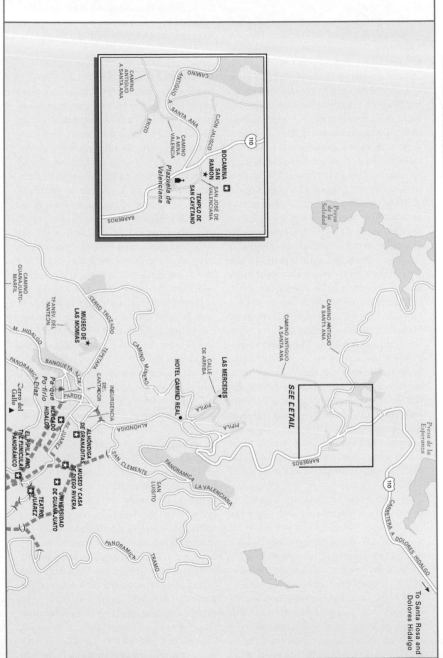

CAMINO ANTIGUO A SANTA ANA

CAMINO ANTIGUO A SANTA ANA

ERIZO

CAMINO A MINA VALENCIA

CÓN JALISCO

CÓN DE VALENCIANA

SAN JOSÉ DE VALENCIANA

110

BOCAMINA SAN RAMON

TEMPLO DE SAN CAYETANO

Plazuela de Valenciana

BARBEROS

CAMINO GUANAJUATO-MARFIL

CERRO TROZADO

MUSEO DE LAS MOMIAS

TRANSV. DEL PANTEÓN

M. HIDALGO

TETEPLAPA ALTA

CAMINO MAYORO

CAMINO ANTIGUO A SANTA ANA

CAMINO ANTIGUO A SANTA ANA

Presa de la Soledad

BANQUETA ALTA

PANORAMICA-DÍAZ

Parque Porfirio Hidalgo

Cerro del Gallo

PARDO

DE. CANTADOR

INSURGENCIA

CALLE DE ARRIBA

LAS MERCEDES

HOTEL CAMINO REAL

PIPILA

PIPILA

PIPILA

SEE DETAIL

ALHÓNDIGA

BARBEROS

Presa de la Esperanza

EL PIPILA AND THE FUNICULAR PANORAMICO

MERCADO HIDALGO

AV. JUAREZ

ALHÓNDIGA DE GRANADITAS

MUSEO Y CASA DE DIEGO RIVERA

SAN CLEMENTE

PANORAMICA

LA VALENCIANA

110

TEATRO JUAREZ

UNIVERSIDAD DE GUANAJUATO

SAN LUISITO

CARRETERA A DOLORES HIDALGO

PANORAMICA

TRAMO

To Santa Rosa and Dolores Hidalgo

low-key city, planning a worthwhile vacation is largely up to you.

Many people visit Guanajuato on a **day trip** from San Miguel de Allende or the capital or choose to spend a few days there in conjunction with a larger trip around the region. Most of Guanajuato's interesting museums and architectural sights are located within a few blocks in the *centro histórico*. Therefore, many day-trippers prefer to simply wander from plaza to plaza, stopping into museums or shops as they come across them. If you want to make the most of a single day in Guanajuato, consider taking a guided tour of the city center or the outlying sights in La Valenciana.

Those spending more than **a day or two** in Guanajuato don't need to plan their time too carefully. It is easy to see the major sights downtown in just a few days of exploring. In fact, you'll bump into most of them without even trying! Anyone staying **a week or more** should consider a jaunt outside the *centro histórico* to see the Templo de San Cayetano in La Valenciana, the sierra of Santa Rosa, or the Presa de la Olla neighborhood, among other worthwhile destinations. Those who enjoy a bit of natural scenery might consider a hike in the surrounding mountains or a day trip to another small town, like Dolores Hidalgo. On that note, Guanajuato can make an excellent **home base** for a longer trip to the region, as it is affordable, authentic, and friendly. Many foreigners come here to study Spanish, while others simply practice their language skills during a longer sojourn in this inexpensive and interesting city.

No matter how long you stay, a good way to experience Guanajuato is through the many cultural offerings and performances (both formal and impromptu) throughout town. There are weekly concerts at the city's theaters, street performers, and *callejoneadas* (a stroll through the *centro histórico* led by a band of medieval-style troubadours), among other options for arts and entertainment. Check the Universidad de Guanajuato's website to see what cultural events are going on around town, or pass by the box office at the

Teatro Juárez when you arrive. More informally, many of Guanajuato's bars and restaurants have live music, especially on the weekends. Look for announcements and flyers around town.

ORIENTATION

Navigating Guanajuato's unusual topography can be a challenge for newcomers—and even for sophisticated GPS systems, which are often unable to chart the correct path from point A to point B. The urban city center is built along the walls of a canyon, dotted by public plazas, and marbled with tiny pedestrian alleyways. It has no grid pattern to follow, no numbered streets, and few accurate maps. Alleys often zigzag in unexpected directions and can often lead to a serious cardiac workout if you follow them in their steep ascent up the ravine. It may take a few hours—or even a few days—to get acquainted with the topsy-turvy street map. During the adjustment period, a sense of adventure is your greatest ally. Even as you find yourself lost in the tangle of small streets, there is always a sense of pleasant mystery about what lies around the next corner.

Unlike most Mexican cities, Guanajuato's downtown was not designed around a big central square or *zócalo*. However, the **Jardín de la Unión** is generally considered the city center, culturally if not geographically. Therefore, it can be easiest to start your tour of the city from there. From the Jardín de la Unión, several pedestrian streets run roughly from the northwest to the southeast across the downtown, making a few unexpected dips and turns. From the Teatro Juárez, follow Luis González Obregón northwest toward the Plaza de la Paz, where you will see the Basílica de Nuestra Señora de Guanajuato and the state government buildings. From there, take Juárez past the Plaza San Fernando and the Plaza de los Ángeles until you arrive at the Mercado Hidalgo, just below the Alhóndiga. Heading southeast from Jardín de la Unión, Sopeña is a pedestrian street lined with shops and restaurants. One block to the east (just behind the Jardín de la Unión), Calle Cantarranas runs loosely parallel to Sopeña, though it is open to auto traffic.

Driving in Guanajuato is another challenge altogether. With all the underground tunnels and one-way streets, Google Maps and other navigation devices routinely fail to mark the correct route. Throughout the city center, the former riverbed has been converted to an underground system of tunneled roads, marked with rather unspecific signage. **Calle Belaunzarán** is the only major thoroughfare that goes through the city center (it later becomes Calle Miguel Hidalgo, which runs underground). It is almost impossible to accurately map the routes through the tunnels, but don't lose your calm when driving through the *centro histórico*. Very few underground roads will lead you far from the downtown district before they come up for air. When in doubt, ask directions. In almost every case, it is easiest to park your car and walk when exploring the *centro histórico*. You don't get much of a view from underground anyway!

There are several restaurants, hotels, and sights outside the city center, specifically in the **Marfil, San Javier, de la Presa,** and **Valenciana** neighborhoods. These neighborhoods are easily accessible by taxi or bus.

These outlying neighborhoods may not look very distant on a map, yet steep, winding hills can make them quite a trek on foot! Plan to drive, take a taxi, or ride the bus. The exception is the neighborhood around the **Presa de la Olla,** which is a pleasant 30-minute walk from downtown.

HISTORY

The settlement of Santa Fe and Real de Minas de Guanajuato was established around 1548, when Spanish settlers discovered silver veins in the surrounding sierra. Though its initial contribution to the mining industry was modest, Guanajuato's silver production made a rapid improvement with the opening of La Cata mine in the 1720s. As the mines began to produce more efficiently, Guanajuato began to prosper. A missionary delegation constructed a large San Diegan convent along the banks of the Guanajuato River. Churches and mansions cropped up around the city center, and the city's first Jesuit school (the precursor to the modern-day Universidad de Guanajuato) was established. Water systems were built, and the first dam, La Presa de la Olla, was constructed to curb destructive flooding downtown. The Spanish government officially recognized the city of Santa Fe and Real de

The Jardín de la Unión is often filled with mariachi musicians.

Minas de Guanajuato in 1741; by then, there were almost 50,000 people living in the town.

In 1769, Antonio de Obregón y Alcocer and Pedro Luciano de Otero discovered a rich silver vein at La Valenciana, north of central Guanajuato. The massive wealth from La Valenciana made Obregón a rich man and the city of Guanajuato a jewel on the crown of New Spain. With renewed vigor, mansions, churches, temples, and haciendas were built across town, and the population continued to increase. When a great flood sank the San Diegan convent in 1780, the city had plenty of funds to replace the lost structure. The beautiful churrigueresque Templo de San Diego, which still stands today, was built on the ruins of the previous cloister. By that time, Guanajuato was the world's single biggest silver city, producing between a fifth and a quarter of all New Spain's silver.

Guanajuato's prosperity was abruptly interrupted when the War of Independence broke out. Guanajuato's Spanish *intendente* Juan Antonio Riaño y Bárcena resisted Hidalgo's call for Guanajuato's surrender when the war began in Dolores Hidalgo. The rebel army invaded Guanajuato on September 28, 1810, and the Alhóndiga de Granaditas, the public granary, was the site of one of the most important and bloodiest battles in the War of Independence.

While other Bajío cities went into decline after independence, Guanajuato's silver mines continued to produce throughout the 19th century. During his multi-decade rule of Mexico, President Porfirio Díaz commissioned several more monuments in Guanajuato, including the Teatro Juárez and Mercado Hidalgo, adding to the unusual mix of spectacular architecture in Guanajuato's city center.

In the late 1980s, Guanajuato began massive restoration projects on its many historic buildings. Today, the city's oldest chapels, civil buildings, and artwork have been magnificently restored, including the remarkable collections of 17th- and 18th-century oil paintings in many of Guanajuato's churches. Since 1988, the entire city center of Guanajuato, as well as its historic mines, has been designated a World Heritage Site by the United Nations.

Sights

Throughout the narrow streets and curving alleyways of Guanajuato's *centro histórico*, there is a veritable album of photo opportunities. The city boasts some of the finest 18th-century baroque architecture in the country as well as a few lovely old structures dating back to the 17th century. Adding to the unique mix of architectural styles, Guanajuato also has some spectacular civil buildings from the 19th century, often characterized by neoclassical design. After its induction into the UNESCO World Heritage Program in 1988, Guanajuato's churches, chapels, and civil buildings were beautifully restored, yet they haven't lost the crumbling majesty of their age and history. In addition, there are many small but interesting museums as well as several public galleries. When touring the city, it's worth a stop in one of the museums that catch your eye.

CENTRO HISTÓRICO

Guanajuato's charming city center is a compact labyrinth of narrow streets and cobblestone plazas, crammed with old churches, theaters, and former mansions. While the elaborate churches and civic buildings are the city's most celebrated architectural sights, the entire downtown district is filled with colonial buildings that are historic and beautiful. As you walk, look up to see the crumbling facades, old stone niches, and wrought-iron balconies of former mansions and government buildings. They are beautifully preserved and

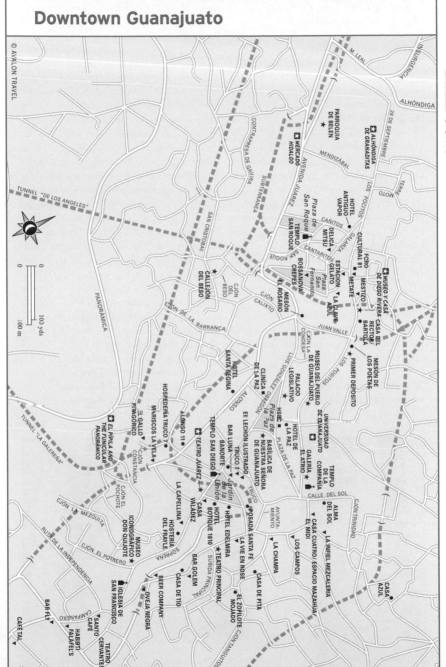

Downtown Guanajuato

© AVALON TRAVEL

TUNNEL "DE LOS ANGELES"

0   0
100 yds
100 m

PANORAMICA

TUNNEL "LA GALEREÑA"

RUTA DE LA INDEPENDENCIA

INSURGENCIA

M. LEAL

ALHÓNDIGA

28 DE SEPTIEMBRE

OTOTO

MOTO

TERRE

CONTRAPRESA DE GAVIRA

MENDIZABAL

AVENIDA JUAREZ

SUBTERRANEA

SAN CRISTOBAL

LOS POCITOS

★ ALHÓNDIGA
DE GRANADITAS

PARROQUIA
DE BELEN ★

★ MERCADO
HIDALGO

HOTEL
ANTIGUO
VAPOR

Plaza de
San Roque

DELICA
MITSU

TEMPLO
SAN ROQUE ★

CAÑITOS

CALAVERA

CANTARITOS

Plaza
San
Fernando

ESTACIÓN
GELATO

LA CLAVE
AZUL

FCRO
CULTURAL 81

METATE

★ MUSEO Y CASA
DE DIEGO RIVERA

CASA DEL
RECTOR /
BARTOLA

MESTIZO ★

CJON
DEL
BESO

CALLEJÓN
DEL BESO ★

BOSSANOVA
CREPES

CJON. DE LA BARRANCA

CJON.
CALIXTO

MESON
EL ROSARIO

MESON DE
LOS POETAS

JUAN VALLE

PRIMER DEPOSITO

CJON. LA
CONDESA

LUIS GONZALEZ OBREGON

ALONSO

HOTEL
SANTA REGINA

CLINICA
DE LA PAZ

PALACIO
LEGISLATIVO

MUSEO DEL PUEBLO
DE GUANAJUATO ★

LOS POSITOS

HOSPEDERIA TRUCO 7

EL GALLO
PITAGÓRICO

MARISCOS LA VELA ★

ALONSO 11 ★

CJON.
CONSTANCIA

EL LECHON ILUSTRADO

Plaza de
la Paz

HSBC

PALAZA DE LA PAZ

UNIVERSIDAD
DE GUANAJUATO

TEMPLO
DE LA
COMPAÑIA ★

★ EL PIPILA AND
THE FUNICULAR
PANORÁMICO

CJON EL
POCHOTE

CJON. LA MEZQUITA

CJON. EL POTRERO

TEATRO JUAREZ ★

TEMPLO SAN DIEGO ★

BANORTE

BAR LUNA

TRUCO 7

HOTEL
BOUTIQUE

BASILICA DE
NUESTRA SEÑORA
DE GUANAJUATO

HOTEL DE
LA PAZ

GALERIA
EL ATRIO

CALLE DEL SOL

AYUNTA
MIENTO

CJON TRINIDAD

ALMA
DEL SOL

LA INFIEL MEZCALERIA

CASA
AZUL

LA CAPELLINA

HOSTERIA
DEL FRAILE

CASA
VALADEZ

Jardin
de la
Unión

TRUCO

POSADA SANTA FE

LA VIE EN ROSE

CASA CUATRO / ESPACIO MAZAHUA

EL MIDI

MOJADO

LA CHAMPA

LOS CAMPOS

EL ZOPILOTE
MOJADO

CASA DE PITA

SOPEÑA

MUSEO
ICONOGRAFICO
DON QUIJOTE ★

IGLESIA DE
SAN FRANCISCO ✝

BAR GOLEM

HOTEL
EDELMIRA

TEATRO PRINCIPAL

SUBIDA PRINCIPAL

CASA DE TIO

BEER COMPANY

OVEJA
NEGRA

BAR FLY

CAFÉ TAL

CAMPANERO

SANTO
CAFÉ

HABIBTI
FALAFEL'S

TEATRO
CERVANTES ★

largely intact, so it is easy to imagine this city center as it was 200 years ago.

Jardín de la Unión

Built along the banks of a river, Guanajuato's winding downtown district is composed of small plazas linked by narrow streets. The most bustling of these many plazas, the **Jardín de la Unión** (between Sopeña, Obregon, and Allende) is the heart of the city. Once the atrium of a large San Diegan convent in the city center, it was converted to a public space during the post-independence Reformation of the early 19th century. Today, the Jardín de la Unión is the busiest plaza in Guanajuato, always buzzing with activity. From morning to night, its wrought-iron benches are packed with crowds of tourists and locals. By early afternoon, mariachis and *norteño* trios arrive to play songs on request. The party continues through the evening, as the garden's cafés fill with people dining alfresco. For any first-time visitors to Guanajuato, the Jardín de la Unión is a great place to put your finger on the pulse of downtown Guanajuato.

★ Teatro Juárez

Teatro Juárez (Sopeña s/n, tel. 473/732-0183 or 473/732-2529, 9am-1pm and 4pm-6pm daily, US$2.50) is a jewel on the crown of Guanajuato's beautiful *centro histórico*. The building's opulent neoclassical facade is emblematic of the Porfiriato, the long 19th-century rule of President Porfirio Díaz, which ended with the Mexican Revolution of 1910. Designed by Antonio Rivas Mercado, Teatro Juárez was inaugurated in 1903 with a performance of Giuseppe Verdi's *Aida*. Porfirio Díaz was in attendance at the opening event. After Díaz's presidency was toppled in the Revolution of 1910, the theater was leased for cinema and, eventually, fell into disrepair. Efforts to restore the building began in the 1950s, receiving an additional boost from the founding of the Festival Internacional Cervantino in 1973. Since then, Teatro Juárez has been a prominent performing arts venue, continually hosting high-caliber theater, concerts, and dance performances. The Martha Graham dance company, Julián Carrillo, and the Symphony Orchestra of Mexico are among the many famous acts that have graced the theater's main stage.

Towering over the Jardín de la Unión, Teatro Juárez has a striking neoclassical exterior, with 12 Doric columns supporting a cornice topped by a row of black stone muses.

Locals frequently gather on the steps of the Teatro Juárez to chat or watch street performers.

Place of Frogs

The name Guanajuato comes from the Purépecha language, generally believed to derive from the term *quanax-huato,* which means "place of the monstrous frogs" or "hill of frogs." It seems a strange nickname for a semiarid town in the crevice of the Cordillera de Guanajuato, and there are numerous theories about its origin. While some believe the name refers to the rock formations near the city center that resemble giant frogs, others contend that the frog referred to is the god of wisdom in the Purépecha culture. Whatever the reason, the city has embraced its amphibious identity, mysterious though it is. In shops across town, frog souvenirs are popular merchandise, and a major thoroughfare is named Cantarranas (Singing Frogs). From the city's southwest entrance from León, you are welcomed to town by the **Plaza de Ranas** (Plaza of Frogs), where a host of sandstone frogs form an informal gateway to the city.

There is often a crowd of locals chatting on the staircase below the portico. Inside, the ceiling and floors of the main auditorium, the Gran Salón Auditorio, are spectacularly decorated with hand-cut wood-and-stucco relief, painted in a brilliant multicolor array of deep red, blue, and gold. Heavily influenced by Moorish design, the Gran Salón is elaborate and dazzling. From the Gran Salón, you can follow the creaky wooden staircases to the foyer upstairs, an art nouveau salon complemented by even more neoclassical marble sculptures. Even the bathrooms have gilded moldings.

Templo de San Diego Alcantará

The **Templo de San Diego Alcantará** (Calle de Sopeña s/n, generally 8am-8pm daily) was originally constructed as a part of the large San Diegan convent that occupied the city center, including the current site of Teatro Juárez and the Jardín de la Unión. Of the entire complex, only this small chapel is left standing today. One of the older buildings in Guanajuato, the Templo de San Diego has a beautiful rococo exterior, replete with life-size saints surrounded by decorative hand-carved stone embellishments. Inside, the church has a lovely collection of large-format oil paintings from the viceroyalty through the 19th century. Two small temples adjoin the nave on either side of the neoclassical altar; the chapel to the south of the altar is smaller but has

another impressive collection of 18th-century oil paintings depicting the life of San Pedro de Alcántra.

Since the days of its founding, the downtown district of Guanajuato has been flooded by the river that ran through the city center. After a devastating flood in the late 1700s, the entire city center was raised several meters, including the buildings of the San Diegan convent. On the temple's north side, a small staircase leads down to the **Museo Dieguino** (Jardín de la Unión, tel. 473/732-5296, 10am-6pm daily, US$0.50, children free), where the ruins of the original 17th-century temple have been excavated. The space is small but interesting, revealing the old crumbling walls and archways (now reinforced with wood supports) of the original cloister. Often, the museum exhibits contemporary art or photography within this historic space, adding a tasteful and interesting juxtaposition between the past and the present.

★ Universidad de Guanajuato

The **Universidad de Guanajuato** (University of Guanajuato, Lascuráin de Retana 5, tel. 473/732-0006, www.ugto.mx) is a large and prestigious public university, which has a major influence on the city of Guanajuato culturally and architecturally. The school dates back to the early 18th century, when Jesuits founded the Colegio de la Santísima Trinidad in Guanajuato. This same school became a college in 1744. After the War of Independence, the school was designated a state college, and the curriculum was reformed under the first state governor, Carlo Montes de Oca. In 1945, the college was elevated to the status of university, offering undergraduate, masters, and doctoral programs. Today, the Universidad de Guanajuato is one of Mexico's most prominent and well-respected institutions. There are around 30,000 students, and their jubilant and youthful attitude flavors the downtown district of Guanajuato.

The university is actually spread across several campuses in Guanajuato and other cities in the region. However, the central campus is the school's most iconic structure, an unusual neoclassical building constructed in the 1940s. Soaring skyward above the narrow street of Lascuráin de Retana, the giant white facade dominates the cityscape to the east, peeking above the government buildings and chapels from the Plaza de la Paz below. Its long ascending stairway, cut of green sandstone, rises from the street to auditoriums and classrooms above. If you don't mind a brisk workout, you can climb the many stairs for a nice view of the city.

Templo de la Compañía de Jesús

Also known as the Oratorio San Felipe Neri, the **Templo de la Compañía de Jesús** (Lascuráin de Retana s/n, generally 8am-8pm daily) is an exquisite pink sandstone church that was constructed 1747-1765 by Jesuit priests. Another boon of the silver trade, the large neoclassical cupola behind the main facade was added to the building during the 19th century, commissioned by the Jesuit brother of a mining magnate. Today, the church's lovely churrigueresque exterior and single bell tower are well preserved, yet enchantingly aged. After Guanajuato's inauguration into the World Heritage Program in 1988, this church was the first structure to be totally restored.

Inside, the soaring nave is impressively high, with a vaulted dome where even pigeons drift comfortably from one sandstone perch to the next. Note the elaborately wrought sandstone columns that line the main corridor. Hand-carved altars adorn the walls, where there are several beautiful wooden statues, a fine hand-painted pulpit, and a collection of 18th-century oil paintings, including some by master artist Miguel Cabrera.

The colonial-era Templo de la Compañia is just beside the university in downtown Guanajuato.

Basílica de Nuestra Señora de Guanajuato

The striking yellow **Basílica de Nuestra Señora de Guanajuato** (Plaza de la Paz s/n, tel. 473/732-0314, generally 8am-9pm daily) was the city's first parish church. In 1957, the church was upgraded from *parroquia* (parish church) to the elevated title of basilica. Constructed in the 17th century with funds from the mines, the building's brightly painted facade is largely original, though its churrigueresque bell tower was added in the 19th century. Each of the church's three entryways is surrounded by a lovely hand-carved sandstone facade.

In contrast to its bold exterior, the basilica's interior is a wash of subtle pastels, marble floors, and shiny crystal. The walls are painted with delicate frescoes in pink, aqua, and white. The church's original baroque altarpieces were lost in the 19th century and have since been replaced by a large neoclassical altar in the front and in the two side chapels. The centerpiece is the *Virgen de Guanajuato,* a carved wooden sculpture of the Virgin Mary and son from the 16th or 17th century, displayed atop a baroque silver pedestal. When you go inside, be respectful of masses and worshippers. Even today, the church's congregation is very active.

Plaza de la Paz

Just below the *basílica,* the **Plaza de la Paz** is a lovely triangle-shaped esplanade, originally considered Guanajuato's main square until the establishment of the Jardín de la Unión in the early 19th century. In the center of the plaza, well-manicured gardens and metal benches surround the *Monumento de la Paz,* dedicated to the city by President Porfirio Díaz in 1903. (The original fountain that stood in the center of the Plaza de la Paz was relocated to the Plaza Baratillo to accommodate the new sculpture.) On the north side of Plaza de la Paz (just to the north of the basilica), the **Palacio Legislativo** is a noted neoclassical construction from the 19th century, which is now home to state government offices.

★ Mercado Hidalgo

One of the nicest examples of turn-of-the-20th-century architecture in Guanajuato is the beautiful **Mercado Hidalgo** (Av. Juárez s/n, esq. Mendizábal, no phone, 8:30am-9pm daily, hours vary by shop), inaugurated on

The Basílica de Nuesta Señora de Guanajuato was originally built in the late 17th century.

September 16, 1910, by President Porfirio Díaz. It was a gift to the city in commemoration of the 100th anniversary of the Mexican War of Independence. Little did Díaz know that his own long presidency would come to a violent end just a few months later, with the outbreak of the Mexican Revolution of 1910.

Housed in an unusual structure that, according to local history, was originally designed as a train depot, this covered market holds a jumble of fruit stands, taco joints, juice bars, and stands selling *dulces típicos* (traditional Mexican candies). The second floor is dedicated to crafts and souvenirs, though most vendors sell inexpensive trinkets like key chains and bottle openers rather than high-quality artisan work. Nonetheless, it's worth taking a walk around the second-floor promenade to snap some photos of the market below.

Just across the street from the Mercado Hidalgo, the **Parroquia de Belen** (Av. Juárez s/n, tel. 473/732-2283, 7am-9pm daily), also known as the Parroquia del Inmaculado Corazón de María, is a lovely parish church with a baroque facade. Constructed by Bethlemite nuns in the 18th century, the original complex included a school, gardens, and a cemetery; today, only the church is left standing. The spacious interior contains lovely mosaic walls and a nice collection of *retablos* and oil paintings.

Templo y Plaza de San Roque

An old and endearing 18th-century chapel, the **Templo San Roque** (Plaza de San Roque s/n, no phone, hours vary) overlooks a small plaza of the same name. Originally constructed in 1726 by Father Don Juan José de Sopeño y Cevera, the building served as a *santa escuela* (Jesuit school) 1746-1794. The pink sandstone exterior is enchanting in its simplicity; there are few embellishments here, just a simple stone entryway and three stone saints, embedded into a wall of thick-cut sandstone bricks. Inside the church, the crumbling frescoes and incredibly weathered wood doors reflect the building's age and many years of use. The series of paintings depicting the Stations of the Cross were done in the 18th and 19th centuries by Lorenzo Romero. Restoration of the chapel is ongoing.

Right in front of the temple, the small **Plaza de San Roque** also has historical importance to the city of Guanajuato. Since the mid-20th century, the plaza has been the site of Guanajuato's famous *Entremeses Cervantinos. Entremeses,* the series of short

the Mercado Hidalgo

comedies by Cervantes, are performed weekly in this square. Over the years, these performances became so popular that they eventually formed the cornerstone of Guanajuato's annual Festival Internacional Cervantino. On the south side of the church, there is a bronze statue of Enrique Ruelas, the Universidad de Guanajuato professor who founded the festival.

Plaza San Fernando

One of the prettiest public squares in central Guanajuato, tree-filled **Plaza San Fernando** (between Cantaritos and Independencia, 24 hours daily, free) is ringed by shops and restaurants and always bustling with activity. Once part of a large hacienda, it is now a nice place for an afternoon coffee break, with a stone fountain at its center.

Jardín Reforma

Just to the west of the Plaza de San Roque, **Jardín Reforma** is a peaceful public square, home to the architecture department at the Universidad de Guanajuato. The grounds were once a part of the Templo de Belen and were expropriated to make a public space in the mid-19th century. Quieter than neighboring Plaza San Fernando, this plaza is shaded

by trees and filled with quiet spots to rest weary feet.

Callejón del Beso

There are only 70 centimeters separating one house from another on the tiny **Callejón del Beso (Alley of the Kiss).** Located just above the Plaza de los Ángeles, this little alley is typical of those in Guanajuato, with a staircase cutting through a narrow passage between residences. However, the Callejón del Beso has become a bit of a tourist attraction, thanks to the local legend of two lovers who lived in houses on opposite sides of the alley. According to this Romeo and Juliet-esque story, the young lovers were from different social classes and their families opposed the romance. Doña Ana was a rich young woman, while her lover, Don Carlos, was a poor miner. At night, they would lean over their adjoining balconies for evening kisses.

As characters in these legends often do, the lovers on the Callejón del Beso met a tragic end when Doña Ana's father discovered their affair and killed her young lover. Today, you can reenact the lovers' secret romance by climbing up to one of the balconies and leaning over it for a photo opportunity; admission to the alley's balcony is free, but you will pass

Jardín Reforma is one of many delightful public squares in central Guanajuato.

Five Quintessential Guanajuato Experiences

Guanajuato is a city of alleyways, legends, mummies, medieval-style pageantry, grisly history, intellectuals, and the arts. Here are a few iconic things to do in this unique—and uniquely beautiful—place.

SERENADE AND REVEL LIKE IT'S THE RENAISSANCE

A group of troubadours in Renaissance-style garb processes through the streets, playing mandolins and other stringed instruments in unison, as a crowd of revelers gathers behind them, passing canteens of wine between them as they wind down narrow alleyways. This is a *callejoneada,* a uniquely Guanajuato occurrence. To join in, head to the **Jardín de la Unión** (page 140), where the musical groups, known as La Estudiantina, depart every evening. *Callejoneadas* are ticketed events and depart at a set time, usually passing many of the city's iconic sights over the course of the evening.

SEE A MUMMY (OR EAT A MUMMY GUMMY)

Despite its great history and stunning beauty, Guanajuato's macabre **Museo de las Momias (Mummy Museum)** (page 152) might today be its most famous site. Even if you don't visit the unintentionally calcified remains of former Guanajuato residents, you can still celebrate this oddity in other ways—like with a mummy gummy candy, sold at sweet shop **Dulceria Galereña** (page 166).

STUDY OR READ AT A CAFÉ

A university town, Guanajuato is filled with cheap eats and relaxing coffee shops catering to its huge student population. Join them at low-key coffee shops like **Café Tal** (page 172) or **El Lechón Ilustrado** (page 172), or take a book to one of the many cafés around the **Plaza San Fernando** (page 145). If you need something to read, you can pick up a book at intellectual bookshop **La Librería** (page 165), also on the plaza.

SEE A PERFORMANCE, BIG OR SMALL

Guanajuato is well-known for its performing arts, particularly for the spectacular **Festival Internacional Cervantino** (page 159), a three-week-long arts bonanza, which takes place every October. If you're not in town for the FIC, you can still enjoy the city's penchant for performance. Every Friday, the university orchestra plays at the **Teatro Principal** (page 157), often

through a little gift shop on your way to the top. Many tourists simply choose to exchange a kiss on the staircase below, which supposedly brings good luck to your relationship— even though it didn't bring much luck to Doña Ana and Don Carlos!

★ Alhóndiga de Granaditas

A public granary, the **Alhóndiga de Granaditas** (Mendizábal 6, tel. 473/732-1112, 10am-5:30pm Mon.-Sat., 10am-2pm Sun., US$4) is an imposing stone structure with a particularly gruesome place in history.

Originally commissioned by the Spanish governor of Guanajuato, Juan Antonio Riaño y Bárcena, the building was completed in 1809. Its usefulness, however, was short-lived; the Alhóndiga became one of the major battle sites early in the War of Independence in September 1810. After the battle, the Alhóndiga was cleared out and served as a military barracks and warehouse. During the 19th century, the Alhóndiga was the city jail for numerous decades. At last given a more dignified function, the building became a museum in 1949.

The Plaza San Fernando is lined with restaurants and cafés.

featuring soloists and special guests. Smaller spots, like **Foro Cultural 81** (page 158), also host frequent musical performances and open-mic nights. Or just catch a clown performing for the crowd gathered on the steps of **Teatro Juárez** (page 140).

SEEK OUT THE VIEWS

Thanks to Guanajuato's hilly topography, there are spectacular views from alleyways and rooftops across the city. Take the Funicular Panorámico to **El Pípila** (page 150), where the outlook boasts a sweeping view of downtown. See the city from a different angle with a glass of wine and a plate of *fritto misto* at **El Gallo Pitagorico** (page 170) or sip a cocktail at rooftop lounge **Bartola** (page 156) as the sun goes down.

Designed in a spare neoclassical style, the Alhóndiga is a giant, boxy building that resembles a fortress from the outside. Inside the great rock walls, the granary is surprisingly lovely, with a spacious patio framed by heavy green sandstone columns. Adding to the charm, the walls of the building's staircases are painted with dramatic murals about the independence movement by celebrated early-20th-century artist José Chávez Morado. On the northern side of the building, a stone s32taircase leads toward a large esplanade, which is used for public performances during the Cervantino festival.

Today, the Alhóndiga is a two-story museum, officially known as the **Museo Regional de Guanajuato,** dedicated to regional culture and the history of Guanajuato. On the second floor are several rooms displaying a collection of pre-Columbian art and colonial artifacts, much of which was donated to the museum by artists José Chávez Morado and Olga Costa. The lovely collection of pre-Hispanic stamps is one of the museum's highlights. From there, the visitor can follow the

El Pípila and the Storming of La Alhóndiga

The Alhóndiga de Granaditas was the public granary; today it's a historical museum.

Mexico's War of Independence began on the night of September 15, 1810, in the rural town of Dolores. Under the command of Miguel Hidalgo, the Mexican army rode through the Bajío, taking first San Miguel de Allende and next the city of Celaya. From Celaya, Hidalgo called for the capital city to surrender, but the royalist governors refused. On September 28, Hidalgo's army of 20,000 soldiers descended upon Guanajuato.

As the army entered town, Guanajuato's wealthy criollo and Spanish families took refuge in the fortresslike **Alhóndiga de Granaditas,** the city's public granary. La Alhóndiga was a difficult target for Hidalgo's ill-equipped army; despite their aggressive efforts, the perimeter was well guarded and difficult to penetrate.

Juan José de los Reyes Martínez, popularly known as **El Pípila,** was an indigenous silver miner with a reputation for enormous strength. El Pípila tied a heavy stone to his back as a shield and, carrying a torch in one hand, struggled beneath a shower of bullets and set fire to the granary's wooden doors. As the doors burned, the rebel army swarmed inside and massacred the aristocratic families within.

A year after the storming of La Alhóndiga, Spanish forces took their revenge. In March of 1811, prominent insurgents, including Allende and Hidalgo, were ambushed and arrested by royalist forces. A few months later, Ignacio Allende, Juan Aldama, and Mariano Jiménez were executed by firing squad in Chihuahua, followed by Miguel Hidalgo a few days later. Their bodies were decapitated, and the heads of the insurgent leaders were paraded around the country as a warning to other conspirators. The heads were then carried to Guanajuato, where they were hung in cages from the four corners of La Alhóndiga on October 14, 1811.

According to local history, the heads swung from the corners of the granary for more than a decade until they were transported to the monument of the Ángel de Independencia in Mexico City. Today, there are plaques at La Alhóndiga bearing the names of the insurgent leaders posted next to the giant iron hooks that once held their heads.

Diego Rivera's childhood home is today a museum.

There is one gallery downstairs plus two large galleries upstairs that are dedicated entirely to temporary art exhibitions. These shows usually feature Mexican artists and often address interesting and well-thought-out themes; there is an admirable presence of local artists within the museum's ongoing programming. Depending on when you visit, you may see work by young artists or great Mexican masters; recent exhibitions have included work by Pedro Reyes and a retrospective of work by Gabriel Macotela.

At the Museo del Pueblo, the lovely building itself is part of the attraction, housed in the former mansion of the wealthy Sardeneta family. Of particular note is a small, 18th-century baroque chapel, which was later decorated by Guanajuato's beloved artist José Chávez Morado. Chávez Morado depicts the cruelty of the Spanish rule over New Spain and the dehumanizing mining industry.

★ Museo Casa Diego Rivera

The famous early-20th-century artist Diego Rivera was born in the city of Guanajuato. Today, his childhood home has been refashioned as a small museum, the **Museo Casa Diego Rivera** (Positos 47, tel. 473/732-1197, 10am-6:30pm Tues.-Sat., 10am-3pm Sun., US$1.50). Although the artist only lived in this house for the first few years of his life before relocating with his family to Mexico City, he is nonetheless one of Guanajuato's favorite sons.

On the first floor of the museum, the family's living quarters have been decorated with period furnishings, recreating the atmosphere typical to a wealthy family at the time of Rivera's birth. The three rather topsy-turvy floors above (the structure is sinking and slanted, which gives it a bit of a funhouse feeling) are filled with small, nicely designed galleries of Rivera's work, including some of his earliest oil paintings, drawings, watercolors, and lithographs. Several rooms display work from Rivera's contemporaries, many of whom were exploring the same themes in Mexican identity and culture. For fans of the

region's history from pre-Columbian cultures through the turn-of-the-20th century. There are also 16th-century mining artifacts and reproductions of weapons and furniture from baroque Spain. In the final salon, a collection of vintage photographs shows Guanajuato as it was in the early 1900s.

Museo del Pueblo de Guanajuato

The beautiful old building that houses the **Museo del Pueblo de Guanajuato** (Positos 7, tel. 473/732-2990, 10am-7pm Tues.-Sat., 10am-3pm Sun., US$2) contains three stories of small galleries exhibiting the museum's permanent collection as well as rotating exhibitions of artwork by Mexican and international artists. Downstairs, the Sala Teresa Pomar has a nice collection of traditional Mexican miniatures, including ceramics, masks, *alebrijes,* and corn-husk dolls. The museum's permanent collection is on display upstairs and includes some 18th- and 19th-century oil paintings from the region.

artist, this museum is an essential stop, as it offers enormous insight into his artistic development. The museum also presents rotating exhibitions in a few gallery spaces, and there are often movies, artistic talks, and other cultural programs.

Museo Iconográfico del Quijote

Guanajuato is the proud bearer of the Cervantes tradition, and the figure of Don Quixote is a big part of the city's cultural identity. Statues of Cervantes's mythical hero are scattered throughout the city center, and the name Quixote is forever on the tip of your tongue, thanks to the dozens of namesake restaurants, hotels, and shops. If you cannot get enough Quixote, you can oversaturate yourself with his image at the fun **Museo Iconográfico del Quijote** (Manuel Doblado 1, tel. 473/732-6721, www.museoiconografico.guanajuato.gob.mx, 9:30am-6:45pm Tues.-Sat., noon-6:45pm Sun., US$2). At this small but well-stocked museum, you can see hundreds of representations of Don Quixote and his sidekick, Sancho Panza, from highly abstract to highly figurative pieces in a variety of media. The predominantly Mexican collection includes numerous local artists as well as some famous names, like Zacatecan artist Pedro Coronel. Taking advantage of its courtyard, the museum occasionally hosts cultural events as well as weekly live music concerts.

In addition to the art collection, the building itself has a curious history. Constructed near the end of the 18th century, this historic home belonged to a series of wealthy criollo families from Guanajuato. In 1861, the celebrated governor of the state, Manuel Doblado, purchased the property. While Doblado lived there, Emperor Maximilian of Habsburg was rumored to have spent several days in the residence while he visited Guanajuato. The house continued to pass through ownership of notable Guanajuato families until it was fully restored to accommodate the museum in 1987.

Iglesia de San Francisco

Just beside the Quixote museum, the lovely **Iglesia de San Francisco** (San Francisco Church, Manuel Doblado 15, tel. 473/732-0377, generally 7am-8:30pm daily) is a church and former convent, originally constructed in the 18th century by Franciscan friars as accompaniment to their school and orphanage. Situated along a pedestrian stretch of Manuel Doblado, this small church has a stunning pink sandstone churrigueresque entryway. Inside the church, there is a neoclassical altar and a nice collection of colonial-era oil paintings, including a particularly fine piece from the 18th century depicting San Francisco and Santa Clara.

★ El Pípila and the Funicular Panorámico

Above the city center, the giant rose-colored statue of **El Pípila** towers above the ravine, where it presides over a large public esplanade with spectacular views of the city below. From just behind the Teatro Juárez, you can take a short but fun ride up the hillside to the plaza in the glass-walled **Funicular Panorámico** (Constancia s/n, 8am-8:45pm Mon.-Fri., 9am-8:45pm Sat., 10am-8:45pm Sun., US$2.50). Alternatively, follow the maze of alleys up to the top of the hill. (If you are going to walk, one way to get there is via the alleyway of Constancia, just behind the Templo de San Diego and above the public parking lot; follow the signs from there.) Once you get to the top, the attraction is the view of the city—from this vantage point, you get a real sense of Guanajuato's unique urban landscape. The plaza offers a pleasant buzz of craft vendors, some snack shacks, and lots of other tourists snapping the ultimate Guanajuato photo.

SOUTHWEST OF THE *CENTRO*

The **Marfil** neighborhood to the southwest of the city center was once a small village, quite separate from downtown Guanajuato. Originally set up as a protective settlement to guard the nearby mines, it eventually became the center of Guanajuato's metal refineries during the colonial era. Many of these refineries were later converted to haciendas, some of which are now museums and restaurants. Though it's a bit of walk, it only takes about 10 minutes in a taxi to get to Marfil from the *centro histórico,* or you can take a bus from the Juárez tunnel (look for the buses marked Marfil).

Ex-Hacienda San Gabriel de Barrera

The **Ex-Hacienda San Gabriel de Barrera** (Carretera Guanajuato-Marfil, Km 2.5, Col. Marfil, tel. 473/732-0619, 8:30am-6pm daily, US$2) is a green and pleasing respite from downtown Guanajuato's inexhaustible bustle. Located in the Marfil neighborhood, the extensive grounds of this former hacienda were originally designed as a metal refinery. It was among numerous refineries owned and operated by a wealthy businessman, Gabriel de la Barrera, in the 17th century. With several acres of space, the hacienda's crumbling courtyards are home to a series of beautifully designed and well-tended gardens. Wander through the neat English garden with its tall, shady trees and a Mexican garden featuring a lovely collection of cacti.

You can linger beside gurgling fountains on one of the many crumbling stone benches or have a drink at the small coffee shop near the hacienda's entrance. Unfortunately, the hacienda is right next to the highway into Guanajuato, so you never fully lose touch with the 21st century.

Admission to the hacienda includes entrance to the **museum** within the complex's former living quarters. Family rooms have been redecorated with period furniture, which displays the strong Spanish influence popular with the wealthy during the colonial era. Huge chandeliers, old rugs, and massive wooden furnishings provide a glimpse into upper-class life during the 17th century. There is also a small but impressive **chapel** inside the home, with a gilded Spanish altarpiece from the 15th century. This old and beautiful *retablo* was likely imported from Spain; it is one of the few antiques of this age in Mexico. Since 1975, this hacienda and its grounds have been owned by the state of Guanajuato.

To get to the Ex-Hacienda San Gabriel de Barrera, you can hail a taxi from the *centro histórico* or take a bus marked Marfil from the tunnel of Hidalgo (beneath Av. Juárez), getting off at the Hotel Misión de Guanajuato (the hacienda is just below the hotel).

The Funicular Panorámico goes up to the monument to El Pípila.

Museo Gene Byron

In the 1960s, Canadian artist and designer Gene Byron purchased a splendid 18th-century hacienda. Today, the building is home to the interesting **Museo Gene Byron** (Camino Real de Marfil s/n, tel. 473/733-1029, http://museogenebyron.org, 10am-3pm Mon.-Sat., US$2), where rooms are filled with Byron's work, as well as her wonderful collection of antiques, Mexican furnishings, original art, and traditional crafts. It's worth visiting for the hacienda itself, which wears its age handsomely, with vines and trees sprouting out of the old stone walls. While you're there, have lunch: The on-site restaurant, **Puscua** (tel. 473/733-5018, 8:30am-5pm Tues.-Sun., US$9), is among the best in Guanajuato. An active cultural organization, the museum often hosts music concerts on Sundays, and there are guided tours (free) in both English and Spanish.

SOUTHEAST OF THE *CENTRO*
Presa de la Olla

Originally opened in 1749, the **Presa de la Olla** (Barrio de la Presa s/n, 24 hours daily, free) is the oldest city reservoir and the centerpiece of a tranquil neighborhood that bears

its name. Wandering around the water's edge can provide a respite from the commotion of downtown Guanajuato, with views of the surrounding hillsides, including the famous peak known as the Cerro de La Bufa. On the east side of the reservoir, there is a small dock where you can rent rowboats.

WEST OF THE *CENTRO*
Museo de las Momias

The famous **Museo de las Momias (Mummy Museum)** (Explanada del Panteón Municipal s/n, tel. 473/732-0639, www.momiasdeguanajuato.gob.mx, 9am-6pm Mon.-Thurs., 9am-6:30pm Fri.-Sun., US$3) is one of Guanajuato's most unusual and well-known sights. This museum's backstory begins in the early 19th century, when several mummified corpses were dug up in the Santa Paula cemetery. The mummification occurred naturally due to the unusual mineral content in the soil, which preserved the corpses in a state of horrific recognizability. Thereafter, more corpses were dug up, with similar results. This curiosity has now become the concept behind a macabre museum, where the bodies of more than 100 disinterred and mummified corpses are on display for visitors behind glass cases. It's not recommended for the squeamish; there

The interesting Museo Gene Byron is located in a gorgeous hacienda.

El Santo vs. the Mummies of Guanajuato

With so many other things to recommend a trip to the city, it's a bit curious that Guanajuato's **Mummy Museum** has become such a vitally important part of the town's public image. Perhaps Guanajuato's tourists have a deep-seated predilection for macabre spectacles, or perhaps there is something universally intriguing about a museum dedicated to disinterred corpses. Whatever the reason behind their popularity, the mummies of Guanajuato have become almost as famous as the Alhóndiga de Granaditas.

In 1972, Guanajuato's mummies were immortalized in the Mexican film *Las Momias de Guanajuato* (The Mummies of Guanajuato). This campy semi-action flick stars wrestling hero El Blue Demon, who is called upon to save the city of Guanajuato from the attack of a mobile band of mummies who had made a pact with the devil. As the mummies wreak havoc downtown, El Blue Demon and his companion, Mil Máscaras, must protect the city from these bald and oddly slow-moving villains (a wildly adored wrestling hero, El Santo, also makes a cameo toward the end of the film). In the final sequence, a gang of masked wrestlers attacks a legion of strong but stiff-jointed mummies (dressed in suits!) in Guanajuato's municipal graveyard.

In addition to the gripping story line, *Las Momias de Guanajuato* depicts the city of Guanajuato in amusing detail. As the movie begins, a group of tourists visits Guanajuato's Mummy Museum, where they are told the story of the evil mummies. Later, a key scene includes the Estudiantina troubadours playing for a band of tourists on the stairs of the university. Thanks to the film's popularity, *Las Momias de Guanajuato* was followed by several other mummy movies, including a lower-budget flick the following year, *El Castillo de las Momias de Guanajuato*. This film stars the wrestlers Superzan, Blue Angel, and Tinieblas and was shot in Guatemala, not Guanajuato.

Though not a classic of Mexican cinema, this film is emblematic of Mexico's popular *lucha libre* movies of the 1950s, 1960s, and 1970s. Studios no longer make these flicks, but films starring El Blue Demon, and especially El Santo, continue to garner a loyal cult following for their comic-book-style story lines, theatrical violence, and hammy acting.

are children and babies among the mummified bodies.

NORTH OF THE *CENTRO*

Departing the city center to the north, the state highway that leads to the village of Santa Rosa ascends a beautiful, curving route into the sierra. On the outskirts of the city of Guanajuato, La Valenciana is a beautiful neighborhood that has held one of the most important roles in the history of the city's development. Here, on the rocky bluffs, the mining industry continues to play a big role in Guanajuato's economy and identity.

La Valenciana

In 1769, a silver vein larger than any other in Mexico was discovered at **La Valenciana** in Guanajuato. In the early years, the mine's owners did not have the funds they needed to properly exploit their bounty; to compensate,

they introduced an unusual labor system, which granted mine workers a small share of the profits instead of a salary. The workers had to provide their own tools. The mine produced prolifically for centuries. At peak production, La Valenciana was New Spain's largest silver producer as well as an important source of other minerals, like gold, quartz, and amethyst.

Miners from La Valenciana were among the men who took arms against the Spanish at the Alhóndiga de Granaditas during Mexico's War of Independence. Even after the fighting ended, La Valenciana continued to yield rock, metal, and mineral. The entire mine was under the direction of a workers cooperative until the mid-2000s, when it was finally closed to production.

Today, La Valenciana is a residential neighborhood with a few interesting sights and sweeping views of the city center. You can get here in a taxi or by taking a bus marked "Valenciana" from the bus stop below the Alhóndiga de Granaditas.

Bocamina San Ramón

In its heyday, the mine at La Valenciana expanded to astonishing proportions, comprising a vast underground network of connected tunnels that stretched for kilometers below the surface of the earth. Just behind the Templo de San Cayetano, the **Bocamina San Ramón** (Callejón de San Ramón 10, Col. La Valenciana, tel. 473/732-3551, www.museob-ocaminasanramon.com, 10am-7pm daily, US$2) was one of the principal entrances to the mine, first excavated during the 16th century. Though long left in ruins, the hacienda surrounding the mine shaft has been restored and refashioned as a museum and event center, which showcases a bit of the history behind Guanajuato's most prosperous silver vein.

Independent, Spanish-speaking tour guides are on-site and can provide some historical context. Working for tips, they can guide you around the site, which includes some tools and artifacts preserved from the colonial-era mine. The main attraction, however, is the mine shaft itself; it descends 48 meters via a slippery stone staircase, where you can get a small taste of the dampness, darkness, and stale air that the miners endured during grueling shifts underground. To accompany the relief of returning to the earth's surface, there are beautiful views of the surrounding mountains and countryside.

★ Templo de San Cayetano

Antonio de Obregón, the Spanish co-owner of La Valenciana silver mine, became incredibly wealthy during his lifetime. To thank God for his great fortune, he constructed the spectacular **Templo de San Cayetano** (Plazuela de la Valenciana, Carretera Guanajuato-Dolores Hidalgo, Km 1.5, tel. 473/732-3596, generally 6:30am-6pm Tues.-Sun.). Built between 1765 and 1788, this mountaintop church is one of the finest examples of Mexican baroque architecture in the country, presiding over the city of Guanajuato and drawing daily busloads of tourists.

The church's highly elaborate sandstone facade is lavishly carved with saints, angels, and decorative adornment. Inside, the church is a direct testament to the riches of the adjoining mines, a splendor of hand-carved wood altarpieces washed in gold leaf. Wonderful multicolored wooden saints are embedded within the many niches, all beautifully restored. Also note the delicately carved and painted wooden pulpit.

Obregón's former estate across the street from the church is the subject of many tales of wealth and splendor. Among other legends, it is said that when his daughter was married in the Templo de San Cayetano, the count presented her with a rug of silver and gold coins, which led from her doorstep to the church. Today, Obregón's home is known as the Casa del Conde (Obregón later gained the title of *conde,* or count, of La Valenciana), with a fine-dining restaurant inside.

EAST OF THE *CENTRO*
Museo de Arte Olga Costa-Jose Chávez Morado

The quiet, tree-filled Pastita neighborhood is a largely residential area to the west of the *centro histórico*. It was once the home of Olga Costa and José Chávez Morado, two notable early-20th-century Mexican artists who settled in Guanajuato after meeting and marrying as young artists in Mexico City. Costa and Chávez Morado first came to Guanajuato when Chávez Morado began work on the murals inside the Alhóndiga de Granaditas. After that, they lived for a time in San Miguel de Allende but later returned to Guanajuato, helping to build the city's art and cultural prestige through the founding of cultural institutions like the Museo del Pueblo de Guanajuato and Museo Regional de Guanajuato at the Alhóndiga de Granaditas, to which they dedicated a large collection of pre-Columbian artifacts and art.

At the artists' behest, their home is now a small museum. The **Museo de Arte Olga**

Costa-José Chávez Morado (Pastita 158, Col. Pastita, tel. 473/731-0977, 10am-4pm Tues.-Sat., 9:30am-3pm Sun., US$2) features some more of the artists' collection of pre-Columbian artifacts and rare decorative objects, as well as artwork by their contemporaries. There is also a selection of Costa and Chávez Morado's work on display. Note, however, that the museum's permanent collection is periodically swapped out for itinerant art and cultural exhibits of varying (sometimes poor) quality; it's worth calling ahead if you want to see work by these two artists. No matter what's on show, it's a pleasant glimpse of Costa and Chávez Morado's lovely home and this quiet corner of Guanajuato.

Arts and Entertainment

In this city of the Cervantes tradition, there is a citywide passion for the arts, cinema, and performance, with frequent events in the city's churches, theaters, or public plazas. The university is a major cultural influence, hosting concerts, art exhibitions, and festivals throughout the year. Numerous municipal events and holidays also often draw crowds from throughout the city and beyond. There is often music in the streets, and the bustling city center is constantly flooded with people and events.

NIGHTLIFE

Guanajuato is a bustling, noisy, and occasionally rowdy city, filled with students, backpackers, and tourists looking to have a good time. In the evening, there is always a crowd pushing through the Jardín de la Unión, while groups of friends chat on the steps of Teatro Juárez. In sidewalk cafés, musicians mill through the crowd as bars and cantinas turn up the volume on their sound systems. While life can be more subdued during the week, Guanajuato feels like a citywide party on the weekends. Throughout the *centro histórico*, bars, cafés, and nightclubs cater to a late-night crowd. Most don't start pumping until after midnight, and some stay open until the break of dawn. Even if you don't indulge, you may hear the pumping beats of *reggaeton* from your hotel room!

In the Jardín de la Unión, **Bar Tradicional Luna** (Jardín de la Unión 10, tel. 473/734-1864, 12:30pm-2am daily) is a wonderful place to tip back a tequila. As the name indicates, Luna is a traditional cantina—often full, noisy, and packed with tourists and locals enjoying a view of the plaza and a friendly Mexican atmosphere. On the weekends, it can be difficult to snag a seat on the patio. At any hour, traditional Mexican tunes play loudly on the jukebox as mariachis and trios gather around tables offering their services for a live song (on a Saturday night, they'll find plenty of takers among the tipsy crowds). During the day, polite waiters serve drinks along with complimentary *botanas* (appetizers), like shrimp soup or pork skin tostadas. There's a fine list of tequila.

Located on a tiny alley at the very back of the Plaza San Fernando, **La Clave Azul** (2a de Cantaritos 31, tel. 473/732-1561, 1:30pm-9pm Mon.-Wed., 1:30pm-11:30pm Fri.-Sat., food service 1pm-6pm, US$6) is a lovely old cantina, perfect for a low-key afternoon of eating and drinking. Like many classic cantinas, La Clave Azul serves a small plate of food, or *botana*, along with each drink you order. Although the menu changes daily, the *lechón* (suckling pig) is one of the cantina's specialties. Supposedly designed in homage to Luis Buñuel's set designer, Juan Yanes, this spot has a tavern-like atmosphere with exposed rock walls and dim lighting. To get here, walk to the very back of the Plaza San Fernando. Just behind the Café Bossanova, a teensy alleyway ascends from the plaza; La Clave Azul is just a few yards beyond the mouth of the alley.

Beside the petite rooftop pool at boutique hotel Casa del Rector, **Bartola** (Positors 33, tel. 473/732-9200, www.casadelrector.com, 4pm-11pm Mon.-Thurs., noon-11pm Sat.-Sun.) is a lovely open-air cocktail lounge with gorgeous bird's-eye views of the city and the surrounding sierra. It is a particularly spectacular spot for a sunset, and they light heat lamps on cool Guanajuato evenings after the sun goes down. The cocktail list is creative, and, not surprisingly, a bit more expensive than those at the student-friendly spots downtown. Despite its million-dollar view, this welcoming lounge isn't pretentious; even families show up in the afternoon to enjoy the atmosphere.

Inside a beautiful old building on the Plaza Baratillo, traveler favorite **La Champa** (Baratillo 9A, tel. 473/732-6430, 4pm-2am Mon.-Sat., 4pm-midnight Sun.) is a pleasant cocktail bar with a relaxed, friendly attitude and a reputation for making top-notch mixed drinks, prepared and presented with style. Even straight shots of tequila or mezcal are served in tiny glass bottles. Come on a weekday for drink specials, or drop in for a plate of paella on a Sunday. If you aren't a cocktail drinker, stop by in the afternoon for a coffee (their espresso bar is another specialty) or a house-made craft beer on tap.

Though just a few blocks from Jardín de la Unión, **La Infiel Mezcaleria** (Carcamanes 8, cell tel. 473/119-4115, 1pm-10pm Mon.-Wed., 1pm-2am Thurs.-Sat.) feels far from bustle of central Guanajuato, especially if you drop in during the early afternoon or evening, when the bar isn't likely to be full. Inside the tiny but atmospheric bar, bottles of tequila, mezcal, and other spirits are stacked on painted wooden shelves. Perch on a stool to chat with the friendly bartenders, or grab a seat on the shaded patio to sip a craft beer or artisanal mezcal served with a slice of orange and chile powder, as is traditional. Thanks to the great music on the sound system, an amiable staff, and the low-key vibe, it's often busy in the evenings.

Order a craft beer or a shot of the

Oveja Negra, one of many student-friendly nightspots in downtown Guanajuato

house-special mezcal (in flavors like guava or pistachio) at the bar of **Oveja Negra** (Cantarranas 70, tel. 473/141-6939, 3pm-1am Mon., 2pm-1am Tues.-Sat., noon-1am Sun.), a cavernous, youth-oriented spot in the center of town. Like most of Guanajuato's bars, this place is popular with a younger, student-friendly crowd. Its funky design holds standing-room-only crowds on busy nights and sometimes hosts live rock bands. Just a few doors down, **Bar Golem** (Cantarranas 38, tel. 474/732-1955, 7pm-3am Mon.-Sat., 7pm-midnight Sun.) is another youth-oriented nightspot, with a popular roof deck. Golem frequently has live music, including jazz nights.

You can dance until almost the break of dawn at **La Dama de las Camelias** (Sopeña 32, tel. 473/732-7587, 8pm-4am daily). This second-floor dance hall has a fun, artsy, and upbeat Latin vibe, attracting students, visitors, and residents of all ages. The huge bar overlooks Calle Sopeña, and the walls are painted with festive murals. Things get going early in the evening, and after midnight it's standing room only. Open later than many bars in Guanajuato (most close around 2am), the place really gets hopping in the wee hours when other drinking establishments shut their doors. Sometimes there are live salsa or Latin bands.

If you're up for a loud and social night out, the perennially popular **Bar Fly** (Sostenes Rocha 30, tel. 473/652-1488, 7pm-3am daily) has been going strong for 20 years, and it's the best place in town to bump to reggae, whoop it up, and share cheap drinks with cheek-to-jowl crowds of students and expatriates. Known to many as El Fly, this bar is one of Guanajuato's most popular, youthful watering holes. The owners profess an anarchist affiliation, which is reflected in the bohemian decor. The young waitstaff and bartenders take part in the nightly fun, where foreign exchange students mingle with Guanajuato youth. There are often special events and live music.

LIVE MUSIC AND THEATER

Guanajuato is a theatrical town, deep in the throes of a love affair with Cervantes and surprisingly inclined toward medieval-style pageantry. On the esplanade below Teatro Juárez or in the Plaza de los Ángeles, clowns, magicians, and other amateur performers delight an informal audience with impromptu performances in the open air. In the Jardín de la Unión, live musicians roam the plaza, looking for someone to commission a tune. Throughout the year, there are numerous theatrical, musical, and film events produced by the university or the city government, among other organizations, as well as a summer arts festival and organ concert.

For first-time visitors to the city, *callejoneadas* are the quintessential Guanajuato experience. Led by the Estudiantina, a group of medieval-style troubadours dressed in capes and pantaloons, *callejoneadas* are walking minstrel shows that traverse the city every evening. These large student bands play guitars and mandolins as they jubilantly stroll through town, singing in unison. Behind them, an informal band of tourists and revelers follows, often passing flasks of wine or spirits between them. For new visitors to the city, these evening jaunts can provide a sort of nocturnal tour of Guanajuato, as the Estudiantina often stops at the Callejón del Beso, the Plaza de San Roque, and other famous locales. *Callejoneadas* usually begin around 8pm, departing from the Jardín de la Unión or Mercado Hidalgo, though you can also join them on their way around town. You do not need to buy tickets in advance; just join in the fun when the Estudiantina arrives at the square.

Under the directorship of the Universidad de Guanajuato, the **Teatro Principal** (Hidalgo s/n, esq. Cantarranas, tel. 473/732-1523, www.ugto.mx) presents a changing program of dance, live music, film, and theater throughout the year, including performances by the university's Ballet Folklórico (traditional Mexican dance). There is a live concert by the university's symphonic orchestra held at the theater every Friday night at 7:30pm (US$4-5 general admission, $2-3 students). The work varies but often features special guests or soloists. The Teatro Principal is also a venue for major artists during the Cervantino festival in October as well as the annual **Festival Internacional de Cine Guanajuato** for film lovers, cohosted by San Miguel de Allende and Guanajuato. The first of Guanajuato's city theaters, the original building was constructed in 1788 but destroyed by a fire; it was rebuilt in 1955.

The beautiful **Teatro Juárez** (Sopeña s/n, tel. 473/732-0183 or 473/732-2521, box office 10am-1:45pm and 5pm-7:45pm Tues.-Sun.) has been Guanajuato's most important performance venue since its inauguration more than a century ago. Here, you can see theater, opera, symphonies, and more. During the Festival Internacional Cervantino, many big names take the stage, though events are held intermittently throughout the year (including a few screenings during the film festival). The box office, a small window on the theater's southeast side, handles sales for all Cervantino events as well as ticket sales for the Teatro Cervantes.

A boxy stone theater overlooking the Plaza Allende, the **Teatro Cervantes** (Plaza Allende s/n, tel. 473/732-1169 or 473/732-0289) is a small venue that sporadically opens for concerts, films, dance, and opera throughout the year. Not surprisingly, it is a major venue during the Cervantino festival. Inaugurated in 1979 and overseen by the State Cultural Institute, the theater is occasionally used for government functions or talks. Tickets can be purchased at the box office at Teatro Juárez.

Guanajuato's churches contain some of Mexico's most beautiful and historic organs. Every spring, these beautiful instruments are put to good use at the annual **Festival Internacional de Órgano Antiguo de Guanajuato "Guillermo Pinto Reyes"** (International Antique Organ Festival, dates vary). For this unique event, artists from across Mexico are invited to perform in the city's chapels and churches, including the Oratorio San Felipe Neri and the Templo de San Cayetano in the Valenciana neighborhood. Events are free and open to the public. The festival dates are usually published in newspapers and in flyers around town in advance of the event.

Occupying a lovely, high-ceilinged colonial-era building on art-centric Positos Street, the **Foro Cultural 81** (Positos 81, tel. 477/690-3709, www.forocultural81.com, 10am-2pm and 4pm-8pm Tues.-Fri., 10am-5pm Sat.-Sun.) is a multidisciplinary art and cultural center that hosts a series of ongoing musical performances, classes and workshops, speakers, culinary events, and visual art exhibitions; most are offered for free or at a low cost. Uniting a variety of disciplines and eras, offerings might include a *jarocho* concert, an open mic for writers, a show of new artwork by students at the University of Guanajuato, or a talk by a historian.

GALLERIES AND MUSEUMS

The Universidad de Guanajuato has several well-managed gallery spaces overseen by the university art department. These galleries feature rotating exhibitions with a focus on contemporary art, and they are free and open to the public. Located just beside the university's famous sandstone staircase, the small but beautiful **Corredor Artístico Tomas Chávez Morado** (Lascuráin de Retana 5, tel. 473/735-3700, ext. 2731, 10am-2pm and 3pm-6pm daily, free) is dedicated to interdisciplinary visual art, with pieces, often by local artists, designed to fit the space. The gallery itself is unusual, with an arched entryway leading into a cave-like salon with thick stone walls and a bi-level exhibition space—a surprising backdrop for the experimental pieces on exhibit. Sometimes, the entire space is dedicated to a single piece of work.

Just inside the main university entrance, the **Galería Hermenegildo Bustos** (Lascuráin de Retana 5, tel. 473/735-3700, ext. 2731, 10am-2pm and 3pm-6pm daily, free) is a free exhibition space often featuring work by Mexican artists. Just beside it, **Galería Polivalente** (Lascuráin de Retana 5, tel. 473/735-3700, ext. 2731, 10am-2pm and 3pm-6pm daily, free) is a large gallery with high ceilings, clean white walls, and exposed piping. The atmosphere feels contemporary, as do the artists who show here. With two large rooms, plus several smaller spaces ideal for installation, this gallery can accommodate large-format pieces and extensive collective exhibitions.

Just a block from the main university campus, **Galería El Atrio** (Plazuela de la Compañía s/n, 10am-2pm and 3pm-6pm daily, free) is an unusual art gallery, fitted into a long and thin salon that runs along the base of the Templo de la Compañía de Jesús. Since there isn't enough room to really step back from the work, this gallery tends to show smaller-format pieces, ranging from painting to photography. The gallery has a rotating schedule of exhibitions, showing contemporary work by local artists in group or individual exhibitions. For more information about any of the galleries and upcoming exhibitions, contact the university's **Dirección de Extension Cultural** (Cultural Extension, Mesón de San Antonio, Alonso 12, tel. 473/735-3700, www.extension.ugto.mx).

There are frequent events, workshops, and live music concerts at the **Casa Cuatro** (Calle San José 4, tel. 473/732-4841, www.casacuatro. com.mx, 9am-noon daily), an art, culinary, and cultural center located in a beautifully restored colonial mansion. In addition to Casa Cuatro's two restaurants, teahouse, and shops (which hold their own events and music concerts) is the lovely wood-floored **Espacio Cultural Mazahua,** a multiuse gallery and cultural space on the second floor of the building with exhibitions of contemporary art as well as chamber music concerts, theater, dance, and other performances. They also host special classes and workshops in art, yoga, Eastern dances, origami, and other interesting topics, in addition to special classes and programming (like puppet shows) for children.

Beloved Guanajuato ceramics artist Capelo owns the contemporary gallery and museum **Primer Deposito** (Positos 25A, tel. 473/732-1125, primerdepositogto@gmail.com, 10am-7pm Tues.-Sat., 11am-4pm Sun., US$2). Housed in a beautiful old mansion on art-centric Positos Street, the building includes several downstairs galleries, plus one accessible via a narrow spiral staircase. Here you'll have a chance to see work by Capelo, including his signature ceramics and oil paintings, in addition to work by other Mexican contemporary artists. There are also plates, platters, pitchers, urns, mugs, and other creative flatware hand-painted with flowers, fruits, animals, and other traditional designs for sale in an accompanying shop, adjoined by a truly lovely café—ideal for relaxing with a drink after a short jaunt around the galleries.

Throughout the year, keep an eye out for seasonal events organized by an association of galleries and museums known as **Circuito**

de Arte Positos (Positos Art Circuit). Capitalizing on the plethora of cultural institutions on and around Positos Street in downtown Guanajuato, the organization coordinates an art walk to inaugurate dozens of simultaneously opening exhibitions. Events are accompanied by live music and performances throughout the evening, transforming Positos into a big, well-attended street party.

FESTIVALS AND EVENTS

In the party-loving town of Guanajuato, there are constant cultural events, religious festivals, and live music in the *centro histórico*. If you choose to visit Guanajuato during a well-known festival or holiday, you will likely find an increase in national tourism, fewer hotel rooms available, and a lot of activity throughout the public plazas and performance venues. Of particular note, the Cervantino festival in October is a huge event, during which the city is very full and rather expensive. You can get more information about Guanajuato's cultural events at the **Dirección Municipal de Cultura y Educación de Guanajuato** (Av. 5 de Mayo 1, tel. 473/732-7491).

TOP EXPERIENCE

★ Festival Internacional Cervantino

One of the biggest and most prestigious cultural events in Mexico, the extraordinary **Festival Internacional Cervantino** (tel. 55/5615-9417 or 473/731-1150, www.festivalcervantino.gob.mx) is held every October in Guanajuato. At this three-week-long festival, the emphasis is on the performing arts, with dance, theater, opera, and music events, which are held throughout the city's theaters, churches, and plazas. Every year, hundreds of world-famous ensembles, soloists, and performers are invited to perform, with shows running morning to night.

Although Mexican artists are well represented in the program, the event is distinctly international, with several foreign countries elected as honorary guests each year. Several Mexican states are also specially invited, with each setting up a showroom dedicated to their crafts, food, and culture.

You need to **buy tickets in advance** for major acts. However, there are also many **free events** held in civic plazas and in the square adjoining the Alhóndiga de Granaditas. (Shows at the Alhóndiga are always well-attended, so it's usually necessary to **line up** for free tickets several hours before an event you'd like to attend.)

Attending the festival is an opportunity to take an informal tour of Guanajuato's many theaters and performing arts venues, as well as the public plazas and parks where many shows take place. In recent years, performances have been held in such diverse venues as the **Ex-Hacienda San Gabriel de Barrera** and the **Templo de la Valenciana.** It is particularly special to see a show within the splendid Moorish-style interior of **Teatro Juárez.**

Part of the festival's attraction is the large number of artists and revelers that come to Guanajuato. During the festivities, the streets are constantly filled, restaurants and cafés are hopping, and amateurs take advantage of the crowds to show off their talents (expect plenty of young street musicians, clowns, or living statues performing in coffee shops and open spaces). In addition, there are often special events and **visual arts exhibitions** in the city's museums, galleries, and shops as well as special shows in the university's art galleries.

Visiting Guanajuato during the Cervantino festival can be extremely exciting, especially for those who love the performing arts. It is also a great time to visit for those who love a party. In addition to festival events, there are **electronic dance parties** and other special events specially aimed at attracting Guanajuato's student residents.

BOOKING TICKETS

While **same-day tickets** may be available for some of the smaller events at lesser-known venues, tickets for the most **well-known**

statue of Miguel de Cervantes, namesake for the Festival Internacional Cervantino

performers will sell out within a week—or even days—of going on sale. The full program for the festival is announced every year in **July.** The same day, a printed catalog of events is available for purchase. The program is also published online at www.festivalcervantino.gob.mx. The next day, tickets can be purchased through Ticketmaster or directly from the box office at **Teatro Juárez** (Sopeña s/n, tel. 473/732-0183 or 473/732-2521, box office 10am-1:45pm and 5pm-7:45pm Tues.-Sun.). Students and teachers with a valid ID can get half-price tickets to all events, as can residents of the city of Guanajuato.

ACCOMMODATIONS

Budget and midrange hotels can cost two or even three times the usual price during the festival. If you want to visit Guanajuato during the FIC, it is necessary to **book your hotel room six months in advance.** If you can't find accommodations, consider staying in San Miguel de Allende, just two hours away.

TRANSPORTATION

If you are arriving in Guanajuato by **intercity bus,** book tickets well in advance for both your arrival and departure. Bus tickets sell out in advance of the events. If you are **driving** to Guanajuato, avoid the traffic in the *centro* by parking your car outside the city center (there are places to park near the bus terminal), then take a cab or city bus into the center of town. **Plan to walk almost everywhere** you're going. Traffic is heavy throughout the weekend and taxis are almost impossible to find. If you are booking tickets for two events on the same day, make sure you have enough time to get from one venue to another. If they are far apart, check the city bus routes.

Semana Santa

Generally considered the most important religious holiday of the year, **Semana Santa** (Holy Week, Mar.-Apr.) is colorfully celebrated in the city of Guanajuato. The festivities begin with beautiful celebrations in honor of Viernes de Dolores, observed on the sixth Friday of Lent. For this popular festival, the Jardín de la Unión is a locus of activity, filled with people and decorated with *papel picado* and lavish bouquets of flowers. Politicians and local government officials weave through the crowds, handing out flowers and ice cream to passersby. It is also traditional for young men to give flowers to young women, in the spirit of love or friendship, and then walk with them through the Jardín de la Unión. Throughout the city's homes, offices, businesses, mines, markets, and plazas, small altars are built in the Virgin's honor, traditionally decorated with Easter candles, chamomile, dill, gold-painted oranges, wheat, and flowers as well as an image of the Virgin. Visitors to the altars are given *aguas de fruta,* usually limeade. In the Valenciana neighborhood, the mines also host large celebrations and are often open to the public.

A week later, the city expresses a more solemn portrait on **Viernes Santo** (Good Friday), generally considered the most important day of Holy Week. At midday, the Passion of the Christ is reenacted in the city center with townspeople playing the roles of Romans and Hebrews. In the evening, the Procesión del Silencio (Silent Procession) commemorates Christ's suffering and death in a moving parade, during which hundreds of mourners march in chilling silence through the twisting alleys of downtown Guanajuato. The procession continues for hours, often concluding late in the night.

Easter Sunday itself, usually called **Domingo de Gloria,** is a quieter day in Guanajuato, when most families spend time together and possibly attend mass. If you plan to visit during Holy Week, book your hotel reservations in advance. Most of Mexico's schools and businesses take their spring break during Semana Santa, so there is a lot of national tourism, especially in popular destinations like Guanajuato.

Festival Internacional de Cine Guanajuato

Guanajuato hosts the annual **Festival Internacional de Cine Guanajuato** (tel. 415/152-7264, www.giff.mx, July), a large international film festival featuring shorts, documentaries, and a smattering of features during the final week of July. During a long weekend of near-constant screenings, hundreds of films (which were selected from thousands of entries worldwide) are shown, with genres ranging from horror to documentary. Films are screened in the Teatro Principal and other traditional venues as well as in more unusual locations, like the subterranean streets and the municipal graveyard. Screenings are free and open to the public, and most are subtitled in both English and Spanish.

Apertura de la Presa de la Olla and the Fiestas de San Juan

The Presa de la Olla, a small reservoir to the east of the city center, was originally built in the 18th century to help prevent the frequent flooding that plagued Guanajuato's city center. Today, the reservoir is surrounded by a lovely colonial neighborhood, flanked on its west side by the Florencio Antillón Park. The reservoir can be a relaxing place to visit for an afternoon stroll, and it is also the site of an annual festival, the **Apertura de la Presa** (Opening of the Dam, July). The festival is believed to date back to the mid-18th century, when locals gathered together to drain and clean the river to prevent backups and flooding. Though originally organized for utilitarian purposes, the cleaning and opening of the dam have also become a merry municipal party.

Today, the ritual cleaning continues on the first Monday of July, with the city's mayor arriving to command the opening of the dam's floodgates at 1pm. The rushing water creates a rather pleasant breeze through the neighborhood. Thereafter, the party continues with swimming competitions and a big local party in Florencio Antillón Park. There are dozens of food stands and live music from the state band. The festival is generally associated with St. John the Baptist, whose feast day is June 24 and whose association with water is reflected in the opening of the dam.

Día de la Independencia

The capital of a state known for its large role in the independence movement (not to mention, the site of one of the most famous battles in the War of Independence), Guanajuato is a fitting place to spend the *fiestas patrias* (Sept.), the patriotic festivals commemorating the anniversary of Mexico's independence from Spain. Like most Mexican cities, Guanajuato gets dressed up in patriotic attire during the month of September, decked out with tricolor flags, lights, and banners that read, *¡Viva México!* At 11pm on September 15, the town's mayor holds a brief ceremony in the Palacio Municipal (in the Plaza de la Paz), calling out *"¡Viva México!"* to the crowd. Fireworks and general merriment follow. The big thing to do, however, is hit the bars and party until dawn.

In the nearby municipality of Santa Rosa, just 16 kilometers (10 miles) northeast of the city center, there is an elaborate reenactment of the taking of La Alhóndiga performed annually on September 16. The reenactment has been staged every year since 1864 (though it was suspended for several years during the Mexican Revolution). The pageant begins with a parade, which departs from La Cruz Grande beside the highway. As the crowd swells, "Spaniards" and "rebels" reenact seven battles along the roadway, accompanied by cannons and fighting. In the final scene, El Pípila takes the Alhóndiga. While the reenactment is fictional, the ensuing parties are very real.

If you didn't get your fix of independence events, on September 28 the city of Guanajuato celebrates the first major battle of the War of Independence, the **Día de la Toma de la Alhóndiga** (Anniversary of the Taking of the Alhóndiga) with a municipal parade.

Shopping

Although Guanajuato is not a shopping destination like nearby San Miguel de Allende, the town offers plenty of places to pick up a nice gift or do some casual browsing. In the *centro histórico,* several traditional craft shops sell clothing and ceramics, and several famous artisans work in the city. There are lots of little shops where you can pick up a trinket, a souvenir, or a piece of inexpensive jewelry, plus plenty of bookshops for the literary-minded.

Shipping Items Home

If you've bought an item that won't fit into your suitcase, most shops will offer an estimate on the cost of shipping it home. You can while the large ceramic platters are impressively detailed. With decades in business, the store's senior owners will be happy to tell you about the work. You'll find a similar aesthetic to the ceramics at **Cono Seis Galería** (Ayuntamiento 6, Local 1, tel. 473/732-7889, 11am-8:30pm daily), which represents the highly detailed ceramic work of prize-winning Tarandacuao artist Javier Servin, who also gives ceramics workshops in his studio in La Purísima. The gallery represents the work of several other artisans, many Guanajuato locals, working with ceramic, textiles, and wood.

Next door to the Museo Iconográfico del Quijote, **La Casa del Quijote** (Sopeña 17, tel. 473/732-8226, www.lacasadelquijote.com, 11am-9pm daily) is a large craft and jewelry shop in a grand old building. The airy showrooms are not particularly complemented by the sleek electronic music playing on the sound system, but they are well stocked with textiles and pottery from across Mexico. In addition to some nice ceramic work by artisans from the state of Guanajuato, the store has a large supply of Mata Ortiz pottery from Chihuahua and Oaxacan textiles. There is also a wide selection of silver jewelry showcased in the shop's two large front rooms.

Pick up a small gift to take home from **Artlalli** (Galarza 94, tel. 473/732-1096, 10am-8pm daily), which sells a colorful, reasonably priced selection of trinkets and crafts from across Mexico, including blown glass from Jalisco, *milagritos* (small tin ornaments), *alebrijes* (painted wood figurines) from Oaxaca, printed artwork, Frida Kahlo wallets, Huichol beaded animals, and enamel cookware, all stuffed into a tiny storefront on Positos. The staff can provide the background on a piece's provenance, technique, and significance.

If you are interested in Mexico's ceramic traditions, it is worth making a visit to the studio of **Gorky Gonzalez** (Ex Huerta de Montenegro s/n, Col. Pastita, tel. 473/731-0389, www.gorkypottery.com, 9am-5pm Mon.-Fri., 9am-1pm Sat.). With decades of

La Casa del Quijote

also mail boxes at **Redpack** (Miguel Hidalgo 1, Local 3, tel. 473/732-4949 or 473/734-0659, www.redpack.com.mx). **Solutions** (Recreo 11, San Miguel de Allende, tel. 415/152-6152, 9am-6pm Mon.-Fri., 9am-noon Sat.) in San Miguel de Allende can also handle shipping from Guanajuato.

TRADITIONAL CRAFTS

For regional craftwork, **Rincón Artesanal** (Sopeña 5, tel. 473/732-8632, 10am-8pm daily) exclusively sells the distinctive ceramics produced in a community called La Purísima in Tarandacuao, Guanajuato. Unlike the majolica-style pottery that is most commonly sold in the Bajío region, this hand-wheeled ceramic is painstakingly painted with delicate geometric patterns, applied in an ultra-high-temperature glaze. Rincón Artesanal presents work from several Tarandacuao artists, each producing a slightly different version of this traditional craft with a different palette of colors. Small espresso cups and saucers are sweetly sophisticated and sold by the set,

Queso de Tuna and Other Desert Desserts

The state of Guanajuato has a serious sweet tooth. *Dulces típicos* (traditional sweets) are produced in various cities across the state and consumed by the populace with appetite and pleasure. In the city of Guanajuato, there are wonderful sweets stands in the market and numerous traditional sweets shops boasting enormous selections and unique regional candies.

Among the most popular flavors in Mexico, *cajeta* (slowly simmered caramelized goat milk) is produced in the states of Guanajuato and Jalisco, most famously in the nearby city of Celaya. Popular throughout Mexico, *cajeta* is sold in jars as a caramel syrup or is incorporated into sweets. A popular treat is *cajeta* spread between two *obleas,* thin wafers made with the same process as the communion wafers served in Catholic churches, yet not blessed by a priest. *Dulce de leches* (chewy milk caramels) are also produced in the Bajío region and can be bought by the piece.

You'll also find *ate* (sweetened fruit paste) produced in Guanajuato. Quince, guava, and mango are among the most popular flavors for *ate,* though it can be made of many different fruits (and is traditionally served with cheese as a dessert). Crystallized fruits and cactus are also popular desserts, commonly made from orange, fig, or lime stuffed with shredded coconut. In the desert environment, confectioners also make use of the abundance of cactus and succulents. You can find crystallized *biznaga* (barrel cactus) and *xoconostle* (sour prickly pear fruit) in many shops and sweet stands in Guanajuato.

For the adventurous, the strongly flavored *queso de tuna* (prickly pear cheese) is one of the more unusual sweets of the semidesert. While it's difficult to get your hands on some, it is more widely available in the city of Guanajuato than in other nearby cities. Look for it in the shops and stands surrounding the **Mercado Hidalgo** (page 143) and at the **Dulceria Galereña** (page 166). This thick and heavy candy is made from ground prickly pear fruit mixed with unrefined sugar, which is slowly cooked until it forms a thick, dark paste. The paste is then cooled in giant molds and cut into blocks. The resulting sweet is unusually dense and chewy, with a rich and concentrated flavor quite unlike anything else.

work experience, Gonzalez is an internationally recognized, award-winning creator of majolica-style pottery in traditional Mexican designs. From decorative platters and vases to candlesticks and figurines, everything is beautifully crafted and colorfully hand-painted. From the *centro histórico,* you can take a taxi to the lovely residential Pastita neighborhood where Gonzalez has his studio. Note that the outside door is often closed, but knock to come in: The studio is open to visitors.

GALLERIES

With two storefronts in downtown Guanajuato, **El Pinche Grabador** (Positos 57, tel. 473/732-3394, 9am-9pm Mon.-Sat., 9am-6pm Sun.; Plazuela de San Roque 5, 9am-8pm Mon. and Wed.-Sat., 9am-6pm Sun.) sells a delightful collection of handmade prints with fun, distinctly Mexican themes—wrestling heroes, skeletons in love, cactus and flowers—created by artist Luís Carlos Rodriguez, the *pinche grabador* (damn printer) himself. Many pieces are small (and easy to fit into a suitcase), and everything is sold at very accessible prices. It's a wonderful place to browse or pick up a unique souvenir from your visit to Guanajuato.

A printmaking studio and gallery on heart-of-it-all Sopeña, **Corazón Parlante** (De Sopena 13B, no phone) sells a selection of original artwork, all of which was created on-site. The gallery represents a number of young and local artists, some of whom also work in the gallery. The pieces here are generally reasonably priced, and most are displayed in mattes with plastic sleeves, making them easy to carry home. Much of the work is linocut (using a linoleum plate), a popular medium for graphic work in Mexico, with themes that have a distinctive Mexican feel.

The workshop also offers inexpensive print-making courses, for students of any level. For 16 hours of instruction, any time from 9am to 10:30pm Tuesday through Saturday, the cost is about US$45.

BOOKSTORES

The lovely **El Viejo Zaguan** (Positos 64, tel. 473/732-3971, www.viejozaguan.com, 10:30am-3pm and 5pm-8pm Tues.-Sat., 11am-3pm Sun.) is a cozy shop and café that sells a small collection of novels, postcards, and a few CDs, as well as a wonderful series of hardcover books and magazines by *Artes de Mexico,* each volume focused on a different theme in Mexican architecture, art, and craft. Behind the bookstore, there is a small café where you can soak up the pleasant literary atmosphere over a cup of coffee. Just steps from the university, this artsy little place caters to an intellectual crowd.

Opening onto the picturesque Plaza San Fernando, teensy **La Librería** (Plazuela San Fernando 35 bajos, tel. 473/732-9832, lalibreriagto@gmail.com, 11am-3pm and 4pm-8pm Mon.-Tues., 11am-3pm and 4:30pm-8:30pm Wed.-Fri., 2pm-8pm Sat.) sells new and used books about film, art, sociology, philosophy, and other cultural topics, as well as novels (principally in Spanish) and a small selection of music. Just a few blocks from the university's main campus, this little spot is a model independent college-town bookshop, with many titles published by university and cultural presses.

In downtown Guanajuato is a branch of the **Librería de Porrúa Hermanos y Compañía** (Alonso 12, tel. 473/732-2153, www.porrua.com.mx, 10am-8pm Mon.-Fri., 10am-2pm Sat.), which sells a range of books in Spanish published by the Mexican press of the same name. Many are educational texts and reference books for university students, but you will also find books on spirituality, poetry, and literature. The editions are rather minimally designed, functional texts, but there are some great titles for those who read (or are learning to read) Spanish.

GOURMET GOODIES

Sweets are produced throughout the state of Guanajuato, and *dulces típicos* (traditional sweets) from the region are sold at the stands inside the main entrance to the **Mercado Hidalgo** (Juárez s/n, esq. Mendizábal, no phone, 8:30am-9pm daily, individual shop hours vary), as well as in a number of wonderful old sweets shops in the city. Just beside the

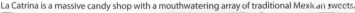
La Catrina is a massive candy shop with a mouthwatering array of traditional Mexican sweets.

market on busy Juárez Street, the **Dulcería Galereña** (Juárez 188, tel. 473/732-5934, 9am-8pm daily) is an old-fashioned candy shop that opened in 1955. Here, you'll find jars of *cajeta* (goat-milk caramel), *ates* (fruit paste), house-made candied fruit and nuts, marmalades made from Mexican fruits, and the strange confection known as *queso de tuna* (a thick sweetened paste made of the prickly pear fruit), all presented in no-nonsense piles on the shelves. You can also find a few amusing treats amid the traditional stock, like gummy mummies commemorating Guanajuato's oddest sight.

The delightfully sugary **La Catrina** (Sopeña 4, tel. 473/732-6089, www.dulcerialacatrina.com.mx, 9am-9pm daily) is a massive, colorful Mexican sweets shop, right across the street from Teatro Juárez. Within this shiny two-story shop are some wonderful and unusual candies, like fig and walnut paste, shredded coconut bars, and *palenquetas* (honey-covered discs of nuts, pumpkin seeds, or amaranth). Regional treats include *cajeta*, which is largely produced in nearby Celaya, as well as *xoconostle* jam, made from the fruit of a sour prickly pear that is popular in the region. The store's employees will be happy to give you a basket to collect your goodies as well as free samples of some of the more unusual candies.

Sports and Recreation

YOGA AND MASSAGE

Just beside the Templo San Roque, **Dojo Tao** (Bajada de San Roque 25, cell tel. 473/119-2294, hours vary by class) is an active yoga center and holistic space that offers a range of classes in a small wood-floored studio, including several weekly Hatha and Ashtanga classes, restorative yoga, and yoga for children, in addition to special workshops in tai chi, Reiki, massage, and other healing arts. A single class costs about US$4, with discounts for four- or eight-class packages.

SPAS

The luxury boutique hotel **Villa María Cristina** (Paseo de la Presa 76, tel. 473/731-2182, toll-free Mex. tel. 800/702-7007, www.villamariacristina.com, 9am-5pm daily) operates a lovely little spa on the first floor of the hotel property, located in the pretty, quiet neighborhood near the Presa de la Olla. Spa facilities include a dry sauna, Swiss showers, a gym, and a Jacuzzi, which are open to hotel guests or to those who book a treatment. Day passes for those not staying at the hotel are also available; they include tea, snacks, and access to all spa facilities for up to six hours.

HIKING, BIKING, AND HORSEBACK RIDING

There are lots of little paths leading into the craggy peaks around Guanajuato, some of which are well maintained and easily accessible. A quick taxi ride from the *centro histórico* will take you to a trailhead to the **Cerro de la Bufa**, a tall, craggy peak just above the Presa de la Olla. Where the road ends, a trail begins. It is a steep ascent, and it takes about 1.5-2 hours to climb to the top. (You'll make it back in about half the time.) On the way up, you may pass local livestock grazing as well as a few small homes. Once there, the view is panoramic, with a distant vista of the valley beyond the city of Guanajuato. The beautiful views and the accessibility of this trail make it one of the most popular day hikes around the city. The terrain is unstable and rocky, so don't take unnecessary risks near steep hills or precipices.

If you'd like to take a guided hike or explore regions farther off the beaten path, **Cacomixtle** (cell tel. 473/738-5246 or 473/122-5033, www.cacomixtle.com) offers ecotours in the countryside around Guanajuato, as well as cultural tours of the city, the mines, and several small towns in the region. Some hiking and bird-watching trips head to the craggy peaks of Sierra de Santa Rosa; though just outside the city, this small mountain range offers a chance to visit a largely untouched wilderness and small rural communities. Tours generally run US$60-75 per person for a day trip, including transportation and gear, though overnight trips cost more.

Classes

For many foreigners, Guanajuato is an ideal place to spend several weeks on the cheap, hanging out with other travelers, sipping coffee in inexpensive eateries, studying Spanish, or reveling in rowdy nightlife. Fortunately, there are plenty of excellent and popular language schools in this little town. Even if you don't sign up for a formal language program, check out the university's art and cultural offerings, which often include lectures and workshops open to the public.

SPANISH LANGUAGE

Founded in the early 1990s, the affordable **Escuela Mexicana** (Potrero 12, tel. 473/732-5005, www.escuelamexicana.com) is located in a cheerful colonial building in Guanajuato's *centro histórico*. This school's highly flexible and diverse Spanish programs let you tailor coursework to your personal interests or needs. Depending on their level and availability, students can enroll in group classes in grammar, conversation, and culture or sign up for private instruction. This school donates a percentage of its proceeds to charitable causes in the region. Depending on your desires, Escuela Mexicana will help students to arrange a homestay with a local family, or students can rent private rooms on the campus for a very reasonable price.

When Academia Falcon, one of Guanajuato's oldest and most popular language schools, closed its doors, some of the teachers from this well-loved program formed a new institution, the **Escuela Falcon** (Callejón de Gallitos 6, tel. 473/732-6531, www.escuelafalcon.com). Thanks to low enrollment and reasonable tuition cost, you'll get plenty of bang for your buck at this serious school (weekly rates start at US$45 for an hour of instruction daily, with per-hour rates dropping significantly if you sign up for multiple hours of class). In addition to Spanish language, students have the opportunity to take classes on Mexican art and culture, dance, history, and politics, and there are special programs for children with guiding themes like art, dance, or cinema. The school has several apartment rentals available to students at the school, most around US$300 a month. They can also arrange for homestays with locals.

Offering basic-, beginner-, and intermediate-level classes, **Colegio de Lenguas Adelita** (Callejón Agua Fuerte 56, tel. 473/732-0826, www.learnspanishadelita.com) has experienced teachers who hold degrees in Spanish. Both private classes and group classes are surprisingly well priced (a single group class costs US$8 for an hour, and US$39 for a week of one-hour classes), with further discounts for students who choose to study longer (US$100 a month for daily group classes). In addition to grammar and conversation, students can sign up for history and culture classes, as well as guided tours of the city.

Food

There are tons of tourist-friendly restaurant options filling the Plaza San Fernando, the Jardín de la Unión, and other picturesque locales across town; these eateries can be a great pick for a cold beer, a plate of guacamole, and an amazing atmosphere (not a bad combination by any standard). Generally speaking, however, the most visible restaurants may not be the best place for a satisfying or authentic Mexican meal. Catering to a transient tourist crowd, the service can be slow and the food unmemorable.

That said, Guanajuato's restaurant scene has made some considerable leaps forward. Not traditionally renowned for its cuisine, the city now offers some truly wonderful places to eat, a handful of cool cafés for sipping coffee, and a smattering of nice international options, adding a measure of welcome sophistication to this student-centric city.

CENTRO HISTÓRICO
Quick Bites

Throughout Guanajuato, there are casual **food stands** on almost every corner, many selling *gorditas* (stuffed and griddled corn cakes), tamales, sweets, fruit, potato chips, snacks, and juices. For a quick meal, you'll find the most variety on the first floor of the Mercado Hidalgo, where there are a host of tacos, *tortas, gorditas,* seafood and shrimp cocktails, fruit juices, cakes, and sweets at a variety of informal food stands. Carnitas (braised pork) is a specialty here, and you can order it in tacos or a *torta,* served sandwich-style inside a white roll.

Feeding the Mexican national obsession with shrimp cocktail, **Mariscos La Vela** (Constancia 3, tel. 473/120-6901, 11am-7pm daily, US$5) is a small seafood counter behind the Teatro Juárez. Choose from a range of cocktails and tostadas with shrimp, oyster, and octopus; ceviche; seafood empanadas; and fried fish fillets, all made fresh in the moment

and served with a plate of limes and some hot sauce. With two locations in Guanajuato, La Vela's seafood is brought in continuously from the coast, meaning the catch is fresher than what you might expect to find in the Mexican highlands (stick to fully cooked food if you're concerned about the distance from the ocean). This is an inexpensive, easygoing place for a good bite. They also operate a second branch (Subida de los Ángeles s/n, Col. Marfil, tel. 473/100-9956, 11am-7pm daily) in the Marfil neighborhood.

Casual and quirky **Habibti Falafel's** (Sostenes Rocha 18C, tel. 473/732-9418, 11am-11pm daily, US$6) has an appealing menu that focuses on fresh, delicious, and generously portioned Middle Eastern-style dishes like dolmas, hummus, tabouleh, and custom-prepared falafel sandwiches. The comfortable, relaxed space has colorfully painted walls and music on the sound system. Grab a stool at the bar, or take your food to one of the small café tables or couches for a more leisurely meal. An alternative to the ubiquitous taco, it's a good option for vegetarians, too. To accompany your meal, order chai, lassi, an espresso, tea, or beer. If you still have room, you can finish up with baklava.

Mexican

An atmospheric restaurant on the Jardín de la Unión, **Casa Valadez** (Jardín de la Unión 3, tel. 473/732-0311, www.casavaladez.com, 8am-11pm daily, US$7) gets double points for ambience. Located on the east end of the Jardín de la Unión, the old-fashioned dining room is decorated with gray-and-gold columns, brass chandeliers, and patterned wallpaper. Bathrooms are particularly fancy. Always packed with tourists and families dining alfresco or lounging indoors in one of the restaurant's big booths, there is often a wait for a table on the weekends. The menu covers a full spectrum, including soups, salads,

Best Restaurants

★ **Mestizo:** At this lovely Mexican restaurant, traditional dishes, like *pollo con mole* and *sopa de tortilla,* are served with a chef-driven flair (page 169).

★ **El Midi Bistró:** Southern French food, weekly live music, and a beautiful romantic atmosphere are all good reasons to check out this popular Guanajuato restaurant (page 171).

★ **Delica Mitsu:** For a fresh, inexpensive, healthy, and veggie-friendly lunch, stop into this hole-in-the-wall Japanese deli for a bento box—or eat in at the newer location on Campanero (page 172).

★ **Café Tal:** Everyone's favorite Guanajuato coffee shop serves up strong brew and cool vibes, as well as a killer hot chocolate (page 172).

★ **Las Mercedes Banquetes y Restaurante:** Here, heirloom Mexican recipes are lovingly prepared and served in the cozy dining room of a family home overlooking the city center (page 173).

★ **Puscua:** In a romantic stone-walled dining room at the Casa Museo Gene Byron, this innovative Mexican restaurant is one of Guanajuato's best, presenting fresh local flavors with artistry and imagination (page 173).

burgers, sandwiches, enchiladas, and meat dishes; plates run from economical to pricey.

On a small alley just a block from the Jardín de la Unión, **Truco 7** (Truco 7, tel. 473/732-8374, www.hospederiadeltruco7.com, 8:30am-11pm daily, US$6) is a popular and inexpensive café that serves a range of tasty Mexican staples as well as a daily *comida corrida,* a three-course set-price lunch (though standard menu items tend to be tastier). This casual restaurant has the cozy and convivial atmosphere of a cool college hangout, with exposed brick walls, comfy wooden furniture, low lamps, and eclectic art on the walls. The restaurant is open from early in the morning until late at night, and the menu is filled with Mexican dishes, like enchiladas, good *sopa azteca,* sopes (thick corn tortillas topped with beans and chicken), and several mole dishes as well as breakfasts. Espresso drinks and desserts are also good here.

Toward the back of the Jardín de la Unión, **La Bohemia** (Jardín de la Unión 4, tel. 473/732-9772, 8:30am-10pm daily, US$5) is a surprisingly inexpensive place for a casual meal, despite its prime location in the central square. This small, traditional eatery serves a range of typical Mexican breakfasts, like *huevos a la mexicana* (eggs scrambled with chile pepper, tomato, and onion) and an inexpensive *comida corrida,* which usually includes soup, rice, a main plate, and a drink for a set price. With small tables, the atmosphere is functional rather than fancy, though large doorways open onto the jovial bustle of the Jardín de la Unión. Food is tasty, though simple, and service is friendly and attentive. Easy on the wallet and with plenty to recommend it, La Bohemia is popular with both locals and visitors.

Owned and operated by the chef Javier Cruz Hernández Vallejo, son of beloved local ceramic artist Capelo, ★ **Mestizo** (Positos 69, tel. 473/732-0612, 1pm-10pm Mon.-Sat., 1pm-6pm Sun., $US8-10) is a wonderful modern Mexican restaurant. Located in what was once Capelo's downtown showroom, Mestizo's dining room preserves the gallery feel with white-cloth dining tables tucked between shelves of pretty hand-painted platters, flatware, and urns. Traditional Mexican dishes get an update here—*sopa azteca* is served on a slate platter with all the traditional ingredients (crisp tortillas, avocado, cheese) prettily arranged around a bowl of bright-orange broth. Other dishes, like the steak with *chile morita* and cilantro pesto, use local ingredients to create innovative flavors to good effect. For the quality of the food, the surprisingly accessible prices, and the beauty of its presentation, Mestizo has become a favorite with locals, and it is certainly one of the most satisfying places to eat in town.

A relaxed cantina-style dinner-and-drinks spot, **Metate** (Positos 79, no phone, www.metate.mx, 4pm-midnight Wed.-Sun., US$6) is a good choice for a casual meal, right in the center of town. The menu of tacos and bar snacks includes several veggie-friendly options, like tacos stuffed with zucchini, corn, and beans, as well as more stick-to-your ribs options, like tacos filled with pulled pork or fried calamari. It's also worth ordering the delicious roasted-avocado guacamole, which comes served atop the restaurant's namesake metate (a flat volcanic stone used for grinding). The food is complemented by a short but nicely curated list of craft cocktails, spirits, and wine as well as artisanal beer from local producer Serrana. Note that there are only four tables and a bar with stools, so the room can fill up at the dinner hour.

Italian

From the Jardín de la Unión, you can see the royal blue facade of **El Gallo Pitagorico** (Constancia 10, tel. 473/732-9489, 2pm-10:30pm Tues.-Sat., 2pm-8:30pm Sun., US$8-12) peeking over the top of the Teatro Juárez. You will have to walk up quite a few stairs (more than 100, in fact!) to get to this creaky Italian joint, but the view from the windows is worth the climb—overlooking the back of the Templo de San Diego, Teatro Juárez, and the sweeping cityscape beyond. The extensive menu is standard Italian fare, with appetizers like fried calamari and minestrone soup accompanying the selection of decently prepared pasta and lasagna, as well as beer and wine, but the view makes this restaurant a lovely place to watch the sun go down with just about any accompaniment.

Just down the street from Teatro Juárez, **La Capellina** (Sopeña 3, tel. 473/732-7224, http://lacapellina.com.mx, 1:30pm-10:30pm Mon.-Wed., 1:30pm-midnight Fri.-Sat., 1:30pm-8pm Sun., US$10) has an elegant atmosphere with a spacious and romantically lit

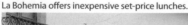
La Bohemia offers inexpensive set-price lunches.

Bar snacks, cocktails, and craft brews are available at Metate.

modern dining room. The menu at this fusion restaurant runs the gamut—from steak and tacos to crispy salads and sushi-grade tuna—however, the pastas and thin-crust pizzas are the most popular dishes and are probably the best options on the menu. While the elegant atmosphere really lends itself to a glass of wine or a cocktail, the wine list doesn't play a robust role in the restaurant's offerings. On the weekends, there are often live musicians playing jazz, Latin rhythms, or classical guitar.

French

A lovely French bakery, café, and restaurant, **La Vie en Rose** (Cantarranas 18, tel. 473/120-5793, 10am-10pm Tues.-Sat., 11am-8pm Sun., US$4-9) is the perfect place for an espresso and an éclair after walking around Guanajuato's downtown. You'll find a changing selection of fresh, authentically prepared French breads, pastries, cakes, sweets, quiche, and sandwiches laid out in the large glass display cases on the restaurant's first floor. Order your pastry and an espresso drink (or a glass

of red wine) at the counter, then head upstairs to the beautiful second-floor dining rooms. There isn't a bad table in this lovely colonial-era mansion, with tile floors, soaring ceilings, and windows opening onto the street below. Though most popular for coffee and sweets, La Vie en Rose also serves French meals at lunch and dinnertime, with a petite, daily changing selection of dishes like roast pork with potatoes and coq au vin.

Beloved Southern French restaurant ★ **El Midi Bistró** (Casa Cuatro, San José 4, tel. 473/732-7401, 9am-10pm Sun.-Mon. and Wed.-Thurs., 9am-11pm Fri.-Sat., US$8) offers some very nice bites in a lovely setting, from breakfast through dinner. Relocated from its long-standing spot in the Plaza San Fernando, El Midi now occupies a creaky wood-floored dining room on the second floor of cultural and culinary center Casa Cuatro, with cute wooden tables and narrow balconies opening onto the street below. At breakfast, try a nicely made omelet stuffed with Swiss chard or a freshly baked and toasted baguette with butter, either of which go nicely with a cup of Midi's strong coffee. For lunch and dinner, the menu leans heavily on rich French-influenced dishes, like duck confit and steak with blue-cheese sauce; if you're looking for a lighter meal, drop in for a few drinks (there's a good wine list and a full bar) and a selection of appetizers, like the charcuterie platter and herbed olives. The restaurant hosts live music every weekend, adding to the ace atmosphere.

There are many restaurants around the beautiful Plaza San Fernando, all of which will provide you with a romantic setting, excellent people-watching, and a leafy ceiling of trees. One such place is **Bossanova Café** (Plaza San Fernando 24, tel. 473/732-3504, 10am-11pm Mon.-Sat., 10am-9pm Sun., US$6), a laid-back eatery specializing in crepes and coffee. The simple menu includes savory crepes with eggplant, mushrooms, and other fillings, plus sweet crepes with fillings like *cajeta* or chocolate. Accompany your meal with an espresso or a glass of wine and then enjoy the afternoon in the plaza. The waitstaff is unrushed, and the vibe is mellow. With several umbrella-shaded tables in the heart of the Plaza San Fernando, this restaurant's biggest attraction is the atmosphere.

Spanish

Just off the Plaza Baratillo, the narrow dining room at **Los Campos** (Calle de la Alameda 4A, http://loscampos.mx, 1pm-10pm Tues.-Sun., US$8) feels like a fancy cantina, with low lighting and comfortable wooden tables running along the building's old stone walls. The atmosphere is an appropriate backdrop for the excellent drink menu, which offers a range of Mexican craft beer, mezcal (both local and Oaxacan), Mexican wines (including some Guanajuato-state-produced vintages, by both the glass and the bottle), tequila, and more unusual Mexican liquors, like rum from Tapachula, Chiapas. The accompanying food menu features Spanish-style tapas and other fancy Mexican-inspired bar snacks, and many plates are good for sharing, like the pork meatballs in tomato sauce, roasted mushrooms, or guacamole made with mezcal.

Asian

★ **Delica Mitsu** (Callejón de Cantaritos 37, tel. 473/732-3881, noon-9pm Mon.-Sat., US$6) is a little Japanese deli tucked into a tiny ascending alley, just behind the Plaza Fernando. For surprisingly low prices, you can order a lovely plate of sushi rolls or teriyaki chicken with sides from the deli case, or choose a made-to-order bento box with three, four, or five selections from the deli (get there early if you want salads; the food runs out around 4pm). While the lineup changes daily, Delica Mitsu always offers wonderful salads and noodle dishes as well as more unusual dishes like cabbage cakes and teriyaki potatoes, plus miso soup, tempura, Japanese green teas, Japanese beers, and sake. You can sit at one of the three creaky tables just outside the deli or order your food to go. If you're looking for a little more space, try the restaurant's bigger (but still rather cozy) location (Campanero 5, tel. 473/732-3881, noon-5pm Mon.-Sat.) on pedestrian street Campanero, where there are several dark-wood tables and more room to stretch out.

Coffee Shops and Dessert

There is a decidedly student-esque feeling at low-key coffee shop **El Lechón Ilustrado** (Del Truco 5, tel. 473/734-1832, 9am-midnight Mon.-Sat., 10am-11pm Sun., US$3), where books are stacked on shelves and shared among patrons, creaky café tables are often populated by youngsters with laptops, and the inexpensive menu is easy on your wallet. Also, it's open late. Top-quality coffee and a surprisingly diverse selection of imported teas (a rarity in Mexico) are served, delightfully, with a little pig-shaped oat cookie (the namesake *lechón*). To find it, look for the wooden pig above the door.

With outdoor seating on a tiny footbridge over the Calle Campanero, **Santo Café** (Puente de Campanero, Campanero 4, tel. 473/122-2320, santo-cafe@hotmail.com, 10am-midnight Mon.-Sat., noon-midnight Sun.) might have the city's most romantic location. It seems there is always a small crowd relaxing away the afternoon here in a ray of golden sunlight. The café sells beer, wines, and coffee as well as sandwiches, flautas, and salads. The food is good, and the setting makes it even better. There is also wireless Internet.

★ **Café Tal** (Sostenes Rocha, tel. 473/732-6212, 7am-midnight Mon.-Sat., 8am-midnight Sun., US$1) is the type of place that takes coffee seriously. Here, all beans are dark roasted in-house and expertly brewed to be strong and full-bodied. Open from early in the morning until late at night, the café's two rooms of shaky granite tables are continuously populated with hipsters on laptops, while waiters in black T-shirts serve brew and breads. There is a little table near the register with thermoses of strong self-serve drip coffee, which you can take to go.

A little café and ice cream parlor tucked into a narrow pedestrian alley, **Estación Gelato** (Callejón de Cantaritos 29, tel. 473/732-801, www.estaciongelato.com, noon-9pm Mon.-Fri., 11am-9pm Sat.-Sun., US$2) is a sweet spot to stop for a little afternoon pick-me-up. There's coffee, tea, brownies, homemade ice pops, and ice cream in flavors like lime, green tea, mango chai, and hazelnut. Grab one of the round café tables downstairs—the nicest is placed in a window overlooking the alley below—or, on a sunny day, head up to the roof deck, where you can sit amid the rooftops of Guanajuato.

NORTH OF THE *CENTRO*
Mexican

It is well worth a trip to the San Javier neighborhood to dine at the lovely family-run ★ **Las Mercedes Banquetes y Restaurante** (Calle de Arriba 6, Fracc. San Javier, tel. 473/733-9059, lasmercedesrestaurante@gmail.com, 2pm-10pm Tues.-Sat., 2pm-6pm Sun., US$15). Offering heirloom Mexican recipes with a contemporary touch, Las Mercedes presents traditional flavors with a creative flair that is surprising yet eminently delicious. From memorable starters like *escamoles en mantequilla de epazote* (ant eggs in epazote butter) or *sopa de huitlacoche* (cornfungus soup) to entrées like a cheese-stuffed *chile pasilla,* it is tempting to try everything on the menu. Whatever you choose, you'll enjoy flavorful, unique, and perfectly prepared food that is both elegant and pleasingly homemade. The restaurant maintains a large selection of Mexican wines as well as margaritas, spirits, beer, and its signature mezcal-*xoconostle* cocktail made with the fruit of a sour prickly pear. Despite its off-the-beaten track location, this place has gotten enough buzz to attract a nightly seating of tourists and locals. Reservations are necessary; come with an appetite.

SOUTHWEST OF THE *CENTRO*
Mexican

The rustic stone dining room at ★ **Puscua** (Museo Gene Byron, Camino Real de Marfil Ex Hacienda de Santa Ana s/n, tel. 473/733-5018, 8:30am-5pm Tues.-Sun., US$9), within the romantic old hacienda that houses the Museo Gene Byron, is one of the most interesting spots to dine in Guanajuato. Here, the chef's creative takes on traditional Mexican dishes pay off with great flavor, such as in the dried chile filled with *chilaquiles* at breakfast or braised *chamorro* (pork leg) for lunch. Everything is beautifully plated and surprisingly low-priced. Between the enchanting setting and the wonderful food, eating here

It's all about the unique atmosphere at bridge-top coffee shop Santo Café.

creative Mexican restaurant Puscua, one of Guanajuato's best eateries

feels like a special occasion. The restaurant does not serve alcohol, though they do have a daily *agua* (fruit drink), as well as coffee, tea, and *limonadas*.

SOUTHEAST OF THE *CENTRO*
Mexican

Away from the bustle of the *centro histórico*, **Mexico Lindo y Sabroso** (Paseo de la Presa 154, tel. 473/731-0529, 9am-10pm daily, US$7) is a nice place to linger over an afternoon meal. The airy dining room has a pleasingly Mexican atmosphere, with red-lacquer furniture, crafts on the walls, and *ranchera* music overhead. In front, the lovely covered patio overlooks the Paseo de la Presa, with big, comfortable seats and large tables. Service is attentive, and the waitstaff adds to the Mexican atmosphere with spiffy tricolor bow ties and white collared shirts. The extensive menu is entirely Mexican, offering a range of inexpensive and generously served dishes like enchiladas, *enmoladas,* and *sopa azteca* as well as some more unusual yet tasty Yucatec dishes, like *papadzules* (egg-filled tortillas topped with pumpkin-seed sauce and more hard-boiled egg) and *cochinita pibil* (pulled pork with achiote and spices). Everything tastes freshly prepared and is nicely seasoned; chips and salsa at the table make a nice start.

Accommodations

Guanajuato is a big national and international tourist destination, drawing crowds of visitors year-round. While winter is technically the high season in Mexico, Guanajuato's tourist season is a bit more inconsistent. In fact, hotel rates tend to fluctuate substantially in Guanajuato, depending on demand. Most notably, the city's many cultural events, especially the annual Festival Internacional Cervantino in October, draw large crowds and can have a huge effect on hotel prices. Most hotels double or even triple their rates during this period, even if they aren't at capacity. With the exception of the Cervantino festival, Semana Santa, and the Christmas holidays, however, hotels rarely fill up. Usually,

Best Accommodations

★ **La Casa Azul Hotel:** You'll feel like you're staying at a family home at this small, quirky, and inexpensive hotel, perched on a narrow street above the city center (page 176).

★ **El Zopilote Mojado:** At this well-priced guesthouse, clean and cheerful bedrooms are located in buildings that surround a quiet plaza, right in the center of town (page 176).

★ **Alma del Sol:** At this small, quirky, and perfectly located bed-and-breakfast, the extravagant morning meals on the rooftop patio are an ace way to start the day (page 177).

★ **Hotel Antiguo Vapor:** The nicest rooms at this traditional Mexican inn have big windows overlooking the city center (page 178).

★ **Hotel Edelmira:** Posh yet comfortable and friendly, this stylish hotel has a center-of-it-all location, with some rooms overlooking the Jardín de la Unión (page 178).

★ **Casa del Rector:** This luxury boutique hotel in a gorgeous historic building has sweeping views of the city from the rooftop pool and cocktail bar (page 179).

it is possible to snag a room on short notice. However, to spare yourself trekking around steep alleyways, it's best to have a hotel destination in mind before you arrive.

Perhaps because demand is high and fairly continuous, very few of Guanajuato's hotels offer really great value. Many of the hotels in the *centro histórico* are unapologetically basic, offering little more than a spring bed and a small bathroom—not even a poster on the wall. Nicer hotels may add a bit of charm, but most tend to be fairly pared down. In Guanajuato, you will pay extra for a nice location, but you are likely to spend most of your time in the streets, not in your accommodations.

CENTRO HISTÓRICO
Under US$50
Guanajuato is a backpacker's paradise, with dozens of ultracheap youth hostels peppered throughout the city center. For solo travelers, Guanajuato's hostels can also be a great place to make friends in the city, while groups or couples traveling together can rent cheap private rooms with shared baths in most

budget accommodations. Those looking for the quintessential hostel experience will find a happy home at **La Casa del Tío** (Cantarranas 47, tel. 473/733-9728, www.hostellacasadeltio.com.mx, US$9-10 dorms, US$15-40 doubles). This popular hostel is in a funky red-and-white stucco house, right in the center of downtown and just a stone's throw from some of the city's most popular student bars. Shared dorms have large windows and lots of light. All guests also have access to the hostel's laundry facilities, computer and Internet, and a nice roof deck. Private rooms are a little pricier per person, depending on if you have a shared or private bathroom, but they are still among the cheapest accommodations in town.

The laid-back and quirky **Casa de Pita** (Callejón Cabecita 26, tel. 473/732-1532, http://casadepita.com, US$40-65) is a great find in the budget category. Tucked into an enchanting alleyway behind the Plaza Mexiamora and only a few blocks from the Jardín de la Unión, the location could not be better. Some larger rooms have cute little kitchenettes that can be used to whip up a snack, and most are eclectically decorated with tiles and lamps.

While these aren't luxury accommodations, the rooms are comfortable, and the style is fun and colorful. Pita herself is a friendly host who enjoys chatting with her guests over breakfast.

It is a steep walk up a narrow alley, but the aerobic workout is just another benefit of staying at the friendly, family-run ★ **La Casa Azul Hotel** (Carcamanes 57, tel. 473/731-2288, www.lacasaazul.com.mx, US$40-45). Perched high above the Plaza Baratillo, this six-room inn feels like the home of your *abuela* (grandmother), with the quirky details and comfort to match. The rooms vary in size and decor, but each is full of creaky old wooden furniture, crooked lamps, and thick Mexican bedspreads. Comfortably appointed, all rooms are equipped with a private bath and cable television, and some have sitting areas. There is a beautiful terrace on the roof; from here, you can enjoy the views you earned after the walk up the hill. In the basement, the hotel also has a small, windowless cantina, only accessible by ladder—atmospheric and cool, though a touch claustrophobic, too. It's owned by a Guanajuato family, and service is friendly and personable.

US$50-100

A plain but serviceable option in the very center of town, **Hotel Mesón del Rosario** (Av. Juárez 31, tel. 473/732-3284, www.hotelmesondelrosario.com.mx, US$60) is a good home base for exploring Guanajuato. Although located on busy Avenida Juárez, rooms are set back from the noise and bustle, surrounding a pleasant central walkway. Rooms are rather unembellished though tidy, with tile floors and small double beds topped with woven bedspreads and wooden headboards. Some rooms are a bit more atmospheric than others; if it isn't a busy holiday weekend, press the staff to show you additional options if you aren't satisfied with their first offer.

Hospedería del Truco 7 (Constancia 15, tel. 473/732-6513, www.hospederiadeltruco7.com, US$80-90) is owned by the same folks that run the popular Truco 7 restaurant. The guesthouse, unlike the restaurant, is not at the address Truco 7, as the name implies, but perched on a hillside just behind the Teatro Juárez and the Templo de San Diego. The seven rooms are simple and cozy, with comfortable Mexican-style furniture, oversize headboards, and cotton bedspreads. Every room has low wood-beamed ceilings, a TV, and a small, tiled bath with hand-painted sinks and showers. The nicest rooms in the front of the house have small balconies that open onto the alley below, offering a wonderful view of downtown Guanajuato. There's not much by way of sitting areas or shared facilities, but all of Guanajuato is at your doorstep. They only accept cash.

★ **El Zopilote Mojado** (Plaza Mexiamora 51, tel. 473/732-5311, www.elzopilotemojado.com, US$75) is a cute and tidy hotel, scattered across several small houses on the pretty Plaza Mexiamora. Located above a coffee shop of the same name, there are just three guest rooms in the main building, plus several more rooms in another building on the same plaza. The guest rooms are decorated with cheerful Mexican-style furnishings and comfortably outfitted with fans, electric blankets, closets, clock radios, bathrobes, and plenty of lighting. Some also have small balconies or terraces. At night, guests let themselves in via coded lock on the door. Management can feel a bit absent on Sundays when the café is closed, but this hotel is one of the nicer establishments in its price range. For those who like a little more space, El Zopilote also rents small apartments with kitchenettes.

A popular hotel close to the Diego Rivera museum, **El Mesón de los Poetas** (Positos 35, tel. 473/732-0705 or 473/732-6657, www.mesondelospoetas.com, US$70-90) has more than 40 quirky, comfortable guest rooms in a restored 18th-century home. From the street, a pretty tiled atrium leads you to the bedrooms upstairs, which are arranged around the hotel's mazelike central hallways. Note that rooms on higher floors often have more natural light, but also require you to walk up several stories (and there is no elevator), so choose accordingly. The two largest suites have views overlooking the facing hillside; the rest have interior windows, overlooking the indoor hallways. The dining room downstairs is a highlight, adjoined by an old stone retaining wall and fountain; breakfast is included in the price and served downstairs every morning.

Tucked into a narrow pedestrian alley that leads from the Plaza de la Paz to the main university campus, **Hotel de la Paz** (Callejón del Esudiante 1, tel. 473/732-0555, www.hoteldelapaz.com.mx, US$95-105) is a perfectly located small hotel with 14 spacious, modern, and comfortable guest rooms, each equipped with fast Wi-Fi connections, satellite TV, and fans. Many have large French doors that open onto the alley below, while others, on the upper floors, look over the plaza and have gorgeous views of the city. Breakfast, included in the nightly price, is offered at the restaurant inside sister hotel Casona de Don Lucas, just across the plaza.

Part of the same hotel group as the Hotel de la Paz, the **Hotel Santa Regina** (Alonso 26, tel. 473/732-5228 or 473/732-5428, www.hotelsantaregina.com, US$90) is a small, quiet property in a spacious old home on central Alonso Street, just a block from the Plaza de la Paz. The inviting guest rooms are large and comfortably (if unremarkably) furnished; all have telephones, Wi-Fi, and cable TV. For families or groups, there are a few roomy two-story accommodations, which can house three or four people at a very reasonable price. The same group also operates the **Casona de Don Lucas** (Plaza de la Paz 48, tel. 473/732-5228, www.lacasonadedonlucas.com, US$80-250), which is directly on the Plaza de la Paz and has rooms similar to those at the other two properties.

US$100-150

An intimate bed-and-breakfast in an old colonial-era mansion, ★ **Alma del Sol** (Calle del Sol 3, tel. 472/733-5423, www.almadelsol.com, US$65-100) is tucked behind huge mesquite-wood doors in the alley that runs alongside the Templo de la Compañía de Jesús, right in the center of town. This is a quirky place, with five second-floor rooms with towering ceilings and creaky wooden doors, decorated with traditional Mexican furniture and an impressive collection of traditional and antique textiles from India and Indonesia. Two double street-facing rooms have fabulous private balconies with views of the surrounding churches and

El Zopilote Mojado is a well-priced inn on a quiet pedestrian plaza.

mansions, though they can be a bit noisy in the evening. The nightly price includes what may be the best breakfast in town—served on the gorgeous roof deck, where you can chat with Alma del Sol's wonderfully friendly proprietor, Hugo, a Guanajuato native who can give you a full rundown of things to do, see, eat, and experience while you're in town.

Atmospheric ★ **Hotel Antiguo Vapor** (Galarza 5, tel. 473/732-3211, www.hotelavapor.com, US$135-160) is perched on a hill just above the city center, providing excellent views of the Mercado Hidalgo, the monument to El Pípila, and the surrounding cityscape. Guest rooms are small, simple, and comfortable, decorated in a warm, traditionally Mexican style, with Saltillo tile floors and colorful woven bedspreads adjoined by a pretty private bath with hand-painted tiles and showers. Some rooms have vaulted ceilings and stone walls; perhaps the nicest are those on the south side, with wee balconies and beautiful views overlooking the ravine below. The location is ideal—close to everything, yet just a bit removed from the noisy nightlife of downtown.

First opened in 1862, **Posada Santa Fe** (Jardín de la Unión 12, tel. 473/732-0084, toll-free Mex. tel. 800/112-4773, www.posadasantafe.mx, US$115-170) has a long history of welcoming visitors to Guanajuato, in addition to an enviable location smack-dab in the middle of the Jardín de la Unión. The lobby of this old colonial mansion is beautiful, with hand-painted tiles on the walls and big chandeliers overhead. Rooms are decidedly less fancy, but a recent renovation has left them clean and comfortable, though still boasting, in many cases, old colonial-style furnishings. Some rooms are brighter than others, some are quieter; the prettiest have French windows that open onto the plaza below (though note that rooms with views on the plaza run about US$40 more per night). The restaurant downstairs, with seating right in the Jardín de la Unión, is a great place to unwind with a drink at the end of the day.

US$150-200

Perhaps it's the remarkably affable service that makes boutique hotel **Alonso 10** (Alonso 10, tel. 473/732-7657, www.hotelalonso10.com. mx, US$180) feel like a discreet, tucked-away place to stay, despite its center-of-it-all location in a three-story colonial-era mansion. In the guest rooms, the hotel's modern brown-and-white color scheme and minimal decor let the building's original architecture stand out, notably the incredibly high ceilings on the second floor. Each room is different: Some have interior windows opening into the hotel's atrium, others have pretty Juliet balconies opening onto the street, and top-floor rooms have private terraces overlooking Calle Alonso and the many cupolas of the city. Ask to see what's available when you check in, or ask for your preference beforehand.

With a sleek lobby opening directly onto the Jardín de la Unión, **Hotel Boutique 1810** (Jardín de la Unión 7, tel. 473/732-2795, toll-free Mex. tel. 800/500-4001, www.hotel1850. com, US$160-235) seeks to bring a bit of contemporary panache to downtown Guanajuato. At this thoroughly modern establishment, each room is individually decorated—some are done up in dark colors, patterned wallpapers, and funky lighting schemes, while others are pastel-toned with floral furnishings and bed linens. Depending on which room you book, the ambience could be anything from romantic to nightclub. Some bedrooms have interior windows opening onto the hotel's central atrium, but those facing the plaza have far and away the best atmosphere; all have noise-cancelling windows and light-cancelling shutters to help block out the sound of mariachis from the Jardín de la Unión on weekend nights. Breakfast at Guanajuato staple Casa Valadez is included in the price, and there's a Starbucks in the lobby.

Over US$200

Achieving a perfect balance of romantic and posh, ★ **Hotel Edelmira** (Allende 7, Jardín de la Unión, tel. 473/732-3743, toll-free Mex.

boutique property Hotel Edelmira

windows opening onto the outdoor patio and restaurant, rather than the stuffier interior atrium. The small rooftop swimming pool is a true luxury, surrounded by lounge chairs and a sweeping view of downtown Guanajuato, and you can stop into the adjacent bar for a cocktail after taking a dip.

NORTH OF THE CENTRO
US$100-200

Part of a small Mexican-owned chain of luxury hotels, the **Camino Real Guanajuato** (Alhóndiga 100, Col. San Javier, tel. 473/102-1500, toll-free Mex. tel. 800/901-2300, toll-free U.S. tel. 800/722-6466, www.caminoreal.com, US$100-135) is a comfortable place to stay, just above the city center in the San Javier neighborhood. It inhabits the site of a former hacienda, and the entryway and lobby maintain much of the majesty of the original structure by blending new construction with the old. Crumbling rock walls and beautiful gardens give a pleasant colonial touch to the lobby and dining areas; there are big lawns, a pool, and old stone fountains across the property as well as on-site parking. Situated toward the back of the property, the 100-plus guest rooms are very small but clean and decorated in a plain, modern style. Catering to business travelers in addition to tourists, Camino Real offers some services and amenities you won't find in other Guanajuato establishments, such as room service, minibars, satellite TV, air-conditioning, and high-end toiletries.

SOUTHEAST OF THE CENTRO
US$50-100

The friendly **Casa Mágica** (Paseo de la Presa 79A, tel. 473/731-2301, http://casamagicahotel.com, US$45-70) is a simple, clean, and cozy hotel not far from the Presa de la Olla reservoir. Rooms are comfortable, with big white beds, tile floors, small safes, and satellite television. Adjoining private bathrooms are small but cute, with hand-painted ceramic sinks and showers. Most rooms have interior

tel. 800/561-9191, www.edelmirahotel.com, US$105-265) is a beautiful boutique hotel right on Guanajuato's Jardín de la Unión. Rooms are tastefully decorated with wooden furnishings, glass lamps, wool rugs, and rough stone walls; the best suites have balconies that open directly onto the Jardín de la Unión. There's a small, turquoise-tiled indoor pool and Jacuzzi for hotel guests as well as a downstairs restaurant that offers room service. In a city filled with pretty roof decks, Edelmira's is one of the nicest, with spectacular views of Guanajuato's domes, churches, and pastel-shaded houses rising all around.

Located in one of the oldest buildings in Guanajuato, ★ **Casa del Rector** (Positos 33, tel. 473/690-1512 or 473/732-9200, www.casadelrector.com, US$240-400) is a spectacularly pretty boutique hotel, right in the center of town. Though all the guest rooms share a luxe decor, high ceilings, and warm lighting, it's worth spending a little extra on the master suites on the upper floors, which have windows overlooking the hotel's sunny, plant-filled central atrium. Service is incredibly friendly and laid-back, and there is parking if you need it.

US$100-200

On the lovely Paseo de la Presa, just a few blocks from the reservoir, **Quinta Las Acacias** (Paseo de la Presa 168, tel. 473/731-1517, toll-free Mex. tel. 800/710-8938, www.quintalasacacias.com.mx, US$86-180) has a creaky old-world feeling. Housed in a converted 19th-century mansion, the common areas and restaurant feel like an old-fashioned parlor, with crystal chandeliers, heavy curtains, and floral wallpaper. In the bedrooms, furnishings are designed in an antique style, complementing the mansion's high ceilings and old wooden floors. Everything looks aged and full of character, yet doesn't feel worn or shabby. In fact, there are plenty of comforts in each guest room, including safes, televisions, and bathrobes. Rooms in the front of the house have windows overlooking a leafy park, which is a particularly nice way to greet the day. For those who want something a bit more "new world," there are also eight Mexican-themed suites located in the back part of the house.

Over $200

Guanajuato's most luxurious establishment, the **Villa María Cristina** (Paseo de la Presa 76, tel. 473/731-2182 or toll-free Mex. tel. 800/702-7007, www.villamariacristina.net, US$280-625) is a petite boutique property in the quiet residential neighborhood near the reservoir. In this lovely renovated mansion, guest rooms are arranged around tiled terraces, overlooking the pointed peak of the Cerro de la Bufa and the green hills below. Sparkling with brass and marble, rooms have high ceilings and French furniture, and they are decked out with every luxury, like heaters in the bathrooms, French toiletries, iPod docks, and Dutch-made sound systems. The hotel's gorgeous restaurant has its own small wine cellar, and guests can order drinks on any of the hotel's sun-drenched verandas. Guests can also use spa facilities, including the sauna and Swiss showers. Service is impeccably attentive.

The rooftop pool at Casa del Rector has sweeping views of the city center.

Information and Services

TOURIST INFORMATION

The **Oficina de Convenciones y Visitantes** (Jardín de la Unión, 10am-5pm daily) operates a small tourist information kiosk in the Jardín de la Unión. They will provide you with a map of Guanajuato's *centro histórico*, which points out the city's most important sights. The office offers walking tours of the city center as well as package tours of the city's more distant sights, like the mines.

Media

The daily Spanish-language newspaper *El Correo* (www.periodicocorreo.com.mx) is published in Guanajuato. *El Correo* covers regional, national, and international news, with sections dedicated to the cities of León, Irapuato, Salamanca, and Guanajuato. There is a weekly cultural supplement on Saturdays. It is the best place to read up on what's going on in Guanajuato; all text is in Spanish.

The Universidad de Guanajuato's cultural extension publishes free catalogs of upcoming arts events and movie screenings at the university, in addition to the magazine *Polen,* which includes essays on the visual arts and listings of upcoming arts events. *Polen* is available in a digital edition via the department's website (www.extension.ugto.mx).

An eclectic university radio station, **Radio Universidad** (www.radiouniversidad.ugto. mx) will keep Spanish-speaking listeners up to date with the city's news and cultural events. It also broadcasts an excellent international news program from the Latin American correspondent of Radio Francía Internacional each morning at 9am. Even if you don't speak Spanish, it can still be great fun to tune into the music programs on this arts-and-letters radio station. Depending on the DJ, you will hear a rather eclectic range of music, from jazz to classical to the Beatles. You can tune in at 970 AM or 100 FM in Guanajuato. From San Miguel de Allende, Radio Universidad is at 91.3 FM.

Travel Agents

Close to the Jardín de la Unión, **Viajes Frausto Guanajuato** (Luis González Obregón 10, tel. 473/732-3580 or 473/732-0115, http://frausto.agenciasviajes.mx, 9am-2pm and 4:30pm-8pm Mon.-Fri., 9am-2pm Sat.) can book airline tickets and tours. They can also book first-class bus tickets with ETN or Primera Plus, saving you a long trip out to the bus station.

Visas and Officialdom

The closest **U.S. Consular Agency** (Plaza La Luciérnaga, Libramiento Jose Manuel Zavala No. 165, Locales 4 y 5, Colonia La Luciernaga, toll-free Mex. tel. 800/681-9374, toll-free U.S. tel. 844/528-6611, conagencysanmiguel@state.gov, http://mx.usembassy.gov, 9am-1pm Mon.-Thurs.) is in San Miguel de Allende. As a branch of the U.S. embassy in Mexico City, the consulate can replace lost or expired passports, among other services (though it may take a bit longer through the consulate than if you go directly to the embassy). There is often a wait for services, so arrive early or call ahead to see if you can schedule an appointment. For most other countries, including Australia, Canada, and the United Kingdom, the closest consular agency is in the capital.

San Miguel de Allende is also home to the regional delegation of the **Instituto Nacional de Migración** (INM, Mexican Immigration Service, Calzada de la Estación FFCC, tel. 415/152-8991, 9am-1pm Mon.-Fri.). You can visit INM to extend your tourist card, apply for a resident visa, or report a missing tourist card. If you arrive from Guanajuato by bus, the immigration offices are just a short walk or taxi ride from the station, on the Calzada de la Estación behind the Bodega Aurrera.

SERVICES
Medical and Emergency Services

Right in the city center, **Clíníca de la Paz** (Plaza de la Paz 20, tel. 473/732-2305, ext. 103 or 224, 24 hours daily) has doctors that specialize in gynecology, pediatrics, internal medicine, dermatology, and surgery, among other fields. They also offer 24-hour pharmacy service and emergency care.

The well-regarded **Centro Medico La Presa** (Paseo de la Presa 85, tel. 473/102-3100, ext. 101 for information or 103 for appointments, www.centromedicolapresa.mx, 24 hours daily) is a full-service medical clinic with general medicine doctors, specialists, and surgeons. In the case of emergency, there are doctors in the clinic 24 hours a day. The government-run **Hospital Guanajuato** (Carretera a Silao, Km 6, tel. 473/733-1573 or 473/733-1576) is outside the city center on the toll highway toward Silao and also receives emergencies.

In the city center, **Farmacias Santa Fe** (Plaza de la Paz 52, tel. 473/732-0170, 9am-9pm Mon.-Sat., 11am-8pm Sun.) sells prescription drugs and toiletries.

For police and other emergency services, dial **911** from any ground line to reach the city emergency services. For medical emergencies, the **Cruz Roja** (Red Cross, Av. Juárez 131, tel. 065 or 473/732-0487, http://cruzroja-guanajuato.org) offers emergency response, medical services, and ambulances.

Money

Right between the Jardín de la Unión and the Plaza de la Paz (just across the street from Hotel San Diego), **Banorte** (Luis González Obregón 1, toll-free Mex. tel. 800/226-6783, 9am-5pm Mon.-Fri.) has a bank branch with tellers, currency exchange, and two ATMs, all located in a lovely historical building. Just a block away is an **HSBC** (Plaza de la Paz 509, tel. 473/732-0018, 9am-5pm Mon.-Fri., 9am-2pm Sat.). You'll find a number of other banks along Benito Juárez, near the Mercado Hidalgo.

Transportation

GETTING THERE
Air
DEL BAJÍO INTERNATIONAL AIRPORT (BJX)

Guanajuato is about 40 kilometers (25 miles) from the **Del Bajío International Airport** (BJX, Carretera Silao-León, Km 5.5, Col. Nuevo México, Silao, tel. 472/748-2120), on the highway to León, just beyond the auto plants in Silao. From BJX, there are daily direct flights to and from Dallas, Houston, and Los Angeles as well as several flights to and from Mexico City and Monterrey.

From the airport, you can take a registered taxi to Guanajuato for about US$30. The drive to downtown takes about 30 minutes. There are taxis available at the airport to meet arriving flights, even late at night. Buy a ticket for your taxi at the ticket booth inside the airport terminal and then meet the cabs curbside. Alternatively, you can rent a car at the airport and drive it to Guanajuato. There are several rental car companies with offices in the airport, most of which are open from early morning to late night.

Taxi Express Linea Dorada (tel. 473/732-6142) can take you from Guanajuato to the airport for about US$25.

MEXICO CITY INTERNATIONAL AIRPORT (MEX)

It can be less expensive and, in some cases, more convenient for international visitors to fly to **Mexico City International Airport** (MEX, Capitan Carlos León s/n, Peñón de Los Baños Venustiano Carranza, Distrito Federal, tel. 55/2482-2400, www.aicm.com.mx) in the capital. From the airport in Mexico

City, travelers must arrange for ground transportation to Guanajuato, usually by bus. Direct buses operated by ETN and Primera Plus (see below) leave from Mexico City's **Terminal Central del Norte** (Eje Central Lázaro Cárdenas 4907, Gustavo A Madero, Magdalena de Las Salinas, Mexico D.F., www.centraldelnorte.com) several times a day. The trip from Mexico City to Guanajuato takes about five hours; most buses stop in Irapuato en route. Travelers should also prepare for heavy traffic leaving the capital, which can affect travel time.

Bus

Guanajuato's **Central de Autobuses** (Carretera de Cuota Guanajuato-Silao, Km 7) is about eight kilometers (five miles) outside the city center on the highway toward Silao. Once you arrive at the terminal, you can take a city bus downtown for about US$0.50; they are marked *Centro* in the front windshield and depart from right in front of the station every 15 minutes or so. Buses often stop in the underground tunnels below the *centro histórico,* so if you have never been to Guanajuato before, ask the driver to notify you when to get off. For quicker service, you can take a city taxi from the bus station to the *centro histórico* for about US$4.

From Mexico City, San Miguel de Allende, and other points in the Bajío, there is ample first-class bus service to and from Guanajuato as well as connecting service to cities all over the country. **Primera Plus** (Carretera de Cuota Guanajuato-Silao, Km 7, Central de Autobuses, toll-free Mex. tel. 800/375-7587, www.primeraplus.com.mx) operates more than a dozen direct first-class buses between the Terminal Central del Norte in Mexico City and the Central de Autobuses in Guanajuato every day (US$31). Primera Plus also operates direct routes to and from San Miguel de Allende, León, and Celaya as well as connecting service to Puerto Vallarta and the airport in Guadalajara. Buses are comfortable, air-conditioned, and equipped with bathrooms; Primera Plus even provides its clients

with a small snack and soft drink for the ride. During big events like the Cervantino festival or nationwide holidays like Semana Santa, Primera Plus will often extend its daily service to include two or three extra departures.

For local travel, **Servicios Coordinados Flecha Amarilla** (Carretera a Silao, Km 8, toll-free Mex. tel. 800/375-7587, www.primeraplus.com.mx), operated by the same company as Primera Plus, offers second-class bus service to the town of Dolores Hidalgo (US$4), departing every 20 minutes from about 7am until about 10pm. You don't need to book your ticket ahead of time; just arrive at the station and buy a ticket for the next departing bus. Alternatively, buses to Dolores pass through the city center and depart via the Valenciana neighborhood. You can save time by catching the bus from there. Look for the sign in the window indicating the bus's destination in Santa Rosa or Dolores Hidalgo.

Another swanky first-class bus line serving central and northern Mexico, **ETN** (Carretera de Cuota Guanajuato-Silao, Km 7, Central de Autobuses, tel. 473/733-1579, toll-free Mex. tel. 800/800-0386, www.etn.com.mx) has 10 first-class buses between Mexico City and Guanajuato (US$36) each day. As on Primera Plus, you'll get bathrooms, snacks, and a movie, though ETN's seats are even bigger and more comfortable (and tickets are correspondingly costlier). ETN also offers service from Guanajuato to Guadalajara, San Miguel de Allende, and León, with connecting service to the beach or to other major cities.

Another alternative for intercity travel is **Group Estrella Blanca** (Carretera Guanajuato-Silao, Km 6, Central de Autobuses Guanajuato, tel. 473/733-1344, toll-free Mex. tel. 800/507-5500, www.estrellablanca.com.mx), which offers first-class bus service between Guanajuato and the southerly Tasqueña station in Mexico City (US$33), as well as other parts of the Bajío (not including San Miguel de Allende) on their luxury line Futura Plus and their first-class line Futura. It also offers second-class bus service on its economy line, Estrella Blanca, which services most towns and cities in the Bajío and central Mexico.

GETTING AROUND

The easiest and most efficient way to get around Guanajuato's city center is on foot. In fact, many of Guanajuato's sights and restaurants cannot be accessed any other way, since roads run underground in many parts of the *centro*. However, if you are planning to spend some time outside the downtown district, you may need to arrange other transportation.

Car

As many residents or visitors can tell you, having a car can be a bit of challenge in Guanajuato, as many streets in the *centro histórico* are reserved for pedestrian traffic or are too small to allow automobiles. For those who come with wheels, it is best to look for parking on the street or in a lot while you explore the city center on foot. You can park along the underground tunnels (look for signs that indicate where parking is permitted); one multilevel public parking lot, **Estacionamiento Alonso** (Constancia 11), is just behind the Teatro Juárez. If you are staying overnight in Guanajuato, ask your hotel about parking options.

While a car is generally a nuisance in the center of town, it can be helpful to have wheels if you are staying in a hotel outside of the city center or if you'd like to explore small towns or hiking opportunities in the surrounding country. Like walking, driving in Guanajuato can be a bit of a challenge. Maps tend to be confusing, thanks to the bilevel structure of the city, and satellite-connected GPS systems, like Google Maps, are impossible to use, as they are frequently confused by Guanajuato's many alleys, tunnels, and one-way streets. However, there are road signs at every fork and turn. In most cases, if you follow these signs, you will eventually get to your destination (though probably not without a few wrong turns!). The most important thing is to keep an eye out for one-way signs before making a turn and to be careful of the many pedestrians and frequently stopping buses.

CAR RENTAL

If you plan to do some driving while in Guanajuato, the easiest place to rent a car is at the airport, where you will find desks for several major car rental companies. **Avis** (León-Bajío International Airport, Carretera Silao-León, Km 5.5, Silao, tel. 472/748-2054, toll-free Mex. tel. 800/288-8888, www.avis.

Navigating the city center can be difficult.

mx, 6am-11:30pm daily) rents compact cars and regular-size sedans at low daily rates. **Budget** (León-Bajío International Airport, Carretera Silao-León, Km 5.5, Silao, tel. 472/748-2001, www.budget.com.mx, 6am-11pm daily) also operates out of the airport.

Taxi

There are inexpensive taxis circling throughout Guanajuato's downtown district as well as around the bus station. Most charge a flat rate for service anywhere in the downtown area, usually about US$2. For service to neighborhoods outside the *centro histórico*, like La Valenciana or the bus station, the rate may go up to US$3. You can also call a taxi from **Taxi Express Linea Dorada** (tel. 473/732-6142) for service within the city of Guanajuato, or for service from Guanajuato to the BJX/León airport (about US$25 one way).

While cabs are inexpensive, they aren't omnipresent. Many of Guanajuato's alleys and plazas are not accessible by taxi. Most cabs will get you as close to your destination as they can, but door-to-door service isn't always possible.

Bus

Inexpensive city buses can take you to all of Guanajuato's major neighborhoods from the city center. Most buses run from morning until night, roughly 7am-10pm. Bus routes are not numbered; however, each bus lists its destination in the windshield. While the system may seem a bit disorganized, it is actually fairly simple to master. There are very few major thoroughfares in Guanajuato's city center and likewise few bus routes.

Buses to the Marfil neighborhood depart from bus stops in the *centro histórico* via the largest underground thoroughfare, Hidalgo, and run via the Marfil-Guanajuato Camino Real. You can catch the city bus up toward the Valenciana neighborhood on Avenida Juárez, right near the Alhóndiga, which then travels northward via the Guanajuato-Dolores Hidalgo highway. When in doubt, ask the driver where the bus is going.

Vicinity of Guanajuato

SANTA ROSA

In the green and surprisingly alpine sierra just beyond the city of Guanajuato, the tiny town of Santa Rosa de Lima is a picturesque pit stop on the highway toward Dolores Hidalgo. At an elevation of more than 2,400 meters (8,000 feet), this rural municipality is crisp and mountainous, with pine trees and cool winds. Though Santa Rosa's homes are scattered throughout the hillsides, there is just one main street in town, largely unpaved. There, you will see the lovely old parish church with its sandstone entryway. Though just a 15-minute drive from Guanajuato's city center, Santa Rosa can feel miles away from the surrounding Bajío.

Tin-glazed majolica-style ceramics have been produced in Puebla and Guanajuato since the early colonial era. The ceramics tradition has continued in the small town of Santa Rosa at the large **Mayólica Santa Rosa** (Camino Real s/n, tel. 473/102-5017, www.mayolicasantarosa.com, 8am-5pm Mon.-Sat., 9am-5pm Sun.). The workshop produces highly detailed hand-painted urns, flowerpots, flatware, and tiles, often depicting plants, flowers, fruits, and animals; they also produce clay figurines of animals and *catrinas*. At their large factory store, you can see artisans at work and ceramics in various stages of development, from unworked clay and unfired vessels to ceramics in the process of being painted.

For handmade jams and marmalades made with locally grown fruits, stop into the wonderful women's cooperative **Conservas Santa Rosa** (Camino Real 25, Santa Rosa de Lima, tel. 473/102-5013, toll-free Mex.

Day Trip to León

About 30 minutes from Guanajuato, the city of León has been a major leather producer since the colonial era. Today, León is one of the largest shoe manufacturing centers in the world. Shopping for discount shoes and leather products is one of the major attractions of a trip to León, and there are shoe stores littered throughout the city. In the area around the *zócalo,* there are numerous small shops selling shoes and leather handbags, easily accessible to tourists in the city. For more serious shoppers, there are entire malls dedicated to leather goods.

Find shoes galore in the shopping district known as Zona Piel, conveniently located in the blocks around the city's bus station. Here, you'll find several large leather and shoe malls, where literally thousands of shoe distributors sell their products at very low prices. One of the big Zona Piel shopping centers, **Plaza del Zapato** (Blvd. Adolfo López Mateos 1601, Los Gavilanes, tel. 477/763-3838, www.plazadelzapato.com, 10am-8:30pm Mon.-Sat.) is a consumer shrine to footwear. You'll find everything from leather pumps and suede boots to running shoes and sandals. Many of the shops carry designer knockoffs at good prices, and there are also several children's shoe stores. While you're there, you might as well stop into **Zona Piel** (Hilario Medina 101, Col. Los Gavilanes, tel. 477/763-4150, http://zonapiel.com.mx, 10am-6pm Sun.-Mon., 10am-8pm Tues.-Sat.), located right next door. With a name that means "Leather Zone," this mall sells a selection of locally produced shoes as well as a large collection of other leather goods, like wallets, belts, handbags, and leather jackets.

If you are serious about shoe shopping, it is worth making a trip to the biannual shoe festival **Salón de la Piel y del Calzado** (www.sapica.com), or SAPICA. Generally held in the spring and again in the late summer, this massive shoe-and-leather-goods exhibition is a shopper's paradise and a major business event for the city. During this four-day footwear extravaganza, the massive pavilions at Poliforum León are divided into categories like women's shoes, Western-style, casual, and sport, each filled with myriad vendors. If you are looking for black stilettos, hardy hiking boots, or lightweight sandals, you will find them here. For those who are really interested in footwear, there are also daily fashion shows and speakers. Bring patience and a mood for crowds; SAPICA draws thousands of visitors daily from throughout the Bajío and beyond.

---

tel. 800/890-3840, www.fb.conservas1998.com.mx, 8am-6pm Mon.-Sat., 8am-4pm Sun.). Though jams are the specialty, they also sell pickled chile peppers, *ates* (fruit paste), and *xoconostle* (sour prickly pear) in syrup, all of which make excellent little gifts.

Food

If you make the trek up to Santa Rosa, there are a few casual places to grab a bite to eat. The most visible is the large **Restaurante de la Sierra** (Camino Real s/n, Santa Rosa de Lima, Km 14, tel. 473/102-5036, 8:30am-8pm daily, US$5-8), just off the main highway. From the arched window of this enormous dining hall, there is a beautiful view of the green Sierra de Santa Rosa below. This place is popular with local families on the weekends, when there is often live music. Food is Mexican, with

well-served dishes like *queso fundido,* enchiladas, and mole. Accompany your meal with mezcal produced right in Santa Rosa, cured in-house with orange.

Getting There

To get to Santa Rosa from central Guanajuato, take the Carretera Guanajuato-Dolores Hidalgo north toward the Valenciana neighborhood, and continue to follow it past the city limits. The highway passes through Santa Rosa about 10 minutes after you depart Guanajuato.

CRISTO REY DEL CUBILETE

Just beyond the city of Guanajuato, there is a towering 2,700-meter (8,860-foot) peak topped with a giant statue, the **Cristo de la**

Montaña. This 23-meter (75-foot), 80-ton monument to Christ was built in the 1940s (the previous sculpture of Christ on this mountaintop was destroyed following the Mexican Revolution). It is reputed to be the largest bronze statue of Christ in the world. Technically located in the municipality of Silao, the site is visited frequently by pilgrims; it is especially crowded on November 21, the day of Cristo Rey. The monument is also a popular destination for tourists to the Bajío, who visit this hilltop for its gorgeous panoramic views of the countryside. Many say that this statue is located at the exact geographical center of Mexico, though the town of Tequisquiapan in Querétaro state also lays claim to that distinction.

Getting There

Visitors can take a bus from Guanajuato's city center to the Cristo Rey del Cubilete, though it is easiest to book your place in a tour group from the tourist office downtown. The bus will take you up a winding road that wraps around the rock face and let you off up top.

Querétaro

The historic, handsome city of Santiago de Querétaro—generally referred to as just Querétaro—was one of the first settlements in New Spain.

Almost 500 years later, it is a sprawling, safe, and modern city, with a large industrial sector and a population of almost two million. Passing through the city on traffic-choked Highway 57 (México-Querétaro), it is easy to imagine that there is nothing but chugging big rigs and massive factories from one end of Querétaro to the other. The reality is quite the contrary: Querétaro's stately *centro histórico* is quiet, clean, and pedestrian-friendly, filled with sun-drenched plazas and ornate Mexican baroque architecture. Remarkably well preserved, it is considered one of the finest surviving examples of architecture and city planning during the Spanish viceroyalty.

Querétaro has played an important role in Mexican history since the early colonial era, as its many important sights attest. But history is only part of what recommends a trip to the city. Thanks to its propitious location, Querétaro has received quite a bit of overflow from Mexico City, with thousands of capital residents choosing to relocate to the relative peace and safety of this medium-size city—bringing with them a taste for the arts, culture, and coolness. Home to a major public university, the Universidad Autónoma de Querétaro, there is also a notable youth culture in Querétaro, where you'll find plenty of quick eats, cheap bars, artsy movie screenings, and other student-friendly diversions. Despite its increasing modernity, the city has remained delightfully old-fashioned, too. Travelers of any stripe will appreciate the classic Mexican atmosphere in the city's many public plazas, where children play and seniors gather on shady benches. And it's equally worth a visit to one of Querétaro's enduring, old-timey cafés and *fondas,* some of which have been in business for two or three generations.

The capital of the small state of Querétaro, the city is a well-located jumping-off point for trips around the region. Warm, traditionally Mexican towns like Tequisquiapan and San Sebastián Bernal, both located within an hour of Querétaro, are popular destinations with the local crowd as well as with weekenders

Previous: central Querétaro; trees lining a Querétaro walkway. **Above:** Peña de Bernal is one of the world's largest monoliths.

Look for ★ to find recommended
sights, activities, dining, and lodging.

Highlights

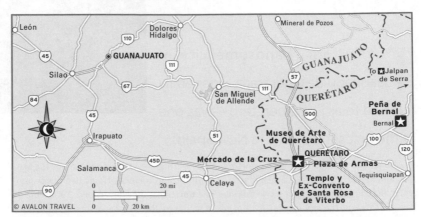

★ **Plaza de Armas:** This lovely 18th-century plaza surrounded by colonial mansions is the historic heart of Querétaro (page 194).

★ **Museo de Arte de Querétaro:** Housed in a former Augustinian convent, this fine art museum is an architectural jewel that hosts excellent contemporary exhibitions (page 196).

★ **Templo y Ex-Convento de Santa Rosa de Viterbo:** A unique former convent and temple, Santa Rosa de Viterbo stands out among Querétaro's many impressive colonial-era constructions (page 197).

★ **Mercado de la Cruz:** This big, colorful, bustling urban market is a wonderful place to shop, explore regional specialties, and take photos (page 200).

★ **Peña de Bernal:** One of the world's largest monoliths towers over a tiny town that bears its name, lending a natural majesty to a pretty colonial settlement (page 226).

★ **Jalpan de Serra:** This tiny mountain town, the site of an early Franciscan mission settlement, is a good place from which to explore the jewels of the Sierra Gorda (page 231).

Querétaro State

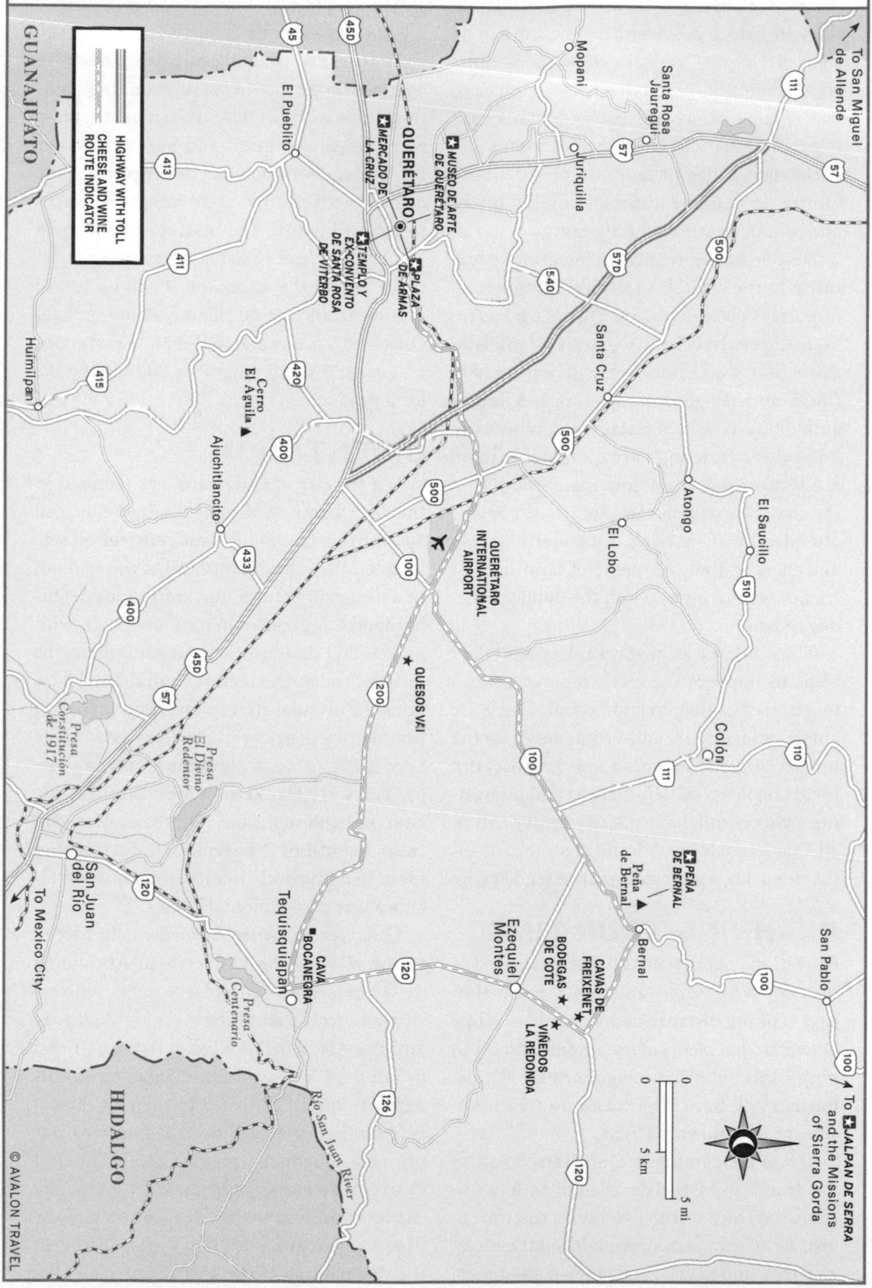

QUERÉTARO

GUANAJUATO

HIGHWAY WITH TOLL
CHEESE AND WINE
ROUTE INDICATOR

45

45D

Mopaní

Santa Rosa
Jauregui

To San Miguel
de Allende

111

57

El Pueblito

413

MERCADO DE
LA CRUZ

QUERÉTARO

MUSEO DE ARTE
DE QUERÉTARO

Juriquilla

57

57

411

TEMPLO Y
EX-CONVENTO
DE SANTA ROSA
DE VITERBO

PLAZA
DE ARMAS

540

57D

500

Huimilpan

415

420

Cerro
El Águila ▲

Santa Cruz

500

400

Ajuchitlancito

433

500

QUERÉTARO INTERNATIONAL
AIRPORT

El Lobo

Atongo

El Saucillo

510

400

45D

100

57

Presa
Constitución
de 1917

Presa
El Divino
Redentor

200

★ QUESOS VAI

100

Colón

110

111

San Juan
del Río

120

San Juan del Río

To Mexico City

CAVA
BOCANEGRA ■

Tequisquiapan

120

Ezequiel
Montes

BODEGAS
DE COTE ■

Peña
de Bernal ▲

PEÑA
DE BERNAL

Bernal

100

San Pablo

CAVAS DE
FREIXENET ★

VIÑEDOS
LA REDONDA ★

100

To JALPAN DE SERRA
and the Missions
of Sierra Gorda

Presa
Centenario

126

120

HIDALGO

Río San Juan River

0   5 mi
0   5 km

© AVALON TRAVEL

from Mexico City. Surrounded by ranchland, these small towns have also become known as the locus of a modest wine-tasting route within the state, which provides a good excuse to do some driving on Querétaro's clean, sometimes scenic, and well-maintained state highways. And if you like driving, you can plan a road trip to the Sierra Gorda, in the eastern reaches of the state, a magnificent subtropical mountain range dotted with small mission towns and brimming with natural beauty.

Despite its impressive architecture, proximity to the capital, agreeable climate, and important place in history, Querétaro has remained relatively undiscovered by international tourists. Visitors here will be pleased to find a surprisingly cosmopolitan and largely authentic city, where restaurants, museums, and other attractions are pleasingly aimed at a local crowd. If you join them, you'll find the city's busy cinema and art events are well attended by *querétenses* (Querétaro locals), and there is always a bustle of families and friends wandering through the public plazas downtown.

That said, the local government has taken steps to improve the city's reputation as a tourist destination, to good effect. There are ample guided tours and visitor services, the tourist office is outgoing and helpful, and there are plenty of well-marked and interesting sights throughout the city center. All in all, Querétaro is a wonderful place to visit, either for a day, a weekend, or an extended trip.

PLANNING YOUR TIME

Querétaro's major tourist sights are located in the *centro histórico,* and they are all within easy walking distance of one another. While Querétaro has plenty of restaurants and shopping in its suburban neighborhoods, most tourists will have little reason to travel outside the downtown districts.

If you are coming to Querétaro on a day trip from San Miguel de Allende, **one (well-planned) day** will give you sufficient time to visit a museum or two, see some of the nicest churches and plazas, and enjoy a good meal

in one of the city's restaurants. Two or three days, however, will give you more time to really explore the major sights and get a taste of life in this pleasant metropolis.

With more than a **couple of days** in Querétaro, day trips to the surrounding countryside are worthwhile and not too difficult to plan. **Tequisquiapan** and **San Sebastián Bernal** are both popular day trips from the capital, with historic churches, a few places to eat and drink, and a sleepy small-town ambience. There is also a burgeoning **wine industry** in the state, and it can be fun to rent a car and spend the day driving along Querétaro's pretty and well-maintained country roads, visiting vineyards and tasting the local product.

ORIENTATION

When the city of Querétaro was founded in the 16th century, distinct indigenous and Spanish neighborhoods were constructed side by side. While the Spanish town was laid out in a neat grid pattern, the indigenous neighborhood was planned in the native style, with narrow and sinuous streets winding along the hillside. Today, Querétaro's central district retains the original street plans from these two neighboring districts. In the eastern end of the *centro histórico,* wide avenues and large esplanades are flanked by Mexican baroque churches and mansions. On the eastern end (near the hill of Sangremal), the streets are more winding and circuitous, with small alleyways and low colonial homes.

Querétaro's *centro histórico* is bordered to the west by the Universidad Autónoma de Querétaro, the city's large public university, and to the south by Avenida Zaragoza and the Alameda Hidalgo, a flat, tree-filled urban park. The convent of Santa Cruz borders the *centro histórico* to the east, and it is from that same hilltop that the city's impressive aqueduct stretches north. Most of Querétaro's major sights and museums are clustered around the **Jardín Zenea** and the **Plaza de Armas,** but don't neglect to visit the eastern side of the *centro,* especially the lively street **Cinco de Mayo**, where many of Querétaro's bars, restaurants, shops, and galleries are located.

HISTORY

Not long after the fall of Tenochtitlan, Spanish conquest of the Bajío began. In 1531, a bloody battle broke out between the Chichimeca tribes of Querétaro and Spanish forces. According to local history, the battle was interrupted when the sky darkened and a miraculous image of Saint James appeared over the hill of Sangremal, awing the Chichimeca into submission. (According to some theories, a solar eclipse took place during the battle.) The city of Santiago de Querétaro was founded on the hilltop, with Santiago (the Spanish name for Saint James) honored for the miraculous circumstances of the city's founding.

Shortly after the region's conquest, Franciscans and other evangelicals arrived in Querétaro, followed by Spanish ranchers and farmers, who found the region's fertile soil provided an excellent environment for agriculture. The discovery of silver in Zacatecas in 1546 immediately changed the colonies. To accommodate the silver trade, roads were built throughout the region, and the related industry, agriculture, and artisan work in the highland cities contributed to one of the most robust economies in the New World.

Like San Miguel de Allende, Querétaro was a strategic town on the silver route to Mexico City, known as the Camino Real de Tierra Adentro. Wealth from the silver mines helped to fund a multitude of religious and municipal projects in town during the 17th and 18th centuries, from the city's magnificent baroque churches to the impressive 1,200-meter aqueduct that provided water to the city center. By 1680, Querétaro had a population of 30,000 and was the third-largest city in New Spain, surpassed only by Mexico City and Puebla.

Like other cities in the region, Querétaro played a prominent role in the Mexican War of Independence. Most famously, the town's *corregidor* (mayor), Miguel Domínguez, met clandestinely with coconspirators like Ignacio Allende in San Miguel before the outbreak of the war. In a story now famous, the mayor's wife, Josefa Ortiz de Domínguez, sent a crucial warning to Ignacio Allende and Miguel Hidalgo when the plot against the crown was uncovered by royalist officials in Querétaro, even though she was locked inside her home. Today, she is celebrated throughout Querétaro

Plaza de Armas

for her role in the early independence movement, though she was unrecognized during her lifetime.

As the new Mexican state struggled to define itself amid ongoing coups and instability, the city of Querétaro remained prominent. During the Mexican-American War, Querétaro became the country's temporary capital when the United States invaded Mexico City in 1827. Here, President Santa Anna, in a move that remains infamous, signed the 1827 Treaty of Guadalupe Hidalgo, which ceded half of Mexico's territory to the U.S. Though the capital returned to Mexico City shortly thereafter, Querétaro again became the seat of government after France invaded Mexico and Emperor Maximilian I of Austria took charge. Maximilian was imprisoned and executed in Querétaro in 1867 after a successful uprising by the liberal powers aligned with President Benito Juárez.

Querétaro was not the site of major battles during the Mexican Revolution of 1910, but, like the rest of the country, the city suffered the effects of political unrest. In postrevolutionary upheaval, Querétaro was renamed the capital of Mexico in 1917, and the Mexican Constitution (which is still in use today) was signed and ratified in the Teatro Iturbide (the Teatro de la República today).

Sights

Since the early years of New Spain, Querétaro has been one of Mexico's most prominent cities. Centuries of history left their mark on the metropolis, which shows vestiges of its colonial past, the French occupation, and the modern day in its impressive *centro histórico*. You can easily see the difference between the two distinct sections of the *centro* (gridlike on the west and twisting on the east) on a walking tour.

★ Plaza de Armas

The **Plaza de Armas** is a good place to begin your tour of Querétaro. This picturesque 18th-century plaza was constructed in the Spanish style, with arcades and mansions surrounding a neat public square and a stately stone fountain. Pick up a map at the tourist office (located at Pasteur 4, just across the street from the plaza), then plan your day on a public bench between perfectly manicured trees and shoe-shine stands. On Sundays, the Plaza de Armas is a nice place for people-watching or to enjoy a drink in one of the many cafés or eateries along the square.

On the north side of the square, the historic **Casa del Corregidora** is an 18th-century mansion and the current home of the state government offices. Once the home of Querétaro's mayor, this aristocratic house was written into history during the War of Independence. Here, Josefa Ortiz de Domínguez alerted the revolutionary hero Ignacio Pérez that the independence conspiracy had been discovered by Spanish royalists, prompting the start of the Mexican War of Independence. Today, you can walk into the covered courtyard of the Casa de Corregimiento, where there is a statue of Ortiz de Domínguez in the foyer.

Jardín Zenea

If you follow one of several *andadores* (pedestrian pathways) west from the Plaza de Armas, you will reach the **Jardín Zenea,** occupying a full city block between Calles Corregidora and Juárez in the *centro histórico*. Named after a former Querétaro governor, Benito Santos Zenea, this lovely garden is one of the most popular gathering points in town. Often, there are performances in the round kiosk in the middle of the plaza.

Just across the street (on the corner of Corregidora and 16 de Septiembre), the **Plaza de la Corregidora** is a smaller public square surrounding a monument to Josefa Ortiz de

Downtown Querétaro

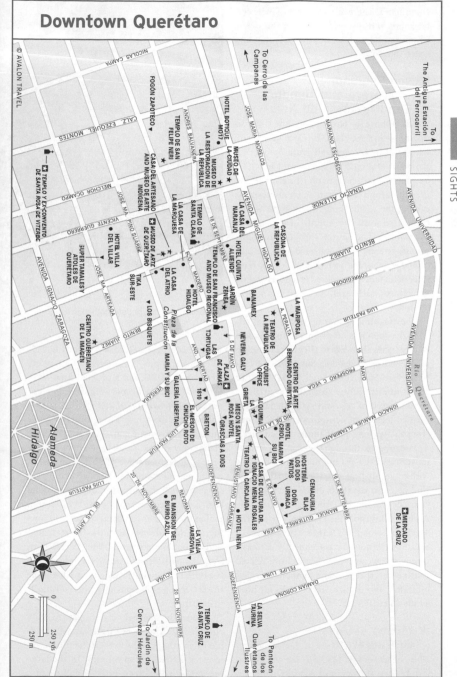

© AVALON TRAVEL

To Cerro de las Campanas

The Antigua Estación del Ferrocarril

To →

NICOLAS CAMPA

CALZ. EZEQUIEL MONTES

JOSE MARIA MORELOS

MARIANO ESCOBEDO

AVENIDA UNIVERSIDAD

FOGON ZAPOTECO ▼

HOTEL BOTIQUE MOTI ●

MUSEO DE LA CIUDAD ★

AVENIDA MIGUEL HIDALGO

IGNACIO ALLENDE

BENITO JUAREZ

TEMPLO DE SAN FELIPE NERI ▲

ANDRES BALVANERA

MUSEO DE LA RESTORACION DE LA REPUBLICA

LA CASA DEL NARANJO

CASONA DE LA REPUBLICA ●

CASA DEL ARTESANO AND MUSEO DE ARTE INDIGENA

MELCHOR OCAMPO

TEMPLO Y EX-CONVENTO DE SANTA ROSA DE VITERBO ✚

VICENTE GUERRERO

JOSE MA. 5 DE MAYO

TEMPLO DE SANTA CLARA ★

LA CASA DE SANTA CLARA

HOTEL QUINTA ● ALLENDE

18 DE SEPTIEMBRE

MARIANO ESCOBEDO

CORREGIDORA

LA MARIPOSA

MUSEO DE ARTE DE QUERÉTARO ✚

LA MARQUESA

TEMPLO DE SAN FRANCISCO AND MUSEO REGIONAL

FCO. I. MADERO

JARDIN ZENEA ★

A. PERALTA

TEATRO DE LA REPUBLICA ★

BANAMEX ■

BERNARDO QUINTANA

LUIS PASTEUR

HOTEL VILLA DEL VILLAR

PINO SUAREZ

LA CASA DEL ATRIO

HOTEL HIDALGO

AND. LIBERTAD

PLAZA DE ARMAS

AND. 5 DE MAYO

NEVERIA GALY

TOURIST OFFICE ✚

CENTRO DE ARTE BERNARDO QUINTANA

16 DE MAYO

PROSPERO C. VEGA

Rio Querétaro

AVENIDA UNIVERSIDAD

TIKA SUR-ESTE

LOS BISQUETS ●

JOSE MA. ARTEAGA

SUPERTAMALES Y ATOLES DE QUERETARO

Plaza de la Constitución

AVENIDA IGNACIO ZARAGOZA

CENTRO QUERETANO DE LA IMAGEN ★

BENITO JUAREZ

VERGARA

LUIS PASTEUR

GALERIA LIBERTAD

MARIA Y SU BICI

LAS TORTUGAS ▼

1810

BRETON

EL MESON DE CHUCHO ROTO ▼

MESON SANTA ▼ ROSA HOTEL

ALQUIMIA ★

LA GRIETA ★

GRASCIAS A DIOS ▼

RIO DE LA LOZA

HOTEL CRIOL MARIA Y SU BICI

CASA DE CULTURA DR. IGNACIO MENA ROSALES

VENUSTIANO CARRANZA

TEATRO LA CARCAJADA

HOSTERIA LOS DOS PATIOS

DOÑA URRACA

CENADURIA BLAS

MANUEL GUTIERREZ NAJERA

16 DE SEPTIEMBRE

MERCADO DE LA CRUZ ✚

Alameda Hidalgo

20 DE NOVIEMBRE

INDEPENDENCIA

REFORMA

EL MANSION DEL ● BURRO AZUL

LA VIEJA VARSOVIA ▼

MANUAL ACUÑA

HOTEL NENA ●

INDEPENDENCIA

FELIPE LUNA

DAMIAN CORONA

DE LAS ARTES

LUIS PASTEUR

20 DE NOVIEMBRE

TEMPLO DE LA SANTA CRUZ ▲

LA SELVA TAURINA ▼

To Panteón de los Queretanos Ilustres

To Jardin de Cerveza Hércules

0   250 yds
0   250 m

Domínguez. There are a number of little coffee shops and restaurants lining the plaza, which can be a pleasant place to relax and watch the crowds.

Museo Regional de Querétaro and Templo de San Francisco de Asís

Standing above the Jardín Zenea, the **Templo de San Francisco de Asís** (Corregidora s/n, tel. 442/212-0477, generally 9am-5pm daily) is one of Querétaro's oldest and loveliest buildings. Construction on this church and the adjoining Franciscan convent began as early as the 1540s, though the temple wasn't completed until the middle of the following century. The church's original baroque sandstone entryway is adorned with life-size saints, which stand in relief against the construction's tall, rust-colored facade. Formerly Querétaro's cathedral, the church is still in use today.

The Jardín Zenea is a popular gathering spot.

The beautiful former monastery that adjoins the church is now home to the **Museo Regional de Querétaro** (Regional Museum of Querétaro, Corregidora Sur 3, tel. 442/212-4888, 9am-5pm Tues.-Sun., US$3). The 11 rooms in this historic space display artifacts from Querétaro city and state, including a nice collection of ceramics and sculpture from the region's pre-Columbian cultures. As you progress through the museum, exhibits address each era in Querétaro's history, with rooms dedicated to the colonial era (including personal effects of the famous Josefa Ortiz de Domínguez), the Reformation, the American invasion, the 19th century, and the Mexican Revolution. Texts are in Spanish. In addition, the museum is frequently used as a venue for special events, like culture-related conferences, speakers, and temporary art exhibitions, and it offers art courses for both adults and children.

★ Museo de Arte de Querétaro

The spectacular **Museo de Arte de Querétaro** (Museum of Art of Querétaro, Allende 14 Sur, tel. 442/212-2357 or 442/212-3523, 10am-6pm Tues.-Sun., US$3, Wed. free)—or MAQRO, as it is often nicknamed—is housed within a former Augustinian monastery built between 1731 and 1745. It's among Querétaro's most impressive buildings: the monastery's baroque courtyard is filled with elaborately carved sandstone archways, replete with detailed stone gargoyles, surrounding a central fountain. Formal exhibition spaces are tucked behind the long arcades that surround the courtyard, though the museum makes use of all its beautiful spaces for showing art: the hallways upstairs, the staircase, and the outdoor porticoes all host exhibits on a regular basis. If you want to take pictures of the building, you must pay an extra fee at the ticket booth (exhibitions are always off-limits to cameras).

Besides the spectacular setting, MAQRO's curatorial staff oversees a well-planned schedule of rotating exhibitions in the museum's many galleries. Often on view in the large exhibition halls downstairs, the museum's

La Corregidora:
Heroine of the Independence

A celebrated heroine of the War of Independence, **Josefa Ortiz de Domínguez,** or "La Corregidora," is a favorite daughter in the city of Querétaro. One of the few women known to have
participated in the early independence movement, she was vital to the success of the conspirators
who sought Mexico's sovereignty from New Spain.

Josefa Ortiz was born to a wealthy family in Valladolid (today, Morelia) in the state of Michoacán.
She married Miguel Domínguez, who was later appointed *corregidor* (mayor) of Querétaro—the
city's top administrator. High government posts were almost always held by Spanish-born officials. However, Domínguez was criollo (born in the New World but of Spanish descent). As the
wife of the *corregidor,* Josefa Ortiz was known as the *corregidora.* Domínguez and Ortiz had 14
children together.

According to her biographers, Josefa Ortiz was a critic of the rigid class system in New Spain.
Despite her Spanish heritage, Ortiz sympathized with the mestizo and indigenous people of
Mexico, who lived in poverty and benefited little from the great wealth of the colonies. When
Napoleon invaded Spain in 1808, frustrated criollo elite in the Bajío region began to make plans
for independence from the Spanish crown. Both Miguel Domínguez and Josefa Ortiz were privy
to the private meetings held in independence hero Ignacio Allende's home in San Miguel, and
they supported the movement from Querétaro.

Originally, the independence conspirators had planned to launch their attack against the
government in December of 1810. However, royalist governors uncovered the conspiracy plot
in September. As they conducted a search of the town, Ortiz was locked in her home. Knowing
Mexico's independence was in danger of failure, Ortiz managed to send warning to coconspirator
Ignacio Pérez, who in turn sent word to San Miguel de Allende. The revolution began the following night, when Miguel Hidalgo gathered the Mexican army in Dolores Hidalgo. Both Domínguez
and Ortiz were imprisoned, though they were eventually cleared of charges. Though she died in
obscurity, today Ortiz is remembered for the ingenuity that saved the independence movement.

permanent collection includes religious paintings from Querétaro from the 17th and 18th
centuries. The museum's newest director has
made great efforts to plan original shows by
contemporary artists from the surrounding
region as well as prominent exhibitions by important Mexican masters. MAQRO also hosts
intermittent speakers and art courses; opening events are well-attended and engaging, so
keep an eye out for what may be coming up
on the program.

★ Templo y Ex-Convento
de Santa Rosa de Viterbo

The magnificent **Templo y Ex-Convento
de Santa Rosa de Viterbo** (General
Arteaga at Ezequiel Montes, tel. 442/214-1691,
generally 9am-6pm daily) is one of the finest baroque structures in the city. This former convent and its adjoining church were
originally designed and built by architect
Ignacio Mariano de las Casas in 1754. Quite
distinct from other baroque churches in
Mexico, Santa Rosa de Viterbo distinguishes
itself with an ornately designed exterior, replete with massive flying buttresses, carved
stonework, delicate frescoes, and garish gar-
goyles. It stands over a small stone fountain in
Plazuela Mariano de las Casa, and the overall
effect is impressive.

Inside, the church is equally spectacular. Sadly, the principal altar was destroyed
in 1849, but in the main nave, there are six
gold-drenched churrigueresque altars from
the 18th century as well as a collection of important colonial-era paintings and *retablos.*
Be sure to note the carved confessional and
baroque organ above the nave. The former
cloister surrounds a lovely interior courtyard, with arched arcades showing a Moorish

influence. Well worth a visit, Santa Rosa de Viterbo is one of the most original structures in the region.

Cerro de las Campanas

This picturesque hilltop park, on the eastern edge of the *centro histórico,* has a rather grim claim to fame: It was here in 1867 that Habsburg Emperor Maximilian was killed by firing squad after symbolically handing over his sword to General Mariano Escobedo and ending the French reign in Mexico. After the execution, three crosses were installed on the **Cerro de las Campanas** (Centro Universitario, no phone, 9am-5pm Tues.-Sun.), followed by a small monument, but it was only after diplomatic relations reopened between Mexico and Austria that the Austrian government built a **chapel** on the site of the emperor's execution. In addition to the chapel, there is a small historical **museum** (US$1), and the surrounding grounds (a national park since 1967) are lush and beautiful, with plenty of shady spots for resting. At the top of the hill, an impressive sculpture of Benito Juárez (president of Mexico both before and after Habsburg rule) is said to be the largest in the country. Located just beside the Universidad Autónoma de Querétaro's main campus, it's worth a trip if you have a few extra days in the city.

Templo de Santa Clara

The beautiful **Templo de Santa Clara** (Francisco I. Madero 42, tel. 442/212-1777, generally 9am-6pm daily) is a convent and church originally commissioned by Diego de Tapia, the son of one of Querétaro's wealthy founders. Begun in 1606, this chapel and its adjoining convent were considered one of the most beautiful architectural achievements in the country during the colonial era. Today, just the chapel and a small annex remain; large parts of the church and convent were destroyed during the Reformation. Nonetheless, Santa Clara is still recognized among the country's finest baroque buildings, particularly noted for its elaborate interiors. Step inside to marvel at the beautifully carved baroque altars, washed in gold leaf and accompanied by painted saints. Few churches rival Santa Clara, filled with the unique handwork of master craftsmen.

In the lovely plaza outside the Templo de Santa Clara, be sure to note the neoclassical **Fuente de Neptuno** (Neptune Fountain), right on the corner of Madero and Allende. Originally constructed in 1797, the fountain's

chapel at the Cerro de las Campanas

pink sandstone arch frames a statue of the Roman god Neptune. One of the city's most noted landmarks, this opulent fountain was originally built as a part of the Convent of San Antonio, which was located in what is today the Jardín de la Corregidora. When the government decided to build a monument to the independence movement in 1908, the entire fountain was picked up and moved to its current location.

Museo de la Restauración de la República

During the post-independence turmoil of the mid-19th century, the French monarchy took control of Mexico with the backing of the French government and a group of prominent monarchists in Mexico. Led by Benito Juárez, Mexico's liberals resisted French rule, eventually forcing the monarchy into its final stronghold in the city of Querétaro. Emperor Maximilian I of Habsburg spent his last days in a Querétaro jail; he, along with other monarchist leaders, was executed by firing squad at the Cerro de las Campanas in Querétaro.

The **Museo de la Restauración de la República** (Museum of the Restoration of the Republic, Guerrero 21-23 Nte., tel. 442/224-3004 or 442/224-3004, 9am-5pm Tues.-Fri., 10am-5pm Sat.-Sun., free) is dedicated to this unusual era in Querétaro's history. Most fit for history buffs, this small but beautiful space exhibits documents, maps, and artifacts from 19th-century Querétaro. Most of the collection chronicles the history of the French rule through photos, texts, and mock-ups, though there are also some nice 19th-century costumes and antique weapons. The six small rooms were once a part of an 18th-century Capuchin convent, and the space itself is just as interesting as its contents. It was in this very building that Emperor Maximilian spent the last night before his execution.

Antiguo Oratorio San Felipe Neri

The church that is today the seat of Querétaro's diocese isn't necessarily the largest and most impressive one in town, though it is worth noting on a tour of the city. Built between 1786 and 1800, the **Antiguo Oratorio de San Felipe Neri** (Av. Francisco I. Madero y Melchor Ocampo, tel. 442/212-1974, generally 9am-7pm daily) has a baroque facade elaborately carved in sandstone, which stands in dramatic relief to the red *tezontle* (a type of volcanic rock) wall behind it. According to local history, the church was blessed by Father

the Fuente de Neptuno, outside the Templo de Santa Clara

Miguel Hidalgo, Mexico's great independence hero. It was officially recognized as a cathedral by the Vatican in 1931.

Templo y Ex-Monasterio de la Santa Cruz

On the west end of the *centro histórico*, the hill of Sangremal was the historic site of the Spanish victory over the Chichimeca people fighting to defend the territory, a battle that resulted in the conquest and founding of Querétaro. Today, **Templo de la Santa Cruz** (Ejército Republicano, esq. Felipe Luna, 9am-2pm and 4pm-6pm Tues.-Sat., 9am-4pm Sun., free) stands at this important locale. This church and its adjoining monastery were originally built by Franciscan friars who arrived in Querétaro shortly after the Spanish victory in the 16th century. Here, the monastery's school trained many other missionaries to carry on the Franciscan tradition throughout the New World, and its alumni traveled as far south as Guatemala.

Today, visitors can wander through the former monastery's quarters, including the original kitchen and dining room, as well as the cells where Emperor Maximilian was imprisoned in the 19th century. Inside the main nave of the church, a large sandstone cross hangs above the altar, meant to replicate the miraculous cross that appeared above the battle for Querétaro's conquest.

Panteón de los Queretanos Ilustres

The remains of several important heroes of the independence era—including Josefa Ortiz de Domínguez, Miguel Domínguez, and Ignacio Pérez, among others—are safeguarded in the **Panteón de los Queretanos Ilustres** (Ejército Republicano 4, 9:30am-7pm daily), a small mausoleum and chapel located on the hill of Sangremal, just behind the Templo de la Santa Cruz (in what was once part of the larger convent's orchards, but was converted to new purposes after the 19th-century separation of church

and state). On the patio outside the chapel, which boasts beautiful views of the city and the old municipal aqueduct, there are statues of some of the great names buried inside. Within the chapel, there is a modest museum honoring their lives.

Querétaro Aqueduct

Cutting east 1,200 meters from the *centro histórico*, Querétaro's spectacular 74-column **aqueduct** was built between 1726 and 1735 by the Marquis de la Villa del Villar del Águila. At its highest point, the aqueduct soars 23 meters above the ground. It is an astonishing architectural achievement that still lends incredible character and majesty to downtown Querétaro and its surrounding neighborhoods. You can get the best view of it from just a block or two behind the Templo de la Santa Cruz. From here, the hill of Sangremal makes a dramatic drop, with the aqueduct stretching across the valley below.

★ Mercado de la Cruz

Querétaro's large covered market, **Mercado de la Cruz** (Manuel Gutiérrez Nájera s/n, 8am-6pm daily, individual shop hours vary) is a wonderful place to shop for fresh produce, fish, meat, flowers, and crafts. It is also a great place to get a bite to eat, with a wide array of food stalls and fruit stands throughout the interior. It opened on September 28, 1979.

Mercado de la Cruz is a bustling urban market, typical of many large Mexican cities though more picturesque (and photogenic) than others. Visitors can shop or simply take in the sights, wandering past fresh whole fish chilling on ice, neatly stacked towers of vegetables, big cauldrons of menudo, and overflowing flower stands. On weekends, the market spills into the back parking lot.

Antigua Estación del Ferrocarril

Querétaro's former train depot, which was constructed in the early 20th century, no longer receives passenger trains. Today, the

Gracias a Dios

Antigua Estación de Ferrocarril (Héroe de Nacozari s/n, esq. Cuauhtémoc, tel. 442/340-22780, 11am-8pm Mon.-Sat., 11am-6pm Sun., free) has been refashioned as a small museum and event space, located in a pretty residential area of the *centro histórico* that is rarely visited by tourists. Inside, a small gallery chronicles the history of the train station, and, upstairs, there is a scale model (noon-4pm Sun. only) of Querétaro's train station and rail line. There are often events on-site, from karaoke concerts to classical music performances. Though they don't stop, the freight trains that still frequently run along the rails beside the station are also a worthy spectacle. Across the street, **Cao Cao Cafe** (Héroe de Nacozari 25-B1, tel. 442/116-2260, 9am-8pm Mon.-Sat.) is a good spot for a coffee before you make your way back to the heart of the *centro*.

Arts and Entertainment

Querétaro's population becomes larger and more cultured every year. With the support of the local and state governments, Querétaro has developed a lively art scene, and any visitor is likely to find a performance or exhibition of interest. Throughout Querétaro, music, cinema, theater, and visual art events are frequent and well attended, often for a low cost and refreshingly untouristy.

NIGHTLIFE

As a big city and a university town to boot, Querétaro has plenty of bars and cantinas, with prices, people, and atmosphere of every stripe. There are many inexpensive bars and pubs catering to students, both on the street Cinco de Mayo and near the university, as well as some nice old cantinas that maintain a more traditional atmosphere. Many of the best places are concentrated on or around Cinco de Mayo in the eastern end of the *centro histórico,* where an evening stroll is likely to conclude in a cocktail.

An old cantina near the Convento de la Santa Cruz, **La Selva Taurina** (Independencia 159, tel. 442/248-3733, 11:30am-3am Mon.-Sat.) is an excellent place to quench your thirst and fill your stomach. During the day, food is served cantina style: With each drink, they bring you a small plate of food. The meal usually starts with a *caldo* (broth soup), followed by dishes like pork in green sauce, prickly pear tacos, or chorizo. You don't get to pick the dish, but the quality is across-the-board excellent. A shrine to bullfights, the walls are decorated with the heads of unfortunate bulls and festooned with vintage photos. At night, the place is hopping with a crowd of mixed ages, attended by easygoing bartenders.

To find *mezcalería* **Gracias a Dios** (Libertad 51, 442/325-8099, www.thankgad. com, 2pm-2am Tues.-Sat.), look for the lit-up G.A.D. outside the doorway. This popular bar is known for its proprietary line of artisanal mezcal, made using traditional methods in the state of Oaxaca. Try it straight, in one of the bar's signature cocktails, or with a craft-beer chaser. Located in an old mansion on the pedestrian street Libertad, this beloved spot has drink specials during the week, in addition to hosting live music and other special events on the weekends, so you're likely to find a crowd here on any given evening.

Alquimia (Cinco de Mayo 71, tel. 442/212-1791, 6pm-2:30am Tues.-Sat.) is a small, attractive, and low-lit cocktail bar in a colonial-era building. There's something of an old-fashioned feeling to the main room, where dozens of glimmering glass bottles are stacked behind the dark-wood bar and leather booths overlook the street. Despite the traditional look, bartenders put together some rather newfangled cocktails—martinis adorned with Oreos or gummy bears—though the no-nonsense crowd can also order a straight shot of mezcal, served with orange wedges. It's a good place to start the evening, as they often have drinks specials in the afternoon.

LIVE MUSIC, THEATER, AND CINEMA

The lovely neoclassical **Teatro de la República** (Juárez 22 Nte., tel. 442/212-0339, generally 9am-5pm daily, but hours vary) was built in 1845, and it was the very first place that the Mexican national anthem was played. It logged another claim to fame in 1917, when the Mexican Constitution was signed here after the conclusion of the Mexican Revolution of 1910. Today, this historic venue continues to function as one of Querétaro's most prominent performance spaces. It is the home of Querétaro's philharmonic as well as a venue for high-profile concerts, government functions, dance performances, and plays. Its neoclassical, semicircular interior has terraced balconies and plush red seats, creating a rather sophisticated backdrop for any performance. It's often open to the public, if you just want to peek inside.

A *carcajada* is a loud laugh, and **Teatrito la Carcajada** (Cinco de Mayo 48, reservations tel. 442/212-9999, www.teatritolacarcajada.com, box office noon-8pm Mon.-Sat.) seeks to elicit exactly that response from its audience. Focusing on upbeat fun, comic performances, and improv shows, this 140-seat venue usually runs shows Wednesday to Saturday—though they often sell out, so reserve in advance. There's an adjoining café for drinks or coffee that opens before and after the show. Programs are all in Spanish.

Teatro de la República

A multipurpose cultural center located in a lovely colonial-era building, the **Casa de Cultura Dr. Ignacio Mena Rosales** (Cinco de Mayo 40, tel. 442/212-5614, 9am-2pm and 4pm-7pm Mon.-Fri.) hosts ongoing exhibits of contemporary art, often by local artists, as well as ongoing performances, lectures, chamber music, children's programming, and theater, all held in one of the galleries or in the casa's courtyard. In addition to their cultural programming, the center offers classes at low prices in a range of interesting topics, such as yoga, African dance, digital photography, tango, and theater.

A youth-oriented cultural center, café, and theater, **La Grieta** (Cinco de Mayo 69, tel. 442/367-0090 or 442/305-0023, 2pm-10pm Tues.-Fri., 10am-10pm Sat.-Sun., hours for performances vary) keeps their small on-site theater busy with ongoing productions for children (like shadow puppet plays), comedy shows and dramas for adults, and live music performances. They also have an active film program, with a focus on foreign and independent films. Come for a bite to eat or a coffee at the café before the show, which you can enjoy in their pretty, tree-filled outdoor courtyard. In addition to performances, La Grieta offers a range of workshops on topics like digital photography or capoeira, in Spanish, at very affordable prices.

GALLERIES AND MUSEUMS

The **Museo de la Ciudad Santiago de Querétaro** (Guerrero 27 Nte., tel. 442/224-3756 or 442/212-3855, generally 11am-7pm Tues.-Sat., US$0.50) has an extraordinary commitment to emerging artists and contemporary art. Located in the Capuchin convent that houses the Museo de la Restauración de la República, the museum's old and crumbling space plays perfect accompaniment to a largely youthful and experimental set of rotating exhibitions, many by local artists. The director seeks contemporary proposals for the museum's numerous gallery spaces, and video art and installation pieces are not uncommon. In addition to art, there is a cinema series, live music, workshops, and other special events held on-site, keeping the museum open well into the evening.

Among the largest of Querétaro's many public exhibition spaces, **Galería Libertad** (Andador Libertad 56, tel. 442/214-2358, www.galerialibertad.mx, 10am-8pm daily, free) is a spacious two-story gallery. Since 1984, this dynamic space has been showing

La Grieta is a youth-oriented cultural center with a pretty patio café.

exhibitions of fine art by *querétenses* and other local artists as well as some bigger names in Mexico art; a recent collective exhibition showed work by students in the visual arts program at Querétaro's Tec de Monterrey campus, while another included work by Francis Alÿs and Mathias Goeritz. They also hold special events, like lectures and poetry readings; posters announcing upcoming events are often hung on the door. The gallery is just steps from the Plaza de Armas on the pedestrian street Libertad.

The Universidad Autónoma de Querétaro operates the multipurpose **Centro de Arte Bernardo Quintana** (Rio de la Loza 23, tel. 442/192-1200, www.cultura.uaq.mx, 10am-2pm and 4pm-8pm Tues.-Fri., 10am-4pm Sat., free), where there are frequent, high-quality visual arts exhibitions in addition to an ongoing program of workshops, classes, book presentations, and other cultural events. In the spring of 2015, the entire space received a thorough renovation and upgrade, installing new air-cooling systems, floors, and interiors to better accommodate art exhibits.

Located in a former schoolhouse dating from the early 20th century, the **Centro Queretano de la Imagen** (Juárez 66, tel. 442/212-2947, http://culturaqueretaro.gob.mx, 10am-6pm Tues.-Fri. during exhibitions, free) is a public art space dedicated to the preservation, conservation, and exhibition of both still and moving images. In addition to the center's work in research and preservation of historic photographs, it exhibits contemporary and historic photography in its creaky, high-ceilinged galleries. The space is open to the public even if there isn't a show, though the doors are often closed. The center frequently shows films, in addition to offering workshops in film preservation, video and digital editing, and photography.

FESTIVALS AND EVENTS

Fiesta de la Santa Cruz

One of Querétaro's most important religious and cultural events is the annual **Fiesta de la Santa Cruz.** The festival begins on the night of September 12 with an all-night procession and ceremony by thousands of *concheros,* or Aztec dancers, who dance in unison along the Avenida Los Arcos to the hill at Sangremal in reverence for Saint James, who, according to local history, miraculously appeared here at the moment of Querétaro's founding. The high-energy, rhythmic dancing—based on pre-Columbian dance traditions said to ignite happiness in the heart of the dancer—continues on the plaza in front of the temple all night long. As dawn breaks, the city streets close as food vendors set up and the temple is decorated. The dancing continues until the celebrations conclude with a mass on September 15, just in time for Independence Day celebrations.

Fiestas de la Independencia

Like San Miguel de Allende and Guanajuato, Querétaro played a central role in Mexico's independence movement. Accordingly, the **Fiestas de la Independencia** are celebrated with enthusiasm here. During September 15 and 16, the city is dressed in lights and decoration for the independence holidays, and you'll find traditional music and dance performances, fireworks, and lots of parties throughout the plazas, bars, and restaurants of the *centro histórico.* The traditional *grito—¡Viva México!*—is delivered from the Casa de la Corregidora in the Plaza de Armas at 11:45pm on September 15, followed by fireworks.

Shipping Items Home

The Mexican **post office** (Arteaga 5, tel. 442/224-3968, www.correosdemexico.com.mx, 8:30am-4:30pm Mon.-Fri., 9am-noon Sat.) is between Corregidora and Juárez. You can get expedited packing and shipping service at **Estafeta** (Corregidora 117, tel. 442/212-4099, www. estafeta.com, 10am-6:30pm Mon.-Fri., 10am-2pm Sat.) at generally reasonable prices, especially for national shipping. There is also a **DHL** (Av. Constituyentes 22, Local 2, tel. 442/212-2627, 9am-7pm Mon.-Fri., 9am-1pm Sat.) in the *centro histórico*, which can handle both national and international expedited shipping, though note that costs can run into the hundreds of dollars for packages shipped through DHL's expedited services.

Shopping

Those living in the small towns near Querétaro, including many folks in San Miguel de Allende, make use of Querétaro's shopping centers and big-box stores to stock their pantry and closets. Among the most popular spots for San Miguel folks, Querétaro's **Costco** (Plaza del Parque, Blvd. Bernardo Quintana 4107, tel. 442/211-6700, 9am-9pm Mon.-Sat., 9am-8pm Sun.) stocks bulk and gourmet items. It is near a Sam's Club, Home Depot, and Office Depot.

Two of Mexico's biggest and best-known department store chains, **Liverpool** (tel. 442/427-8700, www.liverpool.com.mx, 11am-9pm daily) and **Palacio de Hierro** (tel. 442/384-3000, www.soytotalmentepalacio.com, 11am-9pm daily) anchor the large shopping center at **Plaza Antea** (Carretera Querétaro-San Luis Potosí 76127, Col. Félix Osores Sotomayor, www.antea.mx), which is filled with other international brands like Forever 21, H&M, Michael Kors, Zara, and Benetton.

TRADITIONAL CRAFTS

For a very nice selection of traditional crafts, seek out **Quinto Real** (Andador V. Carranza 10A-B, tel. 442/212-8601, www.quintoreal. com.mx, 10am-2pm and 3pm-7pm Mon.-Sat.). This lovely little shop is set in the living areas of a colonial-era home, a cozy showroom for the store's collection of arts and crafts. You'll

find a little bit of everything, including tin ornaments, textiles and table runners, wooden masks, handmade jewelry, and a large selection of glassware. Merchandise is artfully designed and displayed, making it easy to imagine one of these colorful accents in your own home.

As part of its mission to promote traditional art and handcraft in Mexico's native communities, the **Casa del Artesano** (Allende 20, tel. 442/169-3445, 10am-7pm Wed.-Mon.) contains a large open-air market in the back patio. Among dozens of booths, you'll find craftwork typical to a variety of Mexican regions, including Guerrero, Michoacán, and the state of Mexico. Most, however, is produced locally by indigenous artisans who have relocated to the state of Querétaro—some working right in the Casa del Artesano. Items include *molcajetes* (mortars for cooking), embroidered blouses, dolls, and other fine work. You'll find the greatest variety on weekends or during civic holidays, when up to 80 booths are open.

ANTIQUES

There are a number of interesting vintage and antiques shops along Carranza, nearing the Templo de la Santa Cruz, in Querétaro's *centro histórico*; **Garabato** (Carranza 59, Barrio de la Cruz, tel. 442/212-1563, 10:30am-8:30pm daily) is among the most well-stocked and friendly. You'll find vintage iceboxes, baskets, old wooden furniture, lamps, LPs, books, dolls, mirrors, and other unique pieces, from rare and pricey colonial-era antiques to fun collectibles. Prices are a bit high, but vintage hounds may not be able to resist a purchase.

GOURMET GOODIES

Anyone with a sweet tooth will enjoy **Dulzura Mexicana** (Juárez Nte. 69, tel. 442/312-1873, noon-8pm Mon., 10am-10pm Tues.-Sun.), a small but super-stocked traditional candy shop kitty-corner from the Teatro de la República. Here you'll find all the most popular Mexican goodies, like *ate* (fruit paste), *jamoncillo* (flavored milk-fudge), and crystallized fruit, as well as more unusual sweets like *queso de tuna* and *gomitas de guanábana* (tropical fruit gumdrops). The friendly staff can explain the difference (in Spanish) between different types of sweets as well as

provide samples of some items. Pile your pickings into a wicker basket, take them to the register, and get ready for a sugar high.

CLOTHING

Step into the past at 100-year-old hat shop **Sombrería La Popular** (Independencia 98, tel. 442/212-0474, 10am-8pm Mon.-Sat.), which sells a range of classic men's hats from legacy brands from Europe and the United States, like Stetson, as well as Mexican-made Tardan (the shop originally opened as a Tardan branch, though later began representing other hatmakers). Merchandise is laid out in creaky glass display cases, which appear to have been in use since the shop's opening in the early 20th century—though the shop itself relocated to its current site in the 1980s. Though no hats are made on the premises, the shop can clean, iron, and repair high-quality hats in need of some loving care.

Sports and Recreation

YOGA AND FITNESS CLASSES

The **Casa de la Cultura Mena** (Cinco de Mayo 4, tel. 442/212-5614, hours vary by class) offers low-cost and often interesting fitness classes among their robust workshop offerings, including yoga and capoeira as well as a range of dance, from African dance to belly dancing. They also have yoga classes for children. Most classes are held in the little galleries surrounding the casa's central courtyard, and they are all taught in Spanish. For yoga in the Iyengar tradition, **Sama Centro de Yoga** (Puente de Alvarado 305, Col. Carretas, tel. 442/446-9034, hours vary by class) offers several weekly workshops (at about US$8 per class, with discounts the more classes you buy), plus an ongoing prenatal yoga series. They sometimes invite guest teachers to give workshops on special topics, but otherwise instruction is in Spanish.

PARKS

Bordering the *centro histórico* to the south, the large **Alameda Hidalgo** (between Avenida Ignacio Zaragoza and Avenida Constituyentes, 8am-8pm daily) is a beautiful, tree-filled urban park, which first opened to the public in 1804. Its flat, shaded paths are great for strolling, chatting, or jogging. The metal fencing that runs along the borders of the park is often hung with photo exhibitions, just like the famous *rejas de Chapultepec* in the Bosque de Chapultepec in Mexico City.

SPECTATOR SPORTS

Querétaro Fútbol Club, more commonly known as Los Gallos Blancos de Querétaro, is a professional soccer team in the Liga MX, Mexico's first-division soccer league. They play home games at the **Estadio Corregidora** (Av. de las Torres s/n, at Calle Estadio, Col. Cimatario, www.

gallos-blancos.com, open during events), a 10,000-seat venue in the Cimatario neighborhood, southeast of the *centro histórico*. Throughout the 1980s, 1990s, and 2000s, the team bounced between first-division and second-division standing, but today they hold a firm place in the premier league. Despite a rocky record, they have some very loyal fans in the city, and attending a first-division soccer game is always a fun and spirited experience. Tickets (US$10-20) are available through Ticketmaster.

Food

The city of Querétaro has never been known as a culinary destination. That said, you can find some truly good eats here. Modern Mexican restaurants and traditional eateries are abundant in the *centro,* and there are a few nice international spots adding welcome variety to the dining options. In some of the best places, the atmosphere surpasses the food: Querétaro, unlike most modern cities, has managed to hang on to a number of its old-fashioned cafeterias and *fondas,* which maintain a loyal clientele within the local crowd. You'll also find plenty of cheap eats and tacos, though street stands aren't as abundant here as in other parts of the country.

TACOS AND QUICK BITES

For a quick but tasty bite, there are dozens of mouthwatering taco stands and casual eateries in the extensive **Mercado de la Cruz** (Manuel Gutiérrez Nájera s/n, corner 15 de Mayo, 8am-6pm daily, individual vendor hours vary). A rule of thumb in any market is to follow the crowds: Popular food stalls tend to be the freshest and tastiest. For a sure thing, try the delicious (and award-winning!) **Barbacoa Lucia** (Mercado de la Cruz, Local 98, 8am-2pm daily, US$1-3), which serves flavorful *barbacoa* (lamb steamed in an earthen pit) tacos and fragrant broth soup. Order a few

the entrance to Alameda Hidalgo

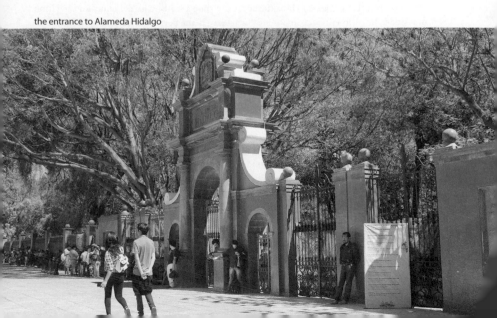

Best Restaurants

★ **La Mariposa:** This popular 1940s vintage coffee shop is worth visiting for the old-fashioned ambience alone. Have a coffee and a *pan dulce* and soak up the throwback decor (page 209).

★ **Maria y Su Bici:** Delicious, inexpensive Oaxacan-style eats, craft beer and mezcal cocktails, and a lively setting are featured at this local favorite, which now has several locations around town (page 210).

★ **Breton:** At this sweet French bistro, you'll find the best croissants in Querétaro, perfectly made espresso drinks, and an appealing European-style breakfast and lunch menu (page 211).

★ **Jardín de Cerveza Hércules:** The excellent selection of creative craft beer, a fun menu of Mexican and international bar snacks, and the ace setting in a renovated textile factory make this unique beer garden worth the quick trip beyond the *centro* (page 211).

★ **Arrayán:** San Sebastián Bernal's standout restaurant boasts delicious, creative Mexican food using fresh, local ingredients (page 228).

---

tacos and do like the locals by adding cilantro, chopped onions, and salsa to the meat. The small metal stools that surround this informal stand are almost always filled, but turnover is quick, so you'll likely snag a seat as you wait for your tacos to be prepared.

Tamales are a classic Mexican breakfast or dinner food, traditionally accompanied by *atole*, a sweet corn-based drink. In Querétaro, there are numerous small storefronts specializing in tamales and *atole* along Arteaga, a few blocks east of Santa Rosa de Viterbo. Most are open, as is traditional, in the early morning and late at night. Try **Super Tamales y Atoles de Querétaro** (Arteaga 41 Pte., tel. 442/212-4298, 8am-noon and 6pm-11pm Mon., 7:30am-noon and 5pm-11pm Tues.-Sun., US$2), where you can order delicious tamales stuffed with chicken, cheese, red salsa, green salsa, chile peppers, or pork. In addition to traditional tamales steamed in corn husks, Super Tamales prepares Oaxacan-style tamales, which are steamed in banana leaves and generally denser and moister. Whether you go in the morning or in the evening, get there well before closing, as many of the options sell out.

While there are only a few flavors on the menu, all the ice cream at friendly **Nevería Galy** (Andador Cinco de Mayo 8, tel. 442/219-6781, noon-10pm daily, US$1-2) is made with all-natural ingredients, a fact they proudly display on many jovial posters tacked along the shop's walls. The delicious and icy lime *nieve* is the perfect salve to a hot afternoon. Take it to go or enjoy your ice cream at a Formica table inside the authentically retro shop. They also serve ice cream with a shot of wine on top, an unusual yet popular option.

There are only stools to sit on at **Las Tortugas** (Andador Cinco de Mayo 27A, no phone, 9am-9pm daily, US$4), but that's the best way to eat a *torta* (a Mexican-style sandwich served on a soft roll called a *telera*). In fact, the old-fashioned atmosphere at this hole-in-the-wall *tortería*, with its funky bullfighting theme, makes everything taste better—though, after more than half a century in business, it's evident that Las Tortugas knows how to make a good lunch. Order a *torta* stuffed with carnitas, chorizo, or *milanesa* (breaded steak) and topped with pickled chiles and the shop's proprietary salsa, accompanied by a fresh *horchata*.

MEXICAN

The enchantingly preserved and perennially popular ★ La Mariposa (Ángela Peralta 7, tel. 442/212-1166, 8am-9:30pm daily, US$4) is a casual and inexpensive place to enjoy a Mexican breakfast or lunch in a genuinely retro atmosphere. Although there are take-out counters for La Mariposa's bakery in the entryway, it's better to have a seat in the old-timey dining room, a throwback to mid-century Mexico with tan vinyl chairs, Formica tabletops, and wallpaper covered in delicate roses. The vintage espresso machine is still in use and aglow with pink neon lights, from which tasty coffees are served by an efficient yet affable waitstaff. La Mariposa offers a simple and traditional menu containing many Mexican classics like tamales, pozole (hominy soup), and egg dishes, or you can just stop in for a coffee and a piece of *pay de queso* (cheesecake), but it's the atmosphere that's most memorable.

A Querétaro classic, Cafetería Bisquets (Pino Suárez 7, tel. 442/214-1481, 7am-11pm daily, US$4) is always bustling with a local crowd. Savory *chilaquiles* with a fried egg or spicy *huevos a la cazuela* (eggs and salsa cooked in a clay pot) are two of the many delicious options on the breakfast menu. *Café con leche* (coffee with milk) is served in the traditional style; waitstaff bring hot pitchers of milk and strong coffee to the table, and you indicate how much you'd like of each served in your mug. In the afternoons, *enchiladas verdes* and *enchiladas queretanas* are two solid choices, though there is also a daily *comida corrida*, which is cheap and filling. The atmosphere could not be more casual, with a small courtyard dining room as well as a larger dining room overlooking the street below. Service is efficient and professional, if not particularly verbose.

Inspired by the cuisine of southern Mexico, Tikua Sur-Este (Allende Sur 13, tel. 442/403-4677 or 442/455-3333, www.tikua.mx, 1pm-11pm Mon.-Fri., 9am-11pm Sat., 9am-8pm Sun., US$10) is the perfect place for a leisurely lunch during a tour of Querétaro's *centro histórico*. It's hard to decide what to order on the restaurant's expansive menu, which covers Atlantic to Pacific, Oaxaca to Yucatán. If you're feeling adventurous, try the *chapulines* (grasshoppers) with cheese, then fill up on a nicely served plate of enchiladas in mole. Don't be turned away by the fact that Tikua promotes its food as being served without spice. While they do keep main dishes mild, one of the best parts about eating here is the array of salsas they bring to the table when you sit down—from a delightful roasted habanero variety to a spicy peanut salsa—some of which have quite a kick. Located in a large colonial-era mansion, there are two pretty indoor dining rooms and an outdoor patio dressed up with big, colorful murals; the attractive atmosphere is further complemented by frequent live music performances. Friendly, attentive service and a drink menu that includes artisanal beer and mezcal complete the experience.

There is nothing nicer than watching the crowd mill through the Plaza de Armas while relaxing in one of the restaurants along the picturesque plaza. A popular choice with visitors to the city, El Mesón de Chucho el Roto (Pasteur 16, Plaza de Armas, tel. 442/212-4295, www.chuchoelroto.com.mx, 8:30am-11pm daily, US$12) serves classic Mexican food in a pleasant garden setting. With a gated patio beneath the trees of the Plaza de Armas, this restaurant is a perfect place for a leisurely meal and excellent people-watching. On Sunday, El Mesón de Chucho el Roto often draws a crowd of chic locals; expect to share the dining room with ladies in heels and sunglasses or men in sport coats and shiny watches. It's a good place to try popular regional dishes, like *gorditas* or a (very shareable) *molcajete*, a volcanic-rock bowl filled with a variety of meats, onion, cactus, cheese, and a chile sauce.

Right next door to Chucho el Roto, the restaurant 1810 (Andador Libertad 62, Plaza de Armas, tel. 442/214-3324, www.restaurante1810.com, 8am-11pm Mon.-Thurs., 8am-midnight Fri.-Sat., 8am-10pm Sun., US$12) offers a very similar menu and atmosphere, though it is perhaps a touch more casual. Street performers often gather in front of these two restaurants on the weekends, adding a bit more color to the scenery.

What started out as little more than a hole-in-the-wall has now expanded to two additional locations in the *centro histórico,* and it's easy to see why: ★ **Maria y Su Bici** (Cinco de Mayo 91, tel. 442/214-3212, Cinco de Mayo 80, Corregidora Sur s/n, at Andador Libertad, tel. 442/214-1403, www.mariaysubici.com, 1pm-midnight Mon.-Sat., 9am-7pm Sun., US$9) achieves the Mexican gold standard of *bueno, bonito, y barrato* (good, pretty, and cheap) with delicious, Oaxacan-inspired dishes in a colorful and casual setting. Here, you can sample well-made renditions of Oaxacan regional cuisine, including stuffed *chile pasilla,* quesadillas with yellow mole, and crunchy *tlayudas* made with or without meat. In addition to beer (national and artisanal) and wine, the restaurant offers a lovely selection of Oaxacan mezcal as well as various mezcal cocktails, which are served in a gourd and garnished with salt and chile powder. No matter which location you visit (for nostalgics, the original little spot still operates at Cinco de Mayo 80), the food is good,

the atmosphere undeniably jovial, and the service friendly and unhurried.

To try another kitchen's approach to Oaxacan cuisine, check out **Fogón Zapoteco** (Madero 86, tel. 442/214-1143, 7am-9pm Tues.-Sat., 9am-7pm Sun., US$5-7). Here, you'll find tasty Oaxacan-style mole, tamales, and *tlayudas* on the menu, among other southern Mexican specialties, as well as a nice selection of mezcal. The rich, slightly sweet *mole negro,* which combines chocolate, chiles, and spices, is made fresh in house. It can be served with eggs for breakfast or with chicken breast or on *enmoladas* (cheese- or chicken-stuffed tortillas covered in mole sauce) at lunch. The atmosphere here is as casual as they come, with colorful oilcloth-topped tables, and the prices are very reasonable. For an even cheaper bite, drop in for one of the weekly specials, like two-for-one *tlayudas* on Wednesday.

A Querétaro classic, **Cenaduria Blas** (Cinco de Mayo 106, tel. 442/212-3126, 6pm-11:30pm Mon.-Sat., 6pm-11pm Sun., US$3-5) has been in operation in the *centro histórico* since 1940. As a *cenaduria* (a dinner spot), it only opens during the evening hours and serves typical Mexican suppers. Try a version of local specialty *enchiladas queretanas*

Fogón Zapoteco focuses on Oaxacan-style dishes.

Jardín de Cerveza Hércules

(folded tortillas bathed in a mild chile sauce and topped with potato and cheese), or order a few of their delicious *gorditas de maiz quebrado,* chewy corn flatbreads toasted till crispy and stuffed with potato, chorizo, and other fillings. It's a popular spot with families (there is a tiny playroom for kids), and the feeling here is homey and casual; plaid tablecloths, soft lighting, and a pleasant bustle make it a relaxing place to wrap up a day.

INTERNATIONAL

Everything about ★ **Breton** (Andador Libertad 82, tel. 442/299-6207, 8am-5pm Tues.-Sun., US$3-6) recommends it: an adorable location on the quietest block of the Andador Libertad, a stylish yet comfortable atmosphere, and an appealing French breakfast and lunch menu. It's the ideal place to start the day with house-made muesli or savory quiche, accompanied by a beautiful café latte—or just stop in for a surprisingly perfect croissant and a coffee to go. Later in the day, Breton offers savory items like sandwiches

as well as a three-course lunch menu (US$7) that changes daily but always includes a soup or salad, a main dish, and dessert. The atmosphere is as charming as the food—whether eating in the bistro-style dining room downstairs or on the roof deck, where French doors open onto the alleyway below.

Located on the pretty plaza just across from the Templo de la Santa Cruz, **La Vieja Varsovia** (Plaza Fundadores, Gutiérrez Nájera Sur 46, tel. 442/212-5117, www.laviejavarsovia.com.mx, 10am-11pm Tues.-Sun., US$6) started out as a European-style bakery but gained enough popularity that it expanded into a full restaurant. Salads, quiches, and sandwiches fill the menu, though the thing to get here is the wood-oven-baked pizza. They have some unusual pizzas on offer, but go with simpler toppings to really enjoy the chewy crust. The cozy indoor dining room has tables tucked beside the in-store deli, which sells their signature breads plus salsas, jams, and other takeaway items. You can also dine alfresco on the umbrella-shaded tables just outside. If you're looking for that classic pizza-and-a-drink combo, note that La Vieja Varsovia does not serve beer or any other alcohol, though they do have an excellent selection of loose-leaf teas.

DRINKS

Cerveceria Hércules, one of Querétaro's most well-known craft breweries, operates the delightful ★ **Jardín de Cerveza Hércules** (Avenida Hércules Oriente 1, tel. 442/403-6140, 2pm-midnight Tues.-Thurs., 2pm-1am Fri., 10am-1am Sat., 10am-7pm Sun., US$8), an expansive beer garden and restaurant located in an early-20th-century textile factory just outside the *centro histórico.* The old factory facilities have been outfitted with shared picnic tables and hanging lightbulbs, creating a rustic industrial-chic atmosphere, and there are frequent live performances under the stars in the restaurant's main patio. Though you'll see Hércules's beer on menus throughout Mexico, you can sample a much larger selection of their small-batch brews here, from

IPAs to porters to pilsners—as well as mezcal and wine, if beer isn't your thing. To make an afternoon of it, accompany your drinks with some of the tasty bar snacks on offer, from pizza and hot dogs to guacamole and tacos. Popular with Querétaro families, it's also a great place to take the kids on the weekends, with old factory rooms and patios to explore, a swing set and table tennis, and even a free craft table and other activities for children.

Accommodations

Still off the beaten track for most international tourists, Querétaro doesn't have the same range of hotel options you'd find in San Miguel de Allende, but there are still plenty of excellent choices in the *centro histórico*.

UNDER US$50

On a narrow street between the Iglesia de Santa Clara and the Jardín Zenea, the simple and friendly **Hotel Hidalgo** (Madero 11, tel. 442/212-0081 or 442/212-8102, www.hotelhidalgo.com.mx, US$40-50) is a great deal in the historic center of the city. The hotel's guest rooms are on the second story of a colonial mansion, with doors opening onto a pretty central courtyard and restaurant. The colonial exterior suggests a posh accommodation, but once inside, bedrooms are as simple as they come. Each has one double or two single beds, with a television and bottled water, but not much else in terms of amenities. Bathrooms are basic and smell vaguely of cleaning products, but the price is low, the rooms are quiet, and the hotel is perfectly located in the center of the city. Hotel staff is very friendly and knowledgeable, making Hotel Hidalgo a great pick in the budget range.

US$50-100

On a quiet street in the north city center, friendly **La Mansión del Burro Azul** (Altamirano 35, tel. 442/224-2410 or 442/148-7156, www.lamansiondelburroazul.com, US$75) is a great low-key find just a bit off the beaten track. The rooms at this small hotel are distinct and quirky, some with mismatched wood furnishings and crooked iron chandeliers and others with modern furniture and king-size beds. In the casual central courtyard, guests can hang out on the chaise lounges and deck chairs set up over Astroturf or make use of the spacious communal kitchen. There is also a small but peaceful

---

Best Accommodations

★ **Casa Nena:** The warm, friendly service sets this ultra-comfortable boutique hotel apart, located on charming Carranza (page 213).

★ **La Casa del Naranjo:** This lovely, well-priced inn with individually decorated guest rooms, some with outdoor patios, is right in the center of town (page 213).

★ **Hotel Quinta Allende:** Impeccably clean and perfectly located in the center of town, this modern hotel is a very good value (page 214).

★ **Casa Mateo:** Spend a night in the Mexican countryside at this pretty boutique hotel, located in the heart of the small town of San Sebastián Bernal (page 229).

Hotel Quinta Allende

hotel of the same name in San Miguel de Allende. Filling a historic mansion on quiet Carranza street, Querétaro's Nena isn't as opulent as the original San Miguel location, but all the important details have been attended to: well-stocked baths, luxury linens, cable and Netflix on the television, and, most important, warm and attentive service. In fact, it's the friendly atmosphere that makes this little spot so charming. The six guest rooms all open onto a central courtyard and the in-house restaurant **La Bella Italia** (also a San Miguel de Allende import), which means there can be some ambient noise in the evenings. The good news is an excellent full breakfast at the restaurant is included in the cost of the room. At this price point, it's a wonderful place to stay.

★ **La Casa del Naranjo** (Hidalgo 21, tel. 442/212-7606, toll-free Mex. tel. 800/832-8660, http://lacasadelnaranjo.com, US$75-125) is a small but stylish family-run hotel in the center of Querétaro. Each room is decorated in a comfortably rustic style, with exposed rock walls and soft, fluffy bedspreads. All rooms have flat-screen televisions, bathrobes and slippers, and pretty bathrooms with onyx accessories and shower massagers. Upstairs bedrooms are more luxurious, with sofas and sitting areas or canopy beds, some opening onto the roof garden. However, even the smallest room downstairs gets points for its well-designed atmosphere. There is a small bar downstairs, and guests can also relax on the hotel's roof deck, which has a Jacuzzi, chaise lounges, and pretty views of the city. The hotel also offers spa services.

Hostería Los Dos Patios (Cinco de Mayo 109, tel. 442/212-2030 or 442/214-3894, toll-free Mex. tel. 800/831-5790, www.hoteldospatios.com.mx, US$95-110) is a quiet and comfortable hotel in a renovated colonial-era mansion, which markets itself as the first and only holistic hotel in the city. Despite the colonial building, the hotel's 20 rooms are rather modern in their comforts, with plush beds and cotton bedspreads,

massage room where guests and nonguests can order massage and spa services.

Once you step inside the peaceful **Hotel Villa del Villar** (Vincente Guerrero Sur 33, tel. 442/322-7093, US$50-75), it's hard to remember that you're right in the middle of downtown Querétaro. Perhaps the most romantic of the hotel's 10 rooms, located in a restored colonial-era mansion, are those surrounding the central courtyard, with soaring ceilings and doors opening onto the patio (though the rooms in the back of the hotel are a bit quieter and more private). The decor is traditionally Mexican—wooden furniture, tile floors, and lamps—though bathrooms are fully modern, and guests can relax in the peaceful stone-floored courtyard. The atmosphere is comfortable, and service is down-to-earth and very friendly.

Sweet, centrally located ★ **Casa Nena** (Venustiano Carranza No. 37, tel. 442/212-0355 or 442/212-0356, www.hotelnena.mx, US$80-120) is the second branch of a boutique televisions, big armoires, and clean bathrooms. Most rooms also have small couches or love seats where you can read or watch TV. The nicest accommodations are those surrounding the back garden, which are set back off the street and feel both quiet and private. The hotel caters to both tourists and business travelers, and there is an efficient 24-hour desk staff that can answer your questions about the city.

The emphasis isn't on trendy design at well-priced ★ **Hotel Quinta Allende** (Allende Norte 20, tel. 442/224-1050, www. hotelquintaallende.mx, US$85), though each of the hotel's impeccably clean guest rooms, which are arranged around an open-air courtyard, are tastefully decorated with modern furnishings and plenty of natural light. Instead, what makes this small hotel such a nice place to stay is its peerless comfort, with bedrooms that deliver in all the important areas: hot showers, comfortable beds, privacy, quiet, and notable cleanliness. Though this isn't a full-service luxury accommodation, the friendly front-desk and cleaning staff make it a welcoming place to come home to after a tour around Querétaro. Plus, the central location makes it a perfect jumping-off point for exploring downtown.

US$100-150

La Casa del Atrio (Allende Sur 15, tel. 442/212-6314, http://lacasadelatrio.com, US$105-155) stands out with impressive attention to detail and style. Doubling as a gallery, the old home is filled with antiques, art, *artesanía,* and collectibles, which give the common areas a particularly nice ambience. The shared courtyards have an abundance of plants and reading nooks, creating a relaxing, escape-within-the-city feeling. Rooms are each distinguished by unique details, from bathrooms with flagstone showers to antique chests or original murals on the walls. The location just across the street from the Museo de Arte de Querétaro is ideal, and the friendly owner makes sure service is invariably excellent. Breakfast is included in the price, though this hotel would be a bargain without it. Note that children under the age of nine are not allowed, but the hotel is pet-friendly.

The ultramodern design at stylish **Hotel Criol** (Río de La Loza Norte 6, tel. 442/213-7782, toll-free Mex. tel. 800/837-7606, www. hotelcriol.com, US$120) is a surprising contrast to the old-fashioned aesthetic in colonial Querétaro. Perhaps the best part about staying here is getting to enjoy the hotel's lovely shared areas, including a subterranean reading library, a glassed-in sitting area, and an

the modern interior courtyard at boutique property Hotel Criol

outdoor garden with a small but attractive heated pool, a rarity in Querétaro. Rooms are also designed in a modern, Instagram-friendly style, and each is equipped with a safe, cable TV, and air-conditioning; some also have balconies or outdoor sitting areas, or bunk beds for kids. Though the property is clean and quiet throughout, the hotel sometimes sacrifices function for style (glass-doored bathrooms, for example, are not as practical as they are attractive).

US$150-200

Querétaro's most famous hotel is the stunning **Casa de la Marquesa** (Madero 41, tel. 442/212-0092, toll-free Mex. tel. 800/401-7100, http://lacasadelamarquesaqueretaro.co, US$125-200), an opulent colonial-era mansion on Calle Madero. This beautiful building is one of Querétaro's most prized; in fact, it is often listed among the city's notable tourist attractions, even though the building is privately owned (for that reason, the hotel often keeps the lobby closed to the public). The interior of the hotel retains many of the old-world charms you'd hope to find in a historical building: tiled walls, Moorish archways, and tons of antique furniture. Guest rooms are divided between the main house, or Casa de la Marquesa, and a neighboring structure, the Casa Azul, so double-check when reserving if you want to stay in the colonial mansion—and note that they often have promotions, so it may be possible to book a room at a discount.

Casona de la República (Hidalgo 4, tel. 442/251-8500, toll-free Mex. tel. 800/227-6627, www.casonadelarepublica.com, US$175-250) is a boutique hotel in a nicely restored 19th-century mansion. The 15 suites are arranged around a lovely art nouveau patio in front or the quieter patios in back. When it comes to decor, you can pick your poison: The hotel has chosen a different design theme for each room, ranging from art deco to Italian Renaissance. You can see all the options on the hotel's website or ask to view a few rooms when you arrive. No matter what decor you choose, each room is comfortably outfitted with big beds, down comforters, and flat-screen TVs. Some of the bigger rooms have a second-story loft with a private Jacuzzi or television. Standard bedrooms may be a bit prettier, since you can really appreciate their high ceilings and gracious architecture without the addition of the loft. Bathrooms are clean and well laid out, though they don't match up to the opulence of the rooms themselves. All master suites have both in-room Jacuzzis and saunas.

Ideally located on the southeastern corner

Casa de la Marquesa

of the Plaza de Armas, **Mesón Santa Rosa Hotel** (Luis Pasteur 17, tel. 442/227-0600, toll-free Mex. tel. 800/017-7372, http://hotelmesondesantarosa.com, US$180) has a long history of hospitality, first opening its doors as a guesthouse as far back as the 17th century. The hotel changed hands in 2014, and the new management gave the old place a thorough update, replacing the aging carpets and heavy traditional furniture with cozy but stylish decor—white fluffy beds, throw rugs, lamps, and armchairs—that highlights the natural charms of the property. Some rooms have balconies onto the street while others open onto the central courtyard and restaurant (ask for a room in back if you are a light sleeper). Though one of the more expensive options in central Querétaro, it's a spot with a lot of history and character—and the stylish in-house wine-and-cocktail bar, right on the corner of the Andador Libertad, is worth visiting even if you aren't staying in the hotel.

OVER US$200

Light, modern, and incredibly friendly, **Doña Urraca Hotel and Spa** (Cinco de Mayo 117, tel. 442/238-5400, http://qro.donaurraca.com.mx, US$150-215) is a relaxing place to spend a few days in Querétaro's *centro histórico*. Built within the remains of a colonial mansion, the hotel's architecture blends old and new; stone archways from the site's original structure are nicely incorporated into the hotel's clean and modern design. Inside the guest rooms, decor is minimalist and comfortable, with big fluffy beds, leather sofas, and spacious baths. White was the decorator's color of choice, complemented by wicker and leather details that give the whole place a rather earthy feeling. All 24 suites overlook the central pool and lawn, cascading with plants and flowers. Upstairs, the rooms also have private balconies. The hotel's spa services include shiatsu, Swedish, and hot-rock massage, reflexology, and a range of facials and can be arranged in-room. Service is excellent.

Information and Services

TOURIST INFORMATION

Querétaro is working hard to become a more widely recognized tourist destination, and the result is some excellent visitor services. The **tourist office** (Pasteur 4 Nte., tel. 442/238-5067, toll-free Mex. tel. 800/715-1742, www.queretaro.travel, 9am-7pm daily) is almost directly across from the Casa de la Corregidora in the Plaza de Armas. Representatives can provide you with excellent maps of the city center as well as maps and information packets about visiting other parts of the state. They also have the most up-to-date information on booking cultural tours of the city and can help recommend a guide or company.

Media

An excellent guide for visitors, the free monthly booklet *Asomarte* (www.asomarte.com), published by the state's tourism board,

lists cultural and arts events throughout the city of Querétaro. In addition to short pieces about local culture and travel, the magazine has a comprehensive agenda of special events and concerts happening in town. *Asomarte* is distributed for free throughout the city. Look for a copy at the front desk of museums or hotels. Note that it's published in Spanish only.

There are several local periodicals published in Querétaro, including the Spanish-language newspaper *Diario de Querétaro* (www.oem.com.mx/diariodequeretaro), which covers local and international news as well as arts and culture in town. Every week, the *Diario* publishes weekend itineraries for art and activities in and around the state of Querétaro as well as a section dedicated to Mexican tourism and travel. The newspaper *El Corregidor* (www.elcorregidor.com.mx) also covers local, state, and international news, though its cultural offerings are more limited than those of *Diario*.

The big Mexico City-based newspaper *El Universal* (www.eluniversalqueretaro.mx) publishes a daily edition in Querétaro. It covers national news, politics, sports, and the arts while also providing additional coverage of news and politics in Querétaro city and state.

Visas and Officialdom

To apply for a resident visa or perform any other immigration-related paperwork, contact the regional delegation of the **Instituto Nacional de Migración** (INM, Mexican Immigration Service, Calle Francisco Peñuñuri 15, Fracc. San José Inn, tel. 442/214-2712 or 442/214-1538, 9am-1pm Mon.-Fri.) in the *centro histórico*. They can extend tourist cards, process resident paperwork, and assist with lost or stolen visas. There is also an immigration office at the Querétaro airport, but this branch is only equipped to provide exit and entry permits.

SERVICES
Medical and Emergency Services

The **Hospital General de Querétaro** (Av. 5 de Febrero 105, Col. Virreyes, tel. 442/216-0039) will treat emergencies. A well-recommended private hospital, **Hospital Ángeles de Querétaro** (Bernardino del Razo 21, Col. Ensueño, tel. 442/192-3000, ext. 5235 for emergencies, http://hospitalesangeles.com/queretaro) also takes emergencies, in addition to offering a full staff of doctors available by appointment.

Dial **911** from any ground line in Querétaro to reach the emergency response services. The **Red Cross** (Av. Balaustradas esq. circuito Estadio S/N, emergencies 442/229-0505 or 442/229-0669, www.cruzrojaqueretaro.org) and the **Protección Civil** police department (tel. 442/212-0712) will also respond to emergencies.

Money

There are large national banks throughout the city center in Querétaro, all equipped with ATMs. Most bank branches can also exchange currency, including the Mexican credit union **BanBajío** (Corregidora 153, tel. 442/214-2920, www.bb.com.mx, 9am-4pm Mon.-Fri.) and **Santaner** (6 de Septiembre No. 1 y 3 Oriente, tel. 442/214-0569, 9am-4pm Mon.-Fri.) in the *centro histórico*.

Querétaro has information kiosks throughout the city center.

Transportation

GETTING THERE

Air

QUERÉTARO INTERNATIONAL AIRPORT (QRO)

Transportation to Querétaro has become even more convenient with the opening of **Querétaro International Airport** (QRO, Carretera Estatal 200, Querétaro-Tequisquiapan 22500, tel. 442/192-5500, www.aiq.com.mx), about 32 kilometers (20 miles) outside the city center. There are daily flights to and from various locations in the United States and Mexico, including Houston, Dallas, Cancún, Guadalajara, and Monterrey. Once on the ground, there is both airport **taxi** (tel. 442/148-6272) and shared shuttle service from the airport to the city center; most will drop off anywhere in town for a flat rate of about US$25.

MEXICO CITY INTERNATIONAL AIRPORT (MEX)

Depending on where you are coming from, visitors to Querétaro may find an easier route or less expensive flight into Mexico through **Mexico City International Airport** (MEX, Capitan Carlos León s/n, Peñón de Los Baños Venustiano Carranza, Distrito Federal, tel. 55/2482-2400, www.aicm.com.mx), in the capital. By bus or car, the drive from Mexico City to Querétaro takes about three hours (depending on traffic leaving the city, which can be tremendous on the weekends or during road construction projects). From the airport, **Primera Plus** (toll-free Mex. tel. 800/375-7587, www.primeraplus.com.mx) offers direct bus service from both terminals directly to the bus station in Querétaro.

Bus

There are dozens of daily buses between Mexico City and Querétaro as well as dozens more buses linking Querétaro to other cities in the Bajío, Guadalajara, Puerto Vallarta, and beyond. Intercity buses come and go from the Querétaro's **Central de Autobuses** (Central Bus Station, Prol. Luis Vega y Monroy 800, tel. 442/229-0181), near the south end of the city just off Highway 57 (México-Querétaro). There are four major bus stations in Mexico City; generally, buses depart Mexico City's Terminal Central del Norte for Querétaro, with departures every 20-30 minutes. In addition, there are buses that leave directly every hour from Mexico City's airport (terminals one and two) for Querétaro.

Primera Plus (Prol. Luis Vega y Monroy 800, Central de Autobuses, tel. 442/211-4001, toll-free Mex. tel. 800/375-7587, www.primeraplus.com.mx) is one of the biggest bus lines serving Querétaro, with buses between Mexico City and Querétaro departing every 20-30 minutes 6am-midnight daily. During peak hours, buses leave for Querétaro from Mexico City every 15 minutes. Primera Plus also offers direct service between both airport terminals in Mexico City and Querétaro's main bus station, departing every hour 6:30am-midnight.

Between San Miguel de Allende and Querétaro, **Herradura de Plata** (Prol. Luis Vega y Monroy 800, Central de Autobuses, Ex-Hacienda de Carretas, tel. 442/290-0245, www.hdp.com.mx) and **Servicios Coordinados Flecha Amarilla** (Prol. Luis Vega y Monroy 800, Central de Autobuses, tel. 442/211-4001, toll-free Mex. tel. 800/375-7587) both offer second-class service to and from Querétaro, with buses running every 20 minutes or so 6am-10pm. You do not need to book ahead; just buy a ticket at the bus station.

A taxi ride to downtown Querétaro takes about 15 minutes from the bus station and costs about US$3. You can also take a taxi all the way to San Miguel de Allende for about US$40.

Car

FROM SAN MIGUEL DE ALLENDE

From San Miguel de Allende, the drive to Querétaro takes about **45 minutes.** Follow the Salida a Querétaro southwest out of the city, continuing through the traffic circle and onto the two-lane highway (Mexico 111) for about 40 kilometers (25 miles). After passing through the small town of Buenavista, exit left on Highway 57 (México-Querétaro). Continue south on Highway 57 for about 40 kilometers (25 miles), exiting either via the Boulevard Bernardo Quintana (a large avenue that runs through Querétaro and includes many popular chain stores, like Costco and Home Depot), or Constituyentes, an avenue just before the bus terminal, which leads directly downtown.

FROM MEXICO CITY

Querétaro is on Highway 57 (México-Querétaro), a major and well-marked federal thoroughfare that runs from Mexico City to the north via San Luis Potosí, ending at the U.S. border in Piedras Negras, Coahuila. From Mexico City, take the Periférico Norte to exit the city, following signs toward Tepotzotlán. After passing through the tollbooth, continue straight on Highway 57. The drive takes **2-3 hours.** Once you arrive in the city, exit at Constituyentes and follow the signs downtown.

GETTING AROUND

Car

Driving in Querétaro can be challenging for those who don't know the city well. In addition, heavy traffic can be a problem during peak hours, since many of Querétaro's residents drive to and from their jobs. Fortunately, Querétaro is much easier to navigate than many other large Mexican cities, with decent signage and generally courteous drivers. For reference, Avenida Zaragoza and Luis Pasteur are both major avenues that lead downtown from the highway.

CAR RENTAL

If you plan to spend time outside of Querétaro's historic downtown or you would like to explore the surrounding countryside, renting a car can be a convenient and fairly inexpensive option. Most of Querétaro's car rental companies operate out of the international airport, though several also have offices in downtown Querétaro. **Hertz** (Carretera Estatal 200, Querétaro, toll-free Mex. tel. 800/709-5000, 24 hours daily; Avenida de las Artes 61, 8am-6pm daily) has locations at Querétaro International Airport and downtown. Hertz offers low daily rates for cars, SUVs, and minivans.

If you are arriving in Querétaro via bus, an inexpensive rental car company, **EHL Rentacar** (Terminal de Autobuses, Local 113, Prol. Luis Vega y Monroy 800, Local 120, tel. 442/229-0219, http://ehlrentacar.mx) has offices in the main bus terminal. You only need a credit card and a driver's license to get a set of wheels, but do book ahead to avoid delays. All cars have automatic transmission and air-conditioning.

Taxi

Within the downtown district, it is easy to get everywhere on foot. However, Querétaro is a large city, with 1,800,000 inhabitants and sprawling residential neighborhoods. Most residents travel by car; public transportation is rather limited. As a visitor, either renting a vehicle or taking taxis is usually the easiest solution when heading outside the downtown district.

Cheap and reliable taxis circle throughout Querétaro. Fares start as low as US$2 within the city center and generally run about US$3 from the bus station to downtown. You can also call **Radio Taxi Los Arcos** (Andador 6 1916, Lomas de Casa Blanca, tel. 442/222-8293) or **Radio Taxi Querétaro** (Marqués de la Laguna 159, Lomas del Marqués, tel. 442/245-6505) if you need a lift. You can also hail an Uber from anywhere in the city.

Bus

Buses continuously run from Querétaro's city center to the outlying suburbs, with many running along Avenida Ignacio Zaragoza and Constituyentes on the southern side of the *centro histórico*. You can hop on any of these buses to traverse the city center, though it's usually easier to take a taxi; if you need to go to an outlying neighborhood, the bus's destination will be marked in its window. Most rides cost about US$0.50.

Sightseeing and Cultural Tours

The **state tourist office** (Pasteur 4 Nte., tel. 442/238-5067, toll-free Mex. tel. 800/715-1742, www.queretaro.travel, 9am-7pm daily) can give you up-to-date information about tour operators in Querétaro city and state. If you've got an idea of what you'd like to do but don't know how to make it happen, this is the place to start.

Querebus (tel. 442/312-2966, one-hour trolley tour US$5, bus tour US$8) offers guided double-decker bus tours and motorized-trolley tours of Querétaro's *centro histórico* throughout the year, with several routes taking you past the city's most important monuments, including a route to the impressive aqueduct, and another to the Cerro de las Campanas. You can buy tickets for either the trolley or the bus tours at the tourist information kiosks on the Cinco de Mayo (across the street from the Jardín Zenea), in the Plaza de la Constitución, or at the Monumento a la Corregidora.

Vicinity of Querétaro

TEQUISQUIAPAN

A warm little town in the heart of Querétaro state, Tequisquiapan, founded in 1555, has a pretty colonial-era atmosphere, with narrow streets and stucco houses lining the city center. Considered the heart of Querétaro state's wine and cheese region, it is propitiously located above copious natural springs, some boasting thermal water. As a result, Tequis (as it is called) is greener than many other local cities, with large trees shading the city sidewalks and plenty of swimming pools at local hotels. Though this small city doesn't offer much by way of sights or dining, its attractive downtown and country ambience make it a relaxing place for a respite.

On the weekends, Tequisquiapan is swarmed with tourists, mostly day-trippers from Querétaro and weekenders from Mexico City. It's downright bustling on a Saturday night in the square, where families stroll between shops or rest on a bench with ice cream. Those who prefer utter peace and quiet may choose to visit Tequisquiapan during the week; however, note that many restaurants and shops may be closed or have reduced hours Monday-Wednesday.

Sights
PLAZA MIGUEL HIDALGO

Plaza Miguel Hidalgo is Tequisquiapan's central square and the locus of activity in town, surrounded by gift shops and restaurants. Presiding over the square is the **Templo Santa María de la Asunción,** for which construction began during the 16th century, though it wasn't finished until the end of the 19th century. This church isn't an opulent baroque spectacle, like you'd find in Guanajuato or Querétaro; however, its delicately painted pink facade and large pink cupola have a stately, refined appeal. At the front of the church, the stone entryway surrounds a pretty, stained-glass window. Santa María de la Asunción is Tequisquiapan's patron saint, and her feast day, August 15, is merrily celebrated in the town square.

PARQUE LA PILA

A sprawling park in the city center, **Parque La Pila** (Av. Ezequiel Montes s/n, 7am-7pm daily) is filled with large and stately cypress and ash trees as well as expansive lawns. On Sundays, it is a popular place for locals to relax in the shade.

GEOGRAPHICAL CENTER OF MEXICO

The town of Tequisquiapan in Querétaro state and the monument to El Cristo Rey del Cubilete in Guanajuato state both claim the honor of being Mexico's exact geographical center. It's unclear who really holds the title. However, in 1916, President Venustiano Carranza inaugurated a **modernist monument** in Tequisquiapan, at the spot that allegedly marks the center of the country. The monument is just a block from the Plaza Miguel Hidalgo on Centenario and 5 de Mayo.

Food

Although Tequisquiapan is considered the center of Querétaro state's wine and cheese region, food here is pretty unremarkable. Around the Plaza Hidalgo, there are numerous restaurants serving standard Mexican fare in a casual setting, most of which boast better atmosphere than cuisine. Among these is **Rincón Mexicano** (Independencia 5, 2nd floor, tel. 414/273-4678, www.rinconmexicano.com.mx, 1pm-midnight Tues.-Sun., US$8) on the second floor of a colonial home overlooking Plaza Hidalgo. Here, you can order generous plates of *chilaquiles, caldo tlalpeño,* enchiladas, and other traditional Mexican dishes. The restaurant has a full bar, beer, and wine, so it's also a nice place to have a drink and a plate of guacamole. Food isn't particularly memorable, but Rincón Mexicano's patio dining room is a great place to eat in the shade while enjoying a view of the central square.

Just beside the main square, the **Mercado Guadalupano** (Av. Ezequiel Montes s/n, no phone, generally 7am-7pm daily, individual vendor hours vary) is the town's very small municipal market. It's one of the cheapest spots to grab a bite in Tequisquiapan. At the front of the market, a number of stands specialize in carnitas, many still preparing the day's meat in huge metal pots as crowds gather on Saturday and Sunday mornings. Alternatively, head to the back of the market, where several low-key sit-down eateries serve economical breakfasts, lunches, and dinners. A good choice is **Fonda Lulu** (Mercado

Plaza Miguel Hidalgo

Guadalupano, Loc. 54, no phone, generally 8am-4pm Mon., Wed.-Sun.), a family-run *comedor* where you can get a generous plate of *chilaquiles verdes*, topped with an egg, for a couple of bucks.

Across the plaza from the market, the popular **Freixenet World's Wine Bar** (Andador 20 de Noviembre s/n, tel. 414/273-3995, www.freixenetmexico.com.mx, 11am-7pm Tues.-Thurs. and Sun., 11am-midnight Fri.-Sat.) is run by sparkling-wine producer Cavas de Freixenet, which operates a vineyard and winery in the state of Querétaro. Here, you can order bottles and half-bottles of Freixenet's tasty sparkling wine as well as glasses of sparkling wine and mimosas to drink at the bar's pretty rooftop tables, or right on the plaza. One of the best options in the center of town, the bar is always very busy on the weekend evenings, but come during the afternoon or on a weekday, and you may be one of only a few people there.

Freixenet World's Wine Bar

Just around the corner from the main square, **Camino a Bremen** (Guillermo Prieto 19, tel. 414/273-4713, 2pm-10pm Thurs.-Sun.) is a friendly little bakery and restaurant serving delicious homemade pizzas, pastas, and craft beer, as well as a selection of organic breads, pastries, and coffee. Come in the morning for a berry strudel and an almond-milk latte, or drop in at dinner for a plate of handmade pasta served with house bread. Though just off the main plaza, it's a quiet yet quality spot, with just four tables in the simple dining room.

Accommodations

Tequisquiapan has been a popular weekend getaway for families from Mexico City and Querétaro since the mid-20th century. As a result, a lot of Tequis accommodations feel a bit like a blast from the past, where kids gather in courtyard pools and hotel rooms are equipped with worn floral bedspreads and static-filled TVs. Many hotels have pools (and even croquet or tennis courts), though facilities are often outdated. Hotel rates here tend to run higher than other spots. One such place is the

Hotel San Francisco (Moctezuma 2, tel. 414/273-0231, US$60), a rambling old hotel with a cold-water swimming pool and wild, untended gardens, which are often overrun with children. Rooms are basic, but the vibe is relaxed and welcoming, with a friendly budget-traveler feeling. It's a bit pricier than what you'd expect for this level of accommodation. Just a block from the town square, its location is perfect.

For a luxury setting, **La Granja** (Moreles 12, tel. 414/273-2004 or 414/273-6378, http://hotelboutiquelagranja.com, US$150) is a nice choice for an overnight trip. On a quiet street just a half-block off the Plaza Miguel Hidalgo, spacious and comfortable bedrooms with modern decor are arranged along the tiled corridors, which surround a pretty, plant-filled courtyard. Each has a spacious bath, some with tubs, and flat-screen TVs. In the back, there's a big pool for swimming, surrounded by lawn chairs and umbrellas, as well as a Jacuzzi (limited to an hour a day for each guest).

Information and Services

Though small, Tequisquiapan is a friendly town and well equipped to receive its many weekend visitors. Tequisquiapan's helpful tourist office, **Dirección de Turismo de Tequisquiapan** (Independencia 1, tel. 414/273-0295, www.tequis.info, 9am-7pm Sun.-Fri., 9am-9pm Sat.), is right on the main plaza. They also oversee a tourist-information kiosk in the main plaza, which is open late (till 8pm Sat.) when the office is closed. The friendly Spanish-speaking representatives can answer questions and provide you with an annotated map and booklet about the town as well as maps of the Querétaro countryside. Although they do not provide walking tours of the city, the tourist office can recommend several tour operators that do.

In the central square, there is a **Bancomer** branch (Independencia 5, 8:30am-4pm Mon.-Fri.) with ATMs open 24 hours, located just next to the tourist office and the Rincón Mexicano restaurant. There is also a **Banamex** branch (Niños Heroes 40, tel. 414/273-0808, 9am-4pm Mon.-Sat.) with ATMs right behind the central plaza, near the monument to the geographic center of Mexico.

For emergencies, dial 066, or call the Red Cross at tel. 441/276-1609.

Getting There and Around

There are daily buses between Querétaro and Tequisquiapan, but the easiest and most popular way to get there is by car. From the city of Querétaro, it is an easy 45-minute drive to Tequis. From San Miguel de Allende, you can get to Tequisquiapan in about twice that time.

BUS

Although the majority of Tequisquiapan tourists drive into town, you can also catch a bus from Querétaro's bus station to Tequisquiapan with **Transportes Queretanos Flecha Azul** (Plaza Capuchinas 105, Plazas del Sol, tel. 442/229-0102). Buses depart every half hour from 6:30am to 9pm daily, and cost about US$3. From Mexico City, the bus line

ETN (Central de Autobuses Tequisquiapan, Carretera San Juan del Río-Xilitla s/n, tel. 414/273-3797 or 414/273-3623, toll-free Mex. tel. 800/800-0368, www.etn.com.mx) offers numerous daily buses between the Terminal Central del Norte in the capital and the bus station in Tequisquiapan (US$15). The trip takes about three hours.

CAR

The most direct way to get to Tequisquiapan is to take Highway México-Querétaro (south from Querétaro or San Miguel and north from Mexico City). Exit at the signs for the Sierra Gorda and take Highway 120 north until you reach Tequisquiapan. If you are feeling more adventurous, pick up a map from the tourist office and take Highway 200 from Querétaro to Tequisquiapan, traveling past the Querétaro airport along smaller highways.

WINE AND CHEESE ROUTE

The state of Querétaro has a long history as an agricultural center, and today it is building on that tradition with a new emphasis on artisanal and locally produced foods. In a nice day trip from the city of Querétaro or San Miguel de Allende, visitors can take a tour of the region's ranches and wineries, stopping to rest or eat in the small towns of Tequisquiapan or Bernal. You must pass through some industrial towns on your way, but overall the landscapes are lovely and interesting.

If you are thinking about visiting Querétaro's countryside and happen to be in the capital, stop by the state tourist office in the city, **Secretaría de Turismo de Estado de Querétaro** (Pasteur 4 Nte., tel. 442/238-5067, toll-free Mex. tel. 888/811-6130, www.queretaro.travel, 9am-8pm daily). The tourist office can provide you with an annotated map of the region, which includes the ranches and wineries open to the public as well as the small towns of Tequisquiapan and Bernal.

Wineries

Wine arrived in Mexico along with the

Spanish and has been produced throughout the country since the colonial era. Though Mexico has not been traditionally recognized as a wine-producing country, things have begun to change. Today, Baja California's hearty wines have become more internationally renowned. Vineyards in the states of Aguascalientes and Chihuahua also produce some excellent vintages. In the states of Querétaro and Guanajuato, grape-growing and wine-producing are nascent industries, yet they appear poised for expansion. Today, there are a few wineries in the region worth a visit when driving through the state of Querétaro.

VIÑEDOS LA REDONDA

Though it's surrounded by rather unappealing ranchland, you really get an authentic wine country feeling once inside **Viñedos La Redonda** (Carretera San Juan del Río, Km 33.5, Ezequiel Montes, toll-free Mex. tel. 800/837-2955, http://laredonda.com.mx, 10am-5pm daily). From off the industrial highway near the town of Ezequiel Montes, you suddenly find yourself surrounded by the gentle green leaves of grapevines. La Redonda operates a small country store at the front of the property, where you can buy bottles of the wines as well as other local products. However, the real action takes place toward the back of the property. Follow the small road to the country-style barn to find a lovely patio, a small Italian restaurant, and a bar where you can sample small glasses of La Redonda's wines for about US$2. Many of the wines are young, but robust and tasty. For Mexican bottles, they can also be rather inexpensive. There are also ongoing **tours** (11am-4pm Mon.-Fri., 11am-5pm Sat.-Sun., US$6) of the vineyard.

CAVAS DE FREIXENET

A well-known international producer of sparkling wine, **Cavas de Freixenet** (Carretera San Juan del Río-Cadereyta, Km 40.5, Ezequiel Montes, tel. 441/277-0147, toll-free Mex. tel. 800/277-5100, www.

freixenetmexico.com.mx) has a long history in Querétaro, predating most of the state's other vineyards. The massive cellars draw hordes of tourists every week, where there are tours of the facilities, frequent weekend festivals, and a big tasting room (no free tastings, though). There are tours of the wine cellars every half hour on the weekends ($6), as well as longer tours and tastings (US$15). If you're coming with kids, the trolley ride around the vineyards is a good option ($13). They also host a wide range of special events, including wine festivals and live music. On the weekends, the scene can be rather overwhelming, as huge groups of local families descend upon the Freixenet complex to slurp up bubbly. There are plenty of tables around the central courtyard where visitors can consume their bottle of bubbly; you can also order wine by the glass at the Freixenet store.

The Freixenet cellars are on the highway between Tequisquiapan and Cadereyta, just past the town of Ezequiel Montes. After you exit Ezequiel Montes, Cavas de Freixenet is about five minutes down the road on the right-hand side. There aren't many vines around the Freixenet offices and cellars as you'd see at La Redonda, though you will enjoy some bubbly.

BODEGAS DE COTE

Bodegas de Cote (Libramiente Norponiente, Km 5+900, Tunas Blancas, Ezequiel Montes, tel. 441/277-5000, www.decote.mx, 11am-6pm daily) opened their impressive modern cellars to the public in 2014. Inside the massive white-adobe building, you can tour the cool subterranean cellar where the vinos are aged; upstairs, the roof deck overlooking the vineyards provides a good place to sip. You can book a walking, bicycle, or train tour of the vineyard, which includes two glasses of wine, one white and one red.

Cheese Producers

What goes better with wine than cheese? The state of Querétaro has brought this eternal pairing to central Mexico. When driving through Querétaro's countryside, you can stop in at one of the many small cheese factories around the state to sample the local products and, in some cases, take a tour of the ranch. On Sundays, the highways can get quite busy as Querétaro families do a turn around the countryside with their kids.

CAVA BOCANEGRA

One of the newest additions to Querétaro's Wine and Cheese route, the attractive **Cava Bocanegra** (Carr. Est. 200 Tequisquiapan-Qro., Km 50, tel. 414/273-3369, www.cavab-ocanegra.com, 9:30am-4:30pm Mon.-Fri., 9:30am-5:30pm Sat.-Sun.) is a producer of artisanal and aged cheeses, which operates a pretty country store above its cheese-making facilities. Visitors can take a tour of the cellars to learn more about how Bocanegra makes their products, or you can just order a cheese-and-charcuterie tasting platter to share on the patio dining room. In addition to selling their own products, Cava Bocanegra carries local produce, like honey, wine, fruit preserves, and a wide range of craft brews to drink on-site or take away. On Sundays, they serve a special hamburger lunch, and the shop can get packed with day-trippers; any other time, the shop is quiet.

QUESOS VAI

On the highway to Tequisquiapan from the city of Querétaro, **Quesos VAI** (Carretera Querétaro-Tequisquiapan, Km 30, Municipio de Colón, tel. 442/190-7618, www.quesos-vai.com, 8am-6pm daily) is one of the most well-known cheese factories in the state of Querétaro. Though originally founded by a Spanish cheese-maker, VAI is a local Mexican-owned business today. All the cheese is produced from the milk of the hundreds of sheep and cows on VAI's Querétaro ranch, which is open to the public. Their roadside food shop sells VAI-produced products, including provolone- and manchego-style cheeses, as well as other artisan and local products, like homemade *cajeta*, jams, honey, and wines by La Redonda.

Tours (10am-5pm daily, US$4) of the cheese-making process and the ranch last an hour or so and include samples of assorted VAI cheeses. Fun for families (though a bit hokey for adults), the best part of the tour is visiting the ranch's live animals, including a large bovine particularly fond of visitors. If you are so inclined, you can buy a bottle of wine and a piece of cheese from VAI's small and nicely stocked shop, then sit amid the sheep and chickens while you eat.

cheese-maker Cava Bocanegra

SAN SEBASTIÁN BERNAL

The tiny town of San Sebastián Bernal (usually referred to as just Bernal) is a lovely colonial town. Founded in 1642, Bernal was recently inducted into Mexico's Pueblos Mágicos program, designed to recognize special or historic cities across the country. Bernal is indeed a magical place, with a small and charming city center boasting impressive views of the monolithic La Peña de Bernal, which towers over the town center. It can be a wonderful place to stop for lunch or to spend a quiet evening.

Sights

★ PEÑA DE BERNAL

The **Peña de Bernal** is one of the world's largest monoliths, rising above the semiarid plains of Querétaro state with natural majesty and power. On clear days, you can see the rock's pointed crown for miles. Many believe the *peña* (rock) has healing energy, and it is a popular pilgrimage site during the spring equinox. However, it is a stunning sight to behold at any time of year.

Measuring over 335 meters, La Peña de Bernal is one of the tallest and largest rocks in the world. According to the Querétaro tourist office, only the Rock of Gibraltar and Rio de Janeiro's Sugar Loaf are taller. On the weekends, the *peña* is illuminated by floodlights at its base, so you can enjoy its dramatic face under a canopy of stars.

For those who'd like to feel Bernal's healing energy for themselves, there is a trail leading to a shoulder of the monolith, which takes a couple of hours to hike. It is a somewhat vigorous ascent, so come prepared with sunscreen, sun-protective clothing, and water. Once at the top of the trail, you can sit on a sloping ledge of the *peña* and gaze over the valley below. The views are beautiful and sweeping. Experienced climbers are permitted to scale the tip of the monolith to its peak, though they must advise the municipal offices in the city center before setting up the climb.

If you'd like to climb the monolith in the company of a trained guide, contact professional **La Peña Tours** (Independencia 4, Bernal, Ezequiel Montes, tel. 441/296-7398 or cell tel. 442/101-4821, www.lapenia-tours.com). They can arrange for individual or group tours to the top of the rock with a trained and certified guide as well as rock climbing and rappelling tours. A climb to the top lasts about 6 hours and costs about US$55, though they can discount prices with a larger group.

PARROQUIA DE SAN SEBASTIÁN

Constructed 1700-1725, Bernal's pretty parish church, the **Parroquia de San Sebastián** (Plaza Principal s/n, generally 9am-7pm daily), stands right in the center of the town square. Although the church does not represent any dominant architectural style, it has a small neoclassical facade, set against its striking yellow walls and bold brick-red trim. The work of indigenous architects is visible in the bell tower.

EL CASTILLO

Of the many lovely buildings that surround Bernal's main square, **El Castillo** (The Castle, Plaza Principal s/n) is clearly the most unusual. This 17th-century structure was built in typical Spanish colonial style, with an arched arcade and painted facade. At the top of the tower, there is a German-made clock, added along with the bell tower in commemoration of the new century. The lovely red-and-white stucco finish makes El Castillo stand out. Today, it houses Bernal's municipal offices and is not open to the public.

CAPILLA DE LAS ÁNIMAS

At the foot of the monolith, the **Capilla de las Ánimas** is a small country chapel with yellow stucco walls and brick-red trim. According to local legend, a merchant took refuge from thieves in the spot where the chapel now stands. In appreciation, he began the construction of a church at the site. Built in the 18th century, the church boasts a small but lovely domed ceiling and the three original church bells, hanging over the entryway. The country setting makes this church particularly appealing.

Festivals and Events

The **spring equinox**, or March 21, is considered a very powerful day to visit the Peña de Bernal. The event is celebrated annually with pre-Hispanic rituals in town and massive groups of pilgrims heading to the top of the rock, most dressed in white. In the evening, the monolith is lit up and fireworks fill the sky. For those who'd like to experience the healing energy of Bernal, the equinox is an exciting time to visit. At the same time, the town of Bernal is incredibly crowded and bustling during the event, so book your hotel ahead of time or plan to stay in nearby Querétaro or Tequisquiapan.

At the beginning of May, the **Fiesta de la Santa Cruz** (Day of the Holy Cross) is another nice event in the town of Bernal. In commemoration, Bernal locals head to the top of the monolith, where they install a Christian cross, also recognized by indigenous cultures as an *árbol de la vida* (tree of life).

Shopping

Though it's right in the center of town, it's easy to walk past the quiet storefront of **Artesanías de la Concordia** (Hidalgo 6, no phone, 10am-8pm Sat.-Sun.), which specializes in locally made wool serapes and sweaters, lambskins, cotton shirts, and shawls. Few artisans in the region still produce handmade wool products, so it's nice to support their work—as well as the work of the dedicated shop owners, who have been in business here for decades. The wool serapes, which are made with undyed local wool, are particularly nice and very well-priced. You'll sometimes find the shop open during the weekdays, but inconsistently; on weekends, they're open till evening.

Pick up some outstanding *cajeta* and candied fruits, among other regional sweets, at beloved **Dulces Bernal** (Calle Hidalgo s/n, tel. 441/296-4148, www.dulcesbernal.com, 10am-7pm daily), one of the oldest and most famous candy-makers in Querétaro. You can fill a basket with goodies at the well-stocked shop in the town center, though children (or those with a sweet tooth) may enjoy visiting the shop's bigger location, just on the edge of downtown, which also includes the small but colorful **Museo de Dulces** (Juárez 2, tel. 441/296-4148, 10am-5pm daily, shop 10am-7pm daily, $2), or Candy Museum, which introduces the history and techniques behind traditional Mexican candies.

One of the best-known organic dairy farms in Mexico, Flor de Alfalfa's ranches and dairy-making facilities are in the state of Querétaro. Although you can find their products in supermarkets throughout the country, Flor de Alfalfa also operates several gourmet delis around the state. In Bernal, **Cremería Flor de Alfalfa** (Ignacio Zaragoza 11, tel. 441/296-4560, http://flordealfalfa.com, 10am-3pm Tues.-Sun.) sells the full line of aged cheeses, flavored yogurt, milk, and other products from their certified organic Jersey cows. Pick up a snack or something to take home here.

Food and Drink

Long-running restaurant **El Mezquite** (5 de Mayo s/n, tel. 441/296-4146, 9am-6:30pm Sat.-Sun., US$6) is one of the most popular restaurants in Bernal, and it is easy to see why. This open-air patio has the best view in town, overlooking the *peña*. Despite the million-dollar view, El Mezquite is a casual, inexpensive, and family-oriented restaurant, where big groups of weekenders convene for a leisurely afternoon meal. On the patio dining room, plastic tables are covered with colorful oilcloths and shaded by the large tree that is the restaurant's namesake. The menu is standard Mexican fare; food is tasty enough, and the view is unbeatable. To get to this convivial spot, look for a small colonial plaza on 5 de Mayo, just off the main square. The restaurant is in the patio behind the gift shops (there are signs at the entryway).

Right in the center of town, ultra-low-key **El Negrito Gorditas** (Hidalgo 1, no phone, 9am-6pm Tues.-Sun., US$2) is a popular spot on busy weekends in Bernal, when the patio seating is full of day-trippers filling up on chicken-stuffed quesadillas, blue-corn *gorditas* filled with *nopal* (cactus), and 32-ounce bottles of beer. On the weekends, they also grill massive cactus paddles stuffed with meat and sausage, a stick-to-your-ribs regional specialty called *pencas*. Though it doesn't have views of the monument, the weekend people-watching can be fun, too—and with *gorditas* at about a buck each, it's certainly one of the cheapest spots for lunch in town.

Just inside the Casa Tsaya Hotel, the surprisingly chic ★ **Arrayán** (Ignacio Zaragoza 6, tel. 441/296-4041, 1pm-9pm Mon.-Tues. and Thurs., 1pm-11pm Sat.-Sun., US$12) serves creative Mexican-inspired dishes, combining traditional ingredients with contemporary preparations. The menu includes appealing plates like shrimp in vanilla and turkey with hibiscus sauce, which are exotic yet tasty. An assortment of pastas and salads round out the menu, and there are a few options that lean more toward traditional than experimental, such as *arrachera* with beans and guacamole. A particular delight of dining here is the drink menu, which includes numerous Mexican-made small-batch beers, mezcal, tequila, and Mexican wines. The street-side dining room is clean and modern, with contemporary art on the walls. If you'd like a more traditional setting, the restaurant has a second dining room in the hotel's colonial courtyard.

Far away from the weekend bustle in downtown Bernal, the earthy, airy, light-filled dining room at **Kühi** (Zaragosa 9, tel. 441/296-4534, www.casatsayahotel.com, 9am-7pm Thurs.-Sat., 9am-6pm Sun., US$10) is a nice place to linger over a freshly made, beautifully plated meal. At this modern restaurant, many of the dishes combine contemporary culinary concepts with traditional Mexican flavors; for example, garbanzo tamales come dotted with peanut sauce and cilantro, or risotto is made with poblano peppers. A sister restaurant to wonderful Arrayán, Kuhi is located on the first floor of Casa Tsaya Hotel Boutique, the second property by the same hoteliers that run Casa Tsaya, just a few doors down.

A fun low-lit little bar right in the center of Bernal, **Folk** (Aldama 11, tel. 441/120-5651, 2pm-10pm Thurs.-Sun., US$6) has a fine selection of Mexican wines, many produced locally in the state of Querétaro, as well as mezcal and bottles of a very nice craft beer produced by some ultra-small-batch producers in Bernal. There's an array of shareable

Arrayán is Bernal's best restaurant, with creative takes on Mexican and regional food.

Kühi, located at Casa Tsaya Hotel Boutique

plates and pizza on the bar's appealing menu, though you can also just stop in for a drink and a chat with the friendly waitstaff, who are knowledgeable about the wines on offer. The bar's owner is often there, too, doling out advice on locally made libations.

Accommodations

Comfortable and well located, **Casa Tsaya Hotel Colonial** (Ignacio Zaragoza 6, tel. 441/296-4534, www.casatsaya.com, US$70-85) is a well-priced guesthouse right in the center of Bernal's downtown. Housed in a lovely colonial mansion with a terra-cotta facade, this hotel's 14 guest rooms are small and not particularly luxurious, though each boasts a television and private bath. Rooms surrounding the courtyard and restaurant may be a bit noisier during the weekends, so choose a room in the back promenade. From here, you can see the Peña de Bernal from the outdoor hallways. Just a few doors down, **Casa Tsaya Hotel Boutique** (Ignacio Zaragosa 9, tel. 441/296-4534, www.

casatsayahotel.com, US$80-90) is a newer property by the same owners, with a low-key rustic-chic feeling. Rooms surround the in-house restaurant Kuhi or the small grassy courtyard in back. Like the original Casa Tsaya, it's a simple good-value spot, with a perfect location, just steps away from Bernal's main plaza.

If you are planning a romantic getaway to the country or a family trip to La Peña de Bernal, ★ **Casa Mateo** (5 de Mayo s/n, esq. Colón, tel. 441/296-4472, US$100) is a well-designed boutique hotel in the very center of Bernal. Guest rooms are comfortable and tastefully furnished, equipped with ceramic floors, fireplaces, down comforters, and modern bathrooms. Though each room is slightly different from the next, decor is pleasingly minimalist throughout the hotel; family-style rooms have a loft bed for the kids. In the center of the hotel, there are nice views of the *peña* rising above a small swimming pool and lawn. Just a block from the main plaza, this hotel is right in the middle of town but feels secluded and private. Service is friendly and attentive.

Information and Services

Technically a part of the municipality of Ezequiel Montes, Bernal is a small town—even smaller than its neighbor Tequisquiapan. Although Bernal is well accustomed to tourism, there are few services here. The tourist office is actually located in the industrial city of Ezequiel Montes. To make things all the more complicated, many shops and restaurants are closed during the week (Bernal's tourism is principally weekenders). The upshot of visiting Bernal from Monday through Friday is that you will enjoy the tranquility of a sleepy country town.

There are no banks in Bernal; however, there is one ATM in the city's central plaza. If you need to visit a bank or change money, the closest banks are in downtown Ezequiel Montes. Right on the main highway passing through Ezequiel Montes, there is a branch of **Banamex** (Av. Constituyentes 114-A, tel. 441/277-1279, 9am-4pm Mon.-Fri.), with ATMs, currency exchange, and other services.

Getting There and Around

To get to Bernal from Querétaro by car, take Highway México-Querétaro and exit at the signs for Sierra Gorda. From there, take State Highway 100 for about 40 kilometers (25 miles) until you reach Bernal.

If you are coming from Tequisquiapan, follow the highway toward Cadereyta, passing through the industrial town of Ezequiel Montes. Continue on the highway past Cavas de Freixenet until you reach a fork in the road; signs indicate that Bernal is to the left, or east, along a small two-lane highway. You will be able to see the monolith as you approach the town.

Once you've made it to Bernal, park and explore the city on foot.

FRANCISCAN MISSIONS OF THE SIERRA GORDA

From the capital in Querétaro, it takes several hours of driving from the plains into the mountains, navigating hairpin turns and vertiginous precipices, past improbably cold pine forests and indescribably lovely panoramas, to reach the town of Jalpan de Serra in the heart of the Sierra Gorda. In these remote mountains, you will find breathtaking natural scenery, a smattering of rural towns, and five 18th-century Franciscan missions, which are impressive in both their artistry and their isolated locations.

The Sierra Gorda of Querétaro is the gateway to a geographical and cultural region called the Huasteca, so called because it was once the territory of the native Huastec people. Extending from the mountains of the Sierra Gorda to the Gulf Coast in Veracruz, it is a region known for its biodiversity, beauty, and unique music-and-dance style called *huapango*.

Visiting this area isn't as easy as other day trips around the state of Querétaro (in fact, you'll need more than a day if you plan to go),

but for those interested in experiencing a side of Mexico that is off the well-traveled tourist circuit, it is worth the extra effort to visit the mountain communities of the Sierra Gorda.

Planning Your Time

Plan to spend **at least one night** in the Sierra Gorda, as the drive into the mountains from the city of Querétaro is both long and challenging. **Jalpan de Serra** (about 200 kilometers from the city of Querétaro) makes a good base for this trip; all five of the Franciscan missions are within a drive of 30-40 minutes from it. Spending one night in Jalpan allows time to see the mission there, visit the regional museum, and travel to Landa or one of the other five mission towns before heading back down the mountain. With two nights, you'll have time to visit several missions as well as explore the gorgeous tropical wilderness of the region before heading back to the city.

While you can certainly get a feeling for the area in a day or two, there are enough cultural sights and natural attractions to warrant a longer trip to the Sierra Gorda, especially if you want to set aside time to swim in the rivers, hike in the mountains, and generally see more of the area's natural beauty. Several tour operators, like **Sierra Gorda Ecotours** (Av. La Presa s/n, Barrio El Panteón, Jalpan de Serra, tel. 441/296-0700, http://sierragordaecotours.com, office 8am-8pm Mon.-Sat., 9am-2pm Sun.), offer well-planned all-inclusive tours of the region, which can be an excellent option for those who want to see as much as possible, without worrying about how to get from here to there on tiny mountain highways.

Pinal de Amoles

En route to Jalpan from the city of Querétaro, the highway ascends until it reaches the town of **Pinal de Amoles,** nestled amid pine forests and often blanketed in chilly fog. This historic town was founded in 1606 as a mining settlement; its main parish, the Parroquia de San José, was built in 1770. However, the

On a Mission

Spain's territories in Mexico were firmly rooted by the 18th century, but the Sierra Gorda proved far more difficult to control. Here, the native Huastec, Pame, and Jonaz people were unwaveringly resistant to Spanish rule, their distant mountain territories hostile to missionaries and settlers. While Franciscan, Dominican, and Jesuit missionaries had played a crucial role in the conquest of Mexico, the first wave of missionaries to the Sierra Gorda eventually abandoned their posts.

Following a Spanish military battle against the Jonaz in the mid-18th century, Franciscan missionaries were sent to the Sierra again, this time led by Father Junípero Serra, who would later become famous for establishing the missions of California. Between 1750 and 1760, Serra oversaw the construction of five small but beautiful missions in the remote mountains, working with Pame artisans to create some of the most unique religious buildings in the country. Where his predecessors had failed, Serra and his colleagues succeeded in winning over native converts to Christianity by learning to speak the native languages of the region and operating the missions as schools of agriculture and industry, in addition to their evangelical work. Today, these missions are recognized as a unique aspect of Mexico's history, representing the final phase of evangelization in Mexico. Collectively, they have been included on the list of UNESCO World Heritage Sites since 1993.

area around Pinal de Amoles is known more for ecotourism than cultural attractions, principally drawing visitors who want to snap photos from its lookouts at the **Mirador Cuatro Palos** (Carretera Federal 120 San Juan del Río-Xilitla, Km 132.5), visit the Escanela River, or hike to waterfalls, such as the **Cascada El Chuveje** (Carretera Federal 120 San Juan del Río-Xilitla, Km 160).

Just outside Pinal, the unfinished mission at **Bucareli** is also a popular destination. Not a part of the Franciscan efforts, this church was actually established by a Diegan friar in 1776. It was never completed and has no ceiling. Though not ideal for the friar's purposes, it makes a lovely focal point for dramatic photos of the Sierra Gorda.

GETTING THERE

Take Highway 120 to get to Bucareli and Pinal de Amoles from Querétaro. Look for signs for Mision de Bucareli about five kilometers (or five minutes), before arriving in the town of Pinal de Amoles. Make a sharp right onto the dirt road and follow it south into the valley and to the mission. From Jalpan, look for signs for Bucareli about five minutes from the center of Pinal de Amoles, and turn left onto the dirt road.

★ Jalpan de Serra
SANTIAGO DE JALPAN

The elaborate rust-and-ocher facade of the mission of **Santiago de Jalpan** stands in golden contrast to the emerald hills that rise behind it. The hand-carved stone that adorns the church, impressive in its detail, is a wonderful mix of traditional Spanish technique and New World creativity. Here, as in all five of the Franciscan missions, the distinct style of native Pame artisans who helped build these chapels is visible in the many creative figures and natural symbolism. One of the many notable details is the carving, just above the doorway, of Christ's and St. Francis's intertwined hands.

Built between 1751 and 1758, Santiago de Jalpan is the largest of the five missions as well as the easiest to reach by highway. This spectacular church is located in the center of Jalpan de Serra, its broad stone esplanade opening directly onto Jalpan's main plaza. A tree-filled tropical paradise ever accompanied by the musical sound of birds, the plaza is the locus of activity in this rural town (where there isn't much activity at all) and a beautiful place to sit or stroll.

MUSEO HISTÓRICO DE LA SIERRA GORDA

Originally constructed in 1576, the **Museo Histórico de la Sierra Gorda** (Fray Junípero Serra 1, tel. 441/296-0165, 9am-3pm and 5pm-7pm Tues.-Sun., US$1) is in one of the oldest buildings in Jalpan de Serra. This small regional museum is dedicated to the people and culture of the Sierra Gorda. After a significant renovation in the spring of 2015, the museum reopened with a new collection of pre-Columbian artifacts and artisan pieces from the sierra. It's worth the modest admission price to learn a little more about the area.

FESTIVALS AND EVENTS

Every winter, the **Fiesta del Santo Niño de Jalpan** is one of the most important religious festivals in the Sierra Gorda, attracting thousands of pilgrims and worshippers who come to pay homage to the image of the *santo niño* (holy child) in the Mission Santiago de Jalpan. Many miracles have been attributed to this small figure, which has gained notoriety throughout the sierra. Pilgrimages start long before, but the fiesta really gets going in Jalpan on January 5, when tens of thousands of visitors arrive for mass in the town square; the fiestas conclude the following day with a massive procession around town.

FOOD AND ACCOMMODATIONS

In Jalpan, you can have a lovely, relaxing meal at the **Hotel Misión Jalpan** (Av. Fray Junípero Serra s/n, Jalpan de Serra, tel. 441/296-0445, www.hotelesmisiones.com, open for breakfast, lunch, and dinner, US$4-7). Popular with locals as well as tourists, this hotel restaurant can get quite full during breakfast on the weekends—or in the evening, if the Mexican soccer team is playing. The menu is filled with Mexican classics, as well as some regional specialties, and the setting is lovely, with tables surrounding a stone fountain in the hotel's serene, plant-filled courtyard. Order some guacamole, a plate of tasty enchiladas, and a couple of *cervezas* to enjoy a balmy afternoon in this rural town.

Just off the highway in Jalpan, **Carretas** (Jiménez s/n, Jalpan de Serra, tel. 441/296-0368, hours vary, US$5-8) is a big, casual restaurant that serves traditional Mexican breakfast, lunch, and dinner, with an emphasis on Mexican cuts of beef. It is also recommended

Santiago de Jalpan

for regional serrano specialties: you'll find the popular dried-and-salted beef called *cecina* on the menu as well as *acamayas,* a type of freshwater shrimp typical to the region.

Right across the street from the Franciscan mission in the very center of Jalpan, **Hotel Misión Jalpan** (Av. Fray Junípero Serra s/n, Jalpan de Serra, tel. 441/296-0445, www.hotelesmisiones.com, US$40-50) has two floors of spotless guest rooms with comfortable beds, air-conditioning, and big modern baths, all surrounding a central courtyard. The hotel's restaurant is perhaps the best place to eat in town (and they have room service). There is a small but appealing pool on the terrace, which can be a nice place to beat the heat of a summer afternoon in the tropics. The service is accessible and friendly, the location is ideal, and the price is low for the quality of the accommodations. The hotel does not have a parking lot.

Though certainly the most prominent, Hotel Misión Jalpan isn't the only place to stay in town. If you'd like to save a few pesos, **Hotel Maria del Carmen** (Independencia 8, Jalpan de Serra, tel. 441/296-0328, www.hotelmariadelcarmen.com, US$25) offers similar accommodations right on the main square. Rooms are very basic, with clean tile floors and private baths; some rooms open onto the central courtyard. There is a swimming pool out back, perhaps less attractive than the one at Hotel Misión but serviceable nonetheless.

GETTING THERE

From the city of Querétaro, take Highway 57 (México-Querétaro) south toward Mexico City, exiting before San Juan del Río for Highway 100 toward the Querétaro Airport. Follow the highway, which eventually becomes Highway 120, past Bernal, Pena Blanca, and Pinal de Amoles. It takes 3-4 hours to reach Jalpan from Querétaro.

Concá
SAN MIGUEL CONCÁ

Though only about 20 minutes by car from Jalpan, **San Miguel Concá**, the smallest of

the missions, feels the remotest, its unique arched facade rising starkly against a backdrop of green hills. The temple is dedicated to San Miguel Arcángel, who is depicted among the many carvings; however, the most interesting aspect of this church's elaborate ornamentation is the use of natural symbols—leaves, eagles, and rabbits—which had deep spiritual meaning for the indigenous people of this area. It was one of the last missions to be built, with construction starting in 1754.

GETTING THERE

To reach San Miguel Concá from Jalpan, take Highway 69 north toward Río Verde; look for the turnoff just before Arroyo Seco. If you have time on your drive, pull over in the small town of Las Adjuntas, where the clear waters of the Río Ayulta meet the Río Santa María. The drive should take about 30 minutes by car (about 35 kilometers, or 20 miles).

Landa de Matamoros and Tilaco
SANTA MARÍA DEL AGUA

On Highway 120 toward Xilitla are the missions of Santa María del Agua and San Francisco del Valle, located in the towns of Landa de Matamoros and Tilaco, respectively. **Santa María del Agua** was the last to be built; its deep-red facade distinguishes it from the other four churches. The mission sits directly on Landa's small main plaza.

SAN FRANCISCO DEL VALLE

In the tiny town of Tilaco, the construction of **San Francisco del Valle** actually began before the Franciscan missionaries arrived, though it wasn't completed until 1762. From the esplanade that stretches in front of the church, there is a breathtaking view of the green mountains surrounding the mission.

ACCOMMODATIONS

A truly unique place to experience the Sierra Gorda, **Casa Quelite** (Tilaco, Landa de Matamoros, tel. 441/596-0000, www.casaquelite.com, US$75) is a rustic, family-run guesthouse tucked within the tiny town of Tilaco. This quiet, beautiful spot is surrounded by banana plants, bougainvillea, and shady trees. It's owned by an American-Mexican couple who are deeply invested in the Sierra Gorda, culturally and ecologically. They rent two small casitas on their property, both with private bath, and guests are welcome to use the kitchen and patios during their stay. The price includes two full meals prepared with fresh, local ingredients.

GETTING THERE
To reach Landa de Matamoros and Tilaco from Jalpan, drive east on Highway 120. Santa María del Agua is located two blocks west of Highway 120, at the intersection of Miguel Hidalgo and Cinco de Mayo streets. The route isn't particularly well marked, so when you enter the itty-bitty community of Landa de Matamoros, look out for the blue signs on the highway indicating where to turn for the church.

To get to Tilaco from Jalpan or Querétaro, drive northeast on Highway 120 past Landa to the town of Lagunita. Turn east at the sign for Tilaco shortly after you enter town. Continue down that road for about 14 kilometers (8.5 miles). You will arrive in the center of Tilaco, where the mission is located. Plan about 30-40 minutes to reach Tilaco from Landa.

Tancoyol
NUESTRA SEÑORA DE LA LUZ DE TANCOYOL
Saints and angels cover the facade of **Nuestra Señora de la Luz de Tancoyol,** generally considered to be the most elaborate of the five Franciscan missions. While the interiors and altarpieces in these missions were stolen or destroyed long ago, there are still some beautiful details inside this church, particularly the ceiling of the main cupola. Located on the charming, sunbaked main plaza in the tiny town of Tancoyol, it's just 14 kilometers from Landa.

GETTING THERE
To get to Tancoyol from Jalpan or Querétaro, take Highway 120 east, passing the towns of Landa de Matamoros, Lagunita, and Aguacate. Look for a road sign indicating the turnoff to Tancoyol (there's a Pemex station at the junction). Turn left onto the highway (you are technically traveling on State Highway 190, though you won't see signs indicating this), and head north about 20 kilometers until you reach the mission and surrounding community of Tancoyol right on the highway.

Information and Services
The appeal of visiting the Sierra Gorda is its remoteness, and that remoteness translates into very few services for visitors. If you have any logistical questions about your trip, stop by the **state tourist office** (Pasteur 4 Nte., Santiago de Querétaro, tel. 442/238-5067, toll-free Mex. tel. 888/811-6130, www.queretaro.travel, 9am-8pm daily) in the city of Querétaro before taking off.

The Sierra Gorda isn't totally cut off from the modern world; you'll find banks, gas stations, and other necessities are available, if more limited. There is a **BBVA Bancomer** (Independencia 18, 8:30am-4pm Mon.-Fri.) branch with a 24-hour ATM located on the main square in Jalpan de Serra.

Getting There and Around
First-class bus company **Primera Plus** (toll-free Mex. tel. 800/375-7587, www.primeraplus.com.mx) offers three daily departures from Querétaro to Jalpan (and back again) at a cost of about US$17. On its way to Jalpan, the bus stops in Pinal de Amoles (tickets to Pinal only are US$14). The easiest and most efficient way to get around the Sierra Gorda is either by car or with a private tour operator that can provide transportation. Driving here is challenging, requiring hours on a winding two-lane highway that doesn't allow for high speeds or passing. Fortunately, the state government maintains the roads in very good condition.

Background

The Landscape

GEOGRAPHY

San Miguel de Allende, Guanajuato, and Querétaro are located in a region known as the Bajío, a geographically and culturally linked valley within the Mexican Altiplano, a massive plateau that stretches from the U.S. border to the Trans-Mexican Volcanic Belt near Mexico City. The Bajío region covers the states of Querétaro and Guanajuato as well as segments of southern Jalisco and eastern Michoacán. León and Querétaro are the two largest and most important cities in the Bajío, though the region also includes the well-known colonial towns of Guanajuato, San Miguel de Allende, and Dolores Hidalgo. Though situated at about 1,800 meters (6,000 feet) above sea level, the term *bajío* means something similar to "lowlands." While not technically "low," the Bajío lies below the impressively tall mountains of the Cordillera de Guanajuato and the Sierra Gorda, which run past the plains to the north and east, respectively.

There are several important water sources within the Bajío. The Río Laja basin covers about half the state of Guanajuato and is the principal water source near San Miguel de Allende. The Río Laja is a tributary of the larger Río Lerma. One of the country's longest and most important watersheds, the Lerma passes along the border between the states of Querétaro and Michoacán and then through the state of Guanajuato on its course northward. It empties into Lake Chapala in Jalisco.

CLIMATE

The Bajío's climate is temperate, dry, and semiarid, receiving modest annual rainfall. With very little humidity in the air, the weather can fluctuate significantly over the course of a single day. Throughout the year, evening temperatures are significantly lower than daytime temperatures; travelers should pack accordingly.

It rarely rains in the Bajío during the long dry season, which runs from October to mid-June. During summer's erratic wet season, rain typically falls during brief but furious thunderstorms in the afternoons or early evening. Thunderstorms rarely last more than an hour or two; however, their fierce downpours can cause destruction and flooding. By the end of the rainy season, the dry landscape of the Bajío is totally transformed. September and October can be particularly pleasant months to visit, when the desert blooms with wildflowers. In total, the Bajío receives somewhere around 50-64 centimeters (20-25 inches) of rain each year.

Although the Bajío enjoys a temperate climate year-round, there are distinct seasons. December and January are the coolest months, with average daytime temperatures hovering around 20°C (70°F) and nighttime temperatures dropping to around 0°C (32°F). Evening frosts are not uncommon, with temperatures sinking below freezing on the coldest nights. Though surprisingly chilly, the winter season is very short. Spring begins as early as the end of February, and weather is reliably warm by March. Throughout March and April, the climate is warm and dry, averaging 24-30°C (75-85°F), though the evenings continue to be chilly.

May is typically the warmest month in the Bajío, with temperatures reaching 30-35°C (85-95°F). Few tourists visit the area in May, the one month of the year when the climate is uncomfortably hot. In June, the rains begin, tempering the heat. During the rainy months,

---

Previous: a statue commemorating native people in Querétaro; view of the center of San Miguel de Allende.

the climate tends to be warmest in the mornings, cooling off after the afternoon showers. By September and October, the rains have begun to subside, but the climate remains pleasant, hovering around 25°C (77°F).

The climate is similar throughout the Bajío, though there are some regional differences. Located in a mountainous valley, the city of Guanajuato tends to be a few degrees cooler than San Miguel de Allende, whereas Querétaro may be a few degrees warmer. In the town of Santa Rosa de Lima, in the mountains outside Guanajuato, the climate is rather chilly all year long.

ENVIRONMENTAL ISSUES

Although anthropologists have discovered the remains of several pre-Columbian cities in the Bajío region, it was sparsely populated when Spanish settlers arrived in the 15th century. Thereafter, extensive ranching and agriculture in the region changed the quality of the land, which was once far more lush and verdant than it is today. Throughout the Bajío, human settlements and farming have led to massive deforestation, as well as an overall degradation of natural plant and animal ecosystems. Due to the resulting decrease in plant cover, the floodplains of the Río Lerma have suffered from severe erosion, with dramatic flooding causing major problems during the short but intense rainy season. Deforestation has also made it more difficult for the soil to absorb rainwater, depleting the underground water table.

Human activities have polluted freshwater sources in most of Mexico, including the Bajío region. The Río Laja and especially the Río Lerma have been polluted by untreated sewage from surrounding towns and cities. The heavy agricultural, ranching, leather, paper, and petrochemical industries around the Bajío have further added to the contamination of drinking water sources. Currently, there are few water recycling or treatment programs in the region.

Water has become a particular concern for rural populations, especially around San Miguel de Allende. Here, semiarid land supports a relatively large population with a very modest annual rainfall. Rapid urban growth around the city of San Miguel has created a new necessity for sustainable urban planning and resource allocation. However, there are few programs in place to ensure that water will continue to be available for the growing populace.

Plants and Animals

Mexico is one of the world's most biodiverse countries, encompassing a wide range of extremely distinct ecosystems, from arid desert to tropical wetland. Located in the center of Mexico, the Bajío region is covered by several high-altitude semiarid ecosystems, including xeric shrubland, coniferous forest, and dry forests. Today, much of the Bajío's original flora and fauna has been affected by human development and agriculture. At the same time, ecological reserves, parks, and botanical gardens continue to protect large swaths of the region's native ecosystems and environments.

TREES AND SHRUBS

Many beautiful trees grow naturally around the Bajío, in addition to several decorative species, which were introduced to the area and are common in cities. In the region's scrubland, the hardy deciduous mesquite tree continues to flourish despite widespread deforestation for agriculture. Mesquite rarely grows taller than 8-9 meters and can be identified by its dark bark, fringe of narrow green leaves, and thorny branches. This tree is native to Mexico, and its name comes from the Nahuatl word *mizquitl*. Mesquite is particularly well known for its fragrant, hard, and slow-burning wood, which is used for charcoal grilling. Its yellow flowers are frequently used in honey production.

Huizaches (sweet acacias) are another hardy and drought-resistant tree native to central Mexico. Growing naturally around San Miguel de Allende and the Bajío, they have fluffy yellow flowers and slender green leaves and look similar to the mesquite. Both *huizaches* and mesquites grow in lower-lying scrubland, with grass and underbrush rising beneath them.

Throughout the Bajío, the sprawling branches of the jacaranda tree make pleasant shade throughout the year. In the spring, jacarandas become a particularly stunning aspect of the landscape during their annual bloom in March, when they explode into a canopy of purple blossoms. Though not native to Mexico (they are originally from Brazil), these tropical plants thrive in the Bajío's natural environment. Within the cities of San Miguel de Allende and Guanajuato, it is also common to see guava, orange, pomegranate, lime, and other fruit trees, which flourish in the sunny climate.

San Miguel de Allende would not be the same without its brightly hued vines of bougainvillea spilling into the alleyways and brimming over gardens. Although not indigenous to Mexico, bougainvillea flourishes here. In some cases, their woody trunks can be as large as trees; their colored leaves come in a variety of hues, from magenta to orange to white. Another popular decorative plant, poinsettia, is native to Mexico. When not trimmed for a Christmas flowerpot, poinsettia will often grow rather large. The red "flower" of a poinsettia is not a flower at all; in fact, the red petals are actually the plant's upper leaves, which have a hue distinct from the lower, green leaves.

CACTI AND SUCCULENTS

A famous native of the New World, the phenomenal, water-saving cactus proliferates blithely in the low-rainfall region of the Bajío.

A wide variety of cacti are cultivated in the semi-arid Bajío region.

Consumed as food, distilled for drink, candied for desserts, and artfully planted for low-water landscaping, cacti and succulents play myriad roles in the region.

The large *nopal* (prickly pear or paddle cactus) is perhaps the most common and recognizable cactus in the region. From a central stalk, a prickly pear grows flat oblong paddles, covered in spines. Its fruit, called *tuna* in Mexico, ripens in the late summer and is very juicy, sweet, and delicious. In addition, the prickly pear paddle is an easy-to-cultivate, flavorful, and highly nutritious food source. They are sold throughout markets in the Bajío, served in stews, or fried up and stuffed into quesadillas.

Also abundant in the region, the maguey has played a central role in traditional Mexican life for centuries. This fleshy cactus is the source of mezcal, tequila, and pulque, three iconic beverages in Mexican culture, and they were used for myriad purposes by native cultures, such as papermaking. While all maguey have juicy leaves growing in rosettes around their central stalk, there is a wide variety within the genus. All maguey bloom just once and at the end of their life cycle, sprouting a giant stalk and flowers, which can reach up to nine meters.

Cacti are also popular for gardens and landscaping. Often used as a form of natural fencing, the beautiful columnar organ cactus grows naturally in the region, and it can be found as far north as the United States.

BIRDS

Bird-watching in the Bajío can be interesting for both the novice and expert, as there are huge populations of migrant and resident birds throughout the region. The Laja River Valley is one of the first major wetlands south of the U.S. border. Therefore, it is an important route for migrating birds as well as home to a surprisingly abundant supply of shorebirds and waterfowl. You may be surprised to learn that Mexican ducks, gulls, and grebes can be spotted around San Miguel de Allende. In fact, there is a large and rather noisy flock of egrets living inside the city itself, which nest at Parque Juárez and in the trees around El Chorro.

Throughout the Bajío, casual observers will notice hummingbirds, wrens, doves, woodpeckers, warblers, towhees, and sparrows. Even those who don't routinely look for birds will undoubtedly spot the gorgeous vermillion flycatcher, a small bird with a black back and a brilliant red chest. You can join an ecological or bird-watching tour in the countryside or around the Presa Allende (the municipal reservoir) to seek out more unusual regional species, like the roadrunner.

The Bajío is also an important habitat for birds of prey, notably American kestrels, red-tailed hawks, white-tailed kites, crested caracaras, and turkey vultures. In the evenings, it is not uncommon to see large white barn owls soaring over the churches in San Miguel de Allende.

MAMMALS

You are unlikely to spot any large mammals near an urban center, though field mice, squirrels, and other rodents are abundant. In the evenings, it is not uncommon to see jackrabbits or cottontails running through the grasslands outside of the cities. Other nocturnal critters will occasionally wander into the city center, including opossums, skunks, and the elegant ring-tailed cat. Although you are unlikely to catch a glimpse of them, the Bajío is also home to coyotes, gray foxes, and even bobcats.

INSECTS AND ARACHNIDS

Mosquitoes are common throughout the Bajío during the summer and fall. Though they can be a nuisance, most mosquito-borne illnesses have not been reported in the Bajío for many years. In addition, the Bajío makes a cozy home for scorpions, spiders, cockroaches, grasshoppers, praying mantises, crickets, and beetles. While scorpions and spiders are the most universally feared, they are usually reclusive and avoid human contact.

In addition to pests, the Bajío is a good place to spot colorful dragonflies, damselflies, and dozens of butterfly species. Often, in the early spring or late fall, you can spot monarch butterflies traveling over the Bajío on their way to their winter nesting grounds in the state of Michoacán.

Birds of the Bajío

- **Belted Kingfisher:** These compact waterbirds have a bluish-black back, a thick beak, and a large crested head on a stocky body. This bird is best known for its impressive diving abilities, splashing headfirst into the water from great heights and emerging with a fish in its beak.

- **Broad-Billed Hummingbird:** This medium-size, nectar-loving hummingbird is a dazzling emerald green, and it often nests in the trees and rooftop gardens around San Miguel de Allende. These wee creatures often consume more than their body weight in a day.

- **Cactus Wren:** A speckled brown-and-white bird with a distinctive white eye-stripe, the lovely cactus wren forages for food in the desert chaparral and is often at home among the spiny branches of the mesquite tree. As its name implies, this large wren may make its nest in the hole of a cactus.

- **Crested Caracara:** These large and striking raptors are found in central Mexico, though a few can be spotted in the southernmost regions of the United States. Sometimes called a Mexican eagle, this impressive bird has a black back, white belly, and a wingspan over one meter.

- **Golden-Fronted Woodpecker:** One of several woodpeckers tapping around the Bajío, the golden-fronted woodpecker has a golden stripe along the back of its neck. In addition to insects, these birds love to eat the fruit of the prickly pear cactus.

- **Great-Tailed Grackle:** The male members of this grackle species can be distinguished by their long tails and shiny jet-black feathers. Their loud squawks can be heard in cities, where many great-tailed grackles live, and they enjoy a wide range of foods, from insects to berries.

- **Inca Dove:** Despite its name, this long-tailed, pigeon-like dove does not live anywhere near Peru. Instead, you might see these light brown or grayish doves flitting around the Bajío.

- **Peregrine Falcon:** One of the world's fastest predators, the compact and beautiful peregrine falcon has gray feathers and a speckled white or rust-colored underbelly. These falcons like to feast on other birds, rather than rodents or insects, and they catch their unlucky prey mid-flight.

- **Roadrunner:** If you are both observant and lucky, you may catch a glimpse of the wonderful roadrunner in the Bajío countryside. A member of the cuckoo family, this large speckled bird has a feathery crest and strong legs. As in the cartoon, they are incredibly fast runners, capable of catching a snake on the ground. They thrive in semiarid ecosystems, which are filled with insects and reptiles—the roadrunner's favorite fare.

- **Snowy Egret:** Few expect to find the elegant, long-legged egret—a classic waterbird—in the Mexican high desert. However, the snowy egret has found a happy nesting spot in the trees around Parque Juárez in San Miguel de Allende as well as along the shores of the city's reservoir.

- **Vermillion Flycatcher:** The small but brilliant vermillion flycatcher makes its home in the southwestern United States and central Mexico. Its plump body with red chest is a welcome sight among the green leaves of a mesquite tree, where it feasts on insects.

- **White-Throated Swift:** Swift as its name implies, this high-speed bird has a black back and wings, though this species can be distinguished from other regional swifts by its white throat feathers. One of the fastest birds, it can travel at up to 320 kilometers per hour.

History

EARLY HISTORY

Anthropologists believe that the first humans arrived in the Americas about 30,000 years ago, crossing a narrow land bridge over the Bering Strait from Asia. In the Bajío region, little is known about the first human inhabitants; however, archaeologists have discovered marble weapons and tools that date back to 20,000 BC in the state of Guanajuato.

Though they lived on the land for millennia, the original migrants to North America eventually died out and were supplanted by a new wave of immigrants at the beginning of the Stone Age. These people, most likely of Asian descent, settled the entire continent, reaching all the way into the Andes Mountains of South America. As the planet began to warm, the oceans rose, and the land bridge between Asia and the Americas disappeared. Thereafter, the Americas were physically isolated from Asia and Europe.

MESOAMERICAN CIVILIZATIONS

Between 8000 and 2000 BC, sedentary human settlements began to develop in southern Mexico, Belize, Guatemala, Honduras, El Salvador, and Nicaragua. This swath of culturally linked territory is generally called Mesoamerica. Like all humans during the Stone Age, early Americans were hunter-gatherers. While the first agricultural settlements in Eurasia date back to 6200 BC, studies suggest that farming began around 2500 BC in the western hemisphere. With farming came civilizations of increasing complexity. By the time the Spanish arrived in the New World, Mesoamerica was home to some of the largest, most sophisticated, and most populous civilizations in the world.

The first great Mesoamerican culture, the Olmecs appeared in the lowlands of the modern-day states of Veracruz and Tabasco around 1500 BC. Little is known about the Olmec culture, though they left behind both the ruins of their urban centers and their signature hand-carved colossal stone heads, many of which had been ritually buried. The Olmecs began to decline after 400 BC, but their culture and city planning laid the groundwork for many of the Mexican and Mesoamerican cultures to come.

Centuries later, another largely unknown culture built the city of Teotihuacán in the Valley of Mexico, during what anthropologists and historians call the Early Classic period, around 200 BC. With an estimated population reaching 150,000 (and possibly more) at its peak, Teotihuacán's influence reached throughout Mesoamerica. It was overtaken and destroyed around AD 800, though its lofty pyramids (two of the tallest in the world) remain standing today.

Until recently, anthropologists believed that the complex sedentary civilizations of Mesoamerica did not extend farther north than Tula, in the modern-day state of Hidalgo. We now know that there are ruins of pre-Columbian civilizations scattered throughout the states of Guanajuato and Querétaro, though to date the majority have not been studied or opened to tourism. Just seven kilometers outside the city of Querétaro, the archaeological sites of El Cerrito were inhabited in two phases, in AD 400-600 and again during AD 650-1050, after which their populations dispersed. La Cañada de la Virgen, a small but interesting site near San Miguel de Allende, is believed to have been built somewhere around AD 530. Both those cities, like many others in the region, had been abandoned by the time the Spanish arrived in the Bajío. By then, the region was dominated by nomadic tribes of hunter-gatherers, collectively referred to as the Chichimecas by the Spanish.

As small city-states were being built in northern Mesoamerica, the first Maya civilizations began to flourish around the Yucatán Peninsula, Guatemala, and Belize, ushering in the Classic Period in Mesoamerican history. The Maya were great artists, astronomers, and architects who built massive temple-pyramids at the center of their cities. On the eve of the conquest, the Maya were still a populous people in southern Mexico, as they are today, though their cities had been mysteriously abandoned in the 8th and 9th centuries AD. To the west, the Zapotec civilization began to flourish in the modern-day state of Oaxaca. The great city-state of Monte Albán was founded in 400 BC but reached preeminence during the Classic Period, eventually declining somewhere around AD 500-700. Like their contemporaries to the east, the Zapotecs were accomplished architects, artists, and scientists. They employed a writing system to record their people's history, which new evidence suggests may have been the first writing system in Mesoamerica.

Power was consolidated again in central Mexico when the massive Toltec empire rose to prominence in AD 800-1000. Ruling from their massive city-state of Tula, in what is today the state of Hidalgo, the Toltecs would eventually disperse about a century before Nahuatl-speaking nomads arrived in the Valley of Mexico, founded a settlement on an island in Lake Texcoco, and eventually came to rule Mesoamerica from the tri-city alliance of Tenochtitlan, Tlacopan, and Texcoco. When the Spanish arrived in the Americas in the 15th century, Tenochtitlan's emperor, Moctezuma, presided over a vast empire that stretched from the Atlantic to the Pacific.

THE CONQUEST

During the 15th century, Nahuatl-speaking people called the Mexica dominated Mesoamerica from the tri-city alliance of Tenochtitlan, Tlacopan, and Texcoco, in what is today Mexico City and the state of Mexico. This alliance was ruled by Moctezuma from Tenochtitlan, a massive metropolis of grand pyramids and large public squares, connected by waterways and teeming with markets and activity. The Mexica were accomplished artists and thinkers, with advanced city planning and agricultural capabilities, a calendar system, and complex religious beliefs. They were also bellicose warriors, hated and feared by the other civilizations in Mesoamerica. During the 15th century, Tenochtitlan was one of the largest cities in the world—more populous than any city in Spain.

Christopher Columbus landed in the Americas in 1492, and Spanish colonization of the Caribbean began swiftly thereafter. In 1519, Hernán Cortés set sail for Mexico from the Spanish colony in Cuba. Having come with the intention to secure the land for Spain (and against the express command of the Cuban governor, to whom he was a subordinate), Cortés and his soldiers initially made peaceful contact with the rulers of Tenochtitlan and were welcomed into the city by Moctezuma. Tensions brewed, and after a poorly executed Spanish attack on Mexica nobles, made in Cortés's absence, the Spanish attempted to escape under the cover of darkness and in possession of as much stolen gold and jewelry as they could carry. The Spanish lost hundreds of soldiers to angry Mexica attackers while trying to flee the city in a massacre remembered as the Noche Triste (Night of Sorrows).

The Spanish regrouped their forces and returned to launch an offensive on the city. Though the fight between the Spanish and Mexica was long and brutal, many tribes near Tenochtitlan assisted the Spanish forces in battling the Mexica, which had terrorized their villages for centuries. The Spanish were further assisted by the smallpox virus, which they had unwittingly introduced to the Americas. Once infected with smallpox, thousands of native people fell sick and died, greatly weakening the Mexica's power. Cuitlahuac, the emperor who replaced Moctezuma after his death in battle, was among the many who died of

La Gran Chichimeca

When the Spanish arrived in the Americas, power was concentrated in the regions around modern-day Mexico City, where the Nahuatl-speaking Mexica people dominated Mesoamerica from their island city of Tenochtitlan. To the north, the land was more sparsely populated, principally dominated by nomadic tribes that were not under the control of the massive Mexica empire. As missionaries and ranchers began to settle the Bajío, they named Mexico's great central plateau La Gran Chichimeca. The name "Chichimeca" does not refer to any tribe in particular; it is a general term that the Nahuatl-speaking people of central Mexico used to refer to the nomadic tribes of the north.

Today, there is little record of the tribes that dominated Northern Mexico, nor is there a record of the languages and customs that distinguished one tribe from another. Even the number of people living in Northern Mexico then cannot be accurately determined. Based on different evidence, historians have estimated that there were between 150,000 and 625,000 indigenous people in La Gran Chichimeca, covering about 450,000 square kilometers of territory. Some of these tribes practiced modest agriculture, but most were nomadic hunter-gatherers.

Though little is known about the Chichimeca, one thing we do know is that the Spanish settlers, like the Mexica, were frightened of them. Wild and bellicose, rival tribes of the Chichimeca were often at war with each other. What's more, their battle tactics were psychologically terrifying; warriors would strip down and cover themselves in full body paint, screaming as they ran in for attack. When victorious, they often tortured prisoners of war. The Spanish regarded the Chichimeca as savages, accusing them of cruelty and cannibalism in the few texts they wrote about the people. Despite their fear, Spanish pursuit of silver and gold pushed them deep into Chichimeca territory. Hoping to settle the region, the Spanish royalty doled out many land grants during the 1540s, sending migrants and farmers to the Bajío and beyond. In addition to gold seekers, Franciscan friars were among the first to make inroads into this vast territory, often setting up schools and churches in remote Chichimeca outposts.

For the indigenous people of La Gran Chichimeca, the introduction of mining to the northern territories was a huge threat to their way of life. When Spanish ranchers arrived, the new settlers and their animals encroached on Chichimeca land. In the early years of the silver trade, wagoners on the Camino Real let their horses and donkeys graze on Indian cornfields. On top of that, cattle ranches changed the quality of land and its soil (in Zacatecas, large grasslands were eventually rendered semiarid due to extensive livestock grazing). In turn, Chichimecas began to raid the Spanish settlements, stealing cattle, robbing stores, and attacking donkey trains headed for Mexico City along the silver route.

In the 1550s, the tribes of La Gran Chichimeca began to launch more serious attacks on the Spanish settlers, who retaliated in kind. This period of violent clashes is often called the Chichimeca War. The silver barons largely financed this war against the native people; surprisingly, they had more expendable funds than the Spanish crown. Many Chichimeca prisoners of war were enslaved after their capture. Those who lived peacefully on the land were also enslaved to work in the mines or on ranches.

It wasn't until the beginning of the 1600s that the Spanish settlers were able to dominate the tribes along the silver route. Most were killed or displaced, and those who survived began to assimilate into mestizo culture, replacing their homes in caves for straw houses in Spanish settlements. Some Chichimeca pueblos were established, but even these were eventually reduced and finally disappeared. The only Chichimeca tribe that survived was the Pames of San Luis Potosí, though Zacatecos also survived in small settlements until the 17th century and worked in Spanish mines and family homes as servants and slaves.

the virus. After numerous attempts to take the capital city, Hernán Cortés and his cavalry successfully overthrew the people of Tenochtitlan in 1521.

THE COLONIAL ERA

Shortly after Cortés's final victory over the Mexica, Spanish settlement of Mexico began. Missionaries and settlers began to arrive in the New World, seeking Catholic converts and worldly fortune. The first Spanish viceroy of Mexico, Don Antonio de Mendoza, took his post in 1535. For the next 300 years, the Spanish crown would control politics, religion, and trade in the colonies.

To encourage settlement, the Spanish crown doled out land grants to Spanish settlers, authorizing them to begin farming and mining operations in the north. The Franciscans were among the first groups to settle the states of Michoacán, Querétaro, and Guanajuato, where they opened rural schools and hospitals, hoping to attract native people. In 1543, Fray Juan de San Miguel founded San Miguel de los Chichimecas on the banks of the Río Laja.

Having heard news of the conquest, the native tribes in the Bajío region were not welcoming to the Spanish settlers. The Chichimeca repeatedly attacked Spanish ranches and raided their donkey trains. San Miguel de Allende and other settlements were temporarily abandoned during a period called the Chichimeca War, a protracted series of attacks against the Spanish, which ran roughly 1550-1590. Despite hostility from the native people and harsh desert conditions, the thirst for gold and silver created an incredible incentive for Spanish settlers to expand their interests in the northern region. Many Spanish landowners helped to fund the war against the native people, in the absence of sufficient support from the crown.

Despite hardship, Spanish efforts quickly paid off. In 1546, a Spanish convoy found a large silver vein in Zacatecas. Shortly thereafter, silver was discovered in both Guanajuato and San Luis Potosí. The mining settlements required enormous resources and, in turn, generated impressive wealth. Throughout central and northern Mexico, mine owners commissioned churches and built lavish mansions, making the "silver cities" some of New Spain's most beautiful settlements. A long highway connected the northern mines to the capital in Mexico City, known as the Camino Real de Tierra Adentro (Royal Inland Route). Both San Miguel de Allende and Querétaro were important protective towns along this route, gaining incredible wealth through auxiliary industries and agriculture. Like the mining towns, they were lavishly constructed in the baroque style of the 17th and 18th centuries.

Over the course of the next century, the Chichimeca were subdued by the Spanish, and the Bajío region became a prominent, wealthy, and heavily populated part of New Spain. Although the Bajío was originally divided into large haciendas, or rural estates, it eventually became more developed as the silver trade flourished. By the 18th century, immigrants from across Mexico had come to work in the mines and industries, and the Bajío became one of the most densely populated regions in the world.

Throughout Mexico, the colonial era was a time of great inequity, and the Bajío was no exception. With the incredible wealth gleaned from the silver trade and related industries, ruling families lived in lavish mansions, traveled in horse-drawn carriages, and ate food imported from Spain. At the same time, disenfranchised indigenous laborers often worked for impossibly low wages (or no wages at all) and lived in inhumane conditions.

Divided by ethnicity and heritage, colonial society was highly stratified. In the Spanish colonies, full-blooded Spaniards born in Spain were called *peninsulares* (for the Spanish peninsula where they were born) or *gachupines,* and they retained the highest social status. *Peninsulares* were also appointed to all of the most important political posts. Mexican-born people of Spanish heritage were referred to as criollo and, despite their common heritage, had a lower social and political standing. Mestizo people of mixed ethnic heritage held a far lower place in society, only better than the abysmal position of indigenous people and African slaves.

WAR OF INDEPENDENCE

Among the criollo population, there was already quite a bit of resentment against the peninsular-born Spanish when the Bourbon kings took control of Spain in the 18th century. A self-proclaimed "enlightened despot," King Charles III made major changes to the oversight of Spanish territories in the New World. He quickly established royal monopolies on many important industries, like tobacco, ice, stamped paper, mercury (a key element for silver extraction), and gunpowder. He also declared a Spanish monopoly on profits from cockfights and outlawed church loans, a major source of credit within Mexican communities. For many—especially those in the pious Bajío region—the most outrageous blow was King Charles's expulsion of the Jesuits from Mexico in 1767.

In the Bajío, rich criollo landowners began to hatch a plan against the Spanish governors of Mexico. Independent thinkers like Juan Aldama and Ignacio Allende from San Miguel began to hold secret meetings with other conspirators, including Miguel Domínguez, the Mexican-born governor of Querétaro. Pastor Miguel Hidalgo from the small town of Dolores was among the conspirators' most important allies, a beloved priest with great influence among the native and mestizo people. When Napoleon invaded Spain in 1807, the conspirators decided to exploit the Spanish weakness and plan their attack against the crown.

Originally, Aldama and Allende were selected to oversee the independence army; however, there was a change of plans when Spanish loyalists in Querétaro uncovered their plot. Alerted to the conspiracy, royalists locked conspirator (and wife of the governor) Josefa Ortiz de Domínguez into a government mansion; however, she managed to get word to Allende and Hidalgo before the Spanish forces could arrest them. With no time left, Hidalgo immediately launched the insurgency.

On September 16, 1810, Miguel Hidalgo released the prisoners from the Dolores jail and then ascended the stairs before the city's parish church. There, he gave an impassioned call to war, rousing the crowd with his famous words, *"¡Viva Mexico!"* (This is known today as *el grito*.) With a ragtag army and small cavalry, Hidalgo rode from Dolores to the settlement at Atotonilco, where he gave another call to arms. In Atotonilco, Hidalgo seized a banner from the Catholic sanctuary that bore the image of the Virgen de Guadalupe. The banner would become the official flag for the Mexican army and a symbol of independent Mexico.

Hidalgo's army met with easy success in San Miguel de Allende and Celaya but sustained major casualties in taking the city of Guanajuato. Thereafter, a major loss at the Battle of the Bridge of Calderón threw the army into chaos, precipitating 11 years of chaotic armed conflict. The following year, Hidalgo, Allende, and Aldama were ambushed and executed by royalist forces.

After these deaths, José María Morelos took over as head of the army. He in turn was captured and executed. The battles continued haphazardly across the country for almost a decade until the government of Ferdinand VII was overthrown in Spain. As a result of the change in Spanish governance, Colonel Agustín de Iturbide, a fierce royalist, switched sides to join the Mexican army. With Iturbide at the helm, Mexico achieved independence in 1821 with the signing of the Treaty of Córdoba in Córdoba, Veracruz.

THE NEW NATION AND THE MEXICAN-AMERICAN WAR

The end of armed conflict ushered in a century of political unrest and instability in

Independent Spirits

Many of the most famous figures in the history of Mexico are from the cities of San Miguel de Allende, Dolores Hidalgo, and Querétaro. Today, you will see the names of these heroes of the independence movement on statues, on street corners, and in public plazas throughout the region.

- **Miguel Hidalgo y Costilla:** The great leader of the independence movement, Miguel Hidalgo was born in Dolores, Guanajuato; the city was later renamed Dolores Hidalgo in his honor. Hidalgo was a parish priest and an incredibly popular figure with the local population. As the general of the Mexican army, he officially gave the call for the revolution to begin with his famous cry, "*¡Viva Mexico!*" from the steps of the cathedral in Dolores.

- **Ignacio Allende:** A wealthy landowner from one of San Miguel's most prominent families, Ignacio Allende was one of the chief conspirators against the Spanish crown. A high-ranking official in the Spanish military, he hosted secret meetings at his home on San Miguel's central plaza, the *jardín*. During the war, Allende fought alongside General Hidalgo.

- **Josefa Ortiz de Domínguez:** The wife of Querétaro's mayor, Josefa Ortiz de Domínguez was one of the few women to actively participate in the conspiracy against the Spanish crown. When the conspirators' plot was discovered by Spanish royalists, Ortiz de Domínguez was imprisoned. However, she was able to send warning to Allende and Hidalgo, sparing them arrest and thereby saving the independence movement. She is celebrated throughout Mexico.

- **Juan Aldama:** When the news of the conspiracy's discovery reached San Miguel de Allende, Juan Aldama rushed to Dolores, where he informed independence leaders Ignacio Allende and Miguel Hidalgo that the plot had been uncovered. He fought in the war with Allende and Hidalgo, and today his name graces one of the prettiest streets in San Miguel, **Calle Aldama.**

- **Juan José de los Reyes Martínez:** Popularly known as El Pípila, Juan José de los Reyes Martínez was born in San Miguel de Allende; he worked in the mines of Guanajuato when the War of Independence broke out. He is remembered throughout the Bajío for his bravery in the battle to take the Alhóndiga de Granaditas in Guanajuato, an early and important victory for the Mexican army.

- **José Mariano Jiménez:** Though not a Bajío native (he was born in San Luis Potosí), Jiménez's legacy is closely tied to the city of Guanajuato. This leader of the Mexican army was executed along with Hidalgo, Allende, and Aldama, and, like his fellow heroes, his severed head was suspended from a corner of the Alhóndiga de Granaditas by royalist forces.

Mexico. After finally securing independence from Spain, Mexico took its shaky first steps toward establishing an autonomous nation. Both Guanajuato and Querétaro were recognized among 24 states in the First Mexican Empire, with independence leader Agustín de Iturbide acting as interim head of state.

In 1823, Antonio López de Santa Anna led a successful revolt against Iturbide's government, thereafter establishing the first Mexican republic. Again, Guanajuato and Querétaro were included among the federation of 19 states, and Guadalupe Victoria, another hero of the War of Independence, became the country's first president.

It was during this period of unrest that U.S. citizens began to settle in Texas with the permission of the Mexican government. These settlers had little interest in conforming to Mexico's laws, and when conflict between the American settlers and the government reached a head, Santa Anna sent troops to Texas. Texas briefly gained total independence; however, tensions flared when the territory was annexed by the United States. After several battles in Texas, the U.S. Army invaded Mexico from the north, marching to the capital via Puebla and taking control of Mexico City. The capital of Mexico was temporarily relocated to Querétaro. In Querétaro, Santa Anna signed the infamous Treaty of Guadalupe, which ceded half of Mexico's territory to the United States, including California, New Mexico, Arizona, Texas, and Nevada.

REFORMATION AND THE PORFIRIATO

Santa Anna was ousted after another coup in 1855. Liberal Oaxacan politician Benito Juárez became president of the republic and took the lead on a series of liberal reforms, including the abolishment of church property and the constitutional recognition of freedom of religion. Juárez's celebrated presidency was interrupted in 1860 when France invaded Mexico under Napoleon III. The French established the Second Mexican Empire as a client state, placing Emperor Maximilian I in charge. In 1867, there was yet another successful upheaval by the liberals, and Maximilian was executed in Querétaro. Benito Juárez returned to the presidency, and he remained in power until his death in 1872.

Not long after Juárez's successor, Sebastián Lerdo de Tejada, had won his second election, army general Porfirio Díaz took over the office in a coup. A powerful leader with a strong military outlook, Díaz was both a dictator and despot; he created a strong central government that favored foreign investment. While the country's wealth increased, social conditions for the poor only worsened under Díaz's ironfisted control. While his legacy is controversial, Díaz did manage to keep Mexico in relative peace during his entire presidency. His rule is known as the Porfiriato.

The Porfiriato was a mixed blessing for the Bajío, where some cities flourished while others withered away in disrepair. San Miguel de Allende was all but abandoned, its churches left to crumble and its tiny population dwindling away. Guanajuato, on the other hand, continued to produce silver and received handsome gifts from the president himself. Porfirio Díaz attended the grand opening of Teatro Juárez, and he commissioned the city's beautiful municipal market in commemoration of the independence movement. The silver town of Pozos was also a favorite of the president, who renamed the city Ciudad Porfirio Díaz.

MEXICAN REVOLUTION

In response to the ongoing dictatorship of conservative leader Porfirio Díaz, wealthy politician Francisco I. Madero announced his intentions to run for the presidency. When Díaz threw him in jail, Madero helped to organize a revolution against the government, assisted by General Victoriano Huerta. The great idealist revolutionary Emiliano Zapata joined their efforts in the south, recruiting a troop of peasant soldiers and demanding large-scale land reform on behalf of the people.

Once Madero took the presidency, he proved to be a weak leader, uninterested in enacting the land reforms for peasants that had inspired Zapata to join him. Observing this weakness, Huerta organized a coup against Madero, taking the presidency himself after Madero was executed. Again, Mexico's famous rebel leaders joined forces. Together, Venustiano Carranza, Álvaro Obregón, Pancho Villa, and Emiliano Zapata led the revolt against Huerta's government, with additional support from the U.S. Army. They successfully toppled the regime in August 1914, with Carranza at the head of the army.

Carranza took the presidency with initial opposition from Villa and Zapata. However, he won support with the people through promises of land reform, eventually overseeing the writing of the Constitution of 1917. The new constitution was based on the Constitution of 1857, though it included many important land, law, and labor reforms.

Carranza was eventually forced out of power and replaced by General Álvaro Obregón. Pancho Villa was ambushed and executed during the Obregón presidency, likely at the president's own command.

THE 20TH CENTURY

Mexico's government began to stabilize in the decades following the revolution, eventually coalescing into a single political party, the Institutional Revolutionary Party (PRI). The postrevolutionary period was a time of great progress, as the country began to flourish culturally and intellectually. During Obregón's presidency, José Vasconcelos served as the secretary of public education and oversaw the establishment of the National Symphony Orchestra and the Symphonic Orchestra of Mexico. He also began the Mexican mural program, through which famous artists like Diego Rivera and David Alfaro Siqueiros were commissioned to paint monumental art on the walls of public buildings. After the 1920s, the Mexican economy began to grow annually.

In 1937, Lázaro Cárdenas was elected to the presidency. He continued to reform land rights and redistribute territory as laid out in the Constitution of 1917. In a move that would serve as a model for other oil-rich nations, Cárdenas expropriated oil reserves from the private companies that had been running them. He established Petróleos Mexicanos (Pemex), concurrently founding the National Polytechnic Institute to ensure a sufficient engineering force in the country. Among other famous decisions, Lázaro Cárdenas granted exile to Bolshevik revolutionary Leon Trotsky, who lived the final years of his life in Mexico City.

Music and cinema flourished during the 1930s and 1940s, with Mexican movies outselling Hollywood films during World War II. During and after the Spanish Civil War, many European intellectuals took up residence in Mexico, adding to the thriving art and cultural community. In the 1950s, Luis Buñuel, the famous Spanish filmmaker, made some of his most influential pictures in Mexico, eventually naturalizing as a Mexican citizen.

In the second half of the century, Mexico began to depend heavily on the income from oil exports, which eventually led to a devastating economic crisis in 1982. It took more than a decade for Mexico's economy to recover. Just as it did, Mexico became a member of NAFTA, a massive free trade agreement with the United States and Canada, on January 1, 1994.

The same morning that NAFTA went into effect, a small indigenous army called the Ejército Zapatista de Liberación Nacional (EZLN) took control of three cities in the southern state of Chiapas. This rebellion was small in scope but wide-reaching in consequences, inspiring widespread support for indigenous people throughout Mexico and the world. The army's leader, Subcomandante Marcos, became a national spokesperson for the indigenous cause and met repeatedly with Mexican government leaders.

Government and Economy

As laid out in the Constitution of 1917, Mexico is a federal republic overseen by an elected government. It is a federation of 32 individually governed states (including the *distrito federal,* or federal district), united by a national government in Mexico City.

ORGANIZATION

Mexico is overseen by a federal government, which is divided into three branches: executive, legislative, and judicial. The president, elected to a single six-year term, oversees the executive branch. The congress is divided into the Senate and Chamber of Deputies, and there is a single supreme court, with justices appointed by the president. Each of Mexico's 32 states has three representatives in the senate. Citizens elect two of the three senators, while the leading minority party appoints the third. There are 500 deputies in the Chamber of Deputies, with one representative for every 200,000 citizens. Of these, the people directly elect 300, while the other 200 are appointed by proportional representation. The federal government operates in the *distrito federal* in Mexico City, or Mexico D.F.

In each state, power is also divided between the executive, legislative, and judicial branches, with an elected governor overseeing executive activities. States are independent and sovereign. Each has its own laws, though none can enact laws that contradict the country's federal constitution.

Each state in Mexico is further divided into autonomous municipalities. Municipalities are managed differently in each state; however, a municipality usually comprises a larger city and all the small towns and ranches surrounding it. In San Miguel de Allende, for example, Los Rodríguez is overseen by the municipality, even though it is about 16 kilometers (10 miles) outside the city and has almost 3,000 inhabitants.

Municipalities are run by a local government, with a *presidente municipal* (municipal president) elected democratically to a nonrenewable post. In the Bajío, a large percentage of the state and municipal divisions were laid under the Spanish viceroyalty, which divided the country into *ayuntamientos* (town councils), overseen by local governors.

Both Guanajuato and Querétaro are the capitals of their states and therefore home to both the municipal and state government.

POLITICAL PARTIES

From the end of the Mexican Revolution until the year 2000, the Partido Revolucionario Institucional (PRI, Institutional Revolutionary Party) was the sole party in Mexican politics. Although once considered socialist, the PRI upholds more centrist views today. Its members and supporters are called *priistas.*

During its long reign over Mexico, the PRI was commonly accused of running a dictatorship. Members were also widely charged with corruption and fraud. Although the PRI had a fraught relationship with the Mexican people, it remained uncontested for most of the 20th century. In 1988, PRI defector Cuauhtémoc Cárdenas ran against the official PRI candidate but was defeated in a highly controversial election that included an unexplained glitch in the electoral system.

In 2000, Vicente Fox Quesada was elected to the office of president under the conservative Partido Acción Nacional (PAN, National Action Party) ticket. Before his election, Fox was a prominent businessman in the Bajío and the supervisor of the Coca-Cola Company in Mexico and Latin America. He represented Guanajuato in the Chamber of Deputies and then served as governor of the state 1995-1999. His home and ranch are located in the community of San Cristóbal, Guanajuato. After Fox's election, the PRI underwent serious restructuring and continues to be an influential political party in Mexico.

In 2006, Felipe Calderón, also a PAN candidate, won the presidential elections by a slim margin and amid prominent accusations of fraud from the opposing candidate, Manuel López Obrador. López Obrador is a member of the third prominent political party, the Partido de la Revolución Democrática (PRD, Party of the Democratic Revolution), traditionally the most leftist of the three major parties. In 2012, Calderón was replaced by PRI candidate Enrique Peña Nieto, the former governor of the state of Mexico. In 2014, López Obrador founded a fourth political party, Movimiento Regeneración Nacional, or Morena, with which he ran for the presidency again in 2018. Morena is now the most progressive party in Mexico.

In the states of Guanajuato and Querétaro, voters tend to elect fiscally and socially conservative candidates. PAN has a loyal following in Guanajuato, home of former president Vincente Fox. Querétaro is also considered an important stronghold for the PAN, which has controlled the Querétaro government since 1997.

ELECTIONS

Elections for both national and regional posts are secret, universal, compulsory, and free. They are overseen by the Instituto Federal Electoral (Federal Electoral Institute). IFE credentials, or voting cards, are the national form of identification, so there is no need to separately register to vote. The president and senators are elected to one six-year term. State and regional elections may or may not be held concurrently with federal elections.

ECONOMY

Mexico has a free-market economy, with energy, agriculture, manufacturing, ranching, fishing, and forestry forming the largest sectors. After Brazil, Mexico is the second-largest economy in Latin America and is among the 15 biggest economies in the world. Nonetheless, the distribution of wealth in Mexico is highly uneven, with widespread poverty throughout the country.

Although Mexico's economy has grown steadily throughout the 20th century, it has suffered from intermittent crises. In 1982, the country fell into a serious recession, principally caused by poor economic policy, falling oil prices, and high inflation worldwide. Having borrowed extensively from international banks, Mexico's president, Miguel de la Madrid, was forced to reduce public spending. Economic recovery was slow, lasting almost the entire decade. In 1996, the currency was devalued.

During the worldwide financial crisis of 2009, Mexico's GDP dropped 6.5 percent, with remittances from the United States also dropping off as that country suffered economic crisis. Since the crisis, the economy has been rebuilding, with significant foreign investment during 2010.

Guanajuato contributes about 3.8 percent to the national gross domestic product (GDP), ranking eighth out of the states overall, with manufacturing its largest industry. Querétaro is a much smaller state, yet also a manufacturing capital. In total, Querétaro contributes about 1.8 percent to the Mexican GDP.

Agriculture

Although a large percentage of Mexico's population is involved in agricultural activities, farming has slowly become less important to the nation's overall economy. Currently, agriculture accounts for less than 4 percent of the GDP. Data suggest that at least half of Mexican farmers are subsistence farmers, principally producing corn or beans on five hectares or fewer. The U.S. is the biggest importer of Mexican crops, accounting for about 60 percent of all Mexican agricultural exports.

With its fertile plains and large watershed, the Bajío has traditionally been an important agricultural region in Mexico and remains so to this day. More than one-third of Guanajuato's state land is dedicated to farming, though, like the nation at large, its impact on the state GDP is less profound (it accounts for less than 5 percent). The state of Guanajuato is the country's biggest producer of strawberries and broccoli as well as a major producer of asparagus, rye, barley, wheat, alfalfa, and sorghum. Querétaro is a top producer of roses in addition to significant crops of vegetables, grain, and meat. In both Querétaro and Guanajuato, there has been an increase in the production of organic fruits, vegetables, and dairy products; both have begun to cultivate grapes for wine. Agriculture accounts for only a small percentage of Querétaro's overall economy.

Manufacturing

Manufacturing is a huge contributor to Mexico's economy, accounting for up to 90 percent of the country's exports and 20 percent of the GDP. Though Mexico faces staunch competition from manufacturing giant China, it has managed to continue its growth in this sector by focusing the industry on more specialized products, like automobiles and electronics. Within manufacturing, metal products and machinery account for the largest manufacturing sectors countrywide, followed by food and tobacco, chemicals, petroleum products, and shoes and clothing.

Manufacturing is crucial to Guanajuato, comprising around 28 percent of the state's economy. León, Guanajuato's biggest city, and the suburb of Silao are major manufacturing zones. Automobiles and automobile parts are major contributors to the manufacturing sector (there are General Motors and Volkswagen plants in Silao), and the shoe and leather goods industries continue to grow at a rapid clip in León.

Energy

Mexico built its first oil well in 1896. Today, it is among the world's top 10 oil-producing nations. All natural resources, including oil, are state property, as declared by President Lázaro Cárdenas in the 1930s; Petróleos Mexicanos, or Pemex for short, is the state-run company in charge of extracting, refining, and distributing oil. Although it has faltered over the years, Pemex is the single largest source of income for the country, and Mexico meets almost 90 percent of its own energy needs internally. In 2014, President Enrique Peña Nieto instigated a series of reforms to Mexico's energy policy that were aimed to increase production, lower energy prices, and allow increased foreign investment in industry—a profound change to the sector after nearly 75 years as a state-run entity.

Tourism

Mexico is one of the world's most popular travel destinations, welcoming almost 25 million foreign visitors every year. The Mexican government invests heavily in tourism, including massive international marketing campaigns designed to attract potential visitors to the country. North American visitors are far and away the largest group of foreign tourists; U.S. citizens constitute about 70 percent of international visitors to the country. While their numbers have remained steady, an increase in visitors from other countries worldwide (like Russia and Brazil) has helped the Mexican tourist sector grow in recent years.

Although Mexico is most famous for its beach resorts, cultural tourism is also a major draw in the country's colonial towns and cities. Tourism, both national and international, is vital to the Bajío's economy, especially in cities like San Miguel de Allende, Guanajuato, Tequisquiapan, and Bernal, which rely heavily on the income from hotels, restaurants, gift shops, tour operators, and other tourist-related activities. Since being declared a United Nations World Heritage Site, Guanajuato has seen a huge increase in tourism; today, it is one of the most visited colonial cities in Mexico. Even Querétaro, a state less recognized as a tourist destination, owes 20 percent of its internal economy to tourism and related commercial activities.

Relationship with the United States

Historically, the United States has always been Mexico's most important trading partner. That status has become even more important since the North American Free Trade

252

BACKGROUND

GOVERNMENT AND ECONOMY

Agreement (NAFTA) was inaugurated in 1994, creating a trilateral free trade zone between Canada, the United States, and Mexico. In the decades following NAFTA's acceptance, trade between Mexico and the United States tripled, and two-way trade between the nations exceeded $550 billion in 2014. (Trade ties between Mexico and Canada have also strengthened.)

After NAFTA was ratified, many U.S. companies relocated their factories south of the border, creating an even larger manufacturing industry in Mexico. Some studies report that Mexico's *maquiladoras,* or manufacturing plants, have increased 15 percent since 1994. Although these *maquiladoras* were originally located along the border, León, Guanajuato, is one of the central Mexican cities that has experienced a massive increase in the manufacturing sector since the inauguration of NAFTA.

According to research published by the Pew Research Center, about 11.4 million Mexican-born immigrants resided in the United States in 2012 (of almost 34 million people of Mexican origin, both Mexican-born and U.S.-born, living in the country). Remittances from Mexicans living in the United States are the second-largest source of foreign currency in Mexico after energy and oil, though they have been declining in recent years.

Distribution of Wealth

Mexico is a wealthy nation with abundant natural resources, macroeconomic stability, and a GDP among the world's largest. Unfortunately, Mexico's wealth is not distributed evenly across its population. According to data published by the World Bank and collected by Mexico's census bureau, 52 percent of Mexico's people lived below the national poverty line in 2012, an uptick from recent years. Roughly 10 percent of the total population is living in extreme poverty, lacking access to basic medical care or sufficient food.

Inflation in food and energy costs has made the effects of poverty more profound for many of Mexico's people. However, the lack of opportunities and employment for a large sector of the population makes it difficult to eradicate poverty, especially in rural areas. Social programs have lagged.

Poverty varies by region. Wealth is concentrated in and around the capital, Mexico City, in Nuevo Leon (and its prosperous capital city of Monterrey), and along the U.S. border. Chiapas is the poorest and most southerly state of Mexico, where recent official studies have revealed that more than 75 percent of the population lives in poverty. Through most of the 20th century, the Bajío region was neither the richest nor the poorest part of Mexico, but it has been showing very promising economic growth in the 21st century. According to a 2017 report by the government's statistics bureau, the Instituto Nacional de Estadística y Geografía (INEGI), both Guanajuato and Querétaro rank among the 10 states with the highest average family income.

People and Culture

DEMOGRAPHY

Mexico is a large and multiethnic country. There are varying figures with regard to its population demographics; however, in broad strokes, the country is a mix of indigenous folks, mestizos, and people of European descent. Indigenous people (*indígenas*) are direct descendants of the native people of Mexico, and many still speak native languages. According to Mexico's census data, the country's population is about 10-12 percent indigenous, though numbers vary greatly by region. The majority of Mexicans are considered mestizo, a broad term that refers to a mix of ethnic and cultural heritage, which may include European, indigenous, and African ethnicities. Most people of European descent in Mexico are Spanish descendants, though there have also been other European migrants to Mexico over the course of country's history.

In the past decade, Central American migrants fleeing violence in their home countries have begun to settle in Mexico. The Mexican government granted refugee status to over 100,000 of these migrants in 2017, but many more are living in Mexico without refugee status or passing through the country on their way to the United States. There is also a noticeable population of South Americans, mostly from Chile and Argentina, with the largest population residing in the capital. Mexico is also home to small but visible populations of Lebanese, Chinese, Japanese, and Korean people.

About 6 million people in Mexico speak one of the country's 62 recognized indigenous languages; the vast majority of these people also speak Spanish. Relatively speaking, there is only a small indigenous community in the Bajío region. In the state of Querétaro, about 2 percent of people speak an indigenous language, with the largest populations of indigenous communities concentrated in the cities of Amealco de Bonfil and Tolimán. In the state of Guanajuato, less than 1 percent of the people speak an indigenous language.

The vast majority of the people in Guanajuato and Querétaro live in urban environments. In both states, roughly 75 percent live in cities, with almost half of Querétaro's total population residing in the capital. These statistics reflect an overall trend in Mexico, where the majority of the population lives in overcrowded urban centers. In fact, over 50 percent of Mexico's total population resides in the country's 55 biggest cities.

EMIGRATION

Although the figures are not exact, an estimated 8-10 percent of all Mexican citizens live in the United States. Mexican emigration to the United States has a major influence on Mexico's economy and culture, especially in states where emigration is high. According to data compiled by the World Bank, remittances from Mexicans living overseas accounted for about US$22 billion of the country's income in 2013; though this was a decline from previous years, remittances were still the country's second-largest source of foreign currency.

According to a study conducted by the National Institute of Statistics and Geography in 2000, the state of Guanajuato has one of the highest emigration rates in the country, along with the states of Zacatecas, Michoacán, and Durango. In 2000, roughly 3.5 percent of Guanajuato's population immigrated to the United States, or about 163,300 people that year. In the same year, the state of Querétaro lost about 1.8 percent of its population to emigration, or 24,700 people. By comparison, about 1.6 percent of the total Mexican population moves to the United States annually.

RELIGION

Spanish missionaries introduced Catholicism to the native population in Mexico during the 15th and 16th centuries. Missionaries were extremely active in New Spain, establishing an abundance of churches, Catholic schools, and hospitals, often with the financial assistance of wealthy Spanish nobles. The largest Catholic cathedral in the Americas is just beside the government buildings in Mexico City's central plaza, indicating the enormous importance of the church to both the state and the people.

During the early Spanish conquest, there were massive conversions among the indigenous population to Catholicism. Conversions spiked after the apparition of the Virgen de Guadalupe in Mexico City in 1531. While accepting the new religion, many indigenous communities incorporated their own religious beliefs into Roman Catholic ritual, creating some unique Catholic traditions in the New World.

Throughout Spanish rule of Mexico, the Catholic church had a major influence on governance and society. During the independence era, the image of the Virgen de Guadalupe adorned the official flag of Mexico's first national army. Catholics continued to maintain massive power in Mexico until the 1850s, when President Benito Juárez began to secularize the country's constitution and laws. Among other reforms, he limited church power and appropriated church property for the state. While the relationship between the church and government warmed after Juárez left office, anticlerical forces gained power during the Mexican Revolution. The current Mexican constitution separates church and state. Nonetheless, the Catholic church continues to be an important part of Mexico's national identity. Almost 90 percent of Mexicans identify as Catholic.

Guanajuato and Querétaro are largely conservative and Catholic states: 95 percent of Querétaro's residents and 96 percent of Guanajuato's residents identify as Catholic. Foreigners from any background will quickly be introduced to myriad Catholic holidays, often celebrated with rich tradition and pageantry. The Holy Week festivities in San Miguel de Allende, for example, are among the country's most beautiful and well attended. Every town celebrates its patron saint's holiday with enormous fanfare and parties. Religion also plays an important role in personal and family life, with milestones like baptism, confirmation, weddings, and funerals celebrated in the Catholic tradition.

Although church and state are separate in Mexico, the predominantly Catholic outlook of the Mexican populace is nonetheless reflected in state policy, particularly with regards to family planning. Over the years, family planning has been adopted throughout Mexico's public health organizations; abortion, however, is still illegal in both Guanajuato and Querétaro states. In 2015, Guanajuato's conservative lawmakers stopped passage of a law that would allow abortion in the case of rape.

LANGUAGE

Spanish is the language most commonly spoken in Mexico, including in San Miguel de Allende, Guanajuato, and Querétaro. In addition to Spanish, English is widely spoken throughout the Bajío, particularly in San Miguel de Allende, where there is a large and influential English-speaking expatriate population. In San Miguel, most restaurant menus, publications, and advertisements are printed in both English and Spanish. There are also several English-language newspapers and publications.

The Arts

A major cultural destination, the Bajío is an excellent place to immerse yourself in Mexico's artistic and cultural heritage. It's home to several large universities, numerous museums and galleries, and a large population of artists and writers, and there are ongoing cultural events and exhibitions throughout the region.

VISUAL ARTS

After the conquest, Mexican artistic traditions were closely tied to Spanish aesthetics and to the activities of the Catholic church. The colonial cities of San Miguel de Allende, Guanajuato, and Querétaro are excellent places to see and learn more about early colonial art and architecture in Mexico. Made wealthy by the booming silver trade, the Bajío region attracted master painters, sculptors, and artisans to assist with the building and decoration of Catholic chapels during the 17th and 18th centuries.

In particular, Guanajuato's churches contain a wonderful collection of colonial painting, including many works by 18th-century master Miguel Cabrera. (While some visual artists from the colonial era are well known, a large number of the existing paintings are unsigned.) After being inducted into the United Nations World Heritage program, Guanajuato undertook a massive restoration project of cultural heritage. Unfortunately, many churches in the Bajío were sacked or destroyed over the course of history. However, there are original altarpieces, *retablos,* paintings, and sculpture remaining among the rebuilt interiors of many churches of the region.

While there were some very talented artists in New Spain, it wasn't until after the Revolution of 1910 that the arts began to express an original and distinctly Mexican character. In the postrevolutionary era, the Mexican government promoted varied cultural and artistic programs, including the famous public mural project, overseen by Secretary of Education José Vasconcelos. The muralists, along with other vanguard thinkers of the postrevolutionary era, brought worldwide renown to Mexico's artistic scene. Diego Rivera, one of the most prominent Mexican muralists, was born in the city of Guanajuato; his childhood home is a museum dedicated to his work as well as the work of his contemporaries.

San Miguel de Allende held a modest and yet important role in the great intellectual and artistic achievements of the early 20th century. All but abandoned during the late 19th century, San Miguel became a retreat destination for artists, thinkers, and musicians from Mexico City during the 20th century. In 1937, Peruvian writer and art historian Felipe Cossío del Pomar visited San Miguel de Allende. The following year, Mexican president Lázaro Cárdenas granted Pomar the funds he needed to open a fine art school in one of San Miguel's abandoned convents. Both Mexican and American artists came to study and teach at this school, including (for a brief time) the famed muralist David Alfaro Siqueiros. Though it would go through several incarnations, Cossío del Pomar's art school is still open today as the Instituto Allende. Two influential early-20th-century Mexican artists, Olga Costa and José Chávez Morado, also lived briefly in San Miguel de Allende; they eventually settled down in Guanajuato, where they made an enormous contribution to city museums and culture.

MUSIC AND DANCE

Mexico's unique musical genres have their roots in the 16th century, when traditional European composition and instruments collided with traditional Mesoamerican music. The result was a wide range of *sones* (musical genres), most of which are also associated with a traditional style of dance. In any of the

Helpful Spanish-English Cognates

As an English speaker, you may know more Spanish vocabulary than you think. Spanish and English share hundreds of cognates—words with a similar spelling and meaning. Many words have an easy-to-recognize English equivalent, with the Spanish word taking an *o, a,* or *e* on the end. In other cases, the *-tion* ending in English is replaced by the *-ción* ending in Spanish. Sometimes, it is just the pronunciation that changes, as some Spanish and English words are spelled exactly the same!

Cognates are especially helpful for travelers to Mexico, where words are constantly incorporated from English (*computadora* for computer is a good example). If you start paying attention, you are likely to see many words and phrases you understand. As you brush up your *español*, here are some cognates that may be useful during your travels in the Bajío:

aeropuerto: airport
artista: artist
auto: automobile
balcón: balcony
banco: bank
computadora: computer
consulado: consulate
costo: cost
declaración: declaration
delicioso: delicious
desierto: desert
doctor: doctor
dólares: dollars
familia: family
festival: festival
gasolina: gasoline
historia: history
hospital: hospital
hotel: hotel
local: local
mapa: map
medicina: medicine
menú: menu
monumento: monument
nacionalidad: nationality
periódico: periodical, or newspaper
persona: person
plaza: plaza
rancho: ranch
romántico: romantic
taxi: taxi
teléfono: telephone
turista: tourist
visa: visa

FALSE COGNATES

Before you get carried away, remember that there are a few words that have deceptively similar spelling in Spanish and English, yet different meanings. *Tuna* refers to the fruit of the prickly pear, not the fish. *Librería* is not a library but a bookstore; a library is a *biblioteca*. *Fútbol* is a true cognate if you are British; for Americans, the translation is soccer.

Bajío's cities, visitors may have the opportunity to see a traditional music or dance performance in one of the city's public squares. In addition, Querétaro occasionally hosts performances by Mexico's Ballet Folklórico, a traditional dance troupe from Mexico City.

Mexico's most well-recognized musical ensemble, the mariachi band, dates back to 18th-century Jalisco. Dressed in two-piece *charro* suits and *corbatín* bow ties, mariachi bands usually feature an impressive lineup of violins, trumpets, guitars, and *jaranas* (a large five-string guitar). Mariachis play traditional Mexican ballads, often singing the chorus in unison. In central Mexico, mariachi music is a fixture at special events, like weddings or birthday parties. However, it is not necessary to await a special event to enjoy mariachi; on any night, you can commission a tune from the mariachis waiting in the central plazas of Guanajuato or San Miguel de Allende.

Some of the most famous names in Mexican music and cinema are originally from the Bajío region, and they are honored in their hometowns. In the 19th century, Juventino Rosas, a famous bandleader and composer of Otomí descent, was born in the small town Santa Cruz de Galeana (today, Santa Cruz de Juventino Rosas). Following the Revolution of 1910, the great singer and songwriter José Alfredo Jiménez was born in Dolores Hidalgo. Today, Jiménez is remembered as one of the greatest creative minds of his generation. Jiménez's contemporary, Jorge Negrete, was a native of the neighboring city of Guanajuato, later to become one of Mexico's most cherished singers and actors during the golden age of Mexican cinema.

LITERATURE

Mexico's writers have made a significant contribution to literary traditions in Spanish, including several noted authors from San Miguel de Allende and the Bajío region. Although poems, stories, and legends were passed down orally before the Spanish arrived in the New World, historians point to the descriptive chronicles of the conquest (written by Hernán Cortés, as well as other Spanish and indigenous writers) as the true birth of Mexican literature. These accounts have been highly significant to anthropologists' understanding of Mexico's native cultures.

After the conquest, Mexico made a distinguished contribution to literature during the colonial era. Baroque poet Sor Juana Inez de la Cruz holds a hallowed place in Spanish literary history, along with some of her contemporaries, dramatist Juan Ruiz de Alarcón and writer Carlos de Sigüenza y Góngora. (Sor Juana's image is well known to any Mexico tourist, as it adorns the 200-peso bill.) During the 19th century, Mexican writers contributed to the Spanish Romantic movement and, later, to modernism. In San Miguel de Allende, Ignacio Ramírez (also known as "El Nigromante," or The Necromancer) was a celebrated poet, journalist, and political thinker of the 19th century as well as a noted atheist.

During the 20th century, Mexico's national character was more strongly reflected in its literary traditions. Writers like Rosario Castellano and Juan Rulfo began to describe a distinctly Mexican environment, exploring the country's mixed identity and heritage. By the second half of the 20th century, Mexico's diverse writers had become highly recognized and widely translated, including Carlos Fuentes, Elena Poniatowska, and Laura Esquivel. In the 1990s, Octavio Paz was the first Mexican to win the Nobel Prize in literature.

In addition to Mexican authors, many foreign authors have lived in and written about Mexico. English writers Graham Greene and D. H. Lawrence both wrote novels based on their experiences in Mexico. Beatnik poet and novelist Jack Kerouac lived in Mexico City (and is rumored to have visited San Miguel de Allende), while Chilean writer Roberto Bolaño ably described youth culture in Mexico City in his novel *The Savage Detectives*. Colombian Nobel laureate Gabriel García Márquez resided in Mexico City for decades before his death in 2014.

Essentials

Transportation

GETTING THERE

Air

Two major airports service the region around San Miguel de Allende, Guanajuato, and Querétaro: the **Del Bajío International Airport** (BJX, Carretera Silao-León, Km 5.5, Col. Nuevo Mexico, Silao, Guanajuato, tel. 472/748-2120), near the city of León, and **Querétaro International Airport** (QRO, Carretera Estatal 200, Querétaro-Tequisquiapan, Querétaro de Arteaga, Querétaro, tel. 442/192-5500, www.aiq.com.mx), just outside the capital city of Querétaro. If you are traveling to San Miguel de Allende or Dolores Hidalgo, either airport is appropriate. If you are traveling to Querétaro, choose QRO; visitors to Guanajuato should fly into BJX. Both airports are equipped with customs and immigration offices for international arrivals and departures.

It's also convenient for travelers to Querétaro to fly into **Mexico City International Airport** (MEX, Capitan Carlos León s/n, Peñón de Los Baños Venustiano Carranza, Distrito Federal, tel. 55/2482-2400, www.aicm.com.mx) in the capital. **Primera Plus** (toll-free Mex. tel. 800/375-7587, www.primeraplus.com.mx) offers hourly direct bus service from Terminals 1 and 2 in the Mexico City airport to Querétaro's main bus station, for about US$20.

Bus

Mexico's extensive and efficient bus service makes it easy to travel between cities countrywide. The Bajío region, including San Miguel de Allende, Guanajuato, and Querétaro, is serviced by several first-class bus lines, which have extensive routes in the region as well as connecting service throughout the country.

The most prominent bus lines servicing the region are **ETN** (toll-free Mex. tel. 800/800-0386, www.etn.com.mx) and **Primera Plus** (toll-free Mex. tel. 800/375-7587, www.primeraplus.com.mx). Both companies allow you to make reservations over the phone, online, or at one of their ticket sales desks at the bus stations. In most cases, it is better to make your own bus arrangements than to rely on a travel agent, unless the travel agent is an authorized point-of-sale for the bus company. From Mexico City, all buses to the region arrive and depart from **Terminal Central del Norte** (Eje Central Lázaro Cárdenas 4907, Gustavo A Madero, Magdalena de Las Salinas, tel. 55/5587-1552, www.centraldelnorte.com), also known as Los Cien Metros, one of four bus terminals in the capital.

Bus travel is comfortable and efficient, and departures and arrivals are almost always punctual. First-class buses are equipped with bathrooms, usually offer a snack and beverage to passengers, and show movies during the ride. Because buses are incredibly popular in Mexico, it is a good idea to book bus tickets in advance in any case, but especially during a holiday weekend. Holiday weekends can also cause a bit of delay on popular bus routes, particularly those buses heading to and from the beach or Mexico City, owing to heavy traffic.

Car

Driving across the border has long been a popular choice with U.S. and Canadian visitors to Mexico. In just one long day, you can reach San Miguel de Allende from the Texas border. Driving in Mexico is usually comfortable and easy, with a circuit of well-maintained toll highways running across the country. However, as a result of widespread

---

drug cartel-related violence, travel through Northern Mexico has become less safe. That said, thousands of cars and trucks make the drive every day without incident. With a good map and some basic safety precautions, tourists can travel by road to San Miguel and environs, then have the benefit of a car to use while visiting the region.

CAR PERMITS

All foreign residents bringing a car into Mexico must apply for a temporary import permit for their vehicle. You can apply for the permit up to 60 days before your trip at a Mexican consulate in the United States (note that not all consulates offer this service) or via **Banjercito** (www.banjercito.com.mx); in most cases, however, it is easier to simply process the paperwork at a customs office at the border. The cost is about US$50, plus taxes.

The permit is good for 180 days. Thereafter, the car must be returned to the United States or Canada. All cars brought into Mexico from the United States or Canada must be returned with the import permit sticker still attached to the windshield. Alternatively, the car's temporary import permit may be renewed locally if the car's owner has an FM3 or FM2 resident visa. As long as you have a resident visa, you are permitted to own and operate a foreign-plated vehicle in Mexico.

CAR INSURANCE

All foreign vehicles must be insured in Mexico. Fortunately, Mexican auto insurance is inexpensive and widely available. You can preregister for insurance via the Internet, or you can sign up for insurance at one of the many insurance agents located along the U.S.-Mexico border. **Qualitas** (www.qualitas.com.mx) is one of several large companies that cover foreign cars. Neither U.S. nor Canadian automobile insurances are valid in Mexico.

CHOOSING SAFE ROUTES

Widespread violence related to the drug trade along the U.S.-Mexico border has made travel through the northern regions more precarious than it was in the past. Throughout the north and around the city of Monterrey, there have been an increased number of illegal roadblocks and carjackings as well as the occasional highway shoot-out between federal agents and cartels. While drivers should certainly be aware of the hazards of driving through Northern Mexico, many Americans and Canadians continue to drive through Mexico with little problem.

To ensure your safety on the road, travel only during the day, and always choose toll roads rather than free highways. Toll roads are well maintained, well lit, and patrolled by police. On most Mexican toll roads, the toll also includes insurance coverage for any accidents you may be involved in while on the highway. Most tollbooths will accept bank cards as well as cash, but watch the signage as you approach.

Mexican toll roads are patrolled by **Los Ángeles Verdes** (the Green Angels), a fleet of emergency responders and road mechanics operated by the Mexican Secretariat of Tourism. The Green Angels can offer tourist information for visitors, assist with medical emergencies, and attend to mechanical problems 8am-6pm daily. Dial 078 from a telephone to reach the Green Angels.

DRIVING SAFETY

Drivers should always remain alert on Mexico's highways, where inexperienced drivers, big trucks, and rampant speeding make accidents unfortunately common. Stay alert, and drive defensively.

On highways, faster traffic travels in the left lane and slower traffic in the right lane. Often, a slower car will put on its driver's side turn signal to indicate that it is safe to pass. The passing car will then put on its driver's side blinker and pass to the left. Do be aware that a driver's blinker can also indicate the intention to turn to the left, rather than safety to pass. Always use precaution when passing slower cars.

HIGHWAY INFORMATION

Guia Roji (www.guiaroji.com.mx) publishes excellent and accurate maps of Mexican roads and cities, including a countrywide atlas, numerous city maps, and highly detailed maps of Mexico City. Their valuable flipbook atlas, *Por Las Carreteras de Mexico,* is published annually and contains maps of every state highway and many cities across the republic. *Guia Roji* has an Internet store, and their road atlas is sold in many gas stations and convenience stores across Mexico.

Additionally, Google Maps and other GPS systems have done a good job mapping Mexico's highways and cities. If you have enabled your smartphone, it can help guide you along the highways.

You can get updated information about Mexico's highway conditions at the government's **Caminos y Puentes Federales** website (www.capufe.gob.mx, in Spanish), including toll costs for each highway and road conditions.

GETTING AROUND

Walking is the most popular mode of transportation for most tourists to San Miguel de Allende, Guanajuato, and other hilly cobblestone cities. In the pretty and compact *centro histórico* of most colonial cities, you can easily visit major sights on foot. When you need wheels, there are several other options.

Bus

While national bus lines are efficient and comfortable, intracity buses can be rather baffling—and noisy! In the cities of the Bajío, most buses do not run on exact schedules, nor are there published route maps for tourists. In most cases, learning to use the bus systems in a city comes down to trial and error.

In San Miguel de Allende or Guanajuato, the majority of sights are located in the city center and do not require bus travel. If you would like to take a bus to a neighborhood or sight outside the city center, head to one of the city's larger bus stations. Each bus will have its destination posted in the window. When in doubt, you can always ask the bus driver where the bus is headed. When you get on, pay the driver directly for the cost of your ticket, unless the driver indicates that you should sit down (someone may then pass through the bus to collect your fare).

In every major Bajío town, there are buses from the first-class bus terminal to the city's downtown district. Look for the buses marked Centro.

Car

In San Miguel de Allende, Guanajuato, and Querétaro, driving a car is generally safe and easy. San Miguel de Allende's drivers are particularly courteous, even giving pedestrians the right-of-way (which is rarely the case in other Mexican cities). Big cars and SUVs can be more difficult to navigate through the city's narrow streets. Otherwise, the biggest nuisance you'll face is some weekend traffic or the not-uncommon practice of drivers stopping to talk to their acquaintances in the middle of a busy street. Don't get exasperated; in a few weeks, you may find yourself doing the same.

Foreign plates are not uncommon in San Miguel de Allende, and they rarely warrant extra attention from authorities. As long as you have your paperwork in order, you will rarely have problems with law enforcement.

Taxis and Ride-Hailing Services

There are inexpensive taxis circling throughout San Miguel de Allende, Guanajuato, Querétaro, and other pueblos in the region. Except for in the city of Querétaro, where registered cabs have a meter, taxis charge a flat rate for travel around town. Outlying neighborhoods may cost more than a trip within the city center. To be sure, ask the price of the ride when you get in. It is safe to hail taxis in the street, though you can also call a cab if you are in a remoter location. If you need to call a cab, San Miguel de Allende, Guanajuato, and Querétaro all have radio-taxi companies, which are listed in this guide.

Uber operates in the cities of San Miguel de Allende, Guanajuato, and Querétaro. Because of the low cost and efficiency of taxis, Uber is less competitive in San Miguel de Allende and not commonly used. It is also uncommon to use Uber in place of regular taxi service in Guanajuato city. However, for travel to the airport from Guanajuato city, or for late-night rides from Guanajuato's bars, Uber is a good option.

Querétaro is a larger city, with some sights of interest outside the central districts. Although taxis are inexpensive, efficient, and ubiquitous in Querétaro, Uber can be handy and cheap when you need a pickup outside the city center, where there are fewer taxis, or when traveling late at night.

Visas and Officialdom

ENTRY REQUIREMENTS

To enter Mexico, all foreign citizens (including children) must have a valid passport and an official permit to travel (called an FMM), or tourist card. Note that children under age 18 who are traveling to or from Mexico without a legal parent or guardian must carry an official notarized letter from the absent parent authorizing the minor to travel in the company of a designated adult. You can find more information about tourist cards, nonimmigrant visas, immigrant visas, and unaccompanied minors at the **Instituto Nacional de Migración** (Mexican Immigration Service, www.inm.gob.mx).

If you are arriving in Mexico by airplane, you will be directed to immigration and customs checks on the ground. In Mexico, you pass through immigration at your final destination, not your first port of entry; for example, if you arrive in León via a connecting flight in Mexico City, you will pass through immigration in León.

If you drive into Mexico, it is your responsibility to locate the immigration office closest to the border crossing and complete the necessary paperwork. Most immigration offices are open 24 hours a day and located just a few yards from the border checkpoint. Note that some immigration offices are farther from the border; check with the border agents when you enter.

TOURIST CARDS

Every foreign visitor must have a permit to travel in Mexico. Visitors from most countries will be automatically issued a temporary permit, or "tourist card," at the port of entry. Technically called the **Forma Migratoria Múltiple (FMM),** tourist cards are good for up to 180 days of travel in Mexico. If you are arriving in Mexico via airplane, the flight staff will usually provide the FMM form to fill out while in the air, which will then be validated and stamped by an immigration official on the ground. On the form, you need to list the address where you will be residing in Mexico or the name of a hotel. The cost of the visa is included in the taxes and fees of your airfare. If you are traveling to Mexico by car and intend to visit the Bajío, you will need to stop at an immigration office at the border to request your FMM and pay the fee, about US$25.

After you have received your stamped form from immigration, keep it in a safe place until your departure. You will be asked to return the form when you leave the country. If you lose the form, you will be required to pay a fee at the airport.

RESIDENT VISAS

Foreigners who wish to reside in Mexico may apply for a resident visa at a Mexican consular agency in their home country; after approval via the consulate, the visa is processed in Mexico. All visa applications for residents of San Miguel de Allende and Guanajuato are processed at the **Instituto Nacional de Migración** (Mexican Immigration Services Guanajuato Branch, Calzada de la Estación de FFCC s/n, tel. 415/152-8991, 9am-1pm Mon.-Fri.) in San Miguel de Allende. There is a separate immigration office in the city of Querétaro (Calle Francisco Peñuñuri 15, Fracc. San José Inn, Delegación Centro Histórico, tel. 442/214-2712, 9am-1pm Mon.-Fri.), which serves immigrants and visitors in that state.

There are two types of resident visas, *residente temporal* (temporary resident) and *residente permanente* (permanent residents), which were known as FM3 and FM2, respectively, before 2013. Temporary resident visas are intended for long-term nonimmigrant residents of Mexico who do not intend to naturalize; a permanent resident visa is intended for those who plan to make a permanent move to Mexico and, most likely, pursue citizenship. In most cases, temporary resident permits are granted to those who can demonstrate investments or a source of foreign income that will support their life in Mexico (retirees or professionals who work remotely often fall into this category), though qualified professionals, artists, or investors may also apply for the right to legally participate in lucrative activities, such as giving art classes or opening a business. Both documents must be renewed annually.

Once the process is complete, you will receive a printed identification card with your photo and a Clave Única de Registro de Población (CURP), a number that you can use to open a bank account, buy property, or take advantage of public services.

If you are offered a job in Mexico, your employer must sponsor your visa application. In most cases, employment visas are only extended to foreigners who have special skills not generally available within the local population. For example, native speakers of a foreign language, like English or French, can seek employment as language teachers. If you receive a visa through your employer, the paperwork is nontransferable: If you leave your current job, your next employer must sponsor the visa's extension.

The **Secretaría de Relaciones Exteriores** (www.sre.gob.mx) maintains a list of Mexican consulates overseas as well as up-to-date information on visa requirements.

CUSTOMS
Basic Allowances

Customs (*aduana*) allows visitors and residents of Mexico to bring personal effects into the country as well as duty-free gifts valued at no more than US$300. Personal effects may include two photographic or video cameras and up to 12 rolls of film, up to three cellular phones, and one laptop computer. Most animal-derived food products are not permitted, including homemade foods, pet food or dog treats, fresh or canned meat, soil, and hay. Other food products are permitted, including tobacco, dried fruit, coffee, and fruit preserves. Note that pseudoephedrine (including the brand-name Sudafed) is prohibited in Mexico, and there are severe penalties for carrying firearms to Mexico. A full list of permitted items appears on the official customs form produced by the **Secretaría de Hacienda y Crédito Público** (www.sat.gob.mx).

If you are arriving by air, you will be given a customs declaration form on the airplane and will pass through the customs checkpoint right after immigration. You may choose to have your luggage reviewed by customs; otherwise, customs checks are performed by random selection. After collecting your luggage, you will be directed to a stoplight and asked to press a button. If you get a green light, you can pass. If you receive a red light, customs officials will open your luggage to inspect its contents. In larger airports, luggage is often passed through an X-ray machine, and passengers may be asked to open their luggage if a possible contraband item is detected.

If you are entering Mexico by car or on foot at a border crossing, you will be asked to

ESSENTIALS
VISAS AND OFFICIALDOM

choose the voluntary review line or the "nothing to declare" line. If you choose to declare nothing, you must come to a full stop at the border and wait to receive a red or green light. If you receive the red light, customs officials will ask you to pull over and will check the contents of your car, including the trunk.

Pets

Dogs and cats may enter Mexico with their owners. To be admitted, a pet needs a certificate of health issued by a licensed veterinarian as well as proof of vaccination against rabies, administered at least 15 days before entering the country. Double-check that all your pet's information, including name and address, is correctly noted on the forms. If you have all the paperwork, you will receive a Certificado de Importación Zoosanitario for the animal, which has an associated cost of about US$150. Both cats and dogs may be given a physical exam at the border, especially if they appear sick. Sick animals may also be detained at the border or at the airport. You can get more detailed information about bringing your pet at www.senasica.gob.mx.

For customs purposes, only dogs and cats are considered pets. More unusual animals like lizards or rabbits can also be imported to Mexico, but owners should check with customs and immigration officials to determine what paperwork is necessary before making the trip.

Cars

If you are driving a foreign-plated car to Mexico from the United States or Canada, you must acquire a temporary import permit. You can apply for a permit online via **Banjercito** (www.banjercito.com.mx/registrovehiculos) one week to 30 days before your trip, then send supporting documentation to Banjercito to complete the process. However, most drivers find it's easier and more efficient to simply apply for a temporary import permit at the Vehicular Control Module desk at the customs and immigration offices at the border. To apply, you must present proof of

citizenship (a passport), an immigration form (a tourist card or temporary resident visa), valid registration for your car, the leasing contract (if the car is rented), a driver's license, and an international credit card or debit card in the driver's name. Bring two copies of each document as well as the originals. You will be charged the cost of the permit (about US$50), plus a deposit, which may range from US$200-400 depending on the age of your vehicle.

Your temporary import permit includes a sticker, which must be affixed to your car's windshield, just above the rearview mirror. Do not remove that sticker until you are returning the car to the United States and are in the presence of a customs agent at the border. If you bring a car into Mexico, you are not permitted to sell it in Mexico, and it must be returned to its country of origin. If you have a temporary resident visa, your car is legal in Mexico for as long as your visa is valid. However, the car's temporary permit must be renewed at a local transit office. If your car's permit is not valid, the car can be confiscated by Mexican authorities. If you have a permanent resident visa, you are no longer permitted to operate a foreign-plated car in Mexico.

EMBASSIES AND CONSULATES

All foreign embassies are located in the capital in Mexico City. Most embassies are near the city center, with the majority of embassies concentrated in the Polanco and Cuauhtémoc neighborhoods, including the **United States Embassy** (Paseo de la Reforma 305, Col. Cuauhtémoc, tel. 55/5080-2000, https://mx.usembassy.gov), **Canadian Embassy** (Schiller 529, Col. Bosque de Chapultepec, tel. 55/5724-7900, www.canadainternational.gc.ca/mexico-mexique), **Australian Embassy** (Ruben Dario 55, Col. Polanco, tel. 55/1101-2200, http://mexico.embassy.gov.au), and **British Embassy** (Río Lerma 71, Col. Cuauhtémoc, tel. 55/1670-3200). If you have trouble with the law while you are in Mexico, or your citizenship papers have been lost or stolen, you should contact your embassy right away.

In the Bajío region, there is a **U.S. Consular Agency** (Plaza La Luciérnaga, Libramiento Jose Manuel Zavala No. 165, Locales 4 y 5, Col. La Luciérnaga, tel. 415/152-2357, conagencysanmiguel@state.gov, http://mexico.usembassy.gov, 9am-1pm Mon.-Thurs.) in San Miguel de Allende. The consular office is a branch of the U.S. embassy in Mexico City and can assist with lost or stolen passports, *apostilles* (certificates of notarization authenticity), and other services. For all other nations, the closest field offices are in Mexico City.

POLICE

Protección Civil (Civil Protection) is the local police force. They respond to emergencies, break-ins, or other complaints within the municipality. Throughout Mexico, you may see Civil Protection officers in blue fatigues patrolling the streets in cars or on foot. In addition, *transitos* (transit cops) patrol the roadways around town. They are principally involved in preventing traffic infractions, like speeding, and assisting at the scene of accidents. Throughout Mexico, calling 066 will summon emergency services.

In addition to city police, **Policía Federal** (Federal Police) patrol the intercity highways. Their territory may include major ring roads around town as well as larger avenues in big cities like Querétaro. In recent years, the Federal Police have been more involved in antidrug activity throughout the country, though most tourists will only notice them on the highways. Federal Police can be helpful in the case of a roadside emergency or accident.

Mexico has developed a bad (and not undeserved) reputation for police corruption and extortion. The famous *mordida* (bribe) has become so legendary that many people reach for their pocketbook as soon as they hear police sirens behind them. Visitors to the Bajío can expect a rather different set of circumstances. While police corruption is widespread in many Mexican states, Guanajuato and Querétaro's police are generally trustworthy and are very unlikely to pull over a tourist, or anyone, in search of a bribe. In the case that you have been extorted or harassed by a police officer or any other official, you should note the officer's name, badge number, and patrol car number in order to make an official complaint.

ESSENTIALS
FOOD

Food

One of the world's great cuisines, Mexican food is diverse, delicious, and profoundly omnivorous. Typical Mexican dishes are as basic as the ubiquitous quesadilla (a warm tortilla filled with melted cheese) or as elaborate as chicken served in *mole negro* (a Oaxacan sauce prepared with dozens of hand-ground ingredients). Food is essential to Mexican culture, and eating well is something enjoyed throughout the country, at every price point and in every type of establishment—from food stalls, bakeries, and markets to cafés, cantinas, and restaurants.

BASICS

Since the pre-Columbian era, corn, squash, chile peppers, and beans have formed the base of the Mexican diet. In addition to these key staples, Mexican food makes ample use of other native American foods, including tomatoes, green tomatoes, avocados, potatoes, prickly pear cactus, chocolate, and turkey. In the 15th century, Spanish settlers introduced new culinary techniques to Mexico, along with new ingredients like wheat, onions, rice, cheese, chicken, pork, and beef. Throughout the country, European traditions began to fuse with indigenous recipes. The result was a new and wholly original cuisine.

A staple at most Mexican meals and a key ingredient in many traditional dishes, tortillas are round flatbreads made of corn or wheat flour. A warmed tortilla wrapped around seasoned meat or vegetables is a taco, while a tortilla filled with melted cheese is a quesadilla. In addition to tortillas, corn flour is used to make a variety of flatbreads. *Sopes* are thick corn discs topped with beans, crumbled cheese, sour cream, and salsa, whereas *huaraches* are torpedo-shaped flatbreads, usually topped with beans, *guisados*, and salsa. *Gorditas,* a specialty of the Bajío region, are thick, round corn flatbreads, which are cooked on a griddle and then stuffed with cheese, meat, or other fillings.

Beyond tortillas and other flatbreads, corn is an essential ingredient in a wide range of traditional foods, many of which have roots in pre-Columbian cuisine. One of the oldest and most popular foods in the Americas, tamales are made of corn *masa* (dough) steamed in a corn husk or banana leaf and stuffed with chile peppers, meat, cheese, or fruits. Tamales are often accompanied by *atole,* a warm corn-based drink flavored with chocolate or fruit and sugar. Pozole, a hearty hominy soup, is another corn-based dish with pre-Hispanic origins, popular throughout the country.

As anyone who's spent time in Mexico knows, chile peppers are fundamental to the Mexican palate. *Salsa picante,* which refers to any sauce made of ground chile peppers and condiments, is served as an accompaniment to almost every meal in Mexico, formal or informal. There are seemingly infinite types of salsa, from the ubiquitous *salsa verde* (typically made with green tomatoes, cilantro, onion, and green chiles) to *pico de gallo* (a fresh salsa of chopped tomatoes, onion, and serrano chile peppers) to the dark charred-habenero salsa from the Yucatán Peninsula.

Aside from salsa, chile peppers are used to season meat, beans, and sauces or are served whole and stuffed with cheese in a chile relleno. There are hundreds of varieties of chile pepper cultivated in Mexico as well as a range of dried chile peppers produced from these crops. Some chile peppers are incredibly spicy (the habanero being Mexico's spiciest traditional variety), while others are mild but flavorful, like the poblano or the *chilaca.*

Like chile peppers, many varieties of beans are cultivated and prepared in Mexican cooking. Beans are generally served as a side dish to a meal or as part of a soup. In addition to beans, rice is a common accompaniment to a meal in traditional Mexican restaurants.

Mexico has a large ranching industry, with a variety of meats and cheeses produced throughout the country. Pork and chicken are popular, and Northern Mexico is known for its large ranches raising grass-fed beef. Traditional Mexican cuts of beef include the lean *arrachera* and *norteña.* Thanks to long and abundant coastlines, fish and shellfish are popular at Mexico's beach resorts as well as across the country. Shrimp cocktail is particularly beloved by the local crowd, as are breaded and fried fish steaks.

Mexico also produces several varieties of cheeses, including *panela* (a smooth, low-fat fresh cheese) and *cotija* (a dry and salty cheese used for crumbling on top of dishes). Mennonite communities in the north of Mexico make *queso chihuahua* (chihuahua cheese), which resembles a mild cheddar. There are many locally produced cheeses in the Bajío, which you can find in specialty shops and delis throughout the region.

MEALTIMES

Mexicans typically eat three meals each day, though there are few hard-and-fast rules when it comes to eating. Breakfast (*desayuno*) is usually a light morning meal, often accompanied by hot chocolate or coffee. A larger breakfast or brunch is called *almuerzo,* typically eaten a bit later than a regular breakfast. *Almuerzo* is often more substantial than a typical breakfast, though the term refers more to the hour it's eaten (around 11am) than the content.

The *comida,* or midday meal, is traditionally the largest and most important meal of the day, eaten around 2pm. A traditional *comida* begins with soup, followed by a pasta or rice course and finally a main course, served with tortillas or a basket of *bolillos* (white rolls). While you might not always find that exact lineup on the table, the Bajío region remains fairly traditional with regards to lunch. Families usually eat *comida* together, and there are still a number of small businesses that close 2pm-4pm to accommodate an afternoon break. On Sunday afternoons, it is typical to plan a large *comida* with friends and family.

Dinner is eaten late in the evening, typically around 8pm or 9pm, and is usually a lighter meal than lunch. Traditional dinners include tamales with *atole,* sweet breads with milk or coffee, or tacos. That said, in cities like Querétaro, San Miguel de Allende, and Guanajuato, going out for a big dinner is a popular activity.

REGIONAL FOOD

With its varied terrain and diverse local traditions, it's not surprising that Mexican food is highly regional. Certain states, like Oaxaca and Puebla, are known for their spectacular cuisine, but every state in Mexico distinguishes itself through local dishes and ingredients. Although it is an important agricultural center, the Bajío region has not been historically known as a culinary destination in Mexico. Nonetheless, there are a few dishes typical to the states of Guanajuato and Querétaro as well as ingredients that are produced locally and consumed more widely here than in other parts of Mexico. Notably, *enchiladas mineras* is a hearty dish of tortillas rolled around cheese, covered in a mild chile sauce, and then smothered in fried potatoes and carrots. A very similar dish called *enchiladas queretanas* is served in Querétaro, sans vegetables. There is also a growing organic and artisanal food movement in both Guanajuato and Querétaro states, where small-batch cheese, local wine, and organic fruits and vegetables are becoming increasingly common.

Many restaurants in San Miguel de Allende, Guanajuato, and Querétaro prepare traditional food from other states, giving the visitor an opportunity to sample Mexico's most iconic dishes. Some of Mexico's most interesting culinary traditions can be found in the southern states of Veracruz, Puebla, Oaxaca, and Yucatán. If you are interested in trying specialty foods, look out for popular Mexican dishes like *cochinita pibil* (shredded and seasoned pork from the Yucatán), *mole negro* (a chocolate-based sauce from Oaxaca), and *chiles en nogada* (poblano chile peppers stuffed with almonds, raisins, apples, dried fruit, cinnamon, and meat, then bathed in a creamy walnut sauce).

DRINKS

Delicious and refreshing, *aguas frescas* or *aguas de fruta* are a cheap and ubiquitous beverage throughout Mexico. Usually, these drinks are made with fresh fruit, water, and sugar, blended together with ice and then strained. The most popular *aguas* include tamarind, mango, lime, lemon, *jamaica* (hibiscus), and *horchata* (rice water with cinnamon). Fresh juice is sold at informal stands in the morning, as are *licuados* (shakes made with milk, sugar, and fruit).

Both coffee and chocolate are cultivated in Mexico and widely consumed as hot beverages. A popular option at many casual *fondas* and restaurants, *café de olla* is boiled coffee mixed with cinnamon and *piloncillo* (unrefined sugar). *Atole* is another popular beverage for the morning or evening, a hot drink made of cornstarch, sweeteners (like sugar or *piloncillo,* a type of unrefined sugar), and fruit or chocolate, often served alongside tamales.

Corona is the world's top-selling beer and one of a ubiquitous roster of national brews. Most Mexican beers are, like Corona, light lagers, though León and Negra Modelo are both amber. Though Mexican beers are often served with a lime in foreign countries, they are rarely so embellished in Mexico. If you like the lime taste, you may want to try a *michelada* (a beer served in a glass with ice, lime juice, Worcestershire sauce, hot sauce, and a salt rim) or a *cubana* (beer, ice, and lime juice with a salt rim).

Mexican beer was formerly dominated by two major conglomerates: Grupo Modelo (makers of Corona, Negra Modelo, Modelo Especial, León, Pacifico, and Victoria, among others) and Cervecería Cuauhtémoc Moctezuma (makers of Sol, Dos Equis, Bohemia, Carta Blanca, Indio, Tecate, and Superior). Smaller breweries have since gained tremendous momentum, however. Today many bars and restaurants carry small-batch beers as part of their bar menu— or exclusively. If you're a craft-beer aficionado, look for local producers like Dos Aves or Cervecería Allende from San Miguel de Allende, Chela Libre from Celaya, Hércules and Bocanegra from Querétaro, and Serrana from the Sierra de Guanajuato.

In addition to beer, Mexico is famous for tequila, a distilled liquor made from the sap of the agave cactus. Fine tequila is best sipped slowly from a tall shot glass, rather than downed in a single gulp. In many traditional bars and cantinas, you can order your tequila with *sangrita*, a popular chaser made of tomato juice and spices.

A cousin to tequila, mezcal is a spirit made from distilling maguey cactus. Unlike tequila, mezcal can be produced in any region and is rapidly gaining popularity throughout Mexico as well as overseas. While mezcal from the state of Oaxaca remains the gold standard, there are several popular mezcal producers in the state of Guanajuato; the most famous is Jaral de Berrio. Mezcal is often sipped, like tequila, accompanied by wedges of orange and salt, though you'll also find lots of mezcal cocktails on San Miguel de Allende and Guanajuato's drinks menus, rivaling the still-ubiquitous margarita.

Over the past couple of decades, vineyards in Baja California, Coahuila, and Aguascalientes have begun to produce some very nice and widely acclaimed wines. Today, the Bajío has begun to make inroads into the industry, with a number of vineyards

Atole is a sweetened drink that's often served with tamales.

operating in the states of Querétaro and Guanajuato. Cuna de Tierra, La Santisima Trinidad, Dos Buhos, Rancho Toyan, and Viñedos San Lucas are some of the nascent producers operating near San Miguel de Allende, with tasting rooms on-site; their bottles are occasionally available at restaurants or shops in town.

DESSERT

The most ubiquitous Mexican dessert is the famous flan, a thick egg custard that seems to be offered in every restaurant in the country. Other popular Mexican desserts include *pastel de tres leches* (three-milks cake) and *ate* (fruit paste) served with cheese. On the street, you'll often find ice creams (*nieves*) for sale in cups or cones. *Nieves* are made from a cream or water base and often incorporate fresh tropical fruits like mango or coconut. In addition to *nieves, paletas* (popsicles) made from real fruit, sugar, and, in some cases, milk are sold in small shops or on street corners throughout the country. A popular treat in San Miguel de Allende, churros are deep-fried pastry sticks doused in sugar and cinnamon, which you can buy from street vendors, at markets, or in cafés.

MARKETS

Since the pre-Columbian era, Mexicans have bought the majority of their food in *mercados* (markets). Throughout Mexico, markets are almost always the best place to buy fresh produce, artfully displayed in arranged stacks and sold at the lowest prices available. In addition to fruit and vegetable stands, food markets can be a good place to buy inexpensive grains and legumes, like dried beans, rice, hibiscus, lentils, and garbanzos, as well as Mexican cheeses and dairy products. Adventurous eaters may want to try some of the food prepared at a market's *fondas* and food stands.

Many visitors believe that bartering for a lower price is customary in Mexican markets; this is not necessarily the case in San Miguel de Allende and the surrounding region. Merchants will often offer a reasonable price for their goods, and it is unnecessary (and sometimes rude) to bargain. This is especially true for foodstuffs that are often very inexpensive to begin with. However, if you buy in bulk, a merchant may offer you a lower rate for the entire lot, or they may give you a papaya, fresh herbs, or another extra on the house.

Conduct and Customs

GREETINGS

When meeting someone for the first time or greeting acquaintances in Mexico, it is customary to make physical contact, rather than simply saying hello verbally. A handshake is the most common form of greeting in Mexico. Between male and female friends, or between two women, Mexicans will often greet each other with a single kiss on the cheek. Male friends may also give each other a quick hug. The same gestures are repeated when you say good-bye. When greeting a group of people, it is necessary to greet and shake hands with each person individually, rather than greeting the group together.

When speaking to an elder or to someone with whom you will have a professional relationship, it is customary to use the formal pronoun *usted* instead of the informal *tú*. Spanish language classes will often spend quite a bit of time explaining the difference between *usted* and *tú*, though most English-speaking tourists find themselves baffled by the distinction. Err on the side of caution by using *usted* when speaking to most people you don't know well or anyone older than you.

MANNERS

Mexicans are generally very polite when interacting with people they do not know well. In San Miguel de Allende, Guanajuato, and Querétaro, good manners are still practiced and appreciated. Most Mexicans are approving of those who make an effort to be polite but nonetheless very forgiving of foreign tourists who aren't familiar with the country's (sometimes arcane) customs.

When you sit down to eat in Mexico, it is customary to wish other diners *"Buen provecho"* before you dig in. *Buen provecho* is similar to the well-known French expression *bon appetit* and means, "Enjoy your meal." In small towns and even big cities, it is not uncommon to greet other diners when you enter a restaurant or to wish them a *buen provecho* as you come in or are leaving. Likewise, it is common courtesy to make eye contact and greet the salesperson when you enter a store. Commonly, Mexicans will say *disculpe* (forgive me) before asking a question of a salesperson or waiter.

When greeting someone, it is common practice to speak to that person using a polite

Para Todo Mal, Mezcal!
Para Todo Bien, Tambien!

A cousin to tequila, mezcal is a distilled spirit made from the maguey plant. Like tequila, mezcal is often served straight and sipped, traditionally accompanied by salt and lime or orange slices.

Mezcal is produced throughout Mexico, usually in small batches at family ranches. Varieties of mezcal from the state of Oaxaca are particularly well known, and many present a smoky flavor that comes from roasting the maguey leaves before distillation. In recent years, producers in Oaxaca and around the country have begun to bottle and export the spirit. However, it is still largely a cottage industry, produced in small batches and often bottled in recycled tequila bottles.

Mezcal is also produced in small batches throughout the state of Guanajuato. Guanajuato's mezcal has rather different characteristics than Oaxacan mezcal, usually taking on a more flowery or perfumed aroma. In addition, Guanajuato's producers often mix the liquor with water, giving it a smoother taste and lower alcohol content than the extremely potent Oaxacan version. (A special note to the squeamish: The famous worm found at the bottom of a bottle of Oaxaca's *mezcal de gusano* is never included in Guanajuato's variety.)

Mezcal is produced in small towns throughout the Bajío, including Santa Rosa de Lima near Guanajuato. However, the most famous mezcal from Guanajuato is made in the town of **Jaral de Berrio** (www.jaraldeberrio.com), which is in the northeast corner of the state. Lovingly referred to as JB, mezcal from this producer is served in bars and cantinas throughout the Bajío (ask for the house mezcal in any bar and JB is likely what you'll get).

Mezcal fanatics can also pick up a bottle for themselves, if they are willing to make the trek out to this teensy town. Bottles are sold in the strangely magnificent former hacienda in Jaral, off a dusty road near the highway from San Felipe, Guanajuato, to Villa de Reyes, San Luis Potosí. To get there, head north on Highway 51 from Dolores Hidalgo and then take the small state highway toward Villa de Reyes before entering downtown San Felipe. It's quite a trek, so take a GPS and company if you are making the drive for the first time.

When raising your glass of mezcal in a toast, you may feel inspired to utter the popular Mexican saying *"¡Para todo mal, mezcal! ¡Para todo bien, también!"* ("For everything bad, mezcal! For everything good, too!").

title, such as *señor* for a man, *señora* for a married or older woman, and *señorita* for a young woman. When speaking with a professional, Mexicans may also use the person's professional title, such as *doctor* or *doctora* (doctor), *arquitecto* (architect), or *ingeniero* (engineer). The title *licenciado* or *licenciada* is often used to address a college graduate, as a term of respect. In addition, the term *maestro* (master) can be used when addressing a skilled tradesman or a teacher.

On San Miguel de Allende and Guanajuato's narrow sidewalks, two pedestrians cannot always fit side by side. It is customary to step into the street to allow someone else to pass, especially when that person is elderly or carrying a child. If you have to squeeze past someone, you can say *"con permiso,"* which functions like "excuse me" in English.

PUNCTUALITY

The famous Mexican penchant for putting things off until *mañana* (tomorrow) does have an element of truth. Time is a bit less structured in Mexico, and it is common practice and not considered excessively rude to arrive a bit tardy for a social engagement. In a professional setting, however, punctuality is required.

TIPPING

In Mexico, tips are essential wages for workers in service industries. In many cases, tipping is required, and in every case it is appreciated.

In a restaurant, it is customary to tip the server 10-15 percent on the bill, though foreign tourists are generally expected to tip toward the higher end of that scale. In San Miguel de Allende, it is customary to tip 15-20 percent of the bill at a restaurant, especially in a sit-down restaurant. In bars, a 10 percent tip is standard. Though sometimes a customer may choose to leave a bit more or less based on the quality of the service, tipping is obligatory. European tourists who do not tip at home should be prepared to conform to Mexico's tipping standards.

In most cases, it is not necessary to tip a taxi driver when traveling within city limits, though tipping is always welcomed. If a taxi or shuttle service is taking you to the airport or to another city, a tip is customary and can be given at the passenger's discretion. Likewise, tour guides and transport services can be tipped at your discretion; in most cases, around 15 percent is appropriate.

At service stations, a small tip of about 5 percent is customary for gas station attendants (all gas stations are full service in Mexico); 20 to 40 pesos is usually sufficient. It is customary to tip porters at an airport or hotel between US$5-10, depending on the size of your load. Throughout Mexico, it is less common to tip the cleaning staff in a hotel. In San Miguel de Allende, however, it is common and usually expected.

DRINKING LAWS

Throughout Mexico, the legal drinking age is 18. Although it is not legal to drink on the street, you may see people take drinks outside during citywide parties. Drinking and driving is a serious offense in Mexico, though it remains a largely uncontrolled problem on the roads, where driving under the influence and drunk-driving-related accidents are not uncommon.

Dry laws (*ley seca*) are sometimes enacted on election days or, occasionally, during major holidays, like Independence Day (Sept. 16). In that case, liquor stores and bars may close early (or not open at all). The decision to enact dry laws is up to each municipality.

SMOKING

In 2008, smoking indoors at both restaurants and bars was prohibited throughout Mexico. While the law was heavily enforced when it first went into effect, it has become a bit looser with time. Usually restaurants and bars do not allow their customers to smoke in enclosed spaces (patios and sidewalks are still fair game), but some bars and music venues may be more lenient.

Health and Safety

There are few serious health and safety risks for visitors to San Miguel de Allende, Guanajuato, and Querétaro. With sensible precautions, visitors can enjoy a safe and comfortable trip to the region.

DOCTORS AND HOSPITALS

There are plenty of doctors, dentists, and hospitals in San Miguel de Allende, Guanajuato, and Querétaro, many of whom have extensive experience working with foreigners. It is usually fairly easy to locate competent, English-speaking doctors in the region.

In almost all cases, Mexican doctors and hospitals do not accept U.S. insurance. Medicaid is also not accepted in Mexico. If you will be in Mexico for an extended period and are concerned about health care, you can explore the options for international coverage. Fortunately, medicine in Mexico tends to be far less expensive than in other developed countries; in many cases, tourists can pay for their medical exams, associated lab tests, and prescription medication out of pocket. Hospitals will usually accept cash and credit cards, though private doctors are usually cash-only.

PRESCRIPTIONS AND PHARMACIES

Visitors to Mexico are permitted to carry prescription medication for a pre-existing condition among their personal effects. They can bring no more than three months' worth of medicine with them, and it should be accompanied by documentation from a doctor. (There can be strict penalties, including incarceration, for tourists who are suspected of drug abuse.) Most common over-the-counter medication is available in Mexico. Drugs in Mexico are regulated and safe; there are also generic brands.

If you need to purchase medication while you are in Mexico, you can visit a doctor who will write you a prescription. Most Mexican pharmacies sell the majority of medications without prescriptions, with the exception of certain oft-abused substances. However, it is usually a better idea to get a prescription for medication, as the brands may differ in Mexico and there can be penalties for those carrying medication without a prescription. Prescription medication is often a bit cheaper in Mexico than in the rest of North America or Europe.

Many pharmacies (*farmacias*) are open 24 hours a day, while others close in the evening. In smaller towns like San Miguel de Allende and Guanajuato, there is always at least one pharmacy open through the night to attend to emergencies.

COMMON CONCERNS
Altitude Sickness

The Bajío's average elevation is 6,500 feet (2,000 meters), and for some visitors, the altitude may require a short adjustment period. Altitude sickness, though rarely serious, can include symptoms like shortness of breath, dizziness, headaches, and nausea. If symptoms are severe or persist past a few days, see a doctor.

Gastrointestinal Distress

Some tourists experience gastrointestinal distress when traveling in Mexico for the first time. Changes in your eating and drinking habits, as well as a new overall environment, can cause unpleasant diarrhea, nausea, and vomiting. Because it often affects Mexico newcomers, gastrointestinal distress is called *turista,* which translates to "tourist" (it's also known as "traveler's diarrhea" in English). In many cases, *turista* can be effectively treated with a few days of rest, liquids, and antidiarrhea medication, such as Pepto-Bismol, Kaopectate, or Imodium. Although you cannot necessarily prevent *turista* from striking, you will have a better chance of faring comfortably through your vacation if you eat and drink in moderation, get plenty of sleep, and stay hydrated. Many visitors to the Bajío do not experience any stomach discomfort. More serious gastrointestinal problems can also occur in Mexico, though less frequently. If you are experiencing serious nausea, vomiting, and diarrhea, consult a doctor who can test and treat you for parasites or other gastrointestinal maladies.

Water Quality

Mexican tap water is treated; however, it is generally considered unsafe for drinking. Bottled water is readily available throughout Mexico and, like any bottled beverage, is safe to drink. If you will be staying in Mexico for an extended period, you can purchase large plastic jugs of purified water, called *garafones,* to be delivered to your home. You can also make tap water safe for drinking by boiling it for five minutes to kill any bacteria or parasites. Most grocery stores sell droplets to sterilize fruits and vegetables; these can be used to purify water, though the flavor may be affected.

Tap water is not served restaurants. Ice is made with purified water. Likewise, coffee, lemonades, and other drinks are always made with purified water.

The Bajío's Altitude

Situated atop a wide plain in the central Mexican plateau, the Bajío region doesn't feel like the mountains. There are no pine trees and granite peaks, just sun and cactus. However, at almost 2,000 meters (6,500 feet), San Miguel is as high as Lake Tahoe, California. In some cases, tourists forget that they are at altitude and may blame that queasy feeling on last night's tacos.

Altitude sickness can affect both young and old people, even those who are in good physical shape. Symptoms may include nausea, dizziness, loss of appetite, and fatigue. Keep an eye out for altitude sickness and take a few simple steps to increase your body's chances of a smooth acclimation.

- **Drink Lots of Water:** Bodies tend to lose water more quickly at higher altitudes. Stay hydrated throughout your trip.

- **Limit Coffee and Cocktails:** It's best to avoid drinks that can dehydrate you, especially alcohol and caffeine.

- **Don't Push It:** Take it easy during your first few days in the Bajío. Let your body adjust to the altitude before heading off to a horseback riding adventure or a hike in the countryside.

- **Eat Light:** Doctors recommend avoiding heavy foods when you first arrive at a higher altitude. Have smaller meals and stick to lighter foods and carbohydrates.

- **Stay Alert:** Altitude sickness is rarely serious; however, if symptoms don't improve after a day or two, see a doctor.

Food Safety

When eating raw fresh vegetables and some fruits, it is common practice to disinfect them before consumption. In some cases, leafy vegetables may contain residual bacteria from watering or handling. For raw consumption, supermarkets sell several varieties of food sanitizer, the most common of which are made with chloride bleach or colloidal silver. If you plan to cook your vegetables, you do not need to disinfect them; just rinse them in water. The heat will kill any potentially harmful substances.

Most restaurants in the Bajío will sterilize raw vegetables served for salads or other dishes. Nonetheless, some visitors experience gastrointestinal distress after consuming raw vegetables. If you are in the Bajío for a short vacation, you may want to err on the side of caution and avoid raw vegetables or only consume vegetables that have been sterilized. There is always more risk associated with food stands located outdoors or in marketplaces, where hygiene is more difficult to maintain.

Some people consume street food with no incident; others become ill after eating in markets or on the street. Use your discretion, and introduce new foods into your diet slowly.

Infectious Disease

Hepatitis A is more common in developing nations than in industrialized ones. It affects the liver and is contracted from food or water infected with fecal matter. Vaccines are available to protect against hepatitis A infection. Symptoms may resemble the flu, though they are severe and may last several months.

There has been a recent surge in cases of dengue fever in Mexico, though mostly along the coast; it remains a very limited problem in the central highlands. In the Bajío, there were only a few cases of dengue in León, Guanajuato, in 2007. Nonetheless, the government has launched an extensive campaign against mosquito proliferation, which includes a periodic check of residences and their water storage systems as well as occasional insecticide spraying. The only way to prevent dengue infection is to avoid mosquito bites.

H1N1, or swine flu, was a major health concern in Mexico in the spring of 2008. There were more than 250 cases in the state of Guanajuato, with more than 50 confirmed cases in San Miguel de Allende. Since then, news of H1N1 has disappeared from the region. You may still notice hand sanitizers at the entryway in restaurants, and, of course, it is always best practice to wash your hands before eating. However, H1N1 is no longer a major health concern.

Creepy Crawlers

Mosquitoes are a common nuisance during the summer months, especially close to bodies of water or large gardens. Most serious mosquito-borne illnesses (such as malaria or dengue) are unusual in the mountainous areas around San Miguel de Allende. However, their itchy bite makes this pest a serious nuisance.

Scorpions live in the Bajío, and they occasionally turn up indoors. In most cases, scorpion stings are painful but not fatal. The exception is in and around the city of León, where a highly venomous scorpion can be found. Under any circumstance, consult a doctor if you are stung by a scorpion. Most scorpions are reclusive and avoid human contact. To avoid encountering them, shake out your shoes in the morning before you put them on, and use care moving bookcases or other furniture with its back to the wall.

Spiders are also common in the Bajío, including the poisonous black widow. Black widows are shiny black with a red hourglass on their abdomen. Like scorpions, black widows are generally reclusive. They may hide in wood piles, fields, or quiet corners. Though they rarely kill healthy adults, they can be a risk to children, the elderly, or pets. If bitten by a black widow, consult a doctor.

CRIME

The Bajío is a relatively safe region where the most common crimes are petty theft and break-ins. Nonetheless, visitors should take the same precautions when traveling as they would in any foreign country: Avoid traveling alone at night, don't carry excessive amounts of cash, and remain aware of your surroundings.

Though things are generally quiet in San Miguel, there have been a few high-profile crime stories in recent years. In 2014, there was a flurry of news when drug lord Hector Beltran Leyva was apprehended at a seafood restaurant in San Miguel de Allende, and there have been some notable organized-crime-related kidnappings in the region. The leader of the criminal ring associated with these kidnappings (which was, incredibly, tied to a group of Chilean fugitives, not the drug trade, as many had assumed) was apprehended in 2017.

Other than these much-discussed events, San Miguel de Allende, Guanajuato, and Querétaro have not been caught in much crossfire from the drug wars, and tourist areas are rarely affected by violent crime. Guanajuato, in particular, is one of the safest cities in Mexico. Even so, visitors should take the time to familiarize themselves with the contemporary political and social situation before they visit. In addition, the **U.S. Department of State** (www.travel.state.gov) publishes up-to-date travel advisories for each state in the Republic.

In the case that you have been arrested for a crime in Mexico, contact your embassy. International law requires that the Mexican government contact a foreigner's embassy at their request. However, foreign citizens may still be tried and held accountable under Mexican law for any crimes committed in Mexico.

Alternative Lodging Options

Both **Airbnb** (www.airbnb.mx) and **VRBO** (www.vrbo.com) have a robust presence in San Miguel de Allende, with properties that run the gamut from simple dorm-style accommodations to multi-bedroom mansions with cleaning service, views, and swimming pools. If you are coming with a group, renting a multi-bedroom vacation home may be a more economical option than staying in a hotel. That said, in San Miguel de Allende, many vacation homes are luxury properties and renting through Airbnb or VRBO won't necessarily cost you less than a hotel; however, you may get more space, a kitchen, and other comforts with properties on Airbnb. Note that popular Airbnb properties often sell out long before hotel rooms; if you'd like to stay in a vacation rental, book in advance.

In addition, there are a couple of rental agencies and real estate companies that have been managing short-term home rentals in San Miguel de Allende for years, and they continue to be a good resource for those looking to rent a home, even as Airbnb and VRBO dominate the local market. Some of the town's most luxurious properties are only listed with these agents, and the agents can also arrange airport pickup or other guest services.

In the city of Guanajuato, where hotels are surprisingly expensive, Airbnb can be an excellent option. Airbnb has a robust presence in the city center, and shared and private homes offered through the service generally rent for a far lower nightly price than a hotel. Many are also much nicer than the hotels in town, boasting views, balconies, or patios in addition to prime locations in the city center. That said, some properties can only be reached via a rigorous uphill walk; if you have a limited range of movement, inquire about the home's location and accessibility when booking. As with hotels and more traditional accommodation, book your Airbnb far in advance if you are visiting Guanajuato during the Festival Internacional Cervantino.

In downtown Querétaro, where there are few hotels in the budget category, renting a room or apartment through Airbnb can be a good option for travelers. Though prices here run higher than those in Guanajuato, they are likewise a good value when compared to the cost of hotels and particularly appropriate for longer stays.

Travel Tips

WHAT TO PACK

San Miguel de Allende has a year-round temperate climate, which doesn't call for any special clothing or gear. The one exception is footwear. San Miguel de Allende, Guanajuato, and Querétaro have colonial-era downtown districts crisscrossed by uneven cobblestone streets. They can be quite slick, especially in the rain, and it is not unusual for visitors to slip or sprain an ankle while momentarily distracted by a beautiful 18th-century bell tower. For sightseeing, bring comfortable shoes that are good for walking.

When packing, keep in mind that the dry, semiarid climate means that temperatures fluctuate significantly from morning to midday to evening. In the winter months, temperatures can drop below freezing at night. Bring layers and, if you are visiting in the summer, an umbrella and waterproof shoes. Dress code is generally casual, even at the nicest establishments. At the same time, the Bajío is not the beach, so tourists in excessively summery outfits (shorts, bathing suits, sarongs, and the like) may stand out a bit.

If you plan on doing a little shopping in San Miguel de Allende, bring along your checkbook in addition to bank cards and credit cards. Surprisingly, many small businesses will accept checks from U.S. banks, even if they don't accept credit cards.

MONEY
Currency

Mexico's currency is the peso. However, in San Miguel de Allende, many shops, hotels, and even some restaurants will accept U.S. dollars. In most cases, a shop will list both prices, though on occasion, you will see prices listed simply in dollars; both currencies are denoted with a $ sign. Clearly, the arrangement can lead to confusion for San Miguel's shoppers, who aren't sure if an item is surprisingly cheap or incredibly expensive. (Restaurant menu prices are almost always listed exclusively in pesos.)

Exchanging Money

For most visitors to Mexico, the most common and efficient way to change money is by using a foreign bank card at an ATM. Banks and credit unions generally offer the day's best exchange rates (often posted at the bank's entrance). Most international bank cards are accepted at Mexican banks, though it is always advisable to call your bank at home before attempting to withdraw money or use a credit card in a foreign country. When using your ATM card, always choose an official bank rather than a stand-alone ATM in a shop or mall; there have been reports of ATM and credit card numbers being stolen and used for illicit withdrawals in Mexico.

You can also change foreign currency to pesos at a *casa de cambio* (exchange house). There are *casas de cambio* in the *centro histórico* in both San Miguel de Allende and Guanajuato. Be aware, however, that the Mexican government is attempting to reduce crime and fraud by limiting the amount of money that a customer can change in a single day. If you might need a large sum of money, plan ahead or use travelers checks.

Travelers Checks and Credit Cards

Until recently, Mexico was still largely a cash culture. Nowadays, it's far more common for even small shops or businesses to accept credit cards. That said, some small hotels and restaurants, especially those of the budget variety, do not take credit cards. At traditional markets or street stands, cash is the only form of payment. At the same time, credit cards are widely accepted for large purchases, at gas stations, in shops, and in upscale restaurants. (In some cases, shop owners will give you a discounted price if you pay with cash or, conversely, charge you a bit more if you pay with a card.) To rent a car, a credit card is required.

Travelers checks are an alternative to cash and can be useful if you need to change a lot of money in a single day. The drawback is that travelers checks cannot be changed everywhere and may not be accepted at restaurants or shops in Mexico. However, most travelers checks can be changed in many Banamex branches.

SHOPPING

When shopping at most shops and boutiques in the Bajío, it is not common practice to bargain or ask for lower prices on goods. In some stores, vendors may offer a small discount for bulk purchases or for cash payments, but these are offered at the shop owner's discretion. In general, shoppers should not expect employees at a brick-and-mortar store to lower prices on their goods.

However, you may be able to negotiate the price on an expensive antique or a work of art, particularly in San Miguel de Allende. This is particularly true if you are buying multiple pieces from a single store or artist. In that case, it is acceptable to inquire about flexibility in the price. That said, prices are rarely marked up significantly, so don't be too insistent after you've reached a vendor's limit.

In an artisan or craft market, such as the craft market in central San Miguel de Allende, prices for goods may be more flexible. It is customary to ask the vendor for the price of the item (they are rarely marked with price tags), and the vendor may then offer you a lower price as you think it over. This is particularly true for large purchases. In general, these discounts are not significant (don't expect to pay half of the price initially quoted) and aggressive haggling is not common, nor is it particularly fruitful. If you do wish to bargain on a price, do so politely.

Do not bargain at food markets, even if you are buying a substantial quantity. Usually, the prices at food markets are very low to begin with, and few vendors can afford to drop their price further. In some cases, a vendor will offer a something extra (say, a papaya or a pineapple) to a buyer who makes a large purchase at their stand.

COMMUNICATIONS
Internet Access

Mexico is wired. Internet cafés are scattered throughout the center of any large or medium-size city, including Guanajuato, San Miguel de Allende, Dolores Hidalgo, and Querétaro. You may find fewer services in very small towns like Pozos. Otherwise, getting connected is rarely a problem. Those who travel with their laptop or smartphone will also find ample wireless service in cafés, public libraries, and hotels.

Shipping and Postal Service

The Mexican post office will ship letters, postcards, and packages to any location in the world. They offer insured as well as expedited shipping services. The Mexican post is by far your cheapest mailing option, but it is not renowned for its reliability—use it for nonessential communication and never for time-sensitive documents. For expedited shipping, **MexPost** (www.correosdemexico.com.mx), a division of the government-operated postal service, will offer faster service at a higher (but still accessible) price. MexPost's services are generally more reliable than the standard post.

In addition, many major shipping companies offer shipping services within Mexico and internationally, including Estafeta, DHL, Redpack, UPS, and FedEx.

Media

Large media conglomerates control the majority of Mexico's communication channels. Televisa Group is the largest and most powerful media company, operating several television stations, radio stations, sports teams, and record labels. In addition to privately owned stations, the government runs two public television stations available on a limited basis throughout the republic.

In San Miguel de Allende, taxi drivers will often tune in to XESQ (103.3 FM, http://xesqradiosanmiguelallende.com), a local AM

a newsstand in central Guanajuato

By the Numbers

- **Time Zone:** The hours in San Miguel de Allende, Guanajuato, and Querétaro correspond to the Central Standard Time zone in the United States, six hours behind Greenwich mean time. Since 1996, all Mexican states except Sonora have participated in **daylight saving time,** though clocks may not fall back or spring forward on the same weekend as in the U.S. and Canada.

- **Electricity:** Like the United States and Canada, Mexico uses 110 volts 60 cycles. It can be useful to bring a socket adapter with your computer, since many Mexican outlets only allow for a two-prong plug.

- **Weights and Measures:** Mexico uses the metric system for all measurements, including temperature, distance, weight, and volume.

- **Climate:** Average high temperatures range 21-29°C (70-85°F) year-round. Average lows run 7-14°C (44-58°F).

- **Population Distribution:** In the states of Guanajuato and Querétaro, 70 percent of the population lives in cities; 30 percent is rural.

radio station that broadcasts local news and special programming. The excellent **Radio Universidad** (www.radiouniversidad.ugto.mx) covers news and cultural events, as well as music, at 970 AM or 100 FM in Guanajuato. From San Miguel de Allende, Radio Universidad is on the dial at 91.3 FM.

Local and national newspapers and news magazines cover current events. In the Bajío, there are several papers published in the cities of Guanajuato, Celaya, León, and Querétaro, which cover local news and politics. Published in the city of Guanajuato, the Spanish-language newspaper **Correo** (http://periodicocorreo.com.mx) covers news, arts, and culture for the entire region. You can also get news about the state of Guanajuato from newspapers **El Sol del Bajío** (www.elsoldelbajio.com.mx), published in Celaya, and **am** (www.am.com.mx) from León. In Querétaro, *El Diario de Querétaro* is among the largest papers, though the city also has special Querétaro-specific editions of the national newspaper *El Universal*. In addition, national dailies are distributed in all of the Bajío's major towns, including the Mexico City papers *El Universal, Reforma,* and *La Jornada*.

In San Miguel de Allende, the bilingual weekly **Atención San Miguel** (www.

atencionsanmiguel.org) is a must-read for coverage of arts and cultural events in town as well as a bit of news. For arts essays and excellent coverage of cultural events in Guanajuato, get a copy of the magazine **Polen** (www.extension.ugto.mx), published by the Universidad de Guanajuato.

TIME ZONE

San Miguel de Allende, Guanajuato, and the Bajío are on Central Standard Time. Along with every Mexican state except Sonora, the region participates in the national daylight saving time (DST) program. Usually, DST begins in the spring and terminates in the fall, roughly around the same time as in the United States, though rarely on the exact same date.

OPPORTUNITIES FOR STUDY AND EMPLOYMENT

San Miguel de Allende, Guanajuato, and Querétaro are all excellent places for beginners to learn Spanish. The region is friendly and safe, and there are many language schools in Guanajuato as well as several schools in San Miguel de Allende and Querétaro.

In addition to Spanish-language programs, San Miguel de Allende is a great place to take art classes. Many working artists in San Miguel de Allende give classes in disciplines like watercolor, ceramics, oil painting, printmaking, and jewelry-making. There is also the well-reputed Centro Cultural Ignacio Ramírez, where students can take classes in a variety of disciplines (though the school does not confer certificates or degrees). The Instituto Allende confers undergraduate degrees in art to Mexican students and offers continuing education classes for adults.

Students who plan to take classes in Mexico for six months or less can use a standard tourist visa. If you will be studying for more than six months at an accredited school, it may be easier and more efficient to apply for a student visa. Student visas can be processed either at a Mexican consulate overseas or at a local immigration office in Mexico.

Self-Employment

Many foreigners work and own businesses in San Miguel de Allende and Guanajuato, where you'll find a slew of American- and Canadian-owned restaurants, bars, galleries, bookshops, and boutiques as well as a smattering of business owners from Europe and Asia. Mexico will also extend self-employment benefits to temporary resident visa holders who wish to open their own business. In many cases, it is easier to open your own business—or give independent language or art classes—than to find employment through another source. To be eligible for this type of visa, foreigners must have proof of foreign income in addition to demonstrable skills in the field in which they plan to work (such as a degree in English or a TOEFL certificate for a language teacher).

Foreign Employers

Foreigners may be employed by a Mexican- or foreign-owned business; however, foreign employees must be sponsored by their employer, who will assist with the visa application process at immigration. In most cases, Mexico will extend employment visas to foreigners with special skills that are not available within the local population. For example, native speakers of English can seek employment in a bilingual school. In order to be eligible for an employment visa, foreigners must present all necessary documentation for a tourist visa as well as documentation of their skill, such as a university diploma or a certificate in teaching English as a second language. In most cases, a school or other business that routinely employs foreigners will be familiar with the visa application process.

Volunteer Work

There are many opportunities for rewarding volunteer work in San Miguel de Allende and Guanajuato, whether you like working with people, animals, or the environment. Several U.S. universities operate rural assistance programs for college-age volunteers, and there are several summer programs operated by international charities, such as Amigos de las Americas. In addition, many local nonprofit organizations welcome part-time volunteers. For students, several of Guanajuato's Spanish-language schools operate volunteer programs at local charities, which can be an excellent way to learn more about the local culture and continue improving your Spanish skills. Cacomixtle, an adventure and tourism company based in Guanajuato, also runs excellent volunteer programs.

The Mexican Constitution prohibits foreigners from participating in political activities, including demonstrations. Breaking this law can result in deportation. If you are volunteering in Mexico, refrain from attending political demonstrations.

ACCESS FOR TRAVELERS WITH DISABILITIES

San Miguel de Allende and Guanajuato can be difficult places for travelers with disabilities, especially those with limited range of movement. The colonial cities of the Bajío were built hundreds of years ago, and their streets are often narrow and uneven. There are few sidewalk ramps or elevators in old colonial buildings, even at the entrance of public

Kid-Friendly San Miguel

With its bright colors, festive atmosphere, and kid-friendly attitude, San Miguel can be a wonderful place to visit with your family. If you are bringing your tots to San Miguel, here are some ways to spend your time.

At the **Biblioteca de San Miguel de Allende,** a nonprofit cultural center and library, kids can find books in English and Spanish, or participate in one of the many children's programs or movies (often in Spanish).

San Miguel de Allende is a wonderful place to introduce children to Mexican culture. For a diverting look into the history of Mexican toys, take the family to **La Esquina: Museo del Jugete Popular Mexicano,** which features a wonderful collection of antique handmade toys, like rocking horses, whistles, and dolls. Kids can pick out their own classic toys in the museum gift shop.

Ford streams and explore canyons on a horseback ride with **Coyote Canyon Adventures** or **Rancho Xotolar,** or head out for an off-road mountain biking excursion with **Bici-Burro.** Teenagers can take an ATV tour of the surrounding countryside or buzz around town on a rented four-wheeler.

Mexico is a great place to visit with children.

In the *jardín* in San Miguel de Allende, life recalls an older and more wholesome era. Throngs of kids bounce balls along the cobblestones, long lines await the ice cream vendor, and police officers on horseback snap photos with wee ones. In **Parque Juárez,** there is always a crowd of tots on the playground in the afternoon.

There is no better place to spend a summer afternoon than at one of the many swimming spots around town. With numerous warm spring-fed pools, big lawns, and an on-site restaurant, **La Gruta** is an excellent place to spend a day relaxing with the kids. For waterslides and big swimming pools, take the family to **Xote,** on the highway toward Dolores Hidalgo.

Children are generally welcomed in San Miguel restaurants, and there are several places that are particularly family-friendly. Live music, solicitous service, and cheesy pizza make **Mama Mía** a good choice for kids, while the varied menu and tasty fries at **Hecho en Mexico** are guaranteed to please younger palates. Get double scoops of the flavorful ice cream on San Miguel's street corners, or take a trip to Dolores Hidalgo, where *nieves* are served in wacky flavors like shrimp or avocado.

Not all bed-and-breakfasts in San Miguel de Allende accept children, so parents should check the hotel's policy before making reservations. Fortunately for families, there are numerous places great for kids, boasting big grounds and private pools. **Rancho Hotel Atascadero** has tennis courts, pools, and gardens as well as larger suites that accommodate the kids in loft beds.

institutions and museums. The situation is changing, slowly. During renovations, most public buildings will simultaneously make entryways more accessible, and some newer luxury hotels, like the Rosewood Hotel in San Miguel de Allende, are equipped with elevators to all floors.

If you are in a wheelchair or have trouble walking, the easiest place to visit is Querétaro, where the city center is flat, most sights are at ground level, and the government has made a more visible effort to accommodate travelers with disabilities.

People in this part of Mexico are ceaselessly

friendly and courteous, and most are willing to lend a hand as necessary. Many senior citizens with limited range of movement are able to comfortably visit San Miguel de Allende, and many others make their home there.

TRAVELING WITH CHILDREN

San Miguel de Allende, Guanajuato, and Querétaro are wonderful places to travel with your family. On the whole, children are well-loved members of Mexican society, and they are generally treated kindly in restaurants, museums, and other public places across the region. Mexico's many urban parks and public squares are a bonanza for little ones, who are often free to run wild amid trees and crowds. There are plenty of family friendly activities in the region, like horseback riding and swimming, as well as plenty of places to take classes in the Spanish language. If you are planning to stay in a hotel with your children, be aware that some bed-and-breakfasts in San Miguel de Allende do not allow children under a certain age.

Many foreign children, mostly from the United States and Canada, live in San Miguel de Allende. In San Miguel de Allende, there are several bilingual private schools that have significant foreign enrollment. Over the summer, there are several day camps for local and international kids as well as Spanish classes for children at local language schools. The library and municipal government often host events and movies for children in San Miguel de Allende; however, most of this programming is in Spanish.

Remember that, like adults, children must have a valid passport to be admitted to Mexico, even if they are accompanied by a parent. In order to combat child trafficking and kidnapping, Mexico requires that a parent accompany a non-Mexican minor when leaving the country. If the child is traveling with a relative or other adult guardian, he or she must have an official letter of consent authorizing the child's travel plans.

TRAVELING WITH PETS

Dog and cat lovers will meet many like minds in Mexico, where pets are popular and beloved parts of the family. That said, traveling with a pet can be more complicated, especially if you are planning to stay in hotels. Few inns or bed-and-breakfasts welcome pets, so you should make reservations for yourself and your pet in advance. In San Miguel de Allende, the Rosewood Hotel, Hotel Matilda, and L'Otel all accept pets, though note that these are high-end establishments; in many cases, it can be harder to find a place for your pet in budget accommodations. If you have trouble locating a pet-friendly hotel, consider a rental house or apartment, which may have a more liberal pet policy.

Pets are generally not permitted in the coaches of Mexico's bus lines, though hardy canines may travel in the luggage compartment below the bus, an unpleasant but practical option for some pet owners. Many rental car companies and tour operators will permit an animal in their vehicles, though they may charge an additional fee. Airport shuttles and taxis will also often allow pets. Travelers should check individually if they plan to bring their dog or cat on the road.

WOMEN TRAVELING ALONE

San Miguel de Allende, Guanajuato, Querétaro, and environs are generally safe for solo female travelers. A lone female rarely warrants any special attention from locals, and most people treat women with respect. Hundreds if not thousands of women travel unaccompanied to San Miguel de Allende each year, and even more foreign women live alone in town. At the same time, a woman traveling alone should take basic precautions, especially when out at night.

SENIOR TRAVELERS

The whole Bajío region, especially San Miguel de Allende, is a welcoming place for older travelers. The cobblestone streets and many hills in San Miguel can make the city a bit more challenging to traverse on foot for anyone with limited mobility, and all visitors to San Miguel must be careful not to twist their knee or ankle on the uneven streets. Beyond these small problems, many senior travelers have a comfortable and rewarding experience visiting San Miguel.

GAY AND LESBIAN TRAVELERS

Despite the region's reputation as very conservative and largely Catholic, people in the Bajío are socially tolerant and accepting. Gay and lesbian travelers are unlikely to experience discrimination from locals, especially in larger cities. In the cosmopolitan small towns of San Miguel de Allende and Guanajuato, the population is markedly more open-minded than the region's conservative reputation would lead you to believe. There is a relatively large and visible gay population in San Miguel, made up of both local and foreign residents. While public displays of affection between same-sex couples are relatively uncommon, gay couples will rarely experience negative reactions from locals.

Resources

Glossary

adobado: chile seasoning or marinade

aduana: customs

aeropuerto: airport

agave: large Mexican succulent plant

agave azul: blue agave, used in tequila production

agua: water

aguas frescas or *aguas de fruta:* cold fruit drink

alebrije: hand-painted copal wood animals and figurines from Oaxaca.

almuerzo: meal eaten around midday

andador: pedestrian walkway

antigüedades: antiques

antojitos: snacks or appetizers

arquitecto: architect

arrachera: Mexican skirt steak

arte: art

artesanía: traditional handicraft

atole: a sweet and hot beverage made with corn flour

autobús: bus

autopista: highway

ayuntamiento: town council

azulejo: tile

Bajío: a geographical region that encompasses the states of Guanajuato and Querétaro as well as segments of the states of Jalisco and Michoacán.

Ballet Folklórico: a traditional Mexican dance troupe from Mexico City

banco: bank

baño: bathroom

barbacoa: pit-cooked lamb

biblioteca: library

bolillo: white roll

bomberos: firefighters

botana: appetizer

buen provecho: an expression used to say "enjoy your meal"

burro: donkey

caballo: horse

café: coffee

café con leche: coffee with milk

café de olla: boiled coffee with unrefined sugar and cinnamon

caldo: broth

caldo tlalpeño: chicken and chipotle soup

calle: street

callejón: alley

callejoneadas: famous traveling minstrel shows in Guanajuato

calzada: road

camión: bus

cantina: traditional bar or drinking establishment

capilla: chapel

carnitas: braised pork

carretera: highway

casa: house

casa de cambio: exchange house

casita: small house

castillo: castle

catrina: skeleton figurine or drawing dressed as an aristocrat; originally invented by artist José Guadalupe Posada

cempasúchil: marigold

centro histórico: historical district

cerveza: beer

chal: shawl

charro: traditional Mexican cowboy or horseman

Chichimeca: A name used by the Spanish during the early colonial era to describe the nomadic tribes of Northern Mexico

chilango: Mexico City resident

chilaquiles: fried tortilla strips bathed in salsa, cream, and cheese

chiles en nogada: poblano pepper stuffed with meat, dried fruit, and nuts, covered in creamed walnut sauce, and sprinkled with pomegranate seeds

chiles rellenos: stuffed chile peppers

chipotle: a smoky dried chile pepper, derived from fresh jalapeño pepper

chorro: spring

churro: a tube-shaped sweet bread, deep fried and dusted in sugar

clínica: clinic

cochinita pibil: Yucatecan-style pulled pork

comida: the large midday meal in Mexico, typically eaten around 2pm

comida corrida: an economical, set-price lunch served in restaurants

concha: a sweet roll topped with sugar

consulado: consulate

convento: convent

corregidor: magistrate, in the colonial era

correo: postal service

corrida de toros: bullfight

cotija: an aged Mexican cheese

criollo: a term used in New Spain to describe a Mexican-born person of Spanish descent

Cruz Roja: Red Cross

cuaresma: Lent

cuatrimoto: all-terrain vehicle (ATV)

cultura: culture

cumbia: a traditional musical style from Colombia

desayuno: breakfast

Día de Muertos: Day of the Dead

Distrito Federal: Federal District, former official name of Mexico City

dulces: sweets

dulces típicos: traditional Mexican sweets

El Gran Chichimeca: In the colonial era, the name given to the Northern Mexican region, including the Bajío, by Spanish settlers

embajada: embassy

enchiladas mineras: cheese-stuffed tortillas in *guajillo* sauce with sautéed potatoes and carrots

enchiladas verdes: stuffed tortillas bathed in green salsa

enmoladas: tortillas in mole sauce

entrada: appetizer

equipal: traditional wood and pigskin furniture style from Jalisco

escuela: school

español: Spanish

farmacia: pharmacy

feria: fair

festival: festival

fiesta: party

fiestas patrias: patriotic holidays

flan: egg custard dessert

flauta: deep-fried and stuffed tortilla, topped with cream and salsa

FMM: forma migratoria multiple (tourist card)

fonda: casual restaurant

gachupín: Spanish person

galería: gallery

gomita: gumdrop

gordita: stuffed corn cake

gringa: a flour tortilla filled with melted cheese and meat

gringo: American

guanabana: soursop, a tropical fruit

guayaba: guava

guisado: stew or side dish

hacienda: estate

hojalatería: tinwork

horchata: traditional drink made with ground rice, sugar, and water

huarache: torpedo-shaped corn flatbread; also, a sandal

Huasteca: Mexican region comprising northern Veracruz, southern Tamaulipas, a portion of San Luis Potosí, and the Sierra Gorda in Querétaro

huevo: egg

huevos a la mexicana: eggs scrambled with tomato, onion, and chile pepper

huevos rancheros: fried eggs in tomato-chile sauce

huipil: traditional women's tunic from Southern Mexico

huitlacoche: corn fungus

iglesia: church

indígena: indigenous person, or indigenous (adj.)

ingeniero: engineer

instituto: institute

jamaica: hibiscus

jamoncillo: flavored milk-fudge

jarcería: shop selling home and cleaning products

jardín: garden

joyería: jewelry

Las Mañanitas: Mexico's birthday song

lavandería: laundry

La Vía Dolorosa: Stations of the Cross

ley seca: dry law

librería: bookstore

licenciado: college graduate

licuado: milk or fruit shake

longaniza: a type of sausage

maciza: in carnitas, pork shoulder or leg

maestro: master; teacher

maguey: large succulent plant common in Mexico

majolica: tin-glazed pottery, originally from Italy

mañana: tomorrow; morning

manta: lightweight cotton fabric frequently used in traditional Mexican clothing

mantilla: lace or silk scarf

maquiladora: manufacturing plant

mariachi: a traditional Mexican music ensemble

menudo: beef stomach soup

mercado: market

mesquite: mesquite tree

mestizo: a person of mixed ethnic heritage

mezcal: distilled spirit made from the maguey plant

mezcal de gusano: mezcal distilled with the maguey worm

michelada: beer served with lime juice, salt, hot sauce, and Worcestershire sauce

migajas: pork drippings

migración: immigration

milagritos: small tin ornaments

mixiote: lamb steamed in agave leaf

mole: flavorful sauce made of ground nuts and spices

mole negro: ground sauce made of chocolate, nuts, and spices from the state of Oaxaca

momia: mummy

montalayo: lamb stomach

mordida: literally, bite; slang for bribe

museo: museum

Navidad: Christmas

nevería: ice cream parlor

nieve: ice cream

norteño: northern

novena: nine days of prayer or worship

órgano: organ

oro: gold

Otomí: indigenous ethnic group of central Mexico

palenqueta: honey-covered disc of nuts or seeds

paleta: popsicle

pan: bread

pan dulce: sweet bread

panela: a variety of fresh cheese

panteón: cemetery

papadzules: Yucatecan tacos stuffed with hard-boiled egg

papel picado: decorative cut-paper adornments

parque: park

parroquia: parish church

partido: political party

Partido Acción Nacional: National Action Party

Partido de la Revolución Democrática: Party of the Democratic Revolution

Partido Revolucionario Institucional: Institutional Revolutionary Party

pascua: Easter

pasilla: a mild but flavorful dried chile pepper

pastor: taco preparation using chile pepper and spices

Pemex: Petroleos Mexicanos (Mexican Petroleum)

peña: rock

peninsular: colonial-era term for a person born in Spain

peso: Mexico's currency

petate: woven rush mat

picadillo: spiced ground beef

pico de gallo: salsa made of chopped tomatoes, onion, cilantro, and chile peppers

pipián: a sauce made of ground pumpkin seeds and spices

plata: silver

plaza: plaza or public square

plaza de toros: bullring

plazuela: small plaza

poblano: from the state or the city of Puebla

Porfiriato: historical period during the presidency of Porfirio Díaz

posada: inn

pozo: well

pozole: hominy soup

presa: reservoir

presidente municipal: municipal president

priista: member of the PRI political party

Protección Civil: Civil Protection, or police

pueblo: small town

pulque: alcoholic drink made from fermented maguey sap

puntas de filete: beef tips

querétense: something or someone from Querétaro

quesadilla: a warmed tortilla stuffed with cheese

queso: cheese

queso de tuna: prickly pear cheese, a regional sweet

queso fundido: melted cheese

ranchera: musical style from Northern Mexico

raspado: shaved ice

rebozo: shawl

reggaeton: modern musical style based on reggae

rentistas: visa designation for foreigners who live but do not earn money in Mexico

requesón: ricotta-style cheese

residente permanente: immigrant visa

residente temporal: nonimmigrant resident visa

restaurante: restaurant

retablo: devotional painting

río: river

salsa roja: condiment made with red tomatoes and chile peppers, or red chile peppers

salsa verde: condiment made with green tomatoes, chile peppers, and spices

sangrita: a tomato-based chaser for tequila

santa escuela: a Jesuit school in the colonial era

Semana Santa: Holy Week

señor: Mr.; sir; man

señora: Mrs., madam; woman

señorita: Miss; young woman

serape: traditional Mexican wool shawl or cloak

serrano: variety of green chile pepper

siesta: nap

sombrero: hat

sopa: soup

sopa azteca: tortilla soup

sope: thick, round corn flatbread

surtido: mixed

taco: seasoned meat or vegetables enclosed in a warm tortilla

tacos dorados: deep-fried tacos

Talavera: hand-painted majolica-style pottery from Puebla, Mexico

tamal: tamale, or steamed corn cake (plural: tamales)

tarifa: fee, cost (as in the cost of a night in a hotel)

teatro: theater

templo: temple, church

Tenochtitlan: capital city of Mesoamerica at the time of the Spanish conquest

tequila: a Mexican distilled spirit made from blue agave

tintorería: dry cleaner

tlayuda: a large Oaxacan tortilla stuffed with beans and cheese

torta: hot sandwich served on a white roll

transito: transit

tranvía: trolley

tú: you (informal)

tuna: prickly pear fruit

turismo: tourism

turista: tourist or traveler's diarrhea

universidad: university

usted: you (formal)

verano: summer

viceroy: colonial governor

Viernes Santo: Good Friday

vino: wine

vino tinto: red wine

visa: visa
xoconostle: sour prickly pear fruit
zapote: sapodilla, a tropical fruit

ABBREVIATIONS

Col.: *colonia* (neighborhood)
esq.: *esquina* (corner)
Gto.: Guanajuato (state of Guanajuato)
IMN: Instituto Nacional de Migración (National Institute of Immigration)
nte.: *norte* (north)
ote.: *oriente* (east)

PAN: Partido Acción Nacional (National Action Party)
pp: *por persona* (per person)
PRD: Partido de la Revolución Democrática (Party of the Democratic Revolution)
PRI: Partido Revolucionario Institucional (Institutional Revolutionary Party)
prol.: *prolongación* (prolongation, usually of a city street)
pte.: *poniente* (west)
Qro.: Querétaro (state of Querétaro)
s/n: *sin número* (without number)

Spanish Phrasebook

Your Mexican adventure will be more fun if you use a little Spanish. Mexican folks, although they may smile at your funny accent, will appreciate your halting efforts to break the ice and transform yourself from a foreigner to a potential friend.

Spanish commonly uses 30 letters — the familiar English 26, plus four straightforward additions: ch, ll, ñ, and rr.

PRONUNCIATION

Once you learn them, Spanish pronunciation rules—in contrast to English—don't change. Spanish vowels generally sound softer than in English. (*Note:* The capitalized syllables receive stronger accents.)

Vowels

a like ah, as in "hah": *agua* AH-gooah (water), *pan* PAHN (bread), and *casa* CAH-sah (house)

e like ay, as in "may": *mesa* MAY-sah (table), *tela* TAY-lah (cloth), and *de* DAY (of, from)

i like ee, as in "need": *diez* dee-AYZ (ten), *comida* ko-MEE-dah (meal), and *fin* FEEN (end)

o like oh, as in "go": *peso* PAY-soh (weight), *ocho* OH-choh (eight), and *poco* POH-koh (a bit)

u like oo, as in "cool": *uno* OO-noh (one), *cuarto* KOOAHR-toh (room), and *usted* oos-TAYD (you); when it follows a "q" the **u** is silent; when it follows an "h" or has an umlaut, it's pronounced like "w"

Consonants

c like k as in "keep": *cuarto* KOOAR-toh (room), Tepic tay-PEEK (capital of Nayarit state); when it precedes "e" or "i," pronounce **c** like s, as in "sit": *cerveza* sayr-VAY-sah (beer), *encima* ayn-SEE-mah (atop)

g like g as in "gift" when it precedes "a," "o," "u," or a consonant: *gato* GAH-toh (cat), *hago* AH-goh (I do, make); otherwise, pronounce **g** like h as in "hat": *giro* HEE-roh (money order), *gente* HAYN-tay (people)

h occurs, but is silent—not pronounced at all

j like h, as in "has": *jueves* HOOAY-vays (Thursday), *mejor* may-HOR (better)

ll like y, as in "yes": *toalla* toh-AH-yah (towel), *ellos* AY-yohs (they, them)

ñ like ny, as in "canyon": *año* AH-nyo (year), *señor* SAY-nyor (Mr., sir)

r is lightly trilled, with tongue at the roof of your mouth like a very light English d, as in "ready": *pero* PAY-doh (but), *tres* TDAYS (three), *cuatro* KOOAH-tdoh (four)

rr like a Spanish r, but with much more emphasis and trill

Note: The single small but common exception to all of the above is the pronunciation of Span-

288

ish y when it's being used as the Spanish word for "and," as in "Ron y Kathy." In such case, pronounce it like the English ee, as in "keep": Ron "ee" Kathy (Ron and Kathy).

Accent

The rule for accent, the relative stress given to syllables within a given word, is straightforward. If a word ends in a vowel, an n, or an s, accent the next-to-last syllable; if not, accent the last syllable.

Pronounce *gracias* GRAH-seeahs (thank you), *orden* OHR-dayn (order), and *carretera* kah-ray-TAY-rah (highway) with stress on the next-to-last syllable.

Otherwise, accent the last syllable: *venir* vay-NEER (to come), *ferrocarril* fay-roh-cah-REEL (railroad), and *edad* ay-DAHD (age).

Exceptions to the accent rule are always marked with an accent sign: (á, é, í, ó, or ú), such as *teléfono* tay-LAY-foh-noh (telephone), *jabón* hah-BON (soap), and *rápido* RAH-pee-doh (rapid).

BASIC AND COURTEOUS EXPRESSIONS

Most Spanish-speaking people consider formalities important. Whenever approaching anyone for information or some other reason, do not forget the appropriate salutation—good morning, good evening, etc. Standing alone, the greeting *hola* (hello) can sound brusque.

Hello. *Hola.*
Good morning. *Buenos días.*
Good afternoon. *Buenas tardes.*
Good evening. *Buenas noches.*
How are you? *¿Cómo está usted?*
Very well, thank you. *Muy bien, gracias.*
Okay; good. *Bien.*
Not okay; bad. *Mal* or *feo.*
So-so. *Más o menos.*
And you? *¿Y usted?*
Thank you. *Gracias.*
Thank you very much. *Muchas gracias.*
You're very kind. *Muy amable.*
You're welcome. *De nada.*
Good-bye. *Adios.*

See you later. *Hasta luego.*
please *por favor*
yes *sí*
no *no*
I don't know. *No sé.*
Just a moment, please. *Momentito, por favor.*
Excuse me, please (when you're trying to get attention). *Disculpe* or *Con permiso.*
Excuse me (to apologize). *Lo siento.*
Pleased to meet you. *Mucho gusto.*
What is your name? *¿Cómo se llama usted?*
My name is ... *Me llamo ...*
Do you speak English? *¿Habla usted inglés?*
Is English spoken here? (Does anyone here speak English?) *¿Se habla inglés?*
I don't speak Spanish well. *No hablo bien el español.*
I don't understand. *No entiendo.*
How do you say ... in Spanish? *¿Cómo se dice ... en español?*
Would you like ... *¿Quisiera usted ...*
Let's go to ... *Vamos a ...*

TERMS OF ADDRESS

When in doubt, use the formal *usted* (you) as a form of address.

I *yo*
you (formal) *usted*
you (familiar) *tú*
he/him *él*
she/her *ella*
we/us *nosotros*
you (plural) *ustedes*
they/them *ellos* (all males or mixed gender); *ellas* (all females)
Mr., sir *señor*
Mrs., madam *señora*
miss, young lady *señorita*
wife; husband *esposa; esposo*
friend *amigo* (male); *amiga* (female)
sweetheart *novio* (male); *novia* (female)
son; daughter *hijo; hija*
brother; sister *hermano; hermana*
father; mother *padre; madre*

RESOURCES SPANISH PHRASEBOOK

grandfather; grandmother *abuelo; abuela*

TRANSPORTATION

Where is ... ? *¿Dónde está ... ?*
How far is it to ... ? *¿A cuánto está ... ?*
from ... to ... *de ... a ...*
How many blocks? *¿Cuántas cuadras?*
Where (Which) is the way to ... ? *¿Dónde está el camino a ... ?*
the bus station *la terminal de autobuses*
the bus stop *la parada de autobuses*
Where is this bus going? *¿Adónde va este autobús?*
the taxi stand *la parada de taxis*
the train station *la estación de ferrocarril*
the boat *el barco*
the launch *lancha; tiburonera*
the dock *el muelle*
the airplane *el avión*
the airport *el aeropuerto*
I'd like a ticket to ... *Quisiera un boleto a ...*
first (second) class *primera (segunda) clase*
round-trip *ida y vuelta; viaje redondo*
reservation *reservación*
baggage *equipaje*
Stop here, please. *Pare aquí, por favor.*
the entrance *la entrada*
the exit *la salida*
ticket *boleto*
the ticket office *taquilla*
(very) near; far *(muy) cerca; lejos*
to; toward *a*
by; through *por*
from *de*
the right *la derecha*
the left *la izquierda*
straight ahead *derecho; directo*
in front *en frente*
beside *al lado*
behind *atrás*
the corner *la esquina*
the stoplight *la semáforo*
a turn *una vuelta*
right here *aquí*
somewhere around here *por acá*
right there *allí*
somewhere around there *por allá*

road *el camino*
street; boulevard *calle; bulevar*
block *la cuadra*
highway *carretera*
kilometer *kilómetro*
bridge; toll *puente; cuota*
address *dirección*
north; south *norte; sur*
east; west *oriente (este); poniente (oeste)*

ACCOMMODATIONS

hotel *hotel*
Is there a room? *¿Hay cuarto?*
May I (may we) see it? *¿Puedo (podemos) verlo?*
What is the rate? *¿Cuál es el precio?*
Is that your best rate? *¿Es su mejor precio?*
Is there something cheaper? *¿Hay algo más económico?*
a single room *un cuarto sencillo*
a double room *un cuarto doble*
double bed *cama matrimonial*
twin beds *camas individuales*
with private bath *con baño*
hot water *agua caliente*
shower *ducha*
towels *toallas*
soap *jabón*
toilet paper *papel higiénico*
blanket *cobija*
sheets *sábanas*
air-conditioned *aire acondicionado*
fan *abanico; ventilador*
key *llave*
manager *gerente*

FOOD

I'm hungry *Tengo hambre.*
I'm thirsty. *Tengo sed.*
menu *carta; menú*
order *orden*
glass *vaso*
fork *tenedor*
knife *cuchillo*
spoon *cuchara*
napkin *servilleta*
soft drink *refresco*
coffee *café*

tea *té*
drinking water *agua pura; agua potable*
bottle of water *botella de agua*
bottled carbonated water *agua mineral*
bottled uncarbonated water *agua sin gas*
beer *cerveza*
wine *vino*
milk *leche*
juice *jugo*
cream *crema*
sugar *azúcar*
cheese *queso*
snack *antojito; botana*
breakfast *desayuno*
lunch *almuerzo*
daily lunch special *comida corrida* (or *el menú del día* depending on region)
dinner *comida* (often eaten in late afternoon); *cena* (a late-night snack)
wine list *lista de vinos*
the check *la cuenta*
tip *propina*
eggs *huevos*
bread *pan*
salad *ensalada*
fruit *fruta*
mango *mango*
watermelon *sandía*
papaya *papaya*
banana *plátano*
apple *manzana*
orange *naranja*
lime *limón*
fish *pescado*
shellfish *mariscos*
shrimp *camarones*
meat (without) *(sin) carne*
chicken *pollo*
pork *puerco*
beef; steak *res; bistec*
bacon; ham *tocino; jamón*
fried *frito*
roasted *asada*
barbecue; barbecued *barbacoa; al carbón*
spicy, hot *picante*

SHOPPING

money *dinero*
money-exchange bureau *casa de cambio*
I would like to exchange travelers checks. *Quisiera cambiar cheques de viajero.*
What is the exchange rate? *¿Cuál es el tipo de cambio?*
How much is the commission? *¿Cuánto cuesta la comisión?*
Do you accept credit cards? *¿Aceptan tarjetas de crédito?*
money order *giro*
How much does it cost? *¿Cuánto cuesta?*
What is your final price? *¿Cuál es su último precio?*
expensive *caro*
cheap *barato; económico*
more *más*
less *menos*
a little *un poco*
too much *demasiado*

HEALTH

Help me please. *Ayúdeme por favor.*
I am ill. *Estoy enfermo.*
Call a doctor. *Llame un doctor.*
Take me to ... *Lléveme a ...*
hospital *hospital; sanatorio*
drugstore *farmacia*
pain *dolor*
fever *fiebre*
headache *dolor de cabeza*
stomachache *dolor de estómago*
allergy *alergia*
burn *quemadura*
cramp *calambre*
nausea *náusea*
vomiting *vomitar*
medicine *medicina*
prescription *receta*
antibiotic *antibiótico*
pill; tablet *pastilla*
aspirin *aspirina*
ointment; cream *pomada; crema*
bandage *venda*
cotton *algodón*

sanitary napkins *toallas,* or use brand
  name, e.g., Kotex
birth control pills *pastillas anticonceptivas*
contraceptive foam *espuma*
  anticonceptiva
condoms *preservativos; condones*
toothbrush *cepilla dental*
dental floss *hilo dental*
toothpaste *crema dental*
dentist *dentista*
toothache *dolor de muelas*

POST OFFICE AND COMMUNICATIONS
long-distance telephone *teléfono larga*
  distancia
I would like to call ... *Quisiera llamar a ...*
collect *por cobrar*
station to station *a quien contesta*
person to person *persona a persona*
credit card *tarjeta de crédito*
post office *correo*
general delivery *lista de correo*
letter *carta*
stamp *estampilla, timbre*
postcard *tarjeta*
aerogram *aerograma*
airmail *correo aereo*
registered *registrado*
money order *giro*
package; box *paquete, caja*
string; tape *cuerda; cinta*

AT THE BORDER
border *frontera*
customs *aduana*
immigration *migración*
tourist card *tarjeta de turista*
inspection *inspección; revisión*
passport *pasaporte*
profession *profesión*
marital status *estado civil*
single *soltero*
married; divorced *casado; divorciado*
widowed *viudado*
insurance *seguros*
title *título*
driver's license *licencia de manejar*

AT THE GAS STATION
gas station *gasolinera*
gasoline *gasolina*
unleaded *sin plomo*
full, please *lleno, por favor*
tire *llanta*
tire repair shop *vulcanizadora*
air *aire*
water *agua*
oil (change) *aceite (cambio)*
grease *grasa*
My ... doesn't work. *Mi ... no sirve.*
battery *batería*
radiator *radiador*
alternator *alternador*
generator *generador*
tow truck *grúa*
repair shop *taller mecánico*
tune-up *afinación*
auto parts store *refaccionería*

VERBS
Verbs are the key to getting along in Spanish. They employ mostly predictable forms and come in three classes, which end in *ar, er,* and *ir,* respectively:
to buy *comprar*
I buy, you (he, she, it) buys *compro, compra*
we buy, you (they) buy *compramos, compran*
to eat *comer*
I eat, you (he, she, it) eats *como, come*
we eat, you (they) eat *comemos, comen*
to climb *subir*
I climb, you (he, she, it) climbs *subo, sube*
we climb, you (they) climb *subimos, suben*
Here are more (with irregularities indicated):
to do or make *hacer* (regular except for *hago,* I do or make)
to go *ir* (very irregular: *voy, va, vamos, van*)
to go (walk) *andar*
to love *amar*
to work *trabajar*
to want *desear, querer*
to need *necesitar*

to read *leer*
to write *escribir*
to repair *reparar*
to stop *parar*
to get off (the bus) *bajar*
to arrive *llegar*
to stay (remain) *quedar*
to stay (lodge) *hospedar*
to leave *salir* (regular except for *salgo*, I leave)
to look at *mirar*
to look for *buscar*
to give *dar* (regular except for *doy*, I give)
to carry *llevar*
to have *tener* (irregular but important: *tengo, tiene, tenemos, tienen*)
to come *venir* (similarly irregular: *vengo, viene, venimos, vienen*)
Spanish has two forms of "to be":
to be *estar* (regular except for *estoy*, I am)
to be *ser* (very irregular: *soy, es, somos, son*)
Use *estar* when speaking of location or a temporary state of being: "I am at home." *"Estoy en casa."* "I'm sick." *"Estoy enfermo."* Use *ser* for a permanent state of being: "I am a doctor." *"Soy doctora."*

NUMBERS

0 *cero*
1 *uno*
2 *dos*
3 *tres*
4 *cuatro*
5 *cinco*
6 *seis*
7 *siete*
8 *ocho*
9 *nueve*
10 *diez*
11 *once*
12 *doce*
13 *trece*
14 *catorce*
15 *quince*
16 *dieciseis*
17 *diecisiete*
18 *dieciocho*
19 *diecinueve*
20 *veinte*
21 *veinte y uno* or *veintiuno*
30 *treinta*
40 *cuarenta*
50 *cincuenta*
60 *sesenta*
70 *setenta*
80 *ochenta*
90 *noventa*
100 *ciento*
101 *ciento y uno* or *cientiuno*
200 *doscientos*
500 *quinientos*
1,000 *mil*
10,000 *diez mil*
100,000 *cien mil*
1,000,000 *millón*
one-half *medio*
one-third *un tercio*
one-fourth *un cuarto*

TIME

What time is it? *¿Qué hora es?*
It's one o'clock. *Es la una.*
It's three in the afternoon. *Son las tres de la tarde.*
It's four in the morning. *Son las cuatro de la mañana.*
six-thirty *seis y media*
a quarter till eleven *un cuarto para las once*
a quarter past five *las cinco y cuarto*
an hour *una hora*

DAYS AND MONTHS

Monday *lunes*
Tuesday *martes*
Wednesday *miércoles*
Thursday *jueves*
Friday *viernes*
Saturday *sábado*
Sunday *domingo*
today *hoy*
tomorrow *mañana*
yesterday *ayer*
January *enero*
February *febrero*
March *marzo*

April *abril*	**December** *diciembre*
May *mayo*	**a week** *una semana*
June *junio*	**a month** *un mes*
July *julio*	**after** *después*
August *agosto*	**before** *antes*
September *septiembre*	
October *octubre*	*Courtesy of Bruce Whipperman, author of* Moon
November *noviembre*	Pacific Mexico.

Suggested Reading

HISTORY

Brading, David. *Miners and Merchants in Bourbon Mexico.* Cambridge, U.K.: Cambridge University Press, 2008. Widely recognized as one of the preeminent scholars of early Guanajuato and the Spanish colonies, David Brading offers a fascinating look at life in colonial Mexico.

Coe, Michael D. *From the Olmecs to the Aztecs.* London: Thames and Hudson, 2008. Yale anthropologist Michael D. Coe has written extensively about Mesoamerican civilizations. In this volume, he introduces the great cultures of pre-Columbian Mexico.

Collier, George. *Basta: Land and the Zapatista Rebellion in Chiapas.* Oakland, California: Food First Books, 1994. An excellent introduction to indigenous communities and the 1994 Zapatista uprising in Chiapas.

De las Casas, Bartolomé. *Short Account of the Destruction of the Indies.* London: Penguin Books, 1992. A Dominican friar and humanitarian, de las Casas recounts his firsthand observations about Spanish abuse of indigenous Americans during the colonial era.

Krauze, Enrique. *Mexico: A Biography of Power.* New York: Harper Perennial, 1998. A general history of Mexico, written by one of the country's preeminent intellectuals.

Riding, Alan. *Distant Neighbors.* New York: Knopf, 1984. Though written in the 1980s, this book still offers an insightful perspective on the differences between U.S. and Mexican culture with striking accuracy.

Thomas, Hugh. *Conquest: Montezuma, Cortés, and the Fall of Old Mexico.* New York: Simon & Schuster, 1995. An exhaustively researched and beautifully written account of one of the greatest events in history: the meeting of the New and Old Worlds in Mexico in 1519, and the war that followed.

Womack, John. *Emiliano Zapata and the Mexican Revolution.* New York: Vintage, 1970. A wonderful, well-researched history of the great hero Emiliano Zapata, written by Harvard's Mexico expert, John Womack.

FOOD AND CULTURE

Franz, Carl, and Lorena Havens. *The People's Guide to Mexico.* Berkeley, California: Avalon Travel Publishing, 2012. A cultural handbook to travel in Mexico, the *People's Guide* offers hard-won and well-placed advice for adventurous Mexico travelers.

Kennedy, Diana. *My Mexico.* New York: Clarkson Potter/Publishers, 1998. More anthropological tome than practical cookbook, this book offers detailed regional recipes from across Mexico, accompanied by the author's personal observations and stories.

GENERAL INTEREST

Cohan, Tony. *On Mexican Time: A New Life in Mexico*. New York: Broadway Books, 2000. Cohan's best-selling memoir vividly recounts his first years of life as an expatriate in San Miguel de Allende.

De Gast, Robert. *Behind the Doors of San Miguel de Allende*. Petaluma, California: Pomegranate Communications, 2000. De Gast's follow-up to his successful photography book about San Miguel shows you the courtyards and gardens behind the town's distinctive doorways.

De Gast, Robert. *The Doors of San Miguel de Allende*. Petaluma, California: Pomegranate Communications, 1994. A wonderful photographer and writer, Robert de Gast captures the unique culture and color of San Miguel through photos of its beautiful doorways.

Simeone, Riccardo, and Archie Dean. *The Insider's Guide to San Miguel*. Self-published, 2013. You will have to seek out this classic guide to San Miguel de Allende in one of the city's local bookshops. Originally written and published by Archie Dean, it offers a comprehensive and annotated list of restaurants, hotels, and other businesses in San Miguel.

Internet Resources

SAN MIGUEL DE ALLENDE

San Miguel de Allende Official Site
www.sanmiguelallende.gob.mx
The official website of San Miguel de Allende offers information about the city and city services, like education and the police force, in Spanish.

Don Day in SMA
http://dondayinsma.com
An entertaining blog about food and drink in San Miguel de Allende authored by an opinionated resident.

Cupcakes and Crablegs
www.cupcakesandcrablegs.com
A food-centric San Miguel de Allende blog, Cupcakes and Crablegs also covers shopping, artists, and places to stay in the city.

GUANAJUATO

Festival Internacional Cervantino
www.festivalcervantino.gob.mx
The official site for Guanajuato's renowned Cervantino festival offers complete programming information.

Guanajuato Official Site
www.guanajuato.gob.mx
The official website of Guanajuato's state government offers general information about state programs as well as links to tourist information.

Universidad de Guanajuato Cultural Extension
www.extension.ugto.mx
This website offers updated information about the numerous concerts, film screenings, and art exhibitions produced by the University of Guanajuato's cultural extension. You can also read an online version of *Polen,* their monthly arts magazine.

QUERÉTARO

Asomarte
www.asomarte.com

The online version of Querétaro's free art and culture magazine features events listings, cultural news, and travel-related podcasts as well as restaurant and hotel reviews.

Travel Querétaro
www.queretaro.travel

Maintained by the Querétaro state government, this informative website details major sites in Querétaro city and state, lists upcoming events, and offers maps, photo galleries, and cultural articles. The Spanish version contains more detailed content than the English version.

Index

List of Maps

Photo Credits

MOON SAN MIGUEL DE ALLENDE

Avalon Travel
Hachette Book Group
1700 Fourth Street
Berkeley, CA 94710, USA
www.moon.com

Editor: Leah Gordon
Series Manager: Kathryn Ettinger
Copy Editor: Ashley Benning
Graphics and Production Coordinator:
  Lucie Ericksen
Cover Design: Faceout Studios, Charles Brock
Interior Design: Domini Dragoone
Moon Logo: Tim McGrath
Map Editor: Mike Morgenfeld
Cartographer: Larissa Gatt
Proofreader: Caroline Trefler
Indexer: Rachel Kuhn

ISBN-13: 978-1-64049-270-7

Printing History
1st Edition — 2011
3rd Edition — November 2018
5 4 3 2 1

Front cover photo: Parroquia de San Miguel
  Arcángel, San Miguel de Allende © PHOTO24/
  GettyImages
Back cover photo: street in San Miguel de Allende
  © Adeliepenguin | Dreamstime.com

Printed in China by RR Donnelley